THE
PREACHER'S
OUTLINE & SERMON
BIBLE®

THE
PREACHER'S
OUTLINE & SERMON
BIBLE®

NEW TESTAMENT

KING JAMES VERSION

Leadership Ministries Worldwide
Chattanooga, TN

Previous Editions of **The Preacher's Outline & Sermon Bible®**,
New International Version NT   Copyright © 1998
King James Version NT   Copyright © 1991, 1996, 2000
by Alpha-Omega Ministries, Inc.

Please address all requests for information or permission to:
Leadership Ministries Worldwide
PO Box 21310
Chattanooga, TN 37424-0310
Ph.# (423) 855-2181   FAX (423) 855-8616   E-Mail info@outlinebible.org
http://www.outlinebible.org

Library of Congress Catalog Card Number: 96-75921
ISBN Softbound Edition: 978-1-57407-003-3
ISBN Deluxe 3-Ring Edition: 978-1-57407-028-6

LEADERSHIP MINISTRIES WORLDWIDE
CHATTANOOGA, TN

Printed in the United States of America

7   8   9   10   11   16   17   18   19   20

DEDICATED

To all the men and women of the world who
preach and teach the Gospel of
our Lord Jesus Christ and
to the Mercy and Grace of God

- Demonstrated to us in Christ Jesus our Lord.

  *"In whom we have redemption through His
  blood, the forgiveness of sins, according to the
  riches of His grace." (Ep.1:7)*

- Out of the mercy and grace of God, His Word has
  flowed. Let every person know that God will have
  mercy upon him, forgiving and using him to fulfill
  His glorious plan of salvation.

  *"For God so loved the world, that he gave His
  only begotten Son, that whosoever believeth in
  Him should not perish, but have everlasting
  life. For God sent not his son into the world to
  condemn the world, but that the world through
  him might be saved." (Jn.3:16-17)*

  *"For this is good and acceptable in the sight of
  God our Saviour; who will have all men to be
  saved, and to come unto the knowledge of the
  truth." (1 Ti.2:3-4)*

6/07

The
Outli
Serm
is writt
servant
study, t
preachi
Word..

- to sh
  with
- to he
  isters
  their
  ing,
  Word
- to do
  bly c
  boys,
  hearts
  Chris
  etern
- to do
  to the
- to gi
  prope
  Word
  no wo
  istries
  line
  ever t

...whose name... have faded from our memory. May our wonderful Lord continue to bless the min... and the ministries of us all—as we diligently labor to reach the world for Christ and to meet the... suffer so much.

THE GREEK SOURCES

Expositor's Greek Testament, Edited by W. Robertson Nicoll. Grand Rapids, MI: Eerdmans ▐

Robertson, A.T. *Word Pictures in the New Testament*. Nashville, TN: Broadman Press, 1930

Thayer, Joseph Henry. *Greek-English Lexicon of the New Testament*. New York: American B▐

Vincent, Marvin R. *Word Studies in the New Testament*. Grand Rapids, MI: Eerdmans Publis▐

Vine, W.E. *Expository Dictionary of New Testament Words*. Old Tappan, NJ: Fleming H. Re▐

Wuest, Kenneth S. *Word Studies in the Greek New Testament*. Grand Rapids, MI: Eerdmans ▐

THE REFERENCE WORKS

Cruden's Complete Concordance of the Old & New Testament. Philadelphia, PA: The John C

Josephus' *Complete Works*. Grand Rapids, MI: Kregel Publications, 1981.

Lockyer, Herbert. Series of books, including his books on *All the Men, Women, Miracles*▐ Grand Rapids, MI: Zondervan Publishing House, 1958–1967.

Nave's Topical Bible. Nashville, TN: The Southwestern Co., n.d.

The Amplified New Testament. (Scripture Quotations are from the Amplified New Testament, by the Lockman Foundation. Used by permission.)

The Four Translation New Testament. (Including King James, New American Standard, Will▐ Language of the People, Beck - New Testament in the Language of Today.) Minneapolis▐ tions.

The New Compact Bible Dictionary, Edited by T. Alton Bryant. Grand Rapids, MI: Zonderva▐

The New Thompson Chain Reference Bible. Indianapolis, IN: B.B. Kirkbride Bible Co., 1964

THE COMMENTARIES

Barclay, William. *Daily Study Bible Series*. Philadelphia, PA: Westminster Press, Began in 1▌

Bruce, F.F. *The Epistle to the Ephesians*. Westwood, NJ: Fleming H. Revell Co., 1968.

_____. *Epistle to the Hebrews*. Grand Rapids, MI: Eerdmans Publishing Co., 1964.

_____. *The Epistles of John*. Old Tappan, NJ: Fleming H. Revell Co., 1970.

Criswell, W.A. *Expository Sermons on Revelation*. Grand Rapids, MI: Zondervan Publishing *by Verse Study*. Greenville, SC: The Gospel Hour, Inc., 1963.

y on the Whole Bible. Old Tappan, NJ: Fleming H. Revell Co.

n Romans & on Corinthians. Grand Rapids, MI: Eerdmans Publishing Co., 1972–1973.

amentary On the Revelation of John. Grand Rapids, MI: Eerdmans Publishing Co., 1972–

Daniel. Grand Rapids, MI: Baker Book House, 1969.

cording to John. Grand Rapids, MI: Eerdmans Publishing Co., 1971.

, Verse by Verse. Chicago, IL: Moody Press, 1947.

Studies in Galatians & Ephesians. Neptune, NJ: Loizeaux Brothers, 1957.

Philippians. Neptune, NJ: Loizeaux Brothers, 1959.

Neptune, NJ: Loizeaux Brothers, 1956.

ation. Neptune, NJ: Loizeaux Brothers, 1964.

fe Bible Commentary, Edited by Charles F. Pfeiffer & Everett F. Harrison. New York: The
Produced for Moody Monthly. Chicago Moody Press, 1962.

*ted by H.D.M. Spence & Joseph S. Exell. Grand Rapids, MI: Eerdmans Publishing Co.,

rews, A Devotional Commentary. Grand Rapids, MI: Eerdmans Publishing Co., 1970.

Acts of the Apostles. Grand Rapids, MI: Eerdmans Publishing Co., 1956.

ie Romans. Grand Rapids, MI: Eerdmans Publishing Co., 1946.

& Philemon. Grand Rapids, MI: Baker Book House, 1973.

mentaries. Grand Rapids, MI: Eerdmans Publishing Co., Began in 1958.

Apostles. Chicago, IL: Moody Press, 1965.

onian Epistles. Grand Rapids, MI: Zondervan Publishing House, 1973.

Tone Dalen, Joel Pando, Colin Brook, Andrea Rocha, Sorangel, César, Alejandro, Vanesa and the many Cubans who generously extended their hospitality to me during my travels around Cuba.

For my research trips to Angola in 1998 I am indebted to Keith Gubbin who arranged visas, put me up for several weeks and provided me with dozens of priceless contacts, and to Aitor Loidi and Nicole Walter from *Newsweek* who put me up for two months and helped sneak me into Nelson Mandela's press conference. Special thanks go to the former British Ambassador Roger Hart and his Embassy staff in Luanda for their exceptional assistance in setting me up with contacts and arranging interviews, and to Professor Mingas and Drumond Jaime at the Agostinho Neto University in Luanda for assisting my research. Thanks also to the following people for their help (and for some great nights out): Rachel Denning, Pedro Guerra Marques, Irene Revilla, Jaques Yeterian, Julia Pasarón, Joan McClean, Sebastian Mackinnon, Tony Moloney, Luís Campos, Father Colin Reidy and Alex Laskaris (at the US Embassy).

For assistance in travelling to some of the remotest parts of Angola, I am indebted to the following people: Ron Savage, Osmond, João, Jackson and Peter at CARE International (Luanda, Menongue and Lubango), César Arroyo at the WFP (Luanda), Clodagh McCumiskey, Ian, Américo and Luís at Trocaire (Luanda and Quipungo), Phil, Rob and Tony from the Greenfield de-mining team (Menongue), Alan, Jorge Leite (who saved me from the Kuito militia) and Julian Waldemar-Brown at the HALO Trust (Kuito-Bié, Bailundo and Huambo), Teresa, Jim and Phil from CONCERN, Alfredo and Pierre at the ICRC's Bomba Alta prosthesis clinic (Huambo), Timo Orkamo and Mark Jones for flying me from Menongue to Jamba (Cuando Cubango), and the MONUA contingents at Cuito Cuanavale, Bailundo and Jamba who looked after me during my stay.

For my three-month trip to South Africa, I am wholly indebted to the kindness and generosity of Angie and Brian Orlin who put me up in Johannesburg, set me up with dozens of contacts and (on more than one occasion) bailed me out of disastrous situations. Special thanks also to Johann Smith for introducing me to many ex-SADF contacts, and to Mike Morkel and the Cochran family for providing me with contacts for my trip across South Africa.

During my research I have carried out many long and detailed interviews, and I am grateful to the following people for their openness, honesty and humour: Holden Roberto, Paulo Jorge, Major Mateus Timóteo (FAA commander in Cuito Cuanavale), Eduardo António Matamata (former UNITA commander in Jamba), Dr Guerra Marques, and the dozen FAPLA veterans I interviewed in Menongue and Cuito Cuanavale, Johann Smith, Helmoed-Römer Heitman, Eric Lamprecht, Andy Kasrils, Johan Lehman, Danie Crowther and P.W. Botha.

While in Cuba I interviewed two dozen internationalist veterans and several writers, representing views from both extremes of the political spectrum. As the information I acquired (much of it still sensitive) was given in good faith, I have not named any of them in this book unless they gave me express permission to do so.

And finally I would like to thank the following people who have supported my project – both morally and intellectually – over the last few years: my Mum and Dad, my sister Lucy, Sebastian Morrison, Dr Hendrik Hinrichsen, Rachel Skinner, Lois Duquesnoy, David Delaney, Greg Wolk, McKenna Richards, Merryn Gamba, Lisa Williams, Kate Rea, Karina Sarmiento, Ben Etridge and Inocência Mata.

On a final note, I would like to acknowledge my enormous debt to the many writers on whose work I have drawn extensively when writing this book. Although I do not necessarily share their political or ideological convictions, were it not for their detailed contributions to this field, this book would be much the poorer.

INTRODUCTION

In November 1975, Cuba launched the largest intervention in its history, sending 36,000 troops into Angola to defend its Marxist ally from twin invasions by South African and Zairian forces. This unprecedented event – which overnight turned Angola into one of the main fronts of the Cold War – did not arise out of a vacuum, however. It was in fact the culmination of more than a decade of uneven cooperation between the Cubans and the MPLA, dating back to Che Guevara's Congo campaign in the mid-1960s. Over the next thirteen years, the Cuban military contingent grew until, by 1988 – when Cuban and South African forces clashed at Cuito Cuanavale in the second largest battle in African history – there were over 65,000 Cuban troops in Angola, proportionally four times the American commitment to Vietnam. The Cubans fighting in Angola professed to uphold the ideals of internationalism, an ideology little understood in the West and often dismissed by their opponents as a mask for Soviet imperialism. Yet despite being labelled 'Moscow's Gurkhas', the Cuban 'internationalists' drew overwhelming support from the majority of African states, catapulting their leader – the charismatic and much maligned Fidel Castro – back onto the international stage, and by the early 1980s turning him into the unofficial spokesman for the Third World. The fifteen-year intervention in Angola would shape the lives of a generation of Cubans, and by its end in 1991 nearly half-a-million Cubans would have served there.

The aims of this book, therefore, are to explain why a Caribbean country sent as many as half-a-million of its citizens 6,000 miles to fight in sub-Saharan Africa, and to examine how a short-term intervention escalated into a lengthy war of intervention, culminating in the spurious Cuban 'victory' at Cuito Cuanavale. Previous studies of the Angolan War have tended to examine Cuba's role in isolation – or as subordinate to Soviet interests – and this book looks at the multidimensional character of the Angolan War, examining how the interaction between the main players affected and shaped the Cuban intervention. The first two chapters look at the roots of the Cuban–MPLA alliance, examining the evolution of Che

1

Guevara's brand of internationalism which spawned the Brazzaville mission (1965–7), and the weakening of this alliance in the early 1970s as both allies underwent internal crises. Following the Portuguese decision to decolonise Angola (in mid-1974), the perspective expands to take in the other main actors in Angola's chaotic decolonisation – South Africa, the Soviet Union, the USA and Zaire – and follows their fruitless struggle to gain ascendancy in Angola, culminating in the New York Peace Accords in December 1988. The book is therefore more than just a study of the Cuban phenomenon in Angola, and is in a broader sense a study of foreign intervention in the Angolan War, attempting to explain Cuba's escalating involvement in relation to the many other competing strategies in Angola.

Like all conflicts of the Cold War, the Angolan War has produced its share of propaganda and disinformation. Throughout thirty years of near-continuous conflict those involved have seen fit to rewrite events after they occurred to further their political agendas. A balanced analysis of Cuba's involvement in Angola is further hampered by the extreme polarisation of opinion on the Cuban Revolution and its most notorious protagonist – Fidel Castro. For, while some depict him as the saviour of the Cuban people and the champion of the Third World, others label him a Soviet puppet and a monstrous dictator who has ruthlessly maintained his grip on the reins of power in Cuba for more than four decades. Such extreme views on Revolutionary Cuba and its outspoken leader fail, however, to shed any light on the ideologies which motivated the hundreds of thousands of men and women who served in Angola. For the Cubans this involved the constantly-evolving model of Guevara's 'internationalism'; for the Angolans (at least on paper), Marxist–Leninism; and, for the South Africans, 'Total Onslaught', an apocalyptic theory which depicted Pretoria as the last bastion of Western values against the 'Communist onslaught'.

Given the vast amount of confused and contradictory reporting from the war zone – and the heavily-biased official accounts produced after the war – it has proved essential to draw on first-hand accounts of those involved in the conflict, from the politicians in Havana, Luanda and Pretoria, to the troops on the ground. For this reason, during a year spent in Cuba between 1997 and 2002 (and two visits to Miami) I interviewed two dozen Cuban internationalist veterans of Angola, among them professional officers, reservists and civilians (who worked on humanitarian projects). Their views span the political spectrum, and their detailed testimonies shed fresh light on the experience of Cubans serving in Angola, painting a bleak picture of Cuban-Angolan relations which contrasts starkly with the harmonious relationship depicted by Havana and Luanda (see Chapter 7).

During a three-month visit to Angola in early 1998 (when there was a lull in the fighting), I visited the main battlefields at Quifangondo, Cuito

2

Cuanavale and Kuito-Bié, and interviewed a dozen Angolan veterans of the 1985–8 campaigns who provided me with detailed information about the fighting in Cuando Cubango. This was countered by interviews in South Africa with former SADF officers and senior politicians which helped to shed some light on South African perspectives of a conflict in which they were internationally reviled as the pariah. Drawing on their first-hand accounts – and on much new material from libraries and private sources in Cuba, Angola and South Africa – this book aims to construct as accurate a picture as possible of the conflict which has plagued Angola since the early 1960s, dispelling the myths associated with Cuba's intervention in November 1975.

In particular, a fresh examination of the launch of Operation Carlota seeks to demonstrate that Havana's decision to intervene in Angola was not so much an heroic gesture of international solidarity, but rather a last-ditch gamble to avert military disaster (see Chapter 4). By the same token, Cuba's much-heralded 'victory' over the South Africans at Cuito Cuanavale is shown to have been no more than a costly stand-off, its real significance lying in the impetus it gave to the American-brokered peace process (see Chapters 9–11). Given the extremity of the ideological clash in Angola – and the disagreement which still exists over the outcome of the fighting – the book's ultimate goal is to explain Cuba's relationship with Angola within the context of the many conflicting agendas in the Angolan War. Only by examining the interplay between the many bickering parties can a more accurate picture be constructed of the chaotic events which escalated Angola's guerrilla insurgency into a full-scale war of intervention, spawning the conflict which was to plague Angola for four decades.

Description of Angola

Angola is nearly half-a-million square miles in area (over five times the size of Britain), and in 1960 was divided into sixteen provinces (see Map 1).[1] North of the Congo river lies the oil-rich enclave of Cabinda, a historical oddity which has provided an economic life-line for the Luanda regime, generating more than three-quarters of Angola's total export revenue.[2] Cabinda's proximity to Congo-Brazzaville and the vast Mayombe jungle encouraged the early development of guerrilla activity, although the extreme difficulty of the terrain in the end forced the MPLA to scale down its insurgency and relocate to other provinces of Angola. In the north of Angola, Zaire and Uíge provinces cling to the border with Congo-Kinshasa (formerly Zaire),[3] and are dominated by the Bakongo ethnic group whose ties with other Bakongos in the region have fostered a close relationship with Kinshasa (to which they have often looked for support).

3

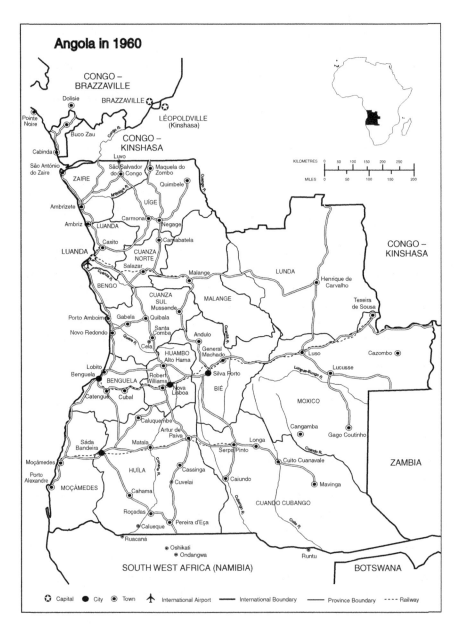

Map 1 Angola in 1960.

Further south Luanda province is dominated by the city of Luanda –
Angola's political, economic and commercial capital – and along with the
neighbouring provinces of Bengo, Cuanza Norte, Cuanza Sul and Malanje
represents the heartland of the Mbundu ethnic group (see p. 6). Further
south still, Benguela province was, until its incorporation into Angola, an
important commercial and political centre in its own right, containing
Angola's two largest commercial ports at Benguela and Lobito. It is the
starting point for the Benguela railway which runs from the coast through
the central highlands and deserted eastern plateau to Luau on the Zairian
border.[4] The two provinces immediately east of Benguela – Huambo and
Bié – are the homeland of the Ovimbundu ethnic group, and were the
location for the last burst of Portuguese colonisation in the 1960s and early
1970s (hence the proposed new capital of Angola – Nova Lisboa – in
Huambo).

South and east of these core Angolan provinces lies the vast and
sparsely-populated periphery, containing many of the smaller ethnic
groups. Directly south of Benguela is Namibe – a barren, desert-like
province served by the small port of Namibe (formerly Moçâmedes) – and
to its east lies the most populous southern province – Huíla – which is
crossed by another railway line stretching to Menongue. One of Angola's
principal rivers – the Cunene – cuts south through Huíla (there is a large
hydroelectric plant at Matala) and forms the western border with Namibia
(after independence, the southern part of Huíla became a separate
province, Cunene). The joint Portuguese and South African hydroelectric
installations at Calueque and Ruacaná have ensured heavy South African
involvement in this province since the late 1960s, and were to provide the
pretext for a South African invasion in 1975 (see Chapter 4).

And finally, on the eastern edge of Angola lie the remotest provinces of
all. In the north-east is Lundas (later divided into Lunda Norte and Lunda
Sul), an area covered in thick jungle terrain which contains some of the
world's richest diamond mines, making it a tempting target for foreign
mining companies, bandits and guerrillas. To the south (forming most of
Angola's border with Zambia) is Moxico – Angola's single largest
province at over 86,000 square miles – and along its southern border is
Cuando Cubango, nicknamed the 'Terras do Fim do Mundo' (Lands at the
End of the Earth) by the Portuguese. The extreme remoteness and size of
Moxico and Cuando Cubango made them ideal for guerrillas, and both the
MPLA (in the 1960s and early 1970s) and UNITA (in the 1980s and 1990s)
used these territories to launch their challenge to the ruling regime, bring-
ing some of the bitterest fighting of the war into these remote areas.

The main ethnic groups in Angola

Angola has a population of around thirteen million,[5] and contains eight main ethnic groups, each with its own language and dialects (see Map 2).[6] The three largest are the Mbundu, the Bakongo and the Ovimbundu, representing over three-quarters of the indigenous population (25 per cent, 15 per cent and 37 per cent respectively).[7] These three ethnic groups dominate the political landscape, and the bitter rivalry between them has often been used by external powers to maintain their grip on the country. Given the proximity of their traditional homeland to the main Portuguese colony of Luanda, the Mbundu have historically had the closest contact with the ruling elite, and to this day the Angolan government is dominated by Mbundus who view Luanda as their official capital. The Bakongo have more in common with their ethnic brothers in the Belgian and French Congos (Congo-Kinshasa and Congo-Brazzaville), and Angola's porous northern border has led to the intermingling of these populations, encouraging both neighbouring countries to interfere in Angola's affairs. The largest ethnic group, the Ovimbundu, remains the most marginalised of the three, basing its power in the central highlands of Huambo and Bié, and viewing the Luanda elite – in particular the *mestiços* (mixed race) and *assimilados* (assimilated Angolans) – with mistrust.[8] The three-way ethnic split in Angola led to the creation of three separate guerrilla movements, each professing to represent all of the Angolan people while, in reality, drawing the bulk of its support from one of the three main ethnic groups (see p. 8).

History of Angola, pre-1950

Like most African countries, Angola is a false construct, and was pieced together in the late nineteenth century from a string of Portuguese colonies along the south-west African coast, principal among them Luanda, Benguela and Cabinda. Since the late fifteenth century, Portugal's interest in Africa was the export of slaves, ivory and precious stones and, as a result, the bulk of Portuguese colonies clung to Angola's 1,000-mile coastline, parts of the interior remaining undiscovered by colonists until the 1920s. Education of the indigenous population was left to the waves of American missionaries who arrived in Angola in the early twentieth century, and the division of Angola between the Baptists in the north, the Methodists in the Luanda hinterland, and the Congregationalists in the central highlands exacerbated the ethnic tensions between the Bakongo, Mbundu and Ovimbundu.[9] Two waves of Portuguese immigrants – in the 1910s and again in the 1950s – dramatically boosted Angola's economic development, but at the expense of the indigenous population which was conscripted into annual forced labour.[10] Following the discovery of vast

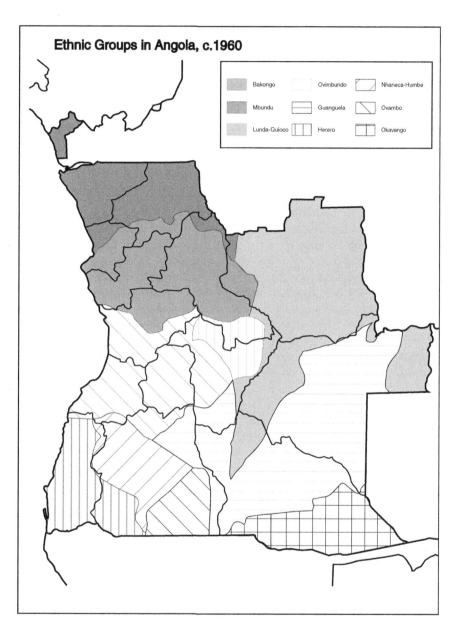

Map 2 Ethnic groups in Angola, *c.*1960.

petroleum reserves off the coast of Cabinda in 1955, Angola underwent an economic boom which, by the early 1970s, had converted it into the jewel of the Portuguese Empire, producing huge revenues for Lisbon from the export of petroleum, diamonds and coffee.[11] Buoyed by the Angolan revenue, the Portuguese dictator Salazar rejected calls to decolonise Portugal's African empire – smothering all discussion of autonomy or independence – and thus it was not until the early 1950s that the first organised resistance appeared in Angola.

The birth of Angolan nationalism, 1950–61

By the time of the Second All African Peoples' Conference in Accra in January 1960, two Angolan liberation movements had emerged. The first was the UPA (*União das Populações de Angola*, Union of the Angolan Peoples) led by Holden Roberto, a Bakongo who had spent most of his life outside Angola and who was at the time President Nkrumah's protégé. Roberto drew his support from northern Angola's Bakongo population (hence the UPA's original name, Union of the *Northern* Angolan Peoples), although his charismatic Foreign Minister, Jonas Savimbi, was an Ovimbundu who would later rise to prominence in Angola (see Chapter 1). Also present at the Conference was the UPA's rival, the MPLA (*Movimento Popular para a Libertação de Angola*, Popular Movement for the Liberation of Angola), an organisation whose cosmopolitan membership Roberto viewed with suspicion. Formed from a collection of nationalist movements (including the Angolan Communist Party), the MPLA was headed by Agostinho Neto – a rising Mbundu nationalist and poet – and contained many intellectuals who would play a prominent role in Angolan history, among them Viriato da Cruz, Lopo do Nascimento and Lúcio Lara.[12] At this stage, there was little to tell the Angolan movements apart, both expounding a nationalist, non-racial and anti-imperialist ideology. But, over time, the Marxist ideology of the MPLA pushed the movement into the socialist camp, while Roberto's ties with the Kinshasa elite effectively allied him with the West.

The outbreak of fighting in Angola, January–March 1961

The spark which set off Angola's insurgency was provided by the wave of nationalism which swept through southern Africa in 1960, starting with Belgium's sudden decision to grant the Congo independence, and culminating in the infamous Sharpeville Massacre on 21 March when South African police shot dead sixty-nine African protesters and wounded 176 others. With the independence of the Congo that June, the MPLA and UPA set up offices closer to Angola in Léopoldville (Kinshasa), and they immediately began preparing to launch the armed struggle the following year. The Portuguese reacted to increased tension in Angola with a clamp-down on activists, arresting Neto on 8 June and then killing and wounding over 200 Angolans in the disturbances which followed. Nevertheless, by the beginning of 1961 the liberation movements were ready, and that year three uprisings rocked Angola, initiating a cycle of violence which has continued to the present day.

The first uprising – led by two mysterious figures called António Mariano and Kula-Xingu – broke out in the Kassanje cotton-growing area (eastern Malanje) in January. It was quickly suppressed with savage reprisals, as many as 7,000 Angolans perishing in the massacre which followed. Of more lasting importance was the bungled launch of the MPLA's guerrilla struggle one month later in Luanda. Capitalising on the presence of a large number of foreign journalists who had come to witness the arrival of the hijacked liner *Santa Maria* (the hijackers eventually sailed it to Recife in Brazil), on 4 February, 250 MPLA guerrillas launched attacks on Luanda's main police station, government buildings and the infamous São Paulo prison. The rebels failed to release any of the eighty-six prisoners, however, and after messy skirmishing they withdrew, leaving behind at least seven Portuguese and forty Angolan dead.[13] The raid failed to spark a general uprising, and the Portuguese responded with a ruthless counter-insurgency campaign in and around Luanda, arresting over 5,000 Angolans while Portuguese settlers ran amok in Luanda's *musseques* (shanty towns), killing dozens of Angolans.

Within weeks the MPLA had been driven out of Luanda – many of its operatives being killed or captured – and the survivors fled to the relative safety of the Dembos, a mountainous area 100 miles north-east of Luanda in the Mbundu heartland. There they set up the MPLA's '1st Military Region' for what was expected to be a protracted guerrilla campaign. They were quickly surrounded by the Portuguese army which eventually stationed 50,000 troops in the region, cutting off the guerrillas from support in Léopoldville. With the Portuguese cordon intercepting all relief columns and correspondence, the situation in the Dembos became desperate, and by late 1964 the MPLA leadership decided to seek foreign help to reinforce the area, initiating the military alliance with Cuba (see Chapter 1).

More serious than either the Kassanje or Luanda uprisings, however, was a third uprising launched by the UPA in northern Angola in March 1961, throwing Angola's unstable situation into chaos. Hoping to spark a national uprising across the Bakongo heartland of Angola, the UPA's leaders got more than they bargained for when the first clashes unleashed a wave of vengeful violence against the Portuguese settlers, as many as a thousand of them being massacred in the first few days. Attending a UN summit in New York, Roberto was embarrassed (and shocked) by the savagery of these attacks, and news of UPA atrocities did much to undermine its legitimacy abroad whilst building sympathy for the Portuguese (whose own brutality received little press attention).[14] Graphic images of raped and mutilated settlers enflamed the Portuguese public's rage, and the army launched a murderous counter-offensive in northern Angola, destroying dozens of villages and killing at least 20,000 Africans before the uprising was put down.[15] When the UPA's last stronghold at Pedra Verde (Uíge) fell to the Portuguese on 20 September 1961, the surviving guerrillas joined the 150,000 Bakongo refugees fleeing over the border into Congo-Kinshasa, and from late 1961 the UPA launched sporadic forays into northern Angola from bases along the frontier.

The Congolese governments are drawn into the Angolan conflict

Almost immediately, however, UPA patrols clashed with MPLA guerrillas attempting to reach the Dembos from Léopoldville. Following the 'Ferreira incident' on 9 October 1961 – when a UPA patrol captured and executed twenty-one MPLA guerrillas en route to the 1st Military Region – open warfare broke out between the MPLA and UPA, undermining their operations against the Portuguese. Over the next three years the insurgency limped on, neither movement making headway against the massively reinforced Portuguese garrison, and gradually Angola's northern neighbours – Congo-Kinshasa and Congo-Brazzaville – were drawn into the conflict, arming their preferred candidates. Congo-Kinshasa had collapsed into chaos less than a week after independence (30 June 1960), an army mutiny and the secession of the copper-rich Katanga province (later re-named Shaba) precipitating a UN intervention which lasted until January 1963. With the withdrawal of the UN, two figures emerged in the Léopoldville elite: Joseph Kasavubu (the Congolese President) and Joseph Mobutu (the Army Chief). Roberto's close relationship with both men ensured military and financial support for his cause,[16] and under their patronage he re-branded the UPA, merging it with a Bakongo nationalist group to form the FNLA (*Frente Nacional para a Libertação de Angola*, the National Front for the Liberation of Angola).

The desire to support the FNLA was more than fraternal, however, as Léopoldville had its eye on the oil-rich Cabinda enclave. While outwardly supporting Roberto's desire to maintain Angola's territorial integrity, it secretly gave military support to the FLEC secessionist insurgency in Cabinda in the hope of strengthening its hand.[17] Léopoldville's bitter rival, Brazzaville – which faced it across the Pool – had similar ambitions on Cabinda, and following the MPLA's expulsion from Léopoldville in November 1963, Brazzaville's Marxist government invited it to set up operations there. With territorial tensions simmering between the Congolese governments, it was only natural that Brazzaville chose to support the FNLA's rival. But the effect was to cement the division between the MPLA and the FNLA, ensuring that, in the long-term, there would be no reconciliation. With a rear-base in Dolisie (Loubomo) – only 25 miles from the border with Cabinda – the MPLA launched its 2nd Military Region in January 1964, and continued to send reinforcements to the Dembos, with frustratingly little success. Meanwhile, tensions between the Congolese governments continued to grow and, by the time Che Guevara arrived for an official visit in January 1965, Brazzaville was braced for an invasion by Léopoldville at any moment (see Chapter 1).

South African involvement in Angola prior to 1974

South Africa's involvement in Angola dates back to the First World War when its troops occupied German South West Africa (Namibia), taking over its administration under a League of Nations mandate.[18] Following the election of the National Party in May 1948, the apartheid system was introduced into South Africa and Namibia, stripping the black and coloured populations of their basic rights and turning the Pretoria government into the pariah of southern Africa. Namibia's 860-mile border with Angola ensured close cooperation between the South African and Portuguese governments, and following the wave of violence which swept southern Africa in the early 1960s, they strengthened their alliance with the appointment of a South African military representative (and Vice-Consul) in Luanda.[19] By the mid-1960s, South Africa's occupation of Namibia was drawing fierce international criticism, and in August 1966 SWAPO (South West Africa People's Organisation) launched a guerrilla insurgency in the Ovambo region of Namibia which borders southern Angola. With SWAPO guerrillas operating back and forth across the border – and with the Angolan guerrillas expanding into Moxico and Cuando Cubango – the Portuguese and the SADF (South African Defence Force) drifted into an alliance, directly involving the South Africans in the fighting in Angola. Finally, in the early 1970s, both governments embarked on a scheme to build a hydroelectric dam on the part of the Cunene river which forms the western border between Angola and Namibia. The installations at Calueque and Ruacaná gave South Africa an economic stake in Angola, and would ultimately provide the pretext for an invasion in late 1975 (see Chapter 4).

Soviet involvement in Angola prior to 1974

Perhaps surprisingly – given the scale of their involvement in Angola during the 1970s and 1980s – the Soviets initially gave only lukewarm support to Angola's liberation movements. Attracted by the MPLA's Marxist sympathies, in late 1961 the Soviet Union started providing it with

11

modest military aid – mostly fire-arms and supplies. But with the Organisation of African Unity (OAU) repeatedly changing its mind over which Angolan movement it would recognise – and with suspicions growing about Neto's suitability to lead the MPLA – Soviet support was shaky. On more than one occasion they withdrew their assistance, only to tentatively restore it at a later date. The Soviets had a troubled relationship with Africa during the 1960s, suffering the embarrassing collapse of several prominent African allies.[20] This led the Soviet premier, Leonid Brezhnev, to re-assess Soviet objectives in sub-Saharan Africa, and to adopt a more geo-strategic approach. As a result, Soviet involvement in Angola tailed off in the early 1970s, and it would take the sudden decision by Lisbon to decolonise Angola to revive Soviet interest in the region. Bereft of reliable foreign support, the MPLA cast its net wide in its search for military assistance, and it was this increasingly desperate search which led them to the Cubans, initiating their military alliance (see Chapter 1).

American involvement in Angola prior to 1974

Following the Second World War, the USA was an outspoken champion of African decolonisation. When in December 1960 it voted in favour of UN General Assembly Resolution 1514 (which called on Portugal to decolonise its empire), it was widely interpreted as a gesture of support for the Angolan insurgents.[21] Washington's relationship with Portugal was complicated, however, by the American military base in the Azores which had been leased from the Portuguese since the early 1940s. Not wishing to inflame Portuguese sensibilities in the run-up to negotiations for an extension of the lease, the Americans withheld aid from the Angolan insurgents, and then sprang to Portugal's defence when Indian troops invaded Goa in December 1961. Viewing Portugal as a necessary bulwark against the spread of Soviet influence in southern Africa, the Americans strengthened their alliance with the Salazar regime, secretly allowing NATO equipment to be used in Angola (in contravention of their own guidelines). By the early 1970s, Washington had come to rely on the Portuguese presence in Angola, leaving it poorly positioned when the decision to withdraw was taken in April 1974 (see Chapter 3). The CIA is nevertheless rumoured to have given the FNLA some financial assistance, and although Roberto has subsequently denied this,[22] it is likely that his close relationship with Mobutu ensured he had some contact with the CIA (who were one of Mobutu's principal sources of foreign support).

Summary of the situation in Angola by late 1964

Once the Portuguese army and the Angolan guerrillas had settled into their protracted and inconclusive struggle, there was little international interest in Angola, and the liberation movements were forced to extend their search abroad for military assistance. By late 1964 – when Che Guevara started a three-month tour of Africa – the MPLA's search had led to the first fledgling contacts with the Revolutionary government in Havana, by then renowned as the leading sponsor of revolution in the world. With a track record of dozens of guerrilla operations across Latin America, Cuba seemed to be the ideal sponsor for the MPLA, and during Neto's first meeting with Guevara in January 1965 he pressed for a programme of Cuban military aid. What neither Guevara nor Neto realised at the time was that the military alliance they were initiating would outlive them both, and last for more than twenty-five years.

1

INTERNATIONALISM IN THE CUBAN REVOLUTION AND THE BIRTH OF THE ALLIANCE WITH THE MPLA, 1959–65

The ideological evolution of the Cuban Revolution has been an improvised and volatile affair, and internationalism is one of many ideologies which have been periodically adopted to fit the Revolutionary government's agenda. The peculiar brand of internationalism which emerged from the Cuban Revolution was the brainchild of its two leading figures – Fidel Castro and Che Guevara – and its contorted evolution mirrored the two men's uneasy relationship during the Revolution's early years. The unusual mix of Castro's cold pragmatism and Guevara's idealism proved a powerful combination, and by the late 1960s had converted Cuba from a docile American satellite into one of the revolutionary centres of the world. Initially focused on overthrowing dictatorships in the Caribbean, Cuban internationalism grew more radical in tandem with the Revolution, and quickly evolved into an anti-imperialist and anti-American call to arms. With the search for allies ever more imperative, Cuban internationalism then spread into Africa, establishing contacts with the revolutionary left and leading to several internationalist missions there (one in support of the MPLA). But in the long term, internationalism's role in the Revolution depended on Guevara's relationship with Castro, and once this started to falter so too did the ideology he cherished.

Background to the Cuban Revolution, 1953–9

Following General Fulgencio Batista's coup in March 1952, many Cuban opposition groups tried unsuccessfully to overthrow the dictator. The most persistent challenge came from M–26–7 (26th July Movement) which launched a quixotic attack against the Moncada barracks in Santiago de Cuba on 26 July 1953. The leader of this movement – who survived the attack unscathed – was Fidel Castro Ruz, a charismatic and overpowering figure from a rich land-owning family in Oriente (eastern Cuba). The two-hour speech he gave at his trial in October 1953 – '*La historia me absolverá* ('History will absolve me') – made his international reputation as a revolutionary figure (and, it must be admitted, as a man who gave long speeches).[1] Under pressure from Washington, Castro and his comrades were released from the Isle of Pines' Model Prison in May 1955, having served only eighteen months of their fifteen-year sentences. Regrouping in Mexico, they started planning an invasion of Cuba with the aim of setting up a guerrilla insurgency in the remote Sierra Maestra (north and west of Santiago) and, while in Mexico City, Castro met Ernesto 'Che' Guevara, an Argentine adventurer who had fled to Mexico the previous year from Guatemala.

The relationship which developed between Castro and Guevara over the following three-and-a-half years was to fundamentally shape the ideology and objectives of the Cuban Revolution, and Guevara quickly emerged as Castro's preferred right-hand man. Guevara was born and raised in Argentina, and from a young age acquired a reputation for determination and puritanical zeal, becoming an accomplished rugby player despite suffering from asthma which was to dog him throughout his life. Leaving Argentina in July 1963 (only three weeks before the Moncada attack) on a journey across Latin America, Guevara grew more radical in his political views – coming into contact with a mixture of Peronist, fascist and left-wing intellectuals – until by his arrival in Guatemala he had adopted Marxist–Leninism as his creed.[2] Though never holding a post in the Arbenz government, in June 1954 Guevara organised a final stand in Guatemala City against the CIA-trained army of Castillo Armas. But resistance fizzled out scarcely after the fighting had begun, and Guevara fled to Mexico. It was there through the Soviet Nikolai Leonov – who travelled back from the International Youth Festival in Moscow with Raúl Castro in mid-1953, shortly before the Moncada attack – that he was introduced to Fidel Castro. Guevara was immediately taken with Castro whose personality and loquacity overpowered him, and by the end of their first meeting he had agreed to join the expedition. The dramatic change from reckless adventurer to ruthless revolutionary would quickly bring Guevara to Castro's attention, and lead to his appointment as the first *comandante* (the guerrillas' highest rank).

The Cuban Revolutionary War, 1956–9

Castro's uprising in Cuba was initially a disaster, however; the crossing from Tuxpán (Mexico) to Cuba turning into a gruelling week-long ordeal for the eighty-two men crammed on board. By the time the crippled yacht ran ashore at Los Cayuelos (Oriente) on 2 December 1956, the uprisings timed to coincide with the landing had already been crushed. Abandoning the yacht with most of the supplies on board, the guerrillas moved inland and were ambushed three days later near Alegría de Pío. Only twenty-two of them survived the hail of bullets and subsequent round-up to escape into the Sierra Maestra. It was at this stage, however, that Castro showed his remarkable tenacity and peculiar ability to convert defeat into victory – something which would become a hallmark of his political career. Over the next two years he built his risibly small band into a competent guerrilla army, and by mid-1958 was posing a direct threat to Batista's power. With Castro's international profile on the rise – in particular after a visit to the Sierra Maestra by *New York Times* journalist Herbert Matthews – relations with the urban leadership of M–26–7 grew strained, triggering a power struggle which encouraged Castro to look towards the Soviets as an alternative source of support (see below). When a last-ditch offensive by Batista in late 1958 failed to dislodge the guerrillas, Castro sent Guevara to capture Santa Clara, and when the city fell on 29 December, the island was effectively cut in two, forcing Batista to flee from Cuba two days later.

The Revolution's first months

The overthrow of Batista was greeted with jubilation by the Cuban population which hoped it would bring an end to the corruption and gangsterism which had come to characterise Cuban political life. The widely anticipated liberal–democratic revolution did not occur, however, and instead the Revolution lurched sharply towards the left under the leadership of Fidel Castro and the Cuban Communists, sparking rebellion from many of Castro's former comrades. Opposition within Cuba was matched by a growing antipathy with the American government which ironically had given backing to the guerrillas during the war's closing stages. Prior to the Revolution, Cuba was one of Washington's most obedient (and lucrative) satellites in the Caribbean – its sugar-based economy dominated by American companies whose influence steadily increased under a string of corrupt Cuban dictatorships. Following Batista's overthrow, however, it became clear that the new Cuban government was seeking a confrontation with the USA and, by the summer of 1959, Washington had already begun plotting Castro's downfall.

Castro had been planning a showdown with the USA whilst in the Sierra Maestra,[3] however, and as early as July 1958 he had sent out feelers to the Soviets via the Cuban Communist, Carlos Rafael Rodríguez.[4] Following Castro's cool reception from the Americans during his visit to the USA in April 1959, relations between the two countries deteriorated sharply, and after Castro and the Cuban Communists seized control of the government in October 1959, Cuba and the Soviet Union concluded a formal alliance through the Soviet Ambassador, Alex Alexiev. When, in February 1960, Khrushchev offered to buy Cuban sugar, Cuba was effectively pulled into the socialist economic bloc, inflaming American sensitivities and setting in motion the Soviet–American confrontation which culminated in the 'Cuban Missile Crisis' (October 1962).

The birth of Cuban internationalism

Against this backdrop of brewing confrontation with the USA and a burgeoning alliance with the Soviet Union, Guevara developed his own model of internationalism, its evolution mirroring the radicalisation of the Cuban Revolution. Although there are many examples of foreigners fighting for other countries for ideological reasons – for example, in the Greek War for Independence (1821–32) – Guevara's ideology drew its inspiration from Karl Marx and Friedrich Engels's *Communist Manifesto*, published in 1848. Urging proletarians to shed their nationality and fight in a common cause against class oppression, Marx's 'Proletarian internationalism' was refined by Lenin, who introduced the concept of the struggle against imperialism, producing the Marxist–Leninist ideology which inspired many liberation movements after the Second World War. Incorporating the concepts of international solidarity with other nations and the constant struggle for revolution, 'Proletarian internationalism' has been described by one Soviet writer as 'Marxist–Leninist theory in all of its constituent parts'.[5] The emergence of a Soviet-controlled socialist bloc after the Second World War strengthened the concept of solidarity between outwardly socialist states, and this gained greater significance when the Cold War divided the world into spheres of Western and Soviet influence.

The internationalism Guevara envisioned when setting up an informal 'Liberation Department' in February 1959 (less than a month after occupying Havana) was of a more localised kind, however, and had more in common with Simón Bolívar than Karl Marx. Although the Cuban regime subsequently claimed that internationalism had deep roots in Cuba – dating back to the Indian chieftain Hatuey who fought against the Spanish in the early sixteenth century – the 'internationalism' practised by folk heroes such as the Dominican Máximo Gómez (a general in Cuba's War of Independence [1895–8]) was of a predominantly Hispanic kind, and was exclusively concerned with the struggle for independence in Spain's remaining American colonies. Guevara's first internationalist operations were similarly concentrated in the Caribbean basin, and were focused on overthrowing neighbouring dictatorships in the Dominican Republic, Nicaragua and Panama. The *ad hoc* nature of the 'Liberation Department' led to poor coordination – precipitating several unauthorised attempts by Cuban guerrillas to invade neighbouring countries[6] – and in late 1959 it was put under the control of the Deputy Chief of MININT (Ministry of Interior), Manuel Piñeiro Losada, known simply as '*Barba Roja*' ('Red Beard').

Under Guevara's supervision '*Barba Roja*' set up the 'MOE section' to oversee all guerrilla training programmes in Cuba, thus avoiding any further embarrassments ('M' was the secret digit for the MININT department, 'OE' stood for *Operaciones Especiales* [Special Operations]). Training camps for Latin American liberation movements were set up across Cuba, and by mid-1960 MOE had begun planning its first two operations: 'Matraca' (a guerrilla insurgency in Peru to be led by the poet Héctor Béjar) and 'Segundo Sombra' (a *guerrilla madre* [guerrilla centre] in northern Argentina which Guevara hoped to command himself). The guerrilla strategy was Guevara's brainchild – *'foquismo'* – a radically new model of guerrilla warfare drawn from his experiences in the Sierra Maestra. Published in April 1960 under the title *'La guerra de guerrillas'*,[7] Guevara's ideology was a major departure from the established Marxist–Leninist model for revolution, and laid down three ground-breaking principles:

1   Popular forces can win a war against a conventional army.
2   It is not necessary to wait for a revolutionary situation to arise – this can be created by the guerrilla forces themselves.
3   In the underdeveloped countries of Latin America, rural areas are the best battlefields for armed struggle.

Providing aspiring revolutionaries with a how-to manual for guerrilla warfare, Guevara's *'La guerra de guerrillas'* based its strategy on infiltrating a small guerrilla cell – or *'foco'* – into a remote rural area, after which it would build itself up with recruits and supplies from the local population. Steadily it would expand its operations until it was strong enough to send out further *'focos'* to spread the insurgency across the country – exactly as Castro's guerrillas had done in the Sierra Maestra. Having been one of only twenty-two survivors of the original landing force, Guevara had witnessed a pitifully small guerrilla band grow into a formidable army which had overthrown a powerful dictatorship, and he believed that Cuba's model of revolution could be successfully exported to the rest of Latin America. Unfortunately for Guevara, *'foquismo'* had several fundamental flaws – not least of which was its open publication, which enabled the CIA to prepare effective counter-measures – and throughout the early 1960s MOE's efforts to set up *'focos'* were continually thwarted, encouraging Guevara to step in and command one himself (see p. 21).

As the confrontation with Washington intensified, the Cuban government grew more radical, and on 2 September 1960 it issued the 'First Declaration of Havana'. Proclaiming Cuba's determination to fight colonialism, capitalism and 'American neo-imperialism' in the world, it was little less than a declaration of war on the USA, and led the CIA to speed up its plans for an invasion by Cuban exiles. With allies in the region deserting Cuba, the search for new ones outside the Western hemisphere became ever more imperative and, in October 1960, Guevara was sent on a two-month tour of the Communist bloc to drum up support. Guevara had already made a highly publicised tour of northern Africa and Asia in late 1959, and his growing international profile quickly turned him into Castro's unofficial ambassador, establishing contact with many of the world's leading revolutionaries. The friendship Guevara developed with Egyptian president Gamal Abdel Nasser opened a gateway into Africa – encouraging ties between Cuba and Africa's left-wing liberation movements – and in early 1961 MOE set up operations in Africa, laying the groundwork for Guevara's Congo mission four years later.

The break between Castro and Guevara

The future of internationalism in the Cuban Revolution depended on Guevara's relationship with Castro, however, and when the confrontation with the USA reached its peak in late 1962 it suffered a fatal rupture. Tit-for-tat expropriations of American-owned businesses and increases in the American embargo continued throughout 1960 and, following the Bay of Pigs invasion in April 1961, Castro strengthened his alliance with the Soviet Union, agreeing in May 1962 to install ballistic missiles in Cuba. This move – which was quickly uncovered by American spy planes – triggered the 'Missile Crisis' of October 1962, a potential nuclear confrontation between the superpowers which was only averted by a last-minute deal under which the Soviets agreed to withdraw their missiles in return for an American commitment not to invade Cuba. Initially both Castro and Guevara were outraged by the deal, as Havana had not been consulted, but in the months following the October crisis their views diverged, rupturing their close alliance.

Privately convinced that the Soviet Union was an imperialist power using Cuba as a pawn, Guevara's response was to reject the Soviet model and look for alternative sources of support (from China and Yugoslavia, for example). Castro, on the other hand, took a more pragmatic view. While angered at being excluded from the negotiations (something he would ensure did not happen during the Angolan War), Castro recognised that the Soviet deal had removed the main threat to his regime's survival – an American invasion. Therefore during a visit to the Soviet Union the following April – where he was fêted for thirty-seven days with offers of economic and technical aid to compensate for the previous year's humiliation – Castro repaired the alliance. On his return to Cuba, he made the radical announcement that Cuba would forgo the rapid industrialisation plans which Guevara as Minister of Industry had been developing, and would instead concentrate on sugar production (for export to the Soviet Union).

In fairness to Castro, Guevara's economic experiments had been disastrous, but the official shift back to the monoculture (sugar) was also a signal that Guevara was becoming a political liability. Increasingly at odds with the Soviet leadership, Guevara's presence in the Cuban government threatened to upset Castro's delicate balancing act with Moscow, while his growing international profile was viewed by Castro's inner circle as a potential threat. Bereft of a role in the new direction the Revolution was taking, the logical solution was for Guevara to leave Cuba and command one of the dozens of guerrilla '*focos*' MOE had set up during the previous three years. But to Guevara's chagrin not a single one of them had been successful,[8] and he quickly pinned his hopes on a '*guerrilla madre*' which was due to be set up in his home country – Argentina – in mid-1963.

The guerrillas had been training in Algeria since January 1963 under the command of Ricardo Masetti, a former Argentine journalist who was Guevara's go-between with the Algerian FLN, helping to smuggle arms to them in the early 1960s. Masetti's column intended to infiltrate northern Argentina and set up a 'liberated area' which could serve as a training ground for other Latin American guerrillas. Learning guerrilla skills from first-hand combat experience (the only way to make a true guerrilla, in Guevara's opinion), cadres would receive invaluable training *in situ* whilst simultaneously bolstering the core guerrilla force, before moving off to set up new '*focos*' elsewhere in Latin America. In this way Argentina would become a '*guerrilla madre*', irradiating out guerrilla '*focos*' across Latin America until it was consumed by a 'Continental Revolution'. Guevara intended to join Masetti once the 'liberated area' was established, but once again the insurgency failed to take hold, and by April 1964 the guerrillas had been surrounded and wiped out.[9] The failure of the Argentine operation was a further demoralising blow for Guevara – seriously calling into question the viability of '*foquismo*' as a model for guerrilla warfare – and left him perilously short of options. With no further guerrilla operations expected to be ready for at least a couple of years – and no clear role in government – Guevara turned his attention to Africa, and started a search which was to bring him into contact with the MPLA.

Cuba's growing involvement in Africa, 1961–4

Since Cuba had first started training African guerrillas in 1961,[10] Havana's contacts with Africa's revolutionary left had expanded dramatically. They were principally channelled through the Cuban embassy in Conakry whose *chargé d'affaires* met regularly with them to discuss policy and strategy, and occasionally offered military assistance.[11] In December 1961 Cuba sent its first internationalist aid – a cache of rifles, machine-guns and mortars – to the Algerian FLN (Front de Libération National).[12] Following independence in July 1962, Cuba set up a military mission in Algeria, and it rapidly became the centre for Cuba's global training programme and the main point of contact with the world's leading revolutionaries. In May 1963, Cuba sent its first internationalist medical brigade (fifty-five doctors and nurses) to Algeria,[13] and in October – following a surprise invasion by Morocco – Cuba launched its first overseas intervention. In response to requests from Ben Bella, a contingent of 686 Cuban troops, twenty-two T-34 tanks and assorted artillery was hastily assembled and sailed to Algeria, completing its arrival by 29 October.[14] Although Cuban troops never saw action – Algeria and Morocco signed a ceasefire the next day – the operation was a powerful demonstration of Cuban solidarity with the Algerian regime, and proved that Cuba had the capability to assemble and transport a sizeable military force to Africa in a remarkably short time. The experience of the Algerian intervention proved crucial to future Cuban interventions overseas, and would serve as the model for the larger military intervention in Angola twelve years later (see Chapter 4).

Guevara's Congo dream

When Guevara turned his thoughts to Africa in late 1964, his attention was caught by the continent's *cause celèbre*, Congo-Kinshasa. Having suffered a string of mutinies, a secessionist war in Katanga (Shaba) and a series of corrupt dictators, Congo-Kinshasa struck Guevara as the ideal location for an African '*guerrilla madre*'. Strategically located at the centre of the continent, Congo's immense jungle-covered territory offered almost unlimited protection for a guerrilla force, while its proximity to allies (such as the newly independent Zambia) guaranteed the guerrillas rear-bases and supplies. Unlike Latin America, sub-Saharan Africa was not in the Americans' 'backyard', and with a wave of nationalism sweeping through the region, the potential for spreading guerrilla '*focos*' across southern Africa seemed limitless. Entirely ignorant of the brutalities of Congo's vicious internecine conflict, Guevara set his sights on the darkest heart of Africa, and in December 1964 he embarked on a two-month African tour to sound out his most trusted allies.

Stopping first at the UN General Assembly in New York to denounce American imperialism, Guevara flew to Algiers to talk with his most trusted North African ally, president Ben Bella. From there he improvised an itinerary which took him through Mali to Congo-Brazzaville for talks with the Congolese leadership on 2 January 1965.[15] President Alphonse Massemba-Débat was by then eager to forge an alliance with the Cubans – fearing an invasion from Léopoldville at any moment – and he requested Cuban help to train the Congolese militia and (if necessary) to defend Brazzaville itself. Guevara readily granted Massemba-Débat's request as it fitted in with his larger mission in the Congo, providing a rear-base which could supply the main front with recruits, weaponry and supplies. Whilst in Brazzaville, Guevara also took the opportunity to meet with an Angolan liberation movement with which Cuba had maintained loose relations since the late 1950s – the MPLA. The talks which followed would transform this relationship, and initiate a military alliance which was to last for more than a quarter of a century.

The birth of the MPLA–Cuban alliance

The MPLA's first informal contacts with M–26–7 began in the late 1950s through the *Casa dos Estudantes do Império* (Imperial Student House) in Lisbon. Originally set up as a hostel, help centre and meeting place for African students from the Portuguese Empire, by the late 1950s the *Casa dos Estudantes* had become a hotbed of revolutionary thought, and a recruiting centre for liberation movements from Portuguese Africa.[16] It was through the *Casa dos Estudantes* that the MPLA made its first tentative contacts with Castro's revolutionaries,[17] and these were followed in 1960 with more formal contacts via the Cuban embassy in Conakry.[18] From its earliest days, the Cuban revolutionary government gave verbal support to the MPLA's cause, and between 1962 and 1964 it offered six scholarships to Angolan students who had fled Portugal. During their stay in Cuba, the Angolans received military training as well as higher education, and among them were several men who became prominent figures in the MPLA, such as N'Dalu (until recently Angolan Ambassador to Washington, DC) and Onanbwe.[19] Once the MPLA had set up an office in Algiers in February 1963, its guerrillas started receiving training from Cuban and Algerian instructors there, and this programme was still continuing when Guevara arrived in Brazzaville in early 1965.

On 5 January 1965, Guevara visited the MPLA's headquarters in Brazzaville, meeting Agostinho Neto (President), Lúcio Lara (Political Secretary) and Luís de Azevedo (Foreign Secretary) for the first high-level talks between the Cuban regime and the MPLA. Guevara outlined his vision for a pan-African revolution, but his suggestion that the MPLA send its own guerrillas to fight in the Congo got a cold reception, and he instead concentrated on Neto's requests for military aid and training.[20] Since launching its insurgency in February 1961, the MPLA had suffered repeated setbacks and was struggling to compete with its rival – the FNLA – based nearby in Léopoldville. Roberto's close contacts with the Léopoldville regime had secured the MPLA's expulsion in November 1963, and the move to Brazzaville had caused considerable disruption, leaving the guerrillas in the Dembos precariously isolated. With FNLA patrols intercepting reinforcement columns – and with the Portuguese cordon cutting off supplies and outside communication – the situation was desperate. Furthermore, hopes of breaking the deadlock in Cabinda had met with failure after the MPLA's guerrillas got bogged down in the tricky terrain of the Mayombe jungle. Although intense diplomatic activity had reversed the OAU's de-recognition of the MPLA in November 1964, it would be some time before the 3rd Military Region (the Eastern Front) could be launched in Moxico, and in the meantime Neto was desperate to prevent the two existing fronts from collapsing.

Neto's requests to Guevara were therefore twofold: first, to send instructors, weaponry and equipment to arm and train a reinforcement column for the 1st Military Region; second, to send experienced Cuban guerrillas to revitalise the 2nd Military Region in Cabinda and – if necessary – to fight alongside the MPLA. Guevara was only too happy to comply with Neto's request as it dovetailed with the subsidiary role Brazzaville was to play as a support base for his Congo operation, and following their meeting he sent instructions to Cuba to start preparing a large military mission for Brazzaville. Promising that Cuban instructors would arrive before the end of the summer, on 7 January Guevara left for Conakry, little realising that the alliance he had concluded with Neto had laid the foundations for the massive intervention in November 1975 (see Chapters 4–5).

Alleged contact between Guevara and Savimbi

While in Africa it has been alleged that Guevara was in contact with Holden Roberto and Jonas Savimbi,[21] a claim that has been consistently denied by the Cubans. Roberto's contact – which involved a brief exchange of letters in March 1965 – does not seem implausible,[22] but Savimbi's claim to have been 'one of the closest friends of Che Guevara' is without foundation.[23] Jonas Savimbi was from Munhango (Bié) on the Benguela railway line (along which his father preached throughout his youth), and had quickly emerged as the FNLA's most prominent Ovimbundu, becoming its Foreign Minister after the formation of the government-in-exile (GRAE) in April 1962. A slippery and ideologically malleable figure, Savimbi resigned his post in July 1964 and briefly flirted with joining the MPLA, visiting their Brazzaville base in December of that year.[24] But he was unimpressed by what he saw and returned to Switzerland to complete his *licence*, leaving immediately afterwards for four months of guerrilla training in China. Any meeting between Guevara and Savimbi was therefore not just unlikely, but actually impossible. In October 1966 Savimbi crossed into Moxico and founded his own liberation movement, UNITA (*União Nacional para a Independência Total de Angola*, National Union for the Total Independence of Angola). UNITA would fail to take hold as its rivals had, however, and it would not be until the early 1980s – long after Angola had achieved independence – that Savimbi rose to prominence in Angola (see Chapter 8).

Guevara fails to drum up African support

Following his ten-day visit to Congo-Brazzaville, Guevara continued on his erratic tour across Africa, receiving only a lukewarm reception for his Congo operation. Determined to press ahead with his plans, on 11 February Guevara reached Dar-es-Salaam – at the time Africa's unofficial revolutionary centre – and arranged a meeting with the leaders of the CNL (*Conseil Nationale de Libération*). Formed in October 1963 from a rainbow coalition of rebel groups in Congo's eastern provinces, the CNL had captured Stanleyville (Kisangani) in September 1964 and set up a 'liberated area' in eastern Congo. This vast area along the western banks of Lake Tanganyika (on the Zambian border) seemed ideal for Guevara's *'guerrilla madre'*, but in his haste to find new allies, Guevara overlooked the power struggle brewing between the president, Christophe Gbenye, and his subordinates, Gaston Soumaliot and Laurent Kabila. Guevara's first meetings with the latter two were not promising. He found Soumaliot vague and inscrutable, and though more impressed with Kabila, Guevara noted his open contempt for his colleagues which did not bode well for the future.

Guevara did manage to convince Kabila that the Congo's struggle was one that should concern *all* African revolutionaries, but he held back from revealing his plans – intending to sound out each of the African liberation movements first – and instead offered thirty Cuban military instructors which Kabila gratefully accepted. With the CNL on board, Guevara arranged to meet the leaders of all the African liberation movements based in Dar-es-Salaam, intending to secure their participation in separate meetings. But due to a misunderstanding by the Cuban Embassy staff, all the movements were called together at the same time, resulting in a tumultuous and confrontational meeting in which their bitter rivalries were given full vent. Stung by Guevara's undiplomatic suggestion that a true guerrilla leader could only be trained in combat (at least half of those gathered there had seen little or none), the guerrilla leaders unanimously rejected Guevara's Congo proposal, some of them reproaching him violently for what he had said.

Guevara breaks with the Cuban government

The rejection of his Congo proposal was a humiliating setback for Guevara's dreams of revolution in Africa, and left him perilously short of options. Unwelcome in Cuba, he had placed all of his bets on the success of the Congo operation, and having received a categorical rejection he was now quite literally a revolutionary without a revolution to fight. Meekly promising Kabila he would still get his Cuban instructors, Guevara left Dar-es-Salaam and for the next month wandered around Africa and

Eastern Europe, meeting trusted allies (among them Nasser and Ben Bella who poured further scorn on his Congo strategy). Eventually he felt it was time to resolve the doubts hanging over his future and, on 24 February 1965, he gave his last public speech in Algiers, breaking with the Cuban government. Described by his supporters as his '*último cartucho*' (last cartridge, or last word), Guevara's speech called on the global community to support the Third World in its struggle against imperialism, and condemned the Eastern Bloc (especially the Soviet Union) for its trade policy which was in his view as imperialist as that of the West. Coming only the day before the Communist Party World Summit in Moscow, the speech was a clear break with Cuban policy, and caused Raúl Castro some embarrassment the next day when he was confronted by indignant Soviet delegates.

By the time Guevara arrived back in Havana on 14 March 1965, his position in Cuba had become untenable. Not only did his calls for revolution in Latin America threaten to undermine the uneasy compromise reached with the Soviets over the issue of Communists parties in Latin America (which opposed armed struggle), but his open Chinese sympathies clashed head-on with Castro who only the previous day had publicly denounced China's split with the Soviets. It was time for Guevara to move on from Cuba, but with all revolutionary avenues in Latin America cut off – and with no African support for his Congo strategy – it was unclear where he could go. Having forced himself into a corner, Guevara was persuaded by Castro to go ahead with the Congo operation anyway – despite its categorical rejection by his African allies.[25] That Guevara should have considered launching the Congo operation under such unfavourable conditions is an indication of his desperation at the time, and he could only trust that his force of character and the eventual success of the enterprise would – in the end – win over his many doubters.

The dual Cuban missions to Congo and Brazzaville

Guevara's role as commander of the Congo operation – indeed his very presence in Africa – had not been authorised by the CNL, however, and in an effort to conceal this, Víctor Dreke was appointed commander of the operation, with José María Martínez 'Papi' Tamayo as second-in-command.[26] Thus Guevara's *nom de guerre* was '*Tatu*' ('three' in Swahili) while Dreke and Tamayo were '*Moja*' and '*Mbili*' ('one' and 'two') respectively. The force under their command – '*Columna 1*' – totalled 113 Cubans (considerably larger than the thirty men promised to Kabila) and was divided into three platoons of infantry and one of artillery. These men would make their way to Dar-es-Salaam in small groups, and from there would be transported to the CNL's liberated area on the western banks of Lake Tanganyika. A second force – '*Columna 2*' (the 'Patrice Lumumba

Battalion') – would simultaneously be sent to Brazzaville to carry out multiple missions, its primary objective to act as a strategic reserve for the Congo operation. This 250-man contingent was placed under the joint command of Rolando Kindelán Bles (the Military Chief) and Jorge Risquet Valdés (the Political Chief).[27] While in Brazzaville, it was charged with providing the assistance Guevara had promised to Massemba-Débat and the MPLA. First, it would send half a dozen experienced cadres to the Cabinda front to fight alongside the guerrillas; second, it would arm and train the Congolese militia to withstand an invasion from Congo-Kinshasa; and third, it would train and equip a reinforcement column for the 1st Military Region. The mission was expected to last for one year, although both the Cubans and Congolese expected to extend it if necessary.

The Cubans who went to the Congo were selected from the ranks of the Cuban army (Fuerzas Armadas Revolucionarias, FAR) in January 1965, and all were strictly volunteers. As was the case during the larger intervention in Angola in the 1970s, men were chosen as much for their ideological soundness as for their technical abilities, and all of them were black, including the officers. This was at the specific request of Soumaliot and Kabila who felt (as did the Cubans) that black instructors were less conspicuous when operating in Africa. Volunteers were told only that they would be performing an internationalist mission abroad which could last for up to two years, and by all accounts the mission was heavily oversubscribed. By late January, around 500 Cuban troops had been selected, and after processing at La Tropical stadium in Marianao (Havana), they were driven to the Piti 1 camp in Pinar del Río (western Cuba) for two month's training. During this period they were visited by Fidel Castro who met the men and explained the objectives of their mission, and this may have contributed to the rather idealistic view they formed of the MPLA's struggle. In March the Cubans divided into three groups – one for Guevara in the Congo, and two for Congo-Brazzaville – and preparations began for their departure in early April.

Guevara burns his bridges before leaving Cuba

Before leaving Cuba – in a gesture which symbolised the end of their partnership – Guevara handed Castro a mournful letter of resignation, admonishing him to release it to the public when he deemed fit. Declaring his intention to carry the fight against imperialism beyond Cuba's shores, Guevara renounced his post in the PCC, the government and the army. Praising Castro's abilities as a leader and mentor, Guevara unequivocally declared that '[n]othing legal binds me to Cuba, only ties of another kind that cannot be broken', and concluded with the phrase which became his epitaph: '¡Hasta la Victoria, siempre!' ('Onwards to victory, always!'). What Guevara did not realise, however, was that earlier that month

Castro had secretly informed the Soviet Ambassador about his Congo operation, sabotaging its already slim chances of success.[28] Possibly Castro was attempting to secure Soviet support for future guerrilla operations in Africa, but the effect of his comments was to alert the Soviets to Guevara's presence in the Congo, enabling them to monitor the progress of their political nemesis until they were ready to pull the plug on the operation.

On 1 April 1965, Guevara left Cuba disguised as a book-seller, and on 19 April he arrived in Dar-es-Salaam with the vanguard of his group. Five days later, he and thirteen Cubans were ferried across Lake Tanganyika to Kibamba where they set up their main camp in expectation of the 100 Cubans who would arrive over the next six months. On 26 April, Cuba's mission to Congo-Brazzaville got underway when the largest ship in the merchant navy – *El Uvero* – left Matanzas as part of 'Operación Triángulo' (Operation Triangle), a complex mission to deliver military supplies to three different Cuban forces in Africa.[29] The ship stopped first in Conakry where it unloaded 315 crates for the PAIGC (see next chapter p. 34) and nine Cuban instructors who immediately flew to Brazzaville. It then sailed to Brazzaville where it unloaded supplies for the Cuban mission, before heading for Dar-es-Salaam to drop supplies for Guevara's column. In late May, Rafael Moracén Limonta and five of the Cuban instructors left Brazzaville for the MPLA's training camp in Dolisie (Loubomo), leaving behind three men to prepare for the arrival of the bulk of the column. Throughout July and August, fifty more Cubans flew into Brazzaville and, on 6 August, the remainder of the battalion set sail from Mariel (Cuba).[30] By the time they reached Pointe-Noire on 21 August, however, Guevara's guerrilla operation in the eastern Congo had gone awry, and very quickly their mission evolved from a rear-guard operation into the centre of Cuban military activity in Africa.

2

THE CUBAN MISSION TO BRAZZAVILLE AND THE COLLAPSE OF THE ALLIANCE, 1965–74

The two-year mission to Brazzaville marked the start of the MPLA's twenty-six-year alliance with Cuba, and forged a bond between the Cubans and Angolans which was to withstand the turbulent and traumatic years which followed. Set up as a rear-base for Guevara's Congo insurgency, the Cuban mission to Brazzaville soon took centre-stage, by 1966 replacing Algiers as the centre of Cuban military operations in Africa. In sharp contrast to the experience of Guevara's guerrillas in eastern Congo – whose exasperation with their African allies and mistrust of the CNL leadership intensified throughout their mission – the Cubans in Congo-Brazzaville built strong relationships with the MPLA which later served as a foundation for the large-scale intervention in November 1975. Over two years the Cubans faced great obstacles, and their attempts to revitalise the Cabinda and the Dembos fronts were constantly hampered by the difficulty of the terrain and bitter infighting within the MPLA. Nevertheless, the Brazzaville mission was to forge an enduring political alliance between Castro and Neto, and this would later prove crucial to the very survival of the MPLA.

Cuban involvement in the 2nd Military Region (Cabinda)

In late May 1965 – before the bulk of the Cuban contingent for Brazzaville had even assembled in Cuba – the first nine Cuban instructors under Rafael Moracén Limonta arrived in Brazzaville incognito. Through the Congolese government they obtained false IDs, and four days later six of them travelled to the MPLA's main camp in Dolisie (Loubomo), thirty miles north of the border with Cabinda. Dolisie was the location of the MPLA's main CIR (*Centro de Instrução Revolucionária*, or training camp), several arms and supply warehouses, and the HQ for the 2nd Military Region. The camp's commander, Hoji Ya Henda, was a charismatic leader and natural guerrilla – despite never having had any formal military training – and he established a strong rapport with the Cubans. Also present in Dolisie was a captain from the Ghanaian army, Kojo Tchikata, who had been sent by President Nkrumah to assist the MPLA, and he teamed up with the six Cubans to form the nucleus of the MPLA's training corps.[1] After acclimatising for a few days, the Cubans were split between two platoons of MPLA guerrillas, and in early June 1965 they crossed into Cabinda, the first Cuban troops to carry out operations in Angola. Within a few days they clashed with a Portuguese patrol in the border area, and over the next five months they criss-crossed the border, training the guerrillas and laying numerous ambushes.

The experience of fighting in the Mayombe jungle was one of 'mutual learning' (as Moracén later put it),[2] the MPLA cadres picking up the skills of guerrilla warfare whilst educating the Cubans on the realities of Angola's inter-tribal conflict. The Angolans received technical training from the Cubans – on the operation and maintenance of rifles and light artillery – as well as irregular tactical instruction, in particular the laying of ambushes. But they were testing times for the Cubans who were accustomed to the regimented FAR and who 'found themselves in a completely alien culture with a very different concept of discipline'.[3] In particular the Cubans were disturbed by the acute tribalism infecting the guerrillas, often putting lives in danger when Umbundus refused to go back for their Bakongo comrades (and vice versa). To the Cubans – all the product of Cuba's explicitly non-racist ideology – the depth of inter-tribal hatred was baffling, and Moracén later admitted that '[t]o me they were all Angolans. But they didn't have this concept'.[4] It was a problem Guevara ran into repeatedly on the Congo front, and Cuban reaction to it – a mixture of confusion and outrage – reflected both their idealistic approach to internationalism and their lack of understanding of African nationalism.[5] Nevertheless, the experience of sharing the same daily risks bred a strong camaraderie between the Cubans and Angolans, and over the months a mutual respect developed between the trainers and their recruits.

Cabinda was a challenging environment for guerrilla operations, and the effectiveness of the Cuban instructors was constantly hampered by the exceptionally difficult terrain. The guerrillas' main infiltration route into Cabinda ran through the Mayombe – the world's second largest (and densest) jungle – and although this afforded them unlimited cover, the thick vegetation made the going very tough. It was at least a day's march to the nearest Portuguese garrison (only just over the border at Sanga Planicie), and up to a week's trek to Belize (forty miles south of Dolisie), the first settlement of note. The sparsely-populated area offered little in the way of local support, especially as the few tribes that did live in the Mayombe were suspicious of the Umbundu-dominated MPLA and tended to support FLEC. The Cuban–MPLA campaign in Cabinda thus involved little more than brief sorties into the enclave, inconclusive clashes with the first Portuguese patrols encountered, and rapid withdrawals to Dolisie for fresh supplies. Although the training the guerrillas received was invaluable, the Cubans' inability to escalate the insurgency in Cabinda convinced Brazzaville that the front had little potential, and that it would be wiser to deploy its forces elsewhere. For this reason, in early 1966 the bulk of the guerrillas were withdrawn from Cabinda to Brazzaville for incorporation into the reinforcement columns destined for the Dembos.[6]

The failure of Guevara's Congo operation, June–November 1965

While the bulk of the back-up force for Brazzaville was making its final preparations to leave Cuba, Guevara's operation ran into trouble. Despite the successful infiltration of over 120 Cubans into eastern Congo during the mission's first six months, Cuban relations with their CNL allies quickly became strained. Guevara grew increasingly frustrated with the Tutsi and Congolese recruits who were undisciplined, racked by tribal divisions and put more faith in black magic than military tactics.[7] Kabila failed to live up to his promises to visit the front, and following the suspicious drowning of Mitoudidi – the only CNL officer in whom Guevara had any faith – communication with the CNL broke down completely. Conscious that Léopoldville was sending a mercenary army into the eastern Congo, Guevara was anxious to carry out an attack to revitalise the crumbling front, and on 20 June he ordered a raid on the 400-man garrison guarding the hydroelectric plant at Bendera, twelve miles south-west of Kibamba. By the time the Cuban–CNL force reached the camp nine days later, half the guerrillas had deserted, and they were easily driven off with the deaths of twenty Congolese and four Cubans. Frustrated by this setback, Guevara's worst fears of a split in the CNL were confirmed two months later when Soumaliot – the man in whose abilities he had the least faith – ousted Gbenye as leader.

Gathering his Cubans together on 12 August, Guevara declared that there was no chance of winning the war with such an undisciplined rabble, and that his dream of training other African revolutionaries in the Congo was totally unfeasible.[8] Coming a fortnight before the bulk of the Cuban military contingent arrived in Brazzaville, Guevara's admission effectively ended Brazzaville's role as a reserve, and enabled the mission to focus on its subsidiary roles (see p. 32). Determined to see his operation through to the bitter end, Guevara stayed on in Kibamba and attempted to reorganise the guerrilla front. But his fortunes took a hammer blow on 13 October when Joseph Kasavubu seized power in Léopoldville, overnight changing the political climate. Ten days later Kasavubu spoke at an OAU meeting in Ghana, promising negotiations with the CNL and announcing that the white mercenaries who had caused such controversy would be withdrawn immediately – and that as a quid pro quo all other foreign forces should do likewise. Kasavubu's message was directed at Tanzania which was providing Guevara with rear-bases and supplies, and under pressure from the Soviets, Tanzania was forced to comply. A few days later President Nyerere summoned the Cuban Ambassador Pablo Rivalta to inform him that Tanzania would henceforth be stopping all aid to the Cubans in the Congo.

On 1 November Rivalta cabled Guevara the devastating news. 'It was the coup de grace for a moribund Revolution,' Guevara wrote later. On 4 November – with mercenaries closing in on his camp – Guevara received a final cable from Castro.[9] Accepting the hopelessness of his situation, Castro left the decision on whether to withdraw or not to Guevara, ordering him to avoid the total annihilation of his Cuban force. Briefly nurturing dreams of trekking across the Congo to link up with Mulele's CNL force in the north, Guevara eventually admitted defeat and on 18 November ordered the evacuation (even as his upper camp was under attack). On 20 November Guevara and all but six of his Cubans were withdrawn by boat from Kibamba, those remaining having volunteered to search for three Cubans who went missing in the retreat.[10] 'It was a desolate, sobering and inglorious spectacle,' Guevara wrote later.[11] Five days later Mobutu overthrew Kasavubu, and for the next thirty-two years Congo-Kinshasa's fate was sealed under his corrupt leadership. Mobutu's seizure of power greatly boosted the FNLA's profile in Kinshasa, and it quickly became the spoiled child of the Zairian Army which provided it with bases and weaponry. But Mobutu would prove a fickle patron, and there were limits to his support, as Roberto would discover to his personal cost during the chaotic scramble for independence which began in mid-1974 (see Chapter 3).

Following the departure of the Cubans from Dar-es-Salaam on 6 December, Guevara ensconced himself in the Cuban Embassy where over the next ten weeks he wrote up his campaign diary. Its opening words – 'This is the story of a failure' – sum up his defeatist mood. What followed was a bitter analysis of the operation's many short-comings, focusing as much on his own as on those of his Congolese allies. There were few crumbs of consolation for Guevara who had seen seven months of effort come to nothing, and he was left bitterly disillusioned by African tribal politics and the wastefulness of the whole enterprise (six Cubans had died). Even before the boat evacuating him from Kibamba had docked in Tanzania, Guevara had set his sights on the Bolivian operation which MOE had been planning since early 1964, but he felt unable to return to Cuba as, by now, his letter of resignation was in the public domain.[12] Having vowed to fight the revolution across the world, Guevara was not prepared to return to Cuba with his tail between his legs, and he retreated to Czechoslovakia where he remained until July, resisting all invitations to return to Cuba. It would take the offer of commanding the Bolivian mission to entice Guevara out, setting in motion his last tragic guerrilla adventure.

The Cuban mission in Brazzaville, 1965–7

With Guevara gone from Africa, Brazzaville became the de facto centre of Cuba's African operations, and in sharp contrast to the Congo operation it proceeded with some success. On 21 August 1965, the bulk of the Cuban force arrived aboard the Soviet liner *Felix Dzerzhinsky* in Pointe-Noire, and most were immediately sent to Madibou, a training camp six miles south-west of Brazzaville, leaving a small contingent in Pointe-Noire to oversee logistics. Work began at once on training the Congolese militia – or CDC (Civil Defence Corps) – which it was hoped would act as a deterrent to an invasion from Léopoldville, whilst also providing Massemba-Débat with a military force independent of the Congolese army which was loyal to him personally. As a result the Congolese army, which at first welcomed the increased security provided by the Cuban military presence, began to resent it, and it was only a matter of time before the Cubans were drawn into the power struggle brewing between Massemba-Débat and his rivals in the army (see pp. 35–6).[13]

In reaction to the overthrow of Ben Bella in a coup in June 1965, the Cubans set up a Presidential Guard for Massemba-Débat, a decision which was to become the hallmark of Cuban military missions in Africa. With army coups and assassinations becoming ever more frequent in the late 1960s, Cuba routinely set up special elite units to protect the African leaders they were supporting (a practice continued to this day in Angola).[14] The loss of Ben Bella was nevertheless a serious blow to Cuba's operations in Africa, and relations with the new regime were cool, prompting a downgrading in the Algiers mission.[15] As a result, Brazzaville quickly became the focus of Cuban operations in Africa, and on his return from Dolisie, Moracén was given the duty of meeting representatives of the African revolutionary movements Cuba was sponsoring.[16]

The Camilo Cienfuegos Column

Shortly after the Congolese militia began training, the Cuban instructors started work on their third mission in Brazzaville – to train a reinforcement column for the stranded 1st Military Region.[17] All of the MPLA's guerrillas were concentrated in Brazzaville for selection (including many who had been training with the Cubans in Dolisie). Around 100 were selected for the relief column, and the experienced Moracén was recalled from Cuba to oversee their training. All of the guerrillas' uniforms, supplies and weaponry – including their first automatic rifles and RPGs (rocket-propelled grenade-launchers) – were provided by Cuba, although it is likely that some guerrillas used Soviet and Yugoslav weaponry. In late 1965, the Cubans helped the guerrillas to smuggle their weaponry into Congo-Kinshasa, burying it in caches close to the Angolan border. Shortly before the column completed its training, the Angolans voted to become the 'Camilo Cienfuegos Column' in honour of the Cuban commander Kindelán (who had served with Cienfuegos in the Revolutionary War). The column was placed under the command of 'Monstro Imortal' (Jacob Alves Caetano), a rising star in the MPLA who had narrowly survived a UPA ambush in April 1963, and whose combat experience and knowledge of the terrain were crucial to the column's chances of success.[18] During training, an envoy from the 1st Military Region arrived in Brazzaville with desperate requests for aid, so it was with a redoubled sense of purpose that the column set out from Brazzaville in August 1966.

Ironically, the most serious danger facing the guerrillas was not from the Portuguese but from the FNLA which viewed northern Angola as its unique area of operations, and which had ruthlessly suppressed all MPLA activity there since late 1961. Using false IDs the Cubans had obtained from the Brazzaville regime, Monstro Imortal's group made the crossing to Kinshasa disguised as locals – a fairly easy task as thousands of people crossed the Pool every day to trade and visit their families. Regrouping near the Angolan border, the column picked up its weapons and began the long trek through northern Angola to the 1st Military Region's HQ at Nambuangongo (190 miles south-west of them). Through a mixture of stealth and sheer luck the column reached the Dembos unscathed, their arrival on 23 September giving a huge morale boost to the region's belea-guered guerrillas. The column brought the first news from the outside world for nearly four years, supplies and sophisticated weaponry, as well as 100 well-armed guerrillas who immediately upset the military balance in the area. The resounding success of the Camilo Cienfuegos Column encouraged the Cubans to train a second relief column later that year, although they little realised that the man they had sent into the Dembos – Monstro Imortal – would later turn against Neto, with bloody results (see Chapter 6).

Cuba and the MPLA wind down the Brazzaville operation

As a result of the good working relationship developing in Brazzaville, more formal political ties emerged between Cuba and the MPLA, and in January 1966 the MPLA was the only Angolan delegation invited to attend the Tricontinental Conference in Havana.[19] Purportedly the brain-child of Guevara, this unprecedented gathering of the world's most notori-ous revolutionary leaders was a bold bid by Castro to assume leadership of the global revolutionary movement. It was thus deeply ironic that the man who gave birth to Cuba's model of internationalism was not present, Guevara missing out on the peak of Cuba's internationalist phase. Africans made up more than 150 of the 512 delegates who attended – a reflection of the importance Africa was expected to play in the war against American imperialism – and shortly after the conference Cuba founded OSPAAAL to coordinate the global revolutionary movement.[20] The MPLA's election to its Executive Committee suggested a tightening in its alliance with Cuba,[21] but appearances were deceptive as, during the conference, Castro had adopted a new African protégé – Amílcar Cabral of the PAIGC.

The PAIGC (African Party for the Independence of Guiné and Cape Verde) had launched its war against the Portuguese in Guiné (modern-day Guinea-Bissau) in January 1963. By 1965 it had taken control of nearly 40 per cent of its territory, and its charismatic leader Amílcar Cabral had established himself as a leading revolutionary. Attracted by his reputation, Guevara met with Cabral in Conakry during his tour of Africa, and following promises of military aid the first supplies were sent to the PAIGC in May 1965 as part of 'Operación Triángulo' (see Chapter 1). By the time Cabral arrived in Havana for the Tricontinental Conference, Castro was keen to upgrade their alliance, and he whisked Cabral off for a three-day tour of the Sierra Maestra where he offered a contingent of Cuban instructors to train his guerrillas in Conakry and, if necessary, to fight alongside them in Guiné. After Guevara's dispiriting failure in the Congo – and with no improvement in Cabinda – Castro was switching his bets, and less than four months later Cuba launched a military mission to Conakry modelled on its sister in Brazzaville.[22] The Conakry mission inevitably shifted Cuba's focus away from Brazzaville – at the time Cuba's largest mission in Africa – and by the summer of 1966 the Cubans were already scaling down their operations there.

Unknown to Havana, however, the MPLA was also planning to pull out of Brazzaville and transfer to Lusaka, having staked its success on the 3rd Military Region (the Eastern Front) which had recently been launched in Moxico. Recognising Brazzaville's poor location for supporting the Dembos – with more than 200 miles of hostile terrain separating the two – the MPLA had decided to re-launch its insurgency in eastern Angola (while scaling back the stagnant Cabinda front). With numerous infiltration routes from rear-bases in Zambia – and a large African population in Moxico – the 'Eastern Front' seemed to offer the key to success. Thus, by the time Neto and Hoji Ya Henda met with Castro in January 1966, both sides were planning to close down their Brazzaville operations. The meeting between Castro and Neto was nevertheless significant – representing the peak of the Cuban–MPLA alliance in the 1960s – and a loyal friendship developed between the two men which would prove a life-line for Neto in his most desperate hour. The success of the Cuban programme was discussed – in particular the Camilo Cienfuegos Column – and it was agreed to prepare a second reinforcement column for the Dembos.

Keen to maintain Cuba's good working relationship with the MPLA, Castro offered to move the contingent of Cuban instructors with the MPLA to Zambia where they could train the large numbers of Angolan recruits gathering in its rear-bases. Neto initially accepted but Lusaka vetoed the move, fearing retaliatory action from its anti-Communist neighbours.[23] Instead, the Cubans proposed setting up a training programme for experienced MPLA cadres in Cuba itself. The most promising MPLA guerrillas would be sent to Cuba's remote Escambray mountains for advanced guerrilla training in the LCB (*Lucha Contra Bandidos*, or counter-insurgency operations), enabling them to return to the 'Eastern Front' as military instructors in their own right. If the programme were successful, the MPLA could meet its own training needs within a few years, obviating the need for Cuban instructors in parts of Africa where they were not welcome. Accordingly, the following October the first ninety MPLA cadres arrived in Cuba to begin seven months of intensive training, and in the summer of 1967 they returned to the Eastern Front to begin work as military instructors.[24] Thus Neto and Henda's visit to Havana in January 1966 – which has often been depicted as the moment when the Cuban–MPLA alliance was cemented at the highest levels – actually marked the moment when it started to wither back to the low-level contacts of the early 1960s.

The attempted coup against Massemba-Débat, 27 June–6 July 1966

Following Neto's return to Brazzaville, the Cuban–MPLA alliance underwent its first serious test when disaffected Congolese officers loyal to Captain Marien Ngouabi launched a coup against Massemba-Débat.[25] Ngouabi was a popular figure in the Congolese army and had recently been demoted by Massemba-Débat who viewed him as a threat to his power. This action inflamed Ngouabi's supporters, and when on 27 June 1966 the president left for a trip to Madagascar, they seized the opportunity to overthrow his government. With the support of Ngouabi's elite paratrooper regiment, the army and the gendarmes took control of central Brazzaville, cutting the ferry service to Kinshasa and arresting the chiefs of the army and security forces. In a panic, Massemba-Débat's government fled to the sports stadium which was located 100 yards from the Cuban camp, and they remained there under Cuban protection for the duration of the coup. With the future of their African operations in the balance, the Cuban contingent teamed up with the CNL and MPLA guerrillas based in Brazzaville to thwart the coup.

Since early 1966, Risquet had feared that a coup was imminent, and as a precaution he had moved the main Cuban camp from Madibou to Bosque on the outskirts of Brazzaville. Moracén was immediately called to Brazzaville, and he hastily assembled one platoon each of MPLA and CNL guerrillas under the command of Henda and Mukudi (the CNL commander in Brazzaville). Hoping to contain the coup before it spread beyond the capital, the two platoons were sent to secure the flank south of the railway line, while a platoon of twenty-five Cubans was dispatched to capture the radio station located 500 yards from the Cuban camp. Simultaneously, small groups of Cubans occupied Brazzaville's main buildings (including the Cuban Embassy, the stadium and the General Hospital) and set up roadblocks at the main intersections. Outmanoeuvred, the plotters held talks with the government inside the Cuban camp (the Cubans reportedly kept their distance), demanding the restoration of Ngouabi, the dissolution of the militia and the departure of the Cubans. A tense stand-off followed, but after one week the mutinous troops unexpectedly returned to their barracks, enabling Massemba-Débat to return to Brazzaville to reassume control of his government.

Though foiled with minimal bloodshed (only one Congolese soldier was killed), the coup attempt severely shook the stability of Massemba-Débat's regime, and it was probably a factor in the decision to extend the Cuban mission four months beyond its August 1966 deadline. Although the Cubans and Congolese had anticipated the mission might extend beyond one year, the four-month extension was nevertheless Cuba's first experience of 'mission creep' in Africa, and encouraged Massemba-Débat to push for a further extension in late 1966 to prop up his government. The focus of the Brazzaville mission would again be on bolstering the CDC (which had proved so ineffective during the coup attempt) and creating a force which could act as a counterweight to the growing power of the army. Anti-Cuban sentiment in the army nevertheless forced Massemba-Débat to make concessions to Ngouabi's supporters – several of them being reassigned to their posts to placate local opinion – and over the following months Ngouabi continued to attract support, encouraging him to try again (see p. 40).

The Kamy Column

Boosted by the success of the Camilo Cienfuegos Column, in October 1966 the Cubans began preparing a second relief column for the 1st Military Region,[26] its guerrillas naming it the 'Kamy Column' after a young guerrilla martyr from the Cabinda front.[27] The column's 150 guerrillas were trained at the MPLA's Kalunga camp – between Dolisie and the border with Cabinda – under the instruction of the chief of the Cuban training contingent, Colonel Augusto Martínez Sánchez. Although the column contained some seasoned veterans, it was for the most part made up of peasants with no military experience, a factor which would have serious repercussions in the gruelling journey ahead. The guerrillas received forty-five days' training, including technical instruction in the use of their Soviet, Chinese and Belgian weaponry, and tactical, physical and political training. In early December the column was placed under the command of 'Ingo' (Benigno Vieira Lopes), an experienced veteran of Cabinda, and included five women from OMA (Angolan Women's Organisation), the most famous of whom – Deolinda Rodrígues de Almeida – was already a senior figure in the MPLA. The Kamy Column would follow the same route taken the previous year by the Camilo Cienfuegos Column, and in mid-January 1967 was seen off personally by Risquet and Neto. Neto's last words to the guerrillas were: 'I hope that when we next embrace it will be in the interior of Angola.'[28]

The Kamy Column was to have a harrowing experience, however. Although the column crossed to Kinshasa without incident, it ran into trouble shortly after crossing into Angola at Luvo (Zaire province) on 12 January 1967 (see Map 3). Due to poor foresight by the Cuban and Angolan planners, no account had been taken of seasonal rains, and the guerrillas abandoned their original plans to reach the M'bridge river by the end of the first week when it took them an entire day to cross the first swollen river they encountered. Wary of increased Portuguese and FNLA vigilance after the Camilo Cienfuegos Column passed through the area, the guerrillas attempted a different route towards Nambuangongo, but they were soon lost and wandered for twenty days, consuming all of their supplies. Eventually reaching a river they believed to be the M'bridge they were ambushed by an FNLA patrol, losing four guerrillas. Once across they learned the dispiriting news from locals that they were still two days from the M'bridge. By the time they reached it on 10 February the column had been reduced to 119 guerrillas (fifteen had died of hunger, several had drowned and some had deserted). Attempts to cross the swollen river failed when their makeshift raft was torn to pieces and one of the guerrillas drowned (most did not know how to swim).

Recognising that many of the guerrillas did not have the strength to continue, Ingo split his force in two – the strongest elements (seventy guerrillas) pushing on under his command to Nambuangongo, while the weakest (including the women) struggled back to Brazzaville under the logistics chief, 'Ludy' (Rodrígues João Lopes). Ingo's larger column pressed on in abysmal conditions – several more guerrillas drowning as they crossed the M'bridge – and their numbers were further depleted by FNLA and Portuguese ambushes. There were scenes of great heroism – one guerrilla fighting for nearly five hours against a Portuguese patrol before using his last bullet on himself – but also of great desperation as the

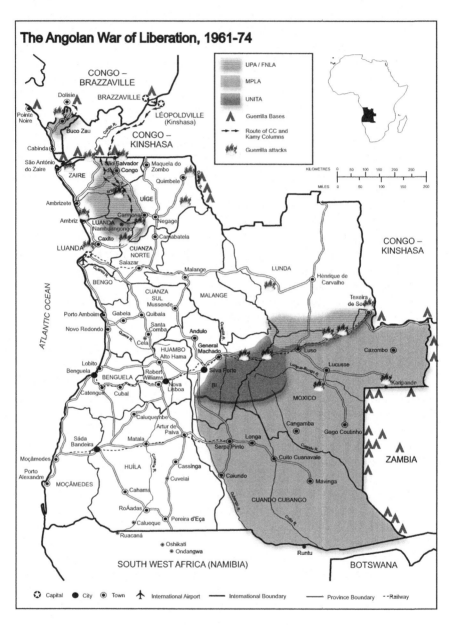

Map 3 The Angolan War of Liberation, 1961–74.

guerrilla force was worn down by attrition. Finally on 1 April 1967 – seventy-nine days after setting out from Songololo – twenty-one bedraggled survivors reached the 1st Military Region. It was a victory of sorts – the arrival of new guerrillas giving a boost to local morale, as did their news that the 3rd Military Region had been launched the previous May, and that a fourth was being planned for the Lundas and Malanje. But their success was immediately undercut by the fate of Ludy's column. Desperately weakened by their ordeal – and lacking even the most basic supplies – Ludy's guerrillas limped back through northern Angola, abandoning dying comrades along the way. When they finally reached the border with Zaire only twenty remained, and in their desperation they asked locals for directions, not realising that they would be betrayed to the nearby FNLA base at Kamuna. As they were approaching the outskirts of Songololo, the guerrillas were captured by the FNLA, and imprisoned in Kinshasa's Kakokol prison (where they were visited by OMA militants and relations). They were then transferred to the FNLA base at Kinkuzu (120 miles south of Kinshasa), after which they were never seen again.[29]

The final extension to the Brazzaville mission, December 1966–July 1967

The departure of the Kamy Column completed the Cuban mission in Congo-Brazzaville, and in mid-December 1966 the bulk of the Cuban contingent was withdrawn. However, again at the request of Massemba-Débat (and also of the MPLA and CNL), sixty Cuban instructors remained behind to train three more columns. The first was destined for the CNL's last remaining foothold in northern Congo, and was commanded by the CNL commander in Brazzaville, Mukwidi. In June 1967 Mukwidi led his column into Zaire, but his guerrillas were quickly intercepted by Mobutu's forces and wiped out. A second Cuban-trained column of twenty-five Cameroonian guerrillas met a similar fate within days of infiltrating Cameroon in the spring of 1967.[30] The third column was destined for the Dembos, the severe losses of the Kamy Column failing to dent the Cubans' determination to break the Portuguese–FNLA stranglehold. Voting to name themselves the Ferraz Bomboko Column (after a guerrilla from the Dembos), the column's 180 men included 98 guerrillas who had just completed their military training in Cuba. Each carried two weapons, one for personal use and the other for a guerrilla in the Dembos. In June 1967, the guerrillas infiltrated Zaire, but due to a basic error (they all got onto one train at the same time) they were discovered by Mobutu's forces who disarmed them and imprisoned them in Kinshasa. Having learned from its previous experience, the MPLA launched a spirited campaign in the OAU to secure the guerrillas' release, and thanks to its efforts they were eventually freed, although without their weapons.[31] The Ferraz

Bomboko Column was thus not a total failure as many of its guerrillas – who now had operational experience – were sent to the Eastern Front where they distinguished themselves over the following years.[32]

Cuba and the MPLA withdraw from Brazzaville

Shortly before the dispatch of these last two columns, the Cuban mission in Brazzaville came to a close, and in July 1967 the last sixty Cuban instructors were withdrawn.[33] The Brazzaville mission could boast several successes – the Camilo Cienfuegos Column, the bloodless crushing of Ngouabi's coup, even the first vaccination campaign against polio.[34] But with the MPLA moving to Lusaka and downgrading the Cabinda Front it was clear that, in the long term, the Cuban mission had been a failure. The crushing of both the Kamy and Bomboko columns convinced the MPLA that the FNLA and Portuguese forces in northern Angola were too strong for reinforcements to get through to the Dembos from Brazzaville. And in Cabinda they were forced to recognise that the enclave was too remote, under-populated and disproportionately garrisoned by Portuguese troops (who were protecting the oil installations off Cabinda city) to develop into a successful insurgency. Furthermore, despite eighteen months' training, the CDC failed to emerge as an effective bulwark for Massemba-Débat, offering only token resistance when Ngouabi launched his second coup in August 1968.

In fairness to the Cubans, the outcome of the mission was not entirely their fault. They had responded to Neto's requests for military assistance, and it was only once the mission was underway that Brazzaville's strategic weakness became apparent. But there was little escaping the fact that after two years of close cooperation, the Cubans and Angolans were moving off to opposite sides of Africa – the Cubans to Conakry, the MPLA to Lusaka – to pursue different agendas. The Cuban withdrawal was followed by the MPLA which moved its HQ to Lusaka in early 1968, hoping to resuscitate its faltering insurgency on the Eastern Front. The move to Zambia was an implicit admission of the failure of the 2nd Military Region, and the Cabinda front was scaled down – although it was not shut down altogether as some writers have suggested.[35] The Cabinda front continued to operate throughout the late 1960s and early 1970s, but it never threatened Portuguese occupation of the enclave and was principally used as a training ground for MPLA recruits, Paulo Jorge later describing it as a 'laboratory of revolutionary warfare'.[36]

By the time Massemba-Débat was ousted from power in early September 1968, the MPLA's move to Lusaka had been completed, and not a moment too soon as its operations in Brazzaville were curtailed by Ngouabi's government. With its departure from Brazzaville, the MPLA's close working relationship with the Cubans was broken, and within months the alliance started to wither away as both parties were consumed by internal crises. For Neto, the rise and sudden collapse of the Eastern Front in Moxico would once again plunge the MPLA into chaos and threaten his leadership, while for Castro the brewing dispute with the Soviet Union would erupt in a dramatic confrontation in 1968, sparking a radical change of direction for the Cuban Revolution. It would not be until Castro re-emerged onto the world stage to make his first tour of Africa in May 1972 that a senior member of the Cuban government met with MPLA officials, by which time the Cuban–MPLA alliance had reverted to the low-level diplomatic contacts of the early 1960s.

The death of Guevara and the internationalist ideal, 1967–72

Since the Missile Crisis of October 1962, a major confrontation had been brewing between Havana and Moscow, fuelled by Cuba's active support for dozens of guerrilla movements across Latin America. While the Soviets were happy to tolerate the bellicose anti-American statements issuing from Havana – most notably the 'Declarations of Havana' (see Chapter 1) – they were concerned that Guevara's guerrilla operations in Latin America would upset the delicate modus operandi they had established with the USA (which allowed them to control most Latin American Communist parties from Moscow). The Soviets raised no objections to the Tricontintenal Conference (hoping it would weaken China's influence in the Third World), but when Castro used the opportunity to blast Moscow's Latin American Communists and stake a claim for the leadership of the global revolutionary movement, relations with Moscow started to deteriorate. The final spark which set off the confrontation came, fittingly enough, from Moscow's nemesis – Che Guevara – who in early 1967 launched his final guerrilla operation in southern Bolivia.

Guevara had remained in Czechoslovakia throughout early 1966 and was only coaxed back to Cuba in July with the offer of commanding the Bolivian operation. Similar in conception to Masetti's doomed Argentine column, Guevara planned to set up a '*guerrilla madre*' in Bolivia which could irradiate guerrilla cells across Latin America, setting the continent ablaze with revolution. For Guevara, now thirty-eight, it was his last throw in the battle to prove that his model of guerrilla warfare – '*foquismo*' – could work in Latin America, and in his impatience to launch the operation he overlooked many crucial weaknesses in his choice of Bolivia, weaknesses which proved fatal.[37] In early 1967, Guevara took command of the mostly Cuban force in south-eastern Bolivia, but they had scarcely completed their first gruelling reconnaissance of the area when their camp was discovered by the Bolivian army – and from then on they were on the run. CIA agents were called in to train a special counter-insurgent force, and after Guevara made the fatal error of splitting his forces, the Bolivians picked off the smaller group in a riverside ambush, and then closed in on Guevara whose acute asthma was slowing his progress. On 8 October he was captured near La Higuera, and after being held overnight he was summarily executed the following morning – under direct orders from the Bolivian High Command.

The death of Guevara marked the death of the internationalist ideal he had championed for nine years, and the Cuban regime quickly set about constructing an elaborate myth around the man and his arguably few achievements, creating what Castro claimed at a candle-lit vigil was the ideal model for Cuba's children. Having upset Moscow in April 1967 with the publication of Guevara's apocalyptic Message to the Tricontinental – which called for 'two, three, many Vietnams' to weaken the imperialist powers in an 'Intercontinental Revolution' – the Cubans were outraged to discover that Mario Monje (the leader of the Bolivian Communist Party) had withheld crucial support from Guevara under pressure from the Soviets (the second operation they had sabotaged). From this point onwards Soviet–Cuban relations took a nose-dive, and following Castro's boycott of the October Revolution's Fiftieth Anniversary Celebrations in Moscow that November, the Soviets retaliated by cutting deliveries of petroleum to Cuba, bringing the economy to a standstill.

Infuriated that Moscow was using the 'oil stick' to bring Cuba into line (it provided Cuba with 99.3 per cent of its petroleum), on 28 January Castro retaliated by arresting and imprisoning an alleged 'micro-faction' in the PCC led by Aníbal Escalante.[38] This thinly disguised purge of pro-Moscow elements in the Cuban government drew further retaliation from the Soviets who withdrew their ambassador, Alexiev. As the oil embargo began to bite, a crazed siege mentality took hold in Cuba, spawning impractical and often ludicrous schemes to escape the Soviet economic stranglehold. But by the end of the summer, Castro was forced to back down, and following the Soviet invasion of Czechoslovakia on 23 August he publicly declared Cuba's support. At once tarnishing his international reputation, Castro's speech signalled the end of Cuba's maverick internationalist phase, and marked the start of its complete absorption into the Soviet bloc. Over the next four years, Cuba would sink into the Soviet embrace, and by the time it emerged in the mid-1970s, little would remain of its previous political or economic system.

The catalyst for radical reform within Cuba came in 1970 when – in a final attempt to escape the Soviet grip – Cuba embarked on a plan to harvest a record ten million tons of sugar. Havana's motivations for launching this plan are still unclear, but it ended in disastrous failure, the conscription of the entire Cuban workforce for the harvest wrecking what little remained of the Cuban economy.[39] Major restructuring of the economic and political systems was needed to repair the damage, and following Castro's trip to the Soviet Union in June 1972, the 'Institutionalisation' process began – converting Cuba into a recognisably Communist state in the Soviet model. Vestiges of 1960s political experimentation (such as Guevara's power base at the INRA) were swept away to be replaced by a centralised political structure with direct control over Cuba's many popular organisations (such as the CDRs).[40] Cuba's armed forces were remodelled along Soviet lines and, in 1970, started a programme to re-equip them with some of the most sophisticated military technology ever provided to a state outside the Soviet bloc. By 1975, the FAR had received over $3 billion worth of Soviet weaponry – twice the amount Cuba had received in Soviet military aid over the previous decade, and all of it free of charge.[41] The modern force which resulted from this programme dramatically enhanced Cuba's ability to project military power abroad, and made possible the massive intervention of November 1975.

The effect on Cuba's foreign policy

The radical changes taking placed within Cuba were matched internationally as Cuba fell into line within the Soviet bloc, siding with Moscow in the Sino-Soviet split and using Cuban influence to bring more Third World countries into the Soviet fold. In July 1972, Cuba joined the Council for Mutual Economic Assistance (CMEA or 'COMECON') – incorporating Cuba into the Socialist economic bloc – and that December, Castro signed a fresh economic agreement with Moscow which included a highly-favourable re-scheduling of Cuba's debt.[42] As a result of Cuba's more rigid foreign policy, the internationalist programme in Latin America was curtailed. Guerrillas who had received Cuban backing since the early 1960s were cut off, while Havana sought rapprochement with the very governments these guerrillas had been trying to overthrow (in Peru, Panama and Argentina). Although some African and Latin American guerrillas continued to be trained in Cuba during the early 1970s, no further Cuban operations would be launched in Latin America until after the intervention in Angola, marking the death of Guevara's internationalist vision for the hemisphere.

The immediate effect of Cuba's less belligerent foreign policy was a dramatic scaling-down in its African operations. Within a year of the withdrawal from Brazzaville only one sixty-man mission remained in Africa, supporting the PAIGC from its base in Conakry. Moving away from backing every African movement which claimed to be Marxist–Leninist, Havana concentrated instead on improving ties with established revolutionary regimes in Africa, restoring its alliance with Algeria, whose president Houari Boumedienne had overthrown Castro's former ally Ben Bella in June 1965.[43] When Castro re-emerged onto the world stage for a tour of Africa, the Eastern bloc and the Soviet Union in May 1972, he therefore took a more cautious approach towards Africa. Keen to balance the need for better diplomatic and commercial relations with the Revolutionary obligation of aiding liberation movements there, Castro visited his most trusted African allies, stopping in Conakry and Algiers for talks with Touré, Boumedienne and several of Africa's leading revolutionary movements (who were still keen to obtain Cuban support).

Castro's visit to Conakry, 3–8 May 1972

The most important meetings Castro held in Conakry were with his principal African protégé – Amílcar Cabral – whose fortunes had taken a turn for the worse since the arrival in Guiné of the new Portuguese military governor, General Antônio Sebastião Ribeiro de Spínola. Successive Portuguese offensives had recaptured much of the territory lost to the PAIGC over the previous five years, and Portuguese experiments with local autonomy were undermining the guerrillas' grass roots support. Spínola was fully aware that any gains made on the ground would be short-lived, but his attempts to persuade the Portuguese Prime Minister Marcello Caetano to enter into negotiations with the PAIGC were rebuffed, leaving Portugal in a Catch-22 situation. If Portugal gave up what was in reality its least important colony, it risked triggering demands for independence in its more lucrative colonies of Angola and Mozambique. But if it continued fighting in Guiné, it would with all certainty lose, and ultimately be ejected by force. The former option – as far as Caetano was concerned – was out of the question, and this left the Portuguese army with the task of fighting a debilitating guerrilla war it knew it could not win, breeding deep resentment which would eventually erupt in April 1974 (see Chapter 3).[44] Recognising Portugal's Achilles heel, Castro stepped up support for the PAIGC, and within a year of their meeting the PAIGC had regained the military initiative, forcing the Portuguese back once more to the coastline.[45]

Castro's talks with the MPLA were less significant than those with the PAIGC, and reflected the downgrading of the Cuban–MPLA alliance.[46] Since late 1967 the MPLA had maintained contact with Havana through its African embassies – in Brazzaville, Conakry and Dar-es-Salaam – and through their shared membership of international organisations such as OSPAAAL. This medium-level contact was complemented by the modest military aid programme started in October 1966, producing Angolan trainers for the MPLA's Eastern Front. In addition, Cuba extended its scholarship programme to more Angolan students, and between 1967 and 1974 trained dozens of economists, doctors and engineers in Cuba, among them Saydi Mingas (later MPLA Minister of Finance) and Enrique dos Santos (a future member of the Central Committee, who married a Cuban).[47] Thus, by the time Castro visited Conakry in May 1972, the MPLA's relationship with Cuba had reverted to its pre-1965 levels, and it was a middle-ranking delegation which met Castro while Neto was conspicuously absent.

The collapse of the Eastern Front, 1970–2

Neto's absence during Castro's first tour of Africa belied his ostensibly close relationship with the Cuban leader, and was probably the result of the acute crisis which had befallen the MPLA. Despite the training programme in Cuba and a significant increase in Soviet aid, the Eastern Front had had mixed fortunes since the MPLA moved its HQ to Lusaka in early 1968. Following the deaths of several gifted cadres – among them the 1st Military Region's former commander Hoji Ya Henda[48] – the leadership had streamlined its executive committee in preparation for a series of large-scale offensives planned for 1971 and 1972.[49] The concentration of effort on the Eastern Front inevitably drew attention away from the 1st Military Region, and after a fourth relief column (the Benedito Column) was intercepted and destroyed by the Portuguese in 1970, the guerrillas in the Dembos were left to their fate, relying on supplies from agents in Luanda and sympathisers in the Portuguese army.[50] The complete isolation of the guerrillas undermined morale – leading to the defection of the Chief Political Officer (and former commander of the Kamy Column) Ingo in September 1972 – and as the months wore on a radical nationalist faction started to emerge, headed by the man who would become Neto's nemesis, Nito Alves (see Chapter 6).

The immediate crisis which kept Neto from Conakry, however, was the collapse of the Eastern Front. Rather unfortunately for the MPLA, its plan to escalate the insurgency in 1970 coincided with the arrival of a new Portuguese Commander-in-Chief, General Costa Gomes. In three successive offensives, the Portuguese swept the guerrillas back towards the Zambian border, encircling the Eastern Front and inflicting crippling casualties. It is therefore strange that the MPLA representatives who met with Castro in May 1972 did not request additional military assistance, either in supplies or in training new recruits to replace the thousands lost in the fighting. It was, after all, the first high-level meeting between the MPLA and the Cubans in Africa since Guevara's summit with Neto seven years earlier. But it was a low-key affair, and when set against Cuba's close alliance with the PAIGC (which, following Conakry, received a substantial boost in Cuban aid), it is clear that MPLA–Cuban relations were more superficial than either side wished to admit.

The brewing factional dispute between Neto and Chipenda, 1970–3

Castro nevertheless reaffirmed his support for Neto's leadership of the MPLA, a gesture which was to have a significant effect on Neto's chances of surviving the factional splits which were surfacing at the time. Castro's support for Neto was curiously at odds with his Soviet patron, however. In contrast to Havana, Moscow had a troubled relationship with the MPLA and, in October 1963, had suspended all military aid when the OAU refused to recognise the movement – only to restore it again the following July. The Soviets disliked Neto's style of leadership (which has been described as cold and hermetic), and they were uneasy at his willingness to seek aid from all sources, including arch enemies such as China. Although the Soviets increased military aid to Neto in July 1970, they were more interested in backing the man who stood the best chance of seizing power in Angola than in protecting Neto's hegemony over the guerrilla movement. When the Eastern Front started to collapse in mid-1972, Neto started to look to the Soviets less like that man, and as splits appeared in the MPLA leadership, they switched their allegiance to the movement's most flamboyant Ovimbundu member, Daniel Chipenda.

Chipenda's star had risen dramatically following the launch of the Eastern Front in May 1966. Credited with having single-handedly ended the stalemate with the Portuguese and expanding the MPLA's influence across a vast section of eastern Angola, Chipenda looked on the Eastern Front as his own fiefdom – and on himself as the real strength behind the MPLA. Following Chipenda's ill-advised escalation of the war into central Angola, however, the Eastern Front collapsed suddenly, sparking bitter recriminations between Chipenda and the leadership in Lusaka, each blaming the other for the military disaster. It was a problem which was to resurface five years later with Nito Alves, the years of isolation and appalling conditions spawning guerrilla factions which viewed the Lusaka leadership as shirkers. Calling on forces loyal to him (around 1,500 men), in early 1973 Chipenda broke away from the MPLA to form the '*Revolta do Leste*' (Eastern Revolt) faction, threatening the disintegration of the MPLA.

The Soviets stopped short of giving Chipenda their full backing, however, and instead they invited Neto to Moscow in January 1973 where they informed him that Chipenda was planning to assassinate him. This was possibly a fabrication, but it showed that the Soviets were keeping their options open, a ploy they were to repeat in the lead-up to the Nito Alves coup attempt four years later (see Chapter 6). Ultimately the Soviets' doubts about Neto had less to do with his leadership of the MPLA and more to do with whether his guerrilla movement would ever seize power in Angola – which by late 1973 seemed a very remote possibility

46

indeed. In particular a number of high-profile defections of leading MPLA cadres had seriously damaged morale, and with acrimonious factional splits crippling the MPLA's operations, in late 1973 the Soviet Union and the OAU suspended military aid altogether.

Castro's support for Neto during this period was therefore crucial, and it is strange that he did not take a greater interest in his fortunes as the MPLA started to implode. Possibly the Soviets pressured Havana to keep contacts with Neto to a minimum. But it is more likely that Havana was too focused on Institutionalisation (which began in 1972) to pay full attention to the MPLA's disintegration. Cuba still went through the paces of its alliance with the MPLA, training cadres in Cuba, maintaining low-level contacts through it embassies in Africa, and publishing favourable propaganda about alleged MPLA military successes. But when factional fighting broke out in early 1973, Havana did not get involved, viewing it as an internal matter which would be resolved in one of the many tumultuous meetings called over the following year in Lusaka, Brazzaville and on the Eastern Front. It would not be until December 1974 that the next high-level meeting occurred between Cuba and the MPLA, by which time the situation in Angola would have changed beyond recognition.

Following the brief meeting in Conakry, therefore, the Cuban–MPLA alliance withered away as both parties concentrated on internal affairs. Following Castro's tour, Cuba stepped up its internationalist operations in Africa, setting up a training mission in Sierra Leone and smaller technical missions in Equatorial Guinea, Somalia, Algeria and Tanzania.[51] This was followed in October 1973 by Cuba's second lightning intervention in Africa – almost a carbon copy of the sea-lift to Algeria ten years previously – when Havana dispatched 1,000 troops to assist Syria in the Yom Kippur War.[52] But the MPLA was not part of Cuba's new internationalist phase, and bereft of outside support it slowly disintegrated, the collapse of the Eastern Front unleashing resentments (and egos) which had lain dormant since the early 1960s. Desperate to rebuild his guerrilla forces, Neto went on an international search for military aid (visiting Hungary, Romania and Yugoslavia) while the MPLA's insurgency was reduced to little more than nuisance value. When, in early 1974, a third faction emerged – the 'Revolta Activa' – the MPLA's demise seemed inevitable, until events in Lisbon dramatically changed the course of war, catching all three independence movements off-guard.

In a coup which took the entire world by surprise, on 25 April 1974 a group of Portuguese officers overthrew Caetano's dictatorship, and promised an immediate end to the wars in Africa and the decolonisation of Portugal's Empire. Faced with the last thing they had prepared for – rapid independence – the Angolan liberation movements were nonplussed, and they scrambled to obtain foreign support for the power struggle they knew would ensue. With Portugal's military presence shortly to be removed from Angola, the door was wide open for foreign interference in its affairs, tempting the superpowers to intervene in a region in which they had previously shown only passing interest. The Carnation Revolution would unleash a chaotic and bloody escalation of Angola's bitter conflict, and provide Cuba with the opportunity to launch a military intervention on a scale previously unimagined by Havana.

3

THE CARNATION REVOLUTION AND THE FAILURE OF ANGOLA'S DECOLONISATION, APRIL 1974–OCTOBER 1975

The period running from the Lisbon coup until Angolan independence was one of escalating violence and political turmoil throughout the Portuguese Empire. By its end, it would have plunged Portugal's most booming colony into a devastating civil war, with three foreign armies fighting it out for supremacy. Portugal's sudden decision to withdraw from Empire after more than a decade of debilitating guerrilla warfare opened the door to foreign intervention, and by Independence Day (11 November 1975) more than thirty countries had become involved in the Angolan War, supplying military equipment, instructors, money, or all three, to the liberation movements.[1] The military escalation in Angola was a tortured and convoluted process, however, and each country improvised its strategy in reaction to its opponents' moves – both real and imagined – until the conflict spiralled out of their control. Throughout Angola's chaotic decolonisation Cuba and the Soviet Union – which by 1974 had reduced or cut off their support to the MPLA – slowly re-engaged in Angola, recognising the opportunity presented by a weak American presidency to expand their influence into sub-Saharan Africa. But with Angola's nearest neighbours – in particular Zaire and South Africa – also determined to manipulate events in Angola to their advantage, they were up against stiff opposition, drawing the battle lines for one of the most dramatic military confrontations in African history.

The Lisbon coup, 25 April 1974

The coup which ended Portugal's forty-year dictatorship and installed General Spínola as president was the culmination of years of military and civilian discontent in Portugal.[2] The long and frustrating wars in Angola, Guiné and Mozambique had taken a severe toll on the Portuguese population, and by April 1974 the Portuguese army had – in Commodore Leonel Cardoso's words – 'reached the limits of physical and psychological exhaustion'. By 1973, fielding nearly 150,000 troops in three war zones (proportionally five times the American commitment in Vietnam), the Portuguese armed forces had been stretched to the limit, and mounting casualties (over 35,000 by 1974) were undermining morale.[3] Domestic opposition to the wars had been growing since the late 1960s, and by early 1974 more than half of those called up for military service failed to report for duty. But with civilian dissent smothered by censorship and the PIDE (secret police), the catalyst for change had to come from the army, and in particular from a new generation of middle-ranking officers who had served in the African wars. Their desire for radical change found figure-heads in Generals Costa Gomes and Spínola, veterans of Angola and Guiné respectively, who were almost unique among high-ranking officers for their public opposition to the wars, a stance which brought them into conflict with Caetano.

Spínola had fallen foul of Caetano two years previously when, as Por-tuguese commander in Guiné, he had requested (and been refused) per-mission to start negotiations with the PAIGC, Caetano declaring rather disturbingly that a military defeat in Guiné better served Portugal's inter-ests than a political capitulation. Returning to Portugal in August 1973, Spínola started writing what would become his political manifesto – *Portu-gal e o Futuro* (*Portugal and the Future*) – and the same month a group of radical middle-ranking officers formed the *Movimento das Forças Armadas* (MFA). Haunted by memories of India's invasion of Goa in December 1961 – when the surrounded 4,000-man Portuguese garrison was ordered by Salazar to fight to the last man (an order their commander disobeyed) – the MFA's officers determined to end the African wars and bring about radical political change in Portugal. The MFA quickly expanded its grip over the armed forces and, following the publication of Spínola's book in February 1974, Caetano tried to purge the army, dis-missing Spínola and Costa Gomes for refusing to demonstrate their support for his government. The MFA reacted with a bungled coup which was easily suppressed by Caetano, but the pressure for change was by then overwhelming, and less than a month later the MFA launched a second coup which brought down the dictatorship.

Reaction of the superpowers

It is hard to overstate the extent to which the Carnation Revolution took the world by surprise, from the superpowers to the Angolan liberation movements themselves. Initially written-off as the sort of coup which first brought the Portuguese military to power in 1926, within days it became clear that a social revolution was underway which would sweep away the previous political system. The American government – hamstrung by the final throes of the Watergate scandal (President Nixon resigned on

9 August 1974) – was nonplussed by the news which overnight invalidated its southern Africa strategy. Five years previously, the National Security Council (NSC) had carried out a review of American policy towards the region, producing National Security Study Memorandum No. 39. Concluding that Southern Africa was not vital to American strategic interests and that the Portuguese could not be defeated by the insurgents (while conversely acknowledging that Portugal could not definitively crush them), it encouraged Nixon to strengthen his alliance with Portugal which was viewed as an ally in the struggle against Communism. Accordingly, as the focus of the Cold War shifted to South-East Asia, the USA cut what little aid it was giving to the FNLA, closed down the CIA office in Lisbon and appointed as US Ambassador to Portugal a friend of Nixon's on a retirement posting. Thus, when the April 1974 coup struck, Washington was caught off-guard, and it could do little more than wait and see what steps the new Portuguese government took next.

The Soviets – like their American counterparts – were also taken by surprise by events in Lisbon, having disbelieved warnings of an imminent coup from sources in Portugal (for example, from the leader of the Portuguese Socialist Party, Mário Soares). The timing of the coup could not have been worse for the Soviets, as only a few months previously they had suspended military aid to the MPLA, leaving them poorly-positioned to influence events in Angola. This made the news that China had initiated a military aid programme for the FNLA more alarming, as the arrival of over 100 military instructors within weeks of the coup not only threatened to tip the balance in the FNLA's favour, but also afforded China a controlling influence in a region which the Soviets had only recently recognised as strategically important.[4] The Soviets immediately rushed to revive their moribund alliance with the MPLA, and they may have been encouraged by Havana which had stood by Neto throughout his leadership crisis.

Cuban reaction to the Carnation Revolution

Havana's reaction to the news that progressive officers had seized power in Lisbon was uncharacteristically muted. The reason for this was that, by early 1974, the Cuban government was focused exclusively on the closing stages of 'Institutionalisation'.[5] High-profile visits from Cuba's most important allies (among them Leonid Brezhnev, Erik Honecker and Houari Boumedienne) further distracted its attention. Though welcoming the new Portuguese government's moves towards independence for Portugal's colonies, Cuba – like many foreign powers subsequently involved in Angola – did not realise the significance of the changes being proposed by the MFA, and made no moves to revive its alliance with the MPLA.[6] Instead, Cuba concentrated on internal matters and ironically – considering the size of its operation in Angola over the next sixteen years – was the last foreign power to intervene militarily in Angola, renewing high-level contacts with the MPLA scarcely a fortnight before the Alvor talks began (see pp. 56–8).

Reaction of the Angolan liberation movements

Of all the parties affected by the Caetano's fall, those least prepared for the radical changes ahead were the Angolan independence movements themselves. Unlike their counterparts in Guiné and Mozambique which had merged to form a united front against the Portuguese (forming the PAIGC and FRELIMO respectively), the Angolan movements had resisted all calls for unity, and after thirteen years of fighting were more bitterly divided than ever. Attempts to merge the FNLA with the MPLA in 1966 and again in 1972 both failed (as would further efforts in the months preceding Alvor),[7] creating a permanent division between the two liberation movements which proved ripe for exploitation by foreign powers. Caught off-guard by the Lisbon coup (Neto was on a fund-raising trip in Canada), the liberation movements scrambled to muster their forces for what quickly developed into a struggle for ascendancy.

Of the three liberation movements, the FNLA was by chance in the strongest military position in April 1974. On the verge of receiving substantial Chinese and Romanian military aid – and strengthened by a political and military restructuring – the FNLA was confidently planning to expand its control over northern Angola, although whether it could have mounted a successful offensive in 1974 is debatable. UNITA was, at the time, a minor military force and had still not extended its influence beyond its power base in the Ovimbundu homelands of Huambo and Bié. Since launching its insurgency in December 1966, UNITA had contented itself with sporadic disruptions of the Benguela railway-line and incursions into Moxico, but it had signally failed to make an impact nationally. Its reputation had also been tarnished by the publication in July 1974 of letters (allegedly written two years before) which detailed UNITA–Portuguese collusion against the MPLA. Though the letters may have been faked, there is no doubt that UNITA had collaborated with the Portuguese, each side agreeing not to attack the other and to concentrate on destroying the MPLA. Militarily insignificant outside its core regions, UNITA was in no position to take on either the FNLA or the MPLA, and it was therefore the keenest supporter of a negotiated independence settlement.

And finally the MPLA was in a state of collapse, struggling to hold itself together under Neto's faltering leadership. Fragile party unity took another hammer blow less than a fortnight after the Lisbon coup when the Andrade brothers announced the formation of another MPLA faction – 'Revolta Activa' (Active Revolt). Backed by seventeen MPLA cadres – who accused Neto of 'presidentialism' – the appearance of a third faction so soon after Chipenda had ruptured party loyalties threatened the complete disintegration of the MPLA as a political entity. Indeed, so dire was Neto's position that, less than a month before the Portuguese coup, the Soviet Ambassador to Brazzaville had informed Moscow that the MPLA had ceased to function as a movement – and that in his opinion Neto had little hope of reuniting it again.[8] Having lost OAU and Soviet aid in December 1973, Neto cast his net wide in the search for new backers, but with poor results, putting the MPLA at an increasing disadvantage to the FNLA. Conscious of the need to strengthen the MPLA's national profile in the run-up to independence, Neto threw his energies into healing the splits in the party, but a rapprochement with Chipenda and the Andrade brothers was to prove beyond his capabilities.

Thus when news of the Lisbon coup reached the world, all those involved for good or worse in the decolonisation of Angola were caught by surprise, and initially they could do little but look towards Lisbon to see how the situation developed. As a result each stage in the radicalisation of the Portuguese Revolution was mirrored by an increase in instability in Angola and a weakening of Portugal's grip on its most lucrative colony, encouraging even greater levels of foreign interference. Tragically for Angola, the new Portuguese government was simply overwhelmed by the task facing it, attempting to decolonise its five African colonies whilst simultaneously reforming Portugal's entire governmental and economic system after forty years of stultifying dictatorship – and all without the support of dependable military and police forces. Within weeks of the Lisbon coup, therefore, a power vacuum opened up in Portugal's African colonies which other foreign powers were quick to exploit.

Foreign powers start to intervene in Angola, mid-1974 onwards

Sensing that divisions between the Angolan independence movements could be played to their advantage, foreign powers were quick to offer support to their preferred clients. Few, if any, however, appreciated the consequences their intervention would have on the Angolan conflict. Their ostensible aim was to bolster their client movement so that it would be in the strongest possible position when independence negotiations began. But they failed to anticipate that, by pouring vast amounts of weaponry and military equipment into Angola, they were initiating an escalation of the conflict which would quickly spiral out of their control. Had the Portuguese government seized the initiative and called tripartite independence negotiations involving the USA, the Soviet Union and China, it could arguably have produced a power-sharing agreement which stood a chance of being implemented. But as all efforts to bring the Angolan movements together met with failure, the Angolans turned to violent means to achieve their aims, calling on their powerful patrons to provide them with the weaponry to do so.

Ironically China – which, of the global powers, had been least involved in Angola – was the first to escalate its involvement, in late 1973 pledging to provide military training and arms to FNLA guerrillas based in Zaire. What the Chinese could not have realised at the time was that within four months Portuguese power would collapse in Angola, putting them in a dominating position which they had neither anticipated nor desired.[9] Possibly in response, on 7 July 1974, the CIA started funding Roberto, although on such a small scale that he was unable to buy arms and instead used the money to purchase Luanda's leading daily newspaper – *A Província de Angola* – and one of its television stations.[10] One month later, South Africa, which had been fighting alongside the Portuguese against SWAPO (and the MPLA) since 1968, initiated contacts with Chipenda's 'Eastern Revolt' faction, although at this stage Pretoria had no plans to invade Angola, and no deal was struck with the Angolans.[11]

In the face of global competition, the Soviet Union resumed its interest in Angola, although it is unclear whether the resumption of military aid to Neto's MPLA preceded or followed the Americans and South Africans. Moscow subsequently claimed that it resumed military aid to the MPLA around October 1974, long after other foreign powers had intervened in Angola.[12] However, recent evidence from Soviet archives reveals that as early as May 1974 the Kremlin was convinced that the Portuguese Empire was on the verge of collapse, and that its interests would best be served by strengthening Neto's MPLA.[13] Soviet aid would be frustratingly slow in coming, however, and in the meantime the MPLA's stockpile of weaponry was stuck in Dar-es-Salaam, with no means of transporting it to Angola. With the FNLA growing increasingly aggressive in Luanda – and with the MPLA's best 250 cadres not due to complete their training in the Soviet Union until mid-1975 – Neto was forced to look elsewhere for support, initiating a search which would lead him back to the Cubans.

The MFA moves towards Alvor

The Soviet decision to resume military aid to the MPLA followed the removal of Spínola on 30 September 1974 and his replacement by a radical MFA government. Spínola had disappointed the MFA once it became clear that he wanted to reform rather than dismantle the Portuguese Empire and, following his attempt to side-step Angolan independence by holding talks with his preferred candidates (Roberto and Chipenda) in Cape Verde, he was replaced by General Costa Gomes who declared his intention to proceed immediately with the decolonisation of the Portuguese Empire. Ceasefires were quickly called with the FNLA (12 October) and MPLA (21 October) – UNITA had suspended military operations back in June – and a concerted effort was made to heal the rift between the Angolan movements so that a tripartite agreement could be signed as quickly as possible. The appointment in November of the MPLA's most outspoken supporter – the 'Red Admiral' Rosa Coutinho – as Angolan High Commissioner signalled Lisbon's open sympathy for the MPLA, however, and he was to play a vital role over the following months in securing its grip on Luanda.

By this stage Neto had reasserted control over the MPLA and expelled (at least for the time-being) its unruly factions. Ironically the Carnation Revolution turned out to be Neto's saviour for, although it caught the MPLA at its weakest, the promise of imminent independence forced Neto to resolve its factional disputes – or face annihilation. Meetings in June and July 1974 between the three factions had only intensified divisions, culminating in the MPLA's first Party Conference for twelve years in Lusaka. With the voting split evenly between Neto and Chipenda, bitter wrangling ensued for the next eleven days until Neto and the 'Active Revolt' faction walked out. Announcing the formation of a new army – the FAPLA (Forças Armadas Populares de Libertação de Angola) – Neto and 250 of his supporters withdrew to the Eastern Front to hold their own Conference. On 21 September they re-elected Neto President of the reformed Neto–MPLA (for want of a better term), and this convinced the Soviets of his legitimacy as leader, leading to their resumption of military aid. A week later Spínola fell from office, and Neto sent a trusted cohort – Paulo Jorge – to Lisbon to begin three months of secret negotiations with the Portuguese.[14]

Fighting breaks out between the FNLA, MPLA and UNITA, November 1974

Meanwhile, rivalry between the independence movements had erupted in open warfare, inaugurating a cycle of violent conflict which was to continue with brief pauses up to and beyond independence. The focus of the fighting was Luanda, Angola's political and economic capital, and an area with traditionally strong MPLA sympathies. Following ceasefires with the Portuguese in October 1974, the MPLA's main rivals had set up offices in Luanda, heightening tensions in the capital. With each group expanding its influence over the local population, the bitter rivalry between them erupted in armed clashes on 10 November, leaving nearly fifty dead.[15] From this date onwards there was fighting almost daily between the MPLA, the FNLA and (unwillingly) UNITA, not only in Luanda but increasingly across the whole of Angola. Within weeks Angola had fractured into spheres of influence, and by mid-1975 the FNLA had effectively taken control of northern Angola, while UNITA retrenched in its Ovimbundu heartland, and the MPLA clung to the coastline, as well as controlling parts of Moxico and (from early November 1974) Cabinda.

The Alvor Accords, 15 January 1975

In this highly-charged atmosphere, the OAU and several African states tried to bring the movements together for talks to stop the fighting and end the bitter feud. Eventually, on 5 January 1975, Neto's MPLA, the FNLA and UNITA were coaxed to Mombassa where they signed an accord pledging to cooperate peacefully, safeguard Angolan territorial integrity and form a common front for independence negotiations with Portugal.[16] This agreement laid the foundations for trilateral independence talks with the Portuguese government at Alvor (in the Algarve) which lasted from 10–15 January 1975. In retrospect, the Alvor talks were Angola's last chance for a peaceful and orderly decolonisation, and despite showing a bias towards the MPLA, Lisbon was genuine in its desire to see an agreement involving the main Angolan movements. The deal signed on 15 January 1975 provided for the establishment of a Transitional Government whose posts would be divided between the three movements and Portugal, the integration of all military forces into a national army, and the drafting of a constitution to be followed by elections before the end of October 1975.[17] Independence day was set for 11 November 1975, the four-hundredth anniversary of the founding of Luanda.

Cuba briefly re-engages in Angola, December 1974

It was only at this late stage – around the time of the Alvor Accords – that Cuba re-engaged in Angola, although it has been alleged that there were Cuban personnel operating in Angola before this date.[18] By then Neto's MPLA was in danger of being overwhelmed by its rivals. For, despite the resumption of Soviet aid in October, it had only been on a modest scale and – crucially – the bulk of the weaponry was not expected to arrive in Angola until May 1975 at the earliest.[19] In the meantime the MPLA faced a growing threat from the FNLA, just as independence negotiations with the Portuguese were about to start in Alvor. The MPLA did have a stockpile of weaponry in Dar-es-Salaam, but could neither get it to Luanda (where it was needed in daily street-fighting) nor find the instructors to train its raw recruits in its use. Two MPLA delegations had been sent to Yugoslavia and Algeria – two of Neto's most stalwart allies over the years – to arrange urgent arms shipments, but even these could not be expected to arrive until March. It was thus in this tricky predicament – lacking both arms and military instructors – that Neto turned to his Cuban allies in late 1974.

On 31 December 1974, an MPLA delegation chaired by Neto met in Dar-es-Salaam with two Cuban officials, Carlos Cadelo (the PCC representative for Angola) and Major Alfonso Pérez Morales 'Pina' (who had served with the PAIGC in Guiné). The Cubans spoke at length with Neto, discussing the MPLA's most pressing needs, and requested Neto's permission to carry out a secret visit to Angola. Cadelo and Pina were on a fact-finding mission for Castro who wanted his own men to assess the situation on the ground before launching a new military aid programme – perhaps reflecting his doubts about the MPLA's true military strength. In recognition of this (and as a demonstration of his trust) Neto readily granted their request, admonishing the Cubans to 'verify everything he had told [them] so that [they] could get an objective view of the real situation in Angola'.[20] While Neto was involved in the Mombassa and Alvor talks, the two Cubans visited the MPLA's main bases of support, meeting leading cadres in Lusaka and Luanda, among them N'Dalu, Xiyetu (Chief of the FAPLA) and Lopo do Nascimento (a leading party ideologue).

Encouraged by what they had seen, Cadelo and Pina met again with Neto in Dar-es-Salaam shortly after he returned from Alvor. They discussed ways in which Cuba could aid the MPLA, and repeatedly returned to the idea of sending Cuban instructors to Angola to train the massive influx of recruits gathering in the MPLA's core areas. No concrete proposals could be drawn up, however, until Neto knew what type of weaponry the Soviets would supply (which suggests that even at this late stage they had not finalised a military aid programme), and this was unlikely for several months. In the meantime, Neto gave the two Cubans a letter for the PCC Central Committee in which he outlined his most pressing needs, principal among them a request for $100,000 to cover the shipping costs of the arms stockpiled in Dar-es-Salaam. Neto also asked for Cuban instructors to establish training centres in Angola, and large amounts of weaponry and uniforms to equip the troops who would form the new FAPLA.[21] Confident that the Cuban government would give his urgent requests its immediate attention, Neto sent the two Cubans back to Cuba where, on 21 March 1975, they presented their lengthy report (forty-two pages).

However – rather puzzlingly – no action was taken by the Cuban government, despite the report's positive tone. Though acknowledging the FNLA's temporary supremacy, Cadelo and Pina optimistically predicted that this would evaporate once Soviet arms started to arrive, and they concluded that the MPLA was 'the best structured politically and militarily' and as a result enjoyed 'extraordinary popular support'. But the Cuban government ignored the report and Neto's letter – not even granting the request for $100,000 – and instead continued with the specialist training programme it had initiated in 1966, training a dozen MPLA cadres in Cuba between March and April 1975.[22] Cuban diplomats in Brazzaville, Lusaka and Dar-es-Salaam did go out of their way to persuade their Soviet counterparts to back Neto and the MPLA, but their action may have been unilateral as Havana's focus was by then fixed on the upcoming National

Assembly elections and the Party Congress.[23] It is even possible that Havana viewed the two-man mission to Angola as little more than a good-will gesture, and had no intention of increasing its involvement with the MPLA. But, whatever Havana's reasoning, the contact lapsed, and Neto would not meet with the Cubans again until May.[24] By that stage the war would have escalated to alarming levels, and Neto's modest requests would have grown into ambitious plans for a Cuban military programme in Angola itself (see pp. 63–7).

The failure of the Transitional Government, January–March 1975

The months following the Alvor Accords were dominated by Portugal's efforts to establish the Transitional Government in Angola, a fruitless endeavour which represented the metropolitan power's last attempt to impose an orderly decolonisation on Angola – before washing its hands of the troubled colony for good. In retrospect, by the time the Portuguese government gathered the liberation movements together at Alvor, it was already too late for a negotiated settlement to resolve the conflict, Lisbon having repeatedly put off Angolan independence while the comparatively simple hand-over to the PAIGC and FRELIMO was effected. By the time the Transitional Government was set up, street-fighting had already broken out in Luanda, and once this spread across Angola its days were numbered, and with them Angola's chance for a peaceful transition to independence. A long-shot at best, the Alvor Accords required the backing of all the parties involved in Angola's decolonisation – which by January 1975 included China, the USA, the Soviet Union, and even Cuba – if they were to be implemented. But the opportunity to involve foreign parties was missed, and given their exclusion from the negotiations (a mistake the Americans would avoid during the 'linkage' negotiations over a decade later), it is unsurprising that they viewed Alvor as nothing more than a smoke-screen for even greater intervention in Angola's internal affairs.

On 22 January 1975 (one week after the Accords were signed) the CIA's 40 Committee met to discuss the situation in Angola, authorising limited funding to Roberto's FNLA ($300,000), but at this stage rejecting requests to fund UNITA which it viewed as a localised phenomenon.[25] This small increase in American funding – coupled with Chinese and Romanian military aid – put the FNLA in the strongest military position, and may be the reason no further increase in American aid was considered until the FNLA started to lose ground to the MPLA in late June 1975. More significantly, one week later (on 30 January) the Soviet Ambassador to Brazzaville met with José Eduardo Dos Santos and promised the MPLA extensive 'technical, military, and civilian assistance'.[26] This was the first indication that the Soviets were planning to step up their assistance to the MPLA, and they would continue hinting at a massive increase in military aid over the coming months.

Any hopes that the Transitional Government might take hold were quickly shattered when street-fighting broke out between FNLA and MPLA less than twenty-four hours after its inauguration. Determined to take control of Luanda the MPLA and FNLA first ganged up on their rivals, attacking Chipenda's 'Eastern Revolt' offices on 3 February and then destroying them ten days later, forcing Chipenda to merge with the FNLA. With Chipenda's challenge snuffed out, the FNLA and MPLA turned on each other, violence erupting on 23 March when FNLA militants hurled grenades through the window of an MPLA office in Vila Alice as Lopo do Nascimento was making an official visit. MPLA activists responded in kind, and this first wave of violence was followed by tit-for-tat killings,[27] an increased FAPLA and FNLA military presence in Luanda, and the perpetual breakdown of ceasefires brokered by Lisbon. Portuguese authority was then dealt another blow with the arrival in northern Angola of 1,200 Zairian troops in support of the FNLA, their presence greatly destabilising the region and presaging the intervention of far greater foreign forces over the following months.

The collapse of the Transitional Government, March–August 1975

The root cause for the collapse in Portuguese authority was not in Luanda, however, but in Lisbon where, on 11 March, the ousted General Spínola launched a failed counter-coup. Alarmed at the Portuguese Revolution's lurch to the left – and feeling that Angola's decolonisation was proceeding too fast – Spínola's coup was a desperate attempt to remove the Communists' growing influence from government. But the coup's failure had the opposite effect, triggering the Revolution's most radical phase – the 'Verão Quente' (Hot Summer) – during which Portugal lost its grip on Angola and became little more than a spectator to the growing crisis. For the Alvor Accords to have succeeded, the Transitional Government needed a strong Portuguese military presence to suppress the violence and give it breathing space to make progress towards elections. But with Portuguese troops refusing to fight in Angola – and with a pro-MPLA stance emerging in the government (headed by Rosa Coutinho) – its authority was fatally undermined. The dismissal on 1 August of the High Commissioner António da Silva Cardoso – whose attempts to restrain the MPLA's aggressive activities in Luanda had made him popular with the FNLA and UNITA – convinced the MPLA's rivals that the Transitional Government was biased against them, and that their interests would be best served on the battlefield.

Having been expelled from Luanda after a week's heavy fighting, the FNLA withdrew to Ambriz where, on 20 July, it announced it would march on the Angolan capital before Independence Day. Its dramatic capture of Caxito (thirty-five miles north-east of Luanda) four days later underlined the reality of its threat, and sparked off the fifth and final wave of violence. Accepting it was pointless to continue when most of the Transitional Government's ministers had fled the capital, on 14 August the Portuguese High Commissioner dissolved it and officially took over its functions. In practice, however, most of the vacant posts were taken up by the MPLA, a clear indication of Portuguese sympathies.[28] When, on 29 August, Lisbon formally annulled the Alvor Accords, to everyone's surprise nothing was offered in their place, merely an insistence that independence would go ahead as planned. Unable to deal with Angola's nascent civil war while undergoing a social revolution at home, Portugal was washing its hands of Angola, its new High Commissioner Commodore Leonel Cardoso announcing within a fortnight of his inauguration that the withdrawal of Portuguese troops had begun. It was an open invitation for all-out warfare between the independence movements, and was the signal their foreign backers had been waiting for to escalate their involvement in Angola to a level beyond which it could neither be contained nor controlled.

Foreign intervention in Angola spirals out of control, March–November 1975

With the collapse of the Transitional Government, fighting immediately intensified between the liberation movements as their foreign backers launched into a 'Scramble for Angola'. Of all the foreign powers involved in Angola, the Soviet Union bears principal responsibility for escalating the violence into a full-scale civil war. Though not the first to intervene, the Soviet decision to massively increase military aid to the MPLA in March 1975 fundamentally altered the nature of the Angolan conflict, the injection of vast amounts of high-tech weaponry unleashing deep-seated hatreds. The Soviets did put pressure on the MPLA to heel its rifts, at one point suggesting a merger with the FNLA. But their simultaneous weapons programme enabled the MPLA to field thousands of well-equipped soldiers, encouraging its leadership to exterminate its rivals rather than negotiate with them. The FNLA shares some responsibility for internationalising the Angolan War, although its rewards for bringing in foreign backers were meagre in comparison to the MPLA.[29] Even when the first American arms belatedly arrived in late July, they were hopelessly outclassed by the FAPLA's modern Soviet weaponry.[30] Between March and November 1975, the Soviets sent a total of twenty-seven shiploads and thirty-to-forty cargo planes of weaponry to the MPLA, providing the raw material for a formidable FAPLA army.[31]

The Soviet weapons programme had to overcome serious obstacles, however. Initially, all military supplies had to be shipped to the MPLA in secret, and this was a complex operation which involved transporting crates to Dar-es-Salaam or Brazzaville, stockpiling them there, and then smuggling them into Angola overland, by private light aircraft or by foreign-registered ship. Attempts to unload cargoes in Luanda were uncovered by the Portuguese authorities which prevented the Yugoslav ship *Postoyma* from unloading jeeps for the MPLA in April 1975. The ship sailed to Pointe-Noire where it unloaded its cargo, setting the pattern for Eastern Bloc arms shipments over the next couple of months.[32] Problems then arose with the Soviets' Congolese ally, President Ngouabi, who like his rival Mobutu had his eye on Cabinda. Fearing the MPLA was taking control of the oil-rich enclave, Ngouabi put a halt to Soviet weapons shipments through Brazzaville, and it took considerable persuasion and a personal visit to Havana to get him to reverse his decision and relinquish his Cabindan ambitions.[33] By July, however, either as the result of a secret agreement with the Portuguese, or simply because of the increasing anarchy in Luanda, the Soviets were able to ship their arms directly to Luanda where they were unloaded under the gaze of the port authorities.

The Soviet military aid programme and Angola's collapse into anarchy did not escape Washington's attention, and on 27 June the NSC requested an options paper on Angola from the 40 Committee. Submitted on 14 July, the paper concluded that the MPLA was strong enough to take control of Luanda and the surrounding area (which it did two days later), and recommended a covert CIA operation to bolster the FNLA which had lost the military advantage.[34] Authorised by President Ford on 18 July, 'Operation IAFeature' would in four months grow from an initial budget of $6 million to $31.7 million. Despite its substantial resources, however, it suffered crippling restrictions. Above all, its objectives were too limited – seeking only to shore up the FNLA rather than install it in power – and as a result of sloppy intelligence (a characteristic of CIA operations throughout the 1970s) these lagged behind events on the ground. Thus, as late as July, the CIA still believed that the Angolan conflict would be resolved by elections in October, when the expulsion of the FNLA and UNITA from Luanda that month had ensured these would never take place. Furthermore, in what would prove a fatal oversight, the CIA did not even consider that the Cubans might intervene in support of the MPLA.[35] Overtaken by events – and with all attempts to expand the operation blocked by Congress – IAFeature would become 'self-limiting: too small to win [whilst] at the same time too large to be kept secret'.[36]

South Africa intervenes in Angola

By this stage, the Americans were coordinating their activities with the South Africans, the first of two foreign powers which were to play a decisive role in shaping the Angolan conflict (the other was Cuba). The SADF had been fighting alongside the Portuguese in southern Angola since the late 1960s, jointly operating an air command post in Cuito Cuanavale and providing aircraft and troops for counter-insurgency operations. The development of the Cunene hydroelectric scheme in the early 1970s gave South Africa a direct stake in southern Angola, the $400m installations providing irrigation and electricity for northern Namibia. The collapse of Portuguese rule in Angola thus caused alarm in Pretoria which not only lost its 'buffer state' on Namibia's northern border, but which also faced the prospect of the MPLA taking power in Luanda. Paranoid that a Marxist, anti-apartheid government would permit SWAPO to set up bases in southern Angola from where it could infiltrate Namibia (a fear which proved well-founded), Pretoria took an increasing interest in Angola and, as Portuguese authority started to crumble, it took matters into its own hands.

South Africa's overriding priority was the security of the Cunene hydroelectric project, part of which was located inside Angola at Calueque, fifteen miles north of the Namibian border.[37] After the withdrawal of the Portuguese garrison in July 1975, security in the area had deteriorated sharply, and following clashes between the MPLA and FNLA on 8 August a small South African detachment crossed the border and occupied Calueque. Four days later, Lisbon was informed that a '30-man patrol' had occupied Calueque in order to protect the workers from factional fighting. Lisbon protested – but only weakly as it was guilty of violating its own security commitments (under which Portugal pledged to protect the installations and workers from attack). With Calueque under South African control – and with SWAPO escalating its operations dramatically throughout 1975 – it was only a matter of time before the SADF was drawn into the fighting in southern Angola.[38]

Given their devoutly anti-Communist ideology, the South Africans quickly drifted into an alliance with the anti-MPLA forces in southern Angola, although the SADF's relations with Chipenda and Savimbi were far from harmonious. Initial contacts with Chipenda's disgruntled MPLA outcasts in August 1974 bore little fruit, as did meetings the following February and March with Savimbi, who rejected South African suggestions that he ally with the FNLA, persuading them to let the contact lapse. However, in April 1975 – under pressure from Foreign Minister P.W. Botha – President Vorster authorised the SADF to try again, and on 31 May Chipenda was coaxed to Windhoek (Namibia) for discussions on setting up a formal alliance. In July Chipenda returned to Windhoek to hammer out a deal with General Hendrik Van den Bergh (Director of BOSS, the Bureau of State Security) and, following this meeting, Vorster approved $14m of weaponry for UNITA and the FNLA. Later that month the South Africans squared the deal with Roberto in Kinshasa, and in September, Savimbi was brought on board, winning over the sceptical Major-General Viljoen and General Van den Bergh who visited him in Kinshasa.[39]

The South African alliance with the FNLA and UNITA was problematic, however. For, although both movements were violently opposed to the MPLA, they were equally suspicious of each other. The three protagonists – Roberto, Savimbi and Chipenda – had been at war with each other for at least a decade, and the bitter enmity between them was never far from the surface. Indeed Savimbi initially rejected out of hand South African suggestions that he unite with the FNLA, only belatedly entering into an alliance with his former patron Roberto after UNITA was dragged against its will into the crossfire. The trick for South Africa would be to keep its Angolan allies apart, using each on separate fronts (and in its traditional area of support) to push the MPLA back towards Luanda. But the South Africans' grasp of Angolan politics was weak, and they took little time to find out about their African proxies before forming their alliance, obsessed with preventing a Communist victory in Angola. Once the tide of war turned against them, this oversight would cost them dear.

Cuba finally re-engages in Angola

Even as South African troops were occupying Calueque, Havana finally decided to intervene in Angola. Since Cadelo and Pina's mission to Angola in January, Havana had shown scant interest in the MPLA, and by the time Neto renewed contacts with the Cubans in May his situation had deteriorated sharply. Still waiting for Soviet arms to arrive in Angola, the MPLA was reeling from a second wave of violence unleashed by the FNLA on 28 April which in five days killed 700 and wounded over 1,000.[40] More ominously, in early May, 1,200 Zairian troops had crossed into northern Angola in support of the FNLA, and their imminent advance on Luanda threatened to overwhelm the MPLA. Thus, by the time Neto approached the Cubans, his requests had evolved into proposals for a Cuban training programme to take place in Angola itself.[41] The MPLA was desperately short of instructors after the Soviets had refused to provide their own, and it is alleged that Moscow suggested Neto ask the Cubans for help as they were perhaps his only other ally qualified to perform this task.[42]

Once again, however, the Cubans failed to respond to Neto's requests, and he repeated them to Cadelo in Maputo in late July during Mozambique's independence celebrations.[43] Only at this late stage did Havana finally take action and authorise a military training programme for the MPLA in Angola itself. It is highly likely that Cuba's decision was influenced by the MPLA's strongest Portuguese supporter – Admiral Rosa Coutinho – who visited Havana in June 1975 for talks with Castro. Although the content of their discussions is unknown, Castro later revealed that he requested permission from Lisbon to send Cuban supplies and instructors directly to Luanda. However, given the fierce divisions in the Portuguese government over which Angolan movement to support, Castro never received a reply, and in late July he dispatched Comandante Senén Casas Regueiro (later Commander-in-Chief of the Cuban operation in Angola) to Lisbon to close a deal. Rosa Coutinho's second visit to Havana in August – precisely when the Cuban decision was taken – suggests that Portuguese compliance was secured, although it may have been unofficial.[44]

The Argüelles mission

The arrival of fifty Cuban weapons specialists in Brazzaville on 25 July to help with deliveries of Soviet arms to the MPLA marked the beginning of Cuba's Angolan operation, a move which did not go unnoticed by Washington.[45] Having decided to provide military aid and training to the MPLA, the FAR sent a seven-man mission to Luanda under Comandante Raúl Díaz Argüelles to draw up plans for a training programme which could meet the objectives laid down by Neto.[46] Perhaps feeling guilty for ignoring his repeated requests over the past six months, on arrival in Luanda on 3 August, Cadelo handed over $100,000 in cash to Neto to pay for transporting the arms stockpiled in Dar-es-Salaam to Luanda.[47] During their six-day visit, the Cuban delegation – which included Cadelo and Víctor Schueg Colás (who four months later commanded the northern offensive) – met with Neto and senior MPLA figures, and discussed the shape of the Cuban mission. Neto envisioned around 100 Cuban instructors spread evenly across Angola, and he requested weapons, uniforms and food to equip and feed the FAPLA recruits during their training. As a result of these meetings, Argüelles drafted a proposal for a ninety-four-man mission which he presented to Fidel and Raúl Castro in Havana on 11 August, three days after his return.[48]

Almost immediately, however, the programme was expanded fivefold, growing to 480 Cuban specialists who would set up and run four camps in Cabinda, Salazar (N'Dalatando), Benguela and Henrique de Carvalho (Saurimo). Over six months they would form 4,800 FAPLA recruits into sixteen infantry battalions, twenty-five mortar batteries and various anti-aircraft units. The Cuban force would be supplemented by a team of doctors, communication experts and 115 vehicles, plus all the necessary food, equipment and supplies to support 5,300 men for six months. The decision to expand the operation reflected a feeling in Havana that if Cubans were going into the middle of a civil war, there had to be enough of them to fulfil their mission as well as defend themselves in the event the operation went awry. It is nevertheless clear that Havana viewed the Angolan mission in the same terms as the mission to Congo-Brazzaville: they expected it to be short term and to last around six months (with an option to extend). The overriding objective was to train the FAPLA to fight for itself, although the FAR accepted that the Cuban instructors might have to fight alongside them.

Early Soviet involvement in the Cuban mission to Angola

Preparations for the Angolan operation began immediately, and between 20 August and 5 September the Chairman of the Joint Chiefs of Staff and the Chiefs of MINFAR and the Air Force were relieved of their posts to begin planning.[49] Contrary to popular belief, the Soviets took no part in the decision and showed a noted reluctance to get involved in Cuba's Angolan operation. On 15 August, Castro sent a message to Brezhnev asking for Soviet transport assistance and staff officers to help plan the FAPLA's operations – requests the Kremlin refused to grant. At this stage Moscow would not commit its own personnel on the ground in Angola, and while happy to attach military advisors to the MPLA in Brazzaville, once they moved to Luanda in early August they refused to accompany them there.[50] Thus the MPLA had to rely entirely on Cuban personnel to train, equip and run the FAPLA, effectively handing over control of their campaign to the Cuban mission in Luanda. As a result, the FAPLA's weaponry was provided by the Cubans, and included 12,000 Czech M-52 rifles, 133 Bulgarian RPG-7's, and dozens of Eastern bloc mortars, light artillery and machine-guns.[51]

The Misión Militar Cubana en Angola (MMCA)

Raúl Díaz Argüelles was appointed commander of the fledgling MMCA (Cuban Military Mission in Angola), reporting to the First Deputy Minister of the FAR, General Abelardo Colomé Ibarra (known by his childhood nickname, 'Furry') who was in overall command of the operation.[52] The 480 Cuban instructors were chosen from the ranks of the FAR as much for their willingness to volunteer as for their ideological soundness, a selection procedure identical to the Congo and Guiné missions.[53] On 21 August, an advance party under Argüelles flew to Luanda via Lisbon (the only viable route at the time), and in early September it was joined there by several other small groups of Cubans (some of whom were held up in Lisbon by visa formalities). The Cubans travelled incognito, were unarmed and their only luggage was clothes, the documents necessary to set up the camps, radio transmitters to maintain contact with Havana and suitcases full of cash.[54] Meeting with Neto the day after their arrival, Argüelles informed him that the Cuban mission had been expanded to 480 men, news Neto received with great emotion. As the commanders of the four camps started to arrive in Luanda, Argüelles held lengthy discussions with Neto and his colleagues, and together they finalised the size and location of the four camps.

The largest – involving nearly half of the Cuban mission's personnel – would be in Cabinda, a decision influenced by Castro himself. During discussions with Argüelles's team in mid-August, Castro had criticised them for failing to take account of the enclave's isolation which made it a prime target for an invasion anywhere along its 130-mile border with Zaire. A well-organised invasion force could sweep in and seize the capital (only fifteen miles north of the border) long before Luanda could send reinforcements. Perhaps for this reason Neto had resigned himself to Cabinda's loss, a decision against which Castro energetically argued. Instead of giving up the enclave, 191 Cubans would be sent to Cabinda under the command of General Ramón Espinosa Martín who was to draw up the defence plan.[55] The remaining 270 Cubans would be split evenly between the other three camps, each of which had a strategic function to play. The second camp in Henrique de Carvalho (Saurimo) – one of the MPLA's core regions of support – was charged with regaining Neto's influence over the Eastern Front after Chipenda's damaging factional split. The third would be set up eight miles south of Benguela – defending the main route from southern Angola – while the fourth in Salazar (N'Dalatando) would defend against incursions from Uíge and Malanje, and provide an emergency reserve which could be withdrawn to Luanda. The mission command – numbering twenty-five men – would be based in Luanda, with support from communications, medical and service teams which moved between Luanda and the camps.

Throughout September – as small groups of Cuban specialists trickled into Luanda on commercial flights – the camps were set up amidst preparations for the arrival of the bulk of the Cuban contingent in early October. Both Argüelles and Neto were keen for Espinosa to travel to Cabinda as soon as possible, and he was sent ahead with Captain Martínez, leaving the five other officers in his group to follow when the opportunity arose. Neto's promises to organise air transport failed to materialise, however, and after waiting for three days, Espinosa hired a Portuguese pilot to fly him there, claiming he was an Argentine journalist reporting on the oil industry. Espinosa arrived in Cabinda in early September, and after meeting the local MPLA commanders he set off on a detailed reconnaissance of the border area.[56] Espinosa was soon joined by a second group of officers who flew in to Cabinda via Moscow, and together they set up the camp at Dinge in the Mayombe foothills (fifty miles north-east of Cabinda city). This was supported by an auxiliary camp at Lândana (Cacongo, Cabinda's second largest port) whose troops could be withdrawn to the capital in an emergency – a wise precaution as it turned out.[57]

On 30 September, the first seventy Cubans of the Cabinda contingent left Havana aboard an ageing Britannia. They flew via Barbados and Bissau to Brazzaville where they transferred to an An-26 (lent by the Congolese army) for the short flight to Pointe-Noire, completing their journey to Cabinda city by road.[58] Their arrival coincided with the first of three Cuban supply ships to reach Angola – the *Vietnam Heroico* – which docked at Porto Amboim on 5 October.[59] These three Cuban ships had been preparing for the mission since early September, and had set sail for Africa two weeks previously.[60] The first two headed for Porto Amboim (where according to one account a Cuban camp had been established),[61] and unloaded their cargo of supplies, weaponry and Cuban instructors for the three camps in southern and eastern Angola. There were, however, problems with the trucks which had been poorly stowed during the crossing and were damaged, requiring several days of time-consuming repairs before they could be driven to the camps.

On 9 October, *La Plata* anchored off Pointe-Noire, and two days later it unloaded military supplies and the final group of Cuban instructors for the Cuban mission, completing Cabinda's 191-man force and bringing the total number of Cubans in Angola to around 500.[62] MMCA worked against the clock to get the camps operational as quickly as possible, and only Henrique de Carvalho (Saurimo) failed to meet the 20 October deadline. Argüelles was upbeat, and on 1 October he reported to Furry that '[t]he present military situation favours the MPLA'.[63] At this stage Argüelles had every reason to believe that, over the next six months, his Cuban team would build the FAPLA into the nucleus of an army which could win the impending battle for supremacy in Angola. Little did he realise that his team would have less than one month – and in some cases only a few days – to prepare their unseasoned recruits for battle. For, unknown to Luanda, the South African government had sent an invasion force into Angola, setting the SADF on a collision course with the Cubans.

4

OPERATIONS SAVANNAH AND CARLOTA, OCTOBER–NOVEMBER 1975

The South African invasion of Angola in October 1975 initiated the final phase in Angola's messy descent into full-scale war, and unleashed the military hardware which had been pouring into Angola over the previous eighteen months. The launch of Operations Savannah and Carlota – as the South African and Cuban interventions in Angola were codenamed – brought the Cold War to the heart of sub-Saharan Africa, and provided each of the warring parties with its own proxy force. The FNLA – whose leader Roberto enjoyed close ties with Mobutu – would draw on several battalions of Zairian troops to strengthen its advance on Luanda. UNITA would rely on South African instructors, weaponry and armour to turn it into a recognisable military force. And the MPLA would receive the backing of the entire Cuban military machine, a devastating weapon which would ultimately prove more than a match for its opponents. Goaded on by the Americans – who were restrained by Congress from escalating their involvement in Angola – Pretoria believed that by invading Angola it could install its proxies and shore up apartheid for the foreseeable future. But, as a result of overconfidence, it failed to define its objectives clearly before launching an open-ended military operation with fractious allies, initiating thirteen years of bitter and inconclusive fighting in southern Angola.

South African involvement in Angola prior to Operation Savannah

One month after occupying the Calueque hydroelectric installations (August 1975), South African military instructors started forming their dispersed Angolan allies into a cohesive fighting force. In late August, Chipenda's guerrillas were moved from Serpa Pinto (Menongue), where they had been inactive, to their camp at M'Pupa (in Cuando Cubango) for a month's training. On 4 September, President Vorster authorised the SADF to give military training, advice and logistical support to UNITA and the FNLA, and three weeks later Savimbi received his first SADF liaison officer – Commandant Van der Waals – who set up a training camp at Calombo (near Silva Porto) and prepared the defences of Nova Lisboa (Huambo).[1] There he was joined by nineteen SADF instructors who set about forming UNITA's thousand-odd recruits into two infantry brigades. Within days of their arrival, however, news arrived that three large FAPLA columns were advancing on Nova Lisboa – from the north (Cela), from the west (Benguela) and from the north-west (Lobito). A mobile attack unit – Battle-Group Foxbat – was hastily assembled using one company of UNITA troops, the SADF instructors and the only three working armoured cars in UNITA's possession (Second World War Pan-hards). On 2 October, Foxbat set out from Silva Porto, and three days later it clashed head-on with the FAPLA at Norton de Matos (Caluita).

The clash at Norton de Matos (Caluita), 5 October 1975

The engagement started badly for the South Africans when their command vehicle was disabled by the FAPLA's first round, and this triggered mass desertion by the raw UNITA troops who had never seen combat. The South African commander rallied his remaining men, and in fierce exchanges they drove off the FAPLA, allegedly killing over 100 soldiers and destroying one of their five armoured cars. Foxbat's success at Norton de Matos saved UNITA's biggest prize – Nova Lisboa – from certain capture. But of greater significance for the South Africans were the first eyewitness reports of Cuban military advisors fighting alongside the FAPLA. Although these reports might have been erroneous, they were sufficient to convince the SADF that Cuban military personnel were intervening on the side of the FAPLA, prompting alarm in Pretoria. Paranoid at the spread of Communist influence into sub-Saharan Africa, the presence of Cuban officers in Angola confirmed Pretoria's worst nightmare, and presaged a Communist victory in Angola which could be followed by an assault on Namibia (and even South Africa itself). It is thus no coincidence that, within days of the clash at Norton de Matos, Pretoria ordered an invasion of Angola.

American collusion in the South African invasion

The South Africans were encouraged to invade by the Americans, although this was to be denied by subsequent administrations. While Washington officially maintained a cool relationship with South Africa throughout the early 1970s, its contacts with Pretoria were, in reality, far closer than it wished to admit, and during this period there were regular security meetings between the CIA and the head of BOSS, General Van Den Bergh.[2] Pretoria shared American paranoia of Soviet expansion into

Africa, and it was keen to establish an informal alliance with the USA to counter this threat even if diplomatically relations were deadlocked over apartheid. By late 1975, the CIA's efforts to expand its Angolan operation were blocked by American public opinion which was hostile to foreign military adventures (following the panicked withdrawal from Vietnam in April) and suspicious of the presidency. Furthermore, in early 1975, Congress had launched two separate investigations into the CIA's covert operations, and by late 1975 they were questioning CIA chiefs about Operation IAFeature even as it was reaching its most critical juncture. The Americans therefore looked on South Africa as a vitally-needed proxy force which could put the FNLA in power, and they actively encouraged Pretoria's plans to invade Angola.

What remains unclear is exactly what was agreed between the American and South African governments before the invasion was launched. Pretoria was quite insistent that the CIA (and, by implication, President Ford) gave the 'green light' for the invasion, promising to extract support for the FNLA and UNITA from Congress over the following months. Their plan envisioned the South Africans capturing as much Angolan territory as possible before Independence Day, after which the FNLA and UNITA would set up a government and call on the Americans for military and financial aid for the final showdown with the MPLA. According to 'Pik' Botha (at the time South African Ambassador to Washington): '[t]he United States at the highest level requested ... South Africa to go in and assist UNITA', and there is little reason to doubt that the rest of the South African leadership shared this belief.[3] The reality was quite different, however, and once news of the South African invasion leaked out, the Americans would be quick to distance themselves, leaving Pretoria precariously isolated.

The decision to invade Angola had one other fatal flaw which was Pretoria's failure to set clear objectives for the invasion force. Instead it opted to extend them on a day-to-day basis as events unfolded. The effect of this strategy was to initiate a tit-for-tat military escalation with the Cubans, each South African advance drawing an equal Cuban response until the war had escalated to a level which Pretoria had neither anticipated, nor had the stomach to match. Pretoria's botched strategy was the result of fierce divisions within the South African leadership over whether the invasion was necessary. While Foreign Minister P.W. Botha and SADF Chief General Viljoen were keen to go ahead (as a means of striking SWAPO which had stepped up its operations in the border region), BOSS Chief General Van den Bergh urged restraint, preferring to arm the FNLA and UNITA and maintain control of Calueque. Caught between the two was President Vorster who was at the time pursuing a policy of détente with southern Africa, and who was loath to jeopardise this just as it was starting to produce tangible results (such as the Victoria Falls Conference that

August). But with four African states privately urging South Africa to intervene, Vorster calculated that an intervention in Angola could actually further détente by convincing South Africa's neighbours that it could be relied on to maintain stability in the region.[4] It was a miscalculation which was to cost Vorster and the South Africans dear.

Task Force Zulu

The invasion force – Task Force Zulu – was hastily assembled from two Angolan groups the SADF had been training since late August.[5] The first was designated Battle-Group Alpha – under Commandant Linford – and consisted of two companies of Bushman soldiers, many of whom had served in the Portuguese Flechas (commandos) as irregular tracking units hunting down the FNLA and UNITA. Their new allies – Battle-Group Bravo under Commandant Breytenbach – would be three companies of Chipenda's troops who had been training at the M'Pupa base for the past month, and who less than a year before had been fighting the Bushmen. The total force numbered roughly 500 men, under the command of fourteen SADF officers.[6] Melding these former adversaries into an effective fighting force would be a tremendous challenge for the South Africans, and Linford's powers of persuasion were tested to the limit the day before his force set off for Angola as he tried to persuade his Bushman troops that the FNLA and UNITA were now their allies. On 9 October Colonel 'Corky' van Heerden flew to the SADF base at Rundu (Namibia) to take command of Operation Savannah, and over the next couple of days the Angolans handed in their kit (to remove all evidence of South African involvement) and were issued with light weaponry, Vickers machine-guns and vegetable trucks for transport. On 13 October, both groups linked up at Katwitwi (on the Angola-Namibia border), and the following morning they crossed into Angola, initiating Operation Savannah.

The first phase of Operation Savannah, 14–24 October 1975

When Zulu Force crossed into Cuando Cubango in mid-October 1975, southern Angola was in chaos. Following the withdrawal of the Portuguese garrison in July 1975, thousands of white settlers had fled the region, creating a power vacuum which was exploited by bands of MPLA, FNLA and UNITA cadres who tried to push their rivals out of the area. The MPLA had taken control of southern Angola's regional capitals – Pereira d'Eça (N'Giva), Sá da Bandeira (Lubango) and Moçâmedes (Namibe) – but was losing ground to UNITA and the FNLA which had much of Cuando Cubango and northern Cunene under their control. UNITA and the FNLA spent as much time fighting each other as they did the MPLA, however, and by October the war in southern Angola had degenerated into a messy stalemate, each movement skirmishing with its opponents whilst making no effort to capture their power bases. The South African invasion would overturn the balance of power, and it would be some time before the FAPLA realised who it was up against.[7]

Operation Savannah's first objective was Pereira d'Eça (N'Giva), Cunene's provincial capital located on the strategic road running from the Namibian border to Sá da Bandeira (Lubango), and beyond to southern Angola's principal ports. Pretoria wanted to give the impression that Zulu Force was Angolan, however, and it ordered the attack to come from the north, forcing Zulu Force to take a roundabout route via Serpa Pinto (Menongue) and Artur de Paiva (Cubango), only getting as far as Cuvelai by dusk on 16 October (see Map 6, page 95). The town was in UNITA hands, but any illusions the South Africans had about their alliance were shattered when the UNITA commander (for reasons known only to himself) ambushed Bravo as it entered the town, being driven off after a noisy fight. The following day Zulu Force had its first contact with the FAPLA, ten miles north of Evale, a brief encounter which descended into farce when Charlie company got into a firefight with itself (there were no casualties). Despite this comical encounter, Zulu Force rapidly improved in proficiency, as was demonstrated two days later when it captured N'Giva with light casualties. The decision to move on N'Giva, however, was, in Linford's opinion, 'a bloody mistake',[8] and he was one of several officers who felt that, if they had kept going, nothing would have stopped them reaching Luanda in a matter of days.

The SADF High Command did not share Linford's view, however, having opted for a staged advance northwards, and following N'Giva's capture they ordered Zulu Force to move at once on Sá da Bandeira (Lubango). Accompanied by a third company of troops – Battle-Group Charlie – Zulu Force launched a two-pronged attack, Alpha clearing the settlements to Sá da Bandeira's south while the rest of the force headed directly north towards the city. Just beyond João de Almeida (Chibia), Bravo ran into the first of several FAPLA positions, driving off the raw troops with crippling casualties. Examining the battlefield after one bloody encounter, the South Africans found what they claimed were Cuban dead (who had been operating the 122 mm rocket launchers), the first physical evidence of Cuban personnel confirming Pretoria's worst suspicions.[9] That night Zulu Force camped at Rotunda, destroying three armoured cars during a night raid, and the next morning it assaulted the city centre. Heavier resistance than expected was met at the airport, and over eighty FAPLA soldiers were killed and thirty captured before it was secured.[10] Bravo then proceeded to clear the town, and by the following morning had captured its last objective – the FAPLA barracks – seizing huge amounts of weaponry and supplies.

Flushed with Zulu Force's success (it had captured over 250 miles of territory in only five days), the SADF ordered it to advance on Moçâmedes (Namibe) – Angola's southernmost port – in order to provide a stronger logistical base for the operation. However, it was still not clear whether Pretoria intended to go the whole way to Luanda, and Breytenbach's account of the time is revealing of the confusion in Zulu Force over its final objectives. Although the troops were told there would be two thrusts northward – Zulu Force moving along the coast to open up the ports for logistics, while Foxbat went inland from Nova Lisboa (Huambo) towards Malanje – no one was told how far north they would go, nor (more crucially) whether they were expected to capture Luanda before Independence Day. Pretoria was playing the situation by ear, confident that the weak resistance Zulu Force had so far encountered would continue as it headed further north. But its indecision over how far north its forces should go played into the Cubans hands, giving them breathing space to reorganise their defences.

The Cuban operation in Angola gets into trouble

Since returning to Luanda on 21 August, Argüelles had been busy setting up the training camps, but he was immediately distracted from his task by the FNLA threat on Luanda. On 30 August, FAPLA troops clashed with the FNLA at Quifangondo, a series of small hills nine miles north of Luanda overlooking the main road from Caxito. The defence of Luanda was vital for the legitimacy of any future MPLA government and, probably as a result of this skirmish, on 18 September the FAPLA attacked Caxito, expelling the FNLA and capturing large amounts of American munitions which were paraded before the world's press as evidence of Roberto's CIA backing. The FNLA responded by calling in Zairian reinforcements and, on 17 September, they recaptured Caxito, putting fresh pressure on Luanda. Over the following weeks, formidable FNLA and Zairian forces built up in Caxito in preparation for a final assault on Luanda, and it is unsurprising that this danger dominated Cuban thoughts, leading them to overlook events in southern Angola.

There were further clashes between the FAPLA and FNLA at Morro do Cal (Chalk Hill) on 26 September, a hilly position between Caxito and Quifangondo which the FNLA intended to use as a springboard for its final assault on Luanda. But the Cubans were too busy dealing with the arrival of hundreds of instructors and equipment to deal with this threat, and it was not until 19 October that they helped the FAPLA draw up a comprehensive defence plan for Luanda, one which recognised the Angolan capital's precarious position.[11] Accepting that the forces defending Luanda were too weak to fight off a determined assault from Morro do Cal, on 21 October the camp at Salazar was shut down and most of its recruits and their Cuban instructors were withdrawn to Luanda. That Argüelles should have considered shutting down the camp only three days after it started operating is an indication of the weakness of his forces in Luanda, and would seem to confirm Cuban accounts that there were only around 500 Cubans in the whole of Angola at the time. Argüelles's priority was to drive the FNLA off Morro do Cal, and two days later he ordered a combined FAPLA–Cuban force to launch their assault.

The attack on Morro do Cal, 23 October 1975

The 1,094-man force was assembled out of the raw recruits from Salazar, fifty-eight Cubans (including forty of their instructors) and two companies of Katangese (roughly 200 men) who had recently allied with the MPLA. They were backed by an assortment of mortars, machine-guns and light artillery. On 23 October (the same day Sá da Bandeira was attacked by Zulu Force) they launched their attack on Morro do Cal against a defending force of as many as 3,500 men.[12] The assault went badly, and the FAPLA troops were driven back to Quifangondo where they managed to dig in and repulse a determined assault that evening. The failure of the attack was as much the result of the FAPLA's lack of training (few soldiers had received more than a week) as it was of poor intelligence, and over the following fortnight the Cubans set about rectifying these weaknesses. Effectively given a two-week breathing-space, the Cubans constructed scaled defences at Quifangondo, digging underground bunkers and installing sophisticated defensive weaponry. In retrospect, had Roberto persisted in his assault on Luanda, he might well have captured the Angolan capital before reinforcements arrived. But the opportunity was missed, and by the time his combined forces launched a further assault on Quifangondo they would find themselves up against a more professional force.

The growing threat from the south

The fighting around Morro do Cal coincided with Zulu Force's attack on Sá da Bandeira, an event which should have alerted the Cubans to a new and more serious threat from the south. The MPLA reacted spiritedly, ordering the mobilisation of the FAPLA and calling on the Angolan people to resist the invaders. Remaining FAPLA forces were withdrawn to Cacula – a strategically vital town forty-five miles north-east of Sá da Bandeira guarding the fork in the road to Benguela and Nova Lisboa – and desperate attempts were made to prepare Benguela's defences against an imminent assault.[13] However, it appears that Argüelles had his attention exclusively focused on Morro do Cal and, on 1 November, he optimistically reported to Furry that '[t]he MPLA still has the advantage, only ten days before independence', while '[t]he enemy, ill-prepared and dispirited, including the Zairian army units ... is giving us the breathing space to train the [FAPLA] battalions.'[14] The reality, however, was that the surprise South African invasion was about to threaten the total extinction of the MPLA in Angola, and with it their 500-man Cuban mission.

Following the capture of Sá da Bandeira (Lubango), Zulu Force spent a couple of days clearing pockets of FAPLA resistance before setting out for Moçâmedes (Namibe) on 27 October. Zulu Force again split into two, Bravo taking the old road while Alpha used the new Leba Gorge pass. Just beyond Caraculo (an important railway junction), Alpha ran into a strong FAPLA position and fought against it into the night, inflicting heavy casualties. The following morning Bravo advanced past the wreckage of the previous night's battle on Moçâmedes itself, and encountered resistance only at the southern edge of the town, occupying Porto Alexandre (Tômbua) later that afternoon. The capture of Angola's southernmost port eased logistical constraints on Zulu Force, and delivered a huge amount of war booty into its hands, including hundreds of new pick-up trucks and tractors. Encouraged by the FAPLA's weak resistance, Zulu Force was ordered to continue on to Benguela and Lobito, and it was probably at this stage that it was decided to go the whole way to Luanda. If so, it was an ironic decision as Zulu Force was about to encounter its first serious resistance.

The South African advance was again split into two fronts, Zulu Force approaching Benguela from the south while Foxbat advanced from Nova Lisboa towards Lobito, cutting off the defenders' retreat. Three days later – after being reinforced by a company of troops and several Eland-90 armoured cars – Zulu Force returned to Sá da Bandeira and headed northwards, running into FAPLA defences at Cacula. That night, Alpha clashed with a FAPLA patrol coming south from Quilengues and destroyed the leading Land Rover, killing five FAPLA soldiers and a Cuban officer.[15] With South African forces advancing on them from the south and the east, the FAPLA pulled back to a new line of defence running from Norton de Matos (Caluita) to the railway junction at Catengue, hoping to halt the South Africans before they reached Benguela. Recognising that Catengue's capture would lay open Benguela's defences, Zulu Force raced north through Quilengues (which the FAPLA had abandoned) and camped just south of Catengue on the night of 1 November, fully expecting a hard fight the next morning.

The clash at Catengue, 2 November 1975

When Zulu Force advanced into Catengue on 2 November, it found the town deserted, and was only alerted to a FAPLA presence to the west when a lone 122 mm Katyusha rocket landed nearby.[16] Charlie Company was dispatched to investigate (another company was also sent east), and it soon came to a bridge over a dry river three miles from Catengue. As it attempted to cross the riverbed, an entire FAPLA battalion dug-in on the hills beyond it suddenly opened fire, driving off most of Charlie Company in a disorganised scramble towards Catengue. Facing a force of up to 1,000 soldiers backed by mortars and artillery, Charlie's commander tried to hold his ground with only forty men in a noisy point-blank firefight. As the first stragglers stumbled into Catengue, Breytenbach realised there was trouble and he rushed to the scene, calling up reinforcements to respond to the barrage being laid down by the FAPLA–Cuban artillery. Fifty-one Cuban instructors from the Benguela camp fought alongside the FAPLA during this battle, and their participation led Breytenbach to conclude that his troops were 'facing the best organised and heaviest FAPLA opposition to date'.

Zulu Force regrouped under heavy artillery fire, while Alpha rushed westwards to set up an ambush on the FAPLA–Cubans' most likely withdrawal route. A staged assault was then launched on the positions on the hills overlooking the bridge, but due to the thickness of the vegetation, several FAPLA trenches were missed, and at one point Breytenbach (armed only with a rifle) found himself fighting off a FAPLA platoon which had been bypassed in the assault. During the battle, the South Africans found the bodies of Cuban instructors lying next to the recoilless guns and heavy machine-guns they had been operating, as well as documents in Spanish which confirmed high-level Cuban participation in the battle. Only after a third assault were the FAPLA–Cubans driven off the hill, and the position was secured by 6p.m. that evening. Further havoc was then wreaked on the retreating forces when they were ambushed by Alpha on the main road to Benguela, precipitating a disorderly rout. The battle had lasted for nine hours, and Zulu Force had suffered at least ten wounded (some of them seriously) while dozens of FAPLA soldiers had been killed. More significant, however, were the first officially recognised Cuban fatalities: four were killed, seven wounded and thirteen were missing-in-action.

The battle at Catengue was the first universally accepted encounter between the two main forces of intervention in Angola – Cuba and South Africa – and its effect was to throw Luanda into panic. If South African accounts are to be believed, the FAPLA–Cuban troops had taken a heavy drubbing, and any hopes they could hold onto Benguela were dashed the next day when Foxbat captured Norton de Matos (ninety miles east of Lobito), threatening their only line of retreat. The Cubans must have been shocked by the news of the deaths of at least half-a-dozen of their comrades (almost as many as had died during the eight-year mission in Guiné),[17] and they realised they would be next if the South African advance were allowed to continue. The Cuban mission in Luanda thus found itself facing not one but two threats – from the north by the FNLA–Zairian forces on Morro do Cal, and from the south by Zulu Force which was advancing on Luanda at the rate of forty miles per day. And to make matters worse, by early November, Cabinda was under threat of invasion by a combined FLEC–Zairian force, threatening to cut off (and possibly annihilate) the 200-man Cuban force defending it.

The decision to launch Operation Carlota, 4 November 1975

By early November 1975, MMCA's small-scale mission to train the FAPLA had been dramatically overtaken by events on the ground, and drastic measures were needed to avoid disaster. On 3 November, the MPLA Politburo met in emergency session and unanimously endorsed a proposal (made by Neto at the urging of Argüelles) to request immediate and massive reinforcements from Havana. The Cuban response came within hours, Castro agreeing to the request after consulting in private with his most trusted colleagues, among them his brother Raúl.[18] From now on all pretence of secrecy would be abandoned as Cuba launched a military intervention on an unprecedented scale. The mission was code-named 'Operation Carlota' after 'Black Carlota', the leader of a slave rebellion which broke out at the Triunvirato plantation (Matanzas) on 5 November 1843. The image of a slave woman rising up to overthrow her racist oppressors – just as Cuba's black troops were taking on the apartheid military machine – was particularly apposite for the Cuban regime which depicted its intervention in Angola as a 'Second Liberation War', the racist 'Boers' replacing the '*Tugas*' as the colonialist oppressors.

What Havana has subsequently chosen to ignore is that it was only forced into launching Operation Carlota as a result of its incompetent Angolan strategy which had ended up placing a lightly armed Cuban force in the path of two foreign armies. Focused exclusively on the closing stages of Institutionalisation, Havana had shown faltering interest in Neto's predicament throughout the first half of 1975, and when belatedly coaxed into re-engaging in Angola in August, it had dispatched a training mission with objectives which had already been overtaken by events on the ground. Indeed, by the time the bulk of the Cubans arrived in Angola, the country had already collapsed into civil war, with the FNLA advancing on Luanda and anarchy engulfing the countryside. This not only made the Cuban mission to train the FAPLA over the next six months impossible, but it put the Cuban force itself in considerable danger. But its predicament was met by an almost total indifference from Havana which failed to spot obvious warning signs (such as the closing of the Salazar camp only three days after it started functioning). Furthermore, the Cuban leadership did not even consider the possibility of a South African intervention, despite newspaper reports of SADF incursions into southern Angola throughout late 1974 and 1975.

The massive disorganisation of the Cuban mission in Angola also played a part in the breakdown of communication between Havana and Luanda. From his earliest reports, Argüelles complained about the disorganised haste of the operation and the chaotic conditions under which it was set up.[19] But he accompanied these with breezily optimistic reports on the MPLA's position, and as late as 1 November (only *three days* before he sent desperate requests for reinforcements), he informed Furry that the MPLA still had the military advantage against an 'ill-prepared and disorganised' enemy. Argüelles no doubt put his woefully inaccurate appraisal of the situation down to a lack of intelligence on southern Angola, but his claims to have been unaware of the progress (or even existence) of Zulu Force strain credibility. After all, the FAPLA had been fighting the South Africans since 17 October and had been driven out of three provincial capitals by them, and MMCA would have known about this from the Cubans spotted by the South Africans fighting alongside the FAPLA during October.

The stunning news that the MPLA (and with it the Cuban contingent) was about to be wiped out could not have come at a worse time for Castro as he was in the final stages of preparing his triumphal First Party Congress. The possibility that dozens (even hundreds) of Cuban personnel would be taken prisoner or killed by the South Africans – and that an anti-Communist regime would take root in Angola – would have been a devastating anti-climax to Institutionalisation, and would certainly have diminished Castro's standing and influence with his Soviet patron. It is thus no surprise that Castro's response was immediate, as he had no other choice. If he allowed the MPLA to be driven out of Luanda and withdraw to Cabinda (as Neto was unwillingly suggesting at this point), it would have been a shattering blow to Neto's legitimacy in Africa, and would have put the Cubans in a hopelessly weak position to influence events in Angola over the following months.

Thus, on 4 November the Cuban leadership faced a military catastrophe of its own creation, for which there were only two solutions: immediate withdrawal to minimise the losses in personnel and equipment, or reinforcement on a massive scale to crush the forces advancing on Luanda. It was a matter of political survival for Castro whose role as supreme Cuban leader and unofficial spokesman for the Third World would be threatened by a defeat in Angola. Faced with impending disaster, he took a massive gamble and ordered a full-scale military intervention in Angola. Hoping to turn potential defeat into overwhelming victory as he had on so many previous occasions in his long political career, Castro was taking once more a leap of faith into Angola (just as he had with Argüelles's training mission). Little did he realise the scale and length of the operation he was initiating.

The Soviet role in the decision to launch Operation Carlota

Soviet involvement in the decision to launch Operation Carlota remains controversial, which is ironic as the evidence suggests they took very little part in it. Although the Soviets did on several occasions suggest the MPLA approach Cuba for military instructors (to avoid sending their own), there is no evidence that they ordered Cuba to launch an intervention in Angola. The Cuban government for its part has been quite insistent that the decision to send combat troops into Angola was purely Cuban, and that the Soviet Union was only informed of the operation once it was already underway.[20] 'The Soviets knew absolutely nothing about it,' Castro recently insisted. 'We took the decision because of our long-standing relations over many years with Neto ... We acted ... but without [Soviet] cooperation. Quite the opposite, in fact. There were criticisms, but we went ahead anyway.'[21] This view might seem far-fetched considering the closeness of Soviet–Cuban relations at the time, but recent testimony from former Soviet officials adds some credence to Cuban claims.

Westad's interview with former Soviet Deputy Foreign Minister, Georgi Kornienko, is particularly revealing. Kornienko claims he first heard about the Cuban airlift to Angola in a cable from the Soviet Ambassador to Conakry, who reported that Cuban aircraft would be refuelling in Conakry en route to Luanda. Having checked with Andrei Gromyko (Soviet Foreign Minister), Yuri Andropov (KGB Chief) and Marshal Andrei Grechko (Defence Minister) – none of whom had any knowledge of the operation – the matter was taken to the Politburo which allegedly opposed it. However, by the time a message was drafted and ready to send to Cuba, the aircraft were already in the air, and the Soviets begrudgingly agreed to go along with the operation.[22] Revealingly, Kornienko mentions that the Soviet personnel who assisted the Cuban airlift were under the impression that the operation had been authorised by the Kremlin, an interesting detail which suggests that the Soviet military might have been working independently on its own agenda. Throughout the 1970s, the Soviet military (bankrolled by Siberian petrodollars) had extended its influence across the world, and in 1975 it may have been keener than the Kremlin to escalate its involvement in Angola. The Kremlin was keen to maintain superpower relations which were still – at least on paper – bound by the Nixon–Brezhnev policy of détente, and it did not want these jeopardised over a region which, up to this point, had escaped all but the most superficial superpower interest.

As a result, throughout 1975, Moscow repeatedly vetoed the use of Soviet personnel in Angola until after Independence Day (even the arrival of the first Soviet advisors in Luanda on 12 November 1975 is disputed).[23]

The Soviet Politburo was prepared to make gestures of solidarity – sending naval units to patrol areas off the Angolan coast in support of the Cuban operation – but it held back from becoming directly involved until the fighting had swung in the Cubans' favour (merely sending arms and a handful of weapons specialists to Brazzaville and Dar-es-Salaam). Only the passing of the controversial Clark Amendment in the USA (on 19 December 1975) changed the Soviet perspective and led to full logistical support for Operation Carlota. Therefore while it is possible that the Soviet military acted independently of the Kremlin in its support for Operation Carlota (as it did during the massive campaigns in Cuando Cubango in the late 1980s), it appears that Moscow – though aware of a Cuban training mission in Angola since late August – was unaware of Operation Carlota until it was already underway.[24]

The launch of Operation Carlota

Immediately following the decision to launch Operation Carlota, frenzied preparations started in Cuba to ship thousands of troops, arms and equipment to Luanda. The Cuban operation would need both short- and long-term objectives to succeed. In the short term, Cuba needed to get as many reinforcements as possible to Luanda before it was overwhelmed, and this meant flying them out immediately, an operation constrained by Cuba's limited air transport capability. In the long term, once Luanda had been secured, Cuba would need to build up a significant military force – backed by heavy artillery, tanks and thousands of troops – which could then drive the enemy out of Angola and extend the MPLA's control over the country. This part of the operation – involving the transport of the bulk of the troops and heavy equipment – would be by sea, and would end up involving all the available shipping in Cuba's merchant marine. The logistical difficulties of transporting a force eventually numbering over 30,000 men (plus equipment) nearly 6,000 miles would strain the Cuban military to its limits, and it would rely on the proven Cuban skill of improvisation to overcome seemingly insurmountable obstacles.

The most pressing need on 4 November was the defence of Luanda which – given the unreliability of Argüelles' reports – could fall at any moment. The defenders of Luanda needed heavy artillery to drive off a determined assault, and troops to prepare a second line of defence in the event enemy forces broke through at Quifangondo. To meet the first need, the FAR turned to one of its newest weapons – the BM-21 missile-launcher. Capable of firing salvoes of forty 122 mm missiles to a range of eight miles, the 'Stalin Organ' was at the time the most advanced artillery system provided by the Soviets, and had only briefly seen combat in the Middle East. The FAR could not provide the MPLA with its own BM-21s – Cuba had, after all, only just received its first units. Instead, twenty of

Cuba's most experienced artillery operators were sent to Luanda to assemble six BM-21s the MPLA had stockpiled in Pointe-Noire (they were ferried to Luanda by the Cuban ship *La Plata*). Following their arrival on 7 November, the Cubans worked around the clock to ensure one set of batteries was ready for the battle at Quifangondo.

To meet the second need, Havana dispatched a battalion of MININT Special Forces to Luanda. Specifically created for special operations anywhere in the world, the elite 628-man battalion was one of Cuba's most experienced professional units, many of the men having obtained doctorates in military or technical sciences. Only cadres with the soundest political convictions were selected for the Special Forces, and their unbending loyalty to the Cuban regime may have been one of the reasons they were chosen to spearhead the intervention (although the short preparation time they required before leaving was also a factor). Transporting this battalion to Luanda was a problem as the only aircraft suitable for personnel – several ageing Bristol Britannias – could not make the 6,000 mile journey non-stop. Each additional soldier and artillery piece reduced the aircraft's range and speed, presenting the Cuban logistics planners with irreconcilable priorities for an airlift which needed to be both rapid *and* on a massive scale. In the end, the Cubans opted for a route previously used for Cabinda which involved refuelling stops in Barbados, Bissau and Brazzaville – a gruelling forty-eight-hour journey but the best solution available at the time. The choice of Barbados would turn out to be controversial, however, and would prompt diplomatic manoeuvring by Washington to deny Cuba landing rights, inspiring original and often desperate alternatives (see Chapter 5).

To meet Operation Carlota's long-term objectives, thousands of Cubans were called up by their local Military Committees to make up the bulk of the intervention force. Although all commanding officers were professionals, the majority of ground troops were reservists, some of them carrying out their military service. As on previous internationalist missions, all personnel were strictly volunteers, and there is ample evidence that the call-up was extremely popular. Indeed, García Márquez records that once news leaked out that volunteers were needed for an internationalist mission '[a] great deal of effort was required to prevent the conversion of this massive solicitude into a state of national disorder'.[25] All available ships in the Cuban merchant marine were commandeered and hastily modified to take as many troops as possible, and on 8 November the first three sailed from Havana bearing 1,200 men with arms and equipment. The first ship would not arrive in Angola until 27 November, however, and in the meantime the Cuban forces in Angola were on their own for the biggest and most decisive battles of the 'Second Liberation War'.

5

THE 'SECOND LIBERATION WAR', NOVEMBER 1975–MARCH 1976

Just after 10 p.m. on 8 November 1975, two Britannias bearing the first 164 men of the MININT Special Forces battalion landed in Luanda, formally initiating Operation Carlota. Their arrival came not a moment too soon, as on all three fronts the situation was critical. That morning, a combined FNLA–Zairian force had launched a third assault on Quifangondo, and there were reports that another force had simultaneously invaded Cabinda, threatening to wipe out the stranded Cuban garrison defending Cabinda city. In the south, Zulu Force was moving inexorably on Benguela and Lobito, threatening the provincial capital of Cuanza Sul, Novo Redondo (Sumbe), which was only a day's drive from Luanda. That evening, the Cuban operation in Angola hung in the balance, and over the following week crucial battles would be fought on all three fronts which would determine the outcome of the bitter fourteen-year struggle between the MPLA and FNLA.

The battle for Cabinda, 8–13 November 1975

The invasion of Cabinda came as no surprise to the Cuban commander, Ramón Espinosa Martín, who had spent the previous month preparing the enclave's defences.[1] By early November, his 232 Cubans had nearly finished training the FAPLA's 1st Infantry Battalion, and they were about to start work on the 2nd, whose recruits had been assembled at Dinge and Lândana (Cacongo). Painfully aware of the weakness of his forces, Espinosa was outraged when Argüelles ordered him to send his most experienced mortar and anti-aircraft instructors to reinforce Luanda. Espinosa refused point-blank, insisting that if he let them go he would jeopardise the defence of Cabinda, and this prompted a visit by Argüelles in person to enforce the order. Inevitably Espinosa acquiesced, but only after Argüelles promised to return the men once the assaults on Luanda had been repelled. In the end, however, the fighting in Cabinda and Quifangondo occurred simultaneously, forcing Espinosa to mount his defence with only one battalion of FAPLA, a handful of experienced guerrillas, five artillery batteries and the reduced contingent of Cubans (a total of around 600 troops).

The challenge for Espinosa was to use his limited forces to defend Cabinda city from a land invasion involving up to five infantry battalions (at least 1,500 men), with possible aerial or naval landings along the coast. Reasoning that the invading force would opt for the quickest route – crossing the border at Iema and taking the main road fifteen miles north to Cabinda city – Espinosa placed his main defences at N'to (Buca), roughly a third of the way along that road (see Map 4). The FAPLA 1st Battalion dug in there in two lines of defence, with anti-tank weapons, mortars and AA guns in support. To guard against secondary attacks along the eastern border – which Espinosa reckoned would converge on Subantando (Baca, fifteen miles east of Cabinda city) – over 500 mines were laid in the border area in the two nights preceding the invasion, while small platoons of experienced guerrillas were deployed to detect and, if possible, halt any invading forces. The 2nd FAPLA battalion was held in reserve at Dinge (where it received a crash-course) under orders to concentrate in Subantando in an emergency. And in Lândana (Cacongo) a small force supported by anti-tank and AA guns was deployed in the old Portuguese base to defend against an amphibious assault.

When the invasion finally came, on the morning of 8 November, Espinosa's strategy appeared to have paid off. The invading army was reportedly made up of four infantry battalions (c.2,000 men) – three FLEC and one Zairian (Mobutu's elite Karmanyola regiment) – and was under the command of 150 French and American mercenaries. Espinosa correctly guessed their plan of attack, but did not anticipate that the FLEC commander (an American mercenary who died in the fighting) planned for all three fronts to converge on Cabinda city simultaneously. Consequently the first attack came from the east (Chingundo), aiming to capture Subantando before the main assault on Cabinda city started. Espinosa scrambled to move his HQ from N'to to Subantando, leaving Comandante Vásquez in command of Dinge and Lândana with orders to follow the agreed defence plan.

Initially the fighting did not go well for the FAPLA–Cubans. Their small groups of guerrillas patrolling the border were quickly driven back almost as far as Subantando (one FAPLA platoon was wiped out), and this prompted Espinosa to send in a company of reinforcements. That night, they were ambushed near the Lulando river (west of Chimbuande) and three FAPLA soldiers were killed, precipitating a disorderly retreat during which three mortars were left behind (but later recovered). The Cubans nevertheless rallied their troops and dug in east of Subantando, laying minefields around their positions. The next morning, patrols were sent out to locate the FLEC–Zairian force, and one was ambushed as it emerged

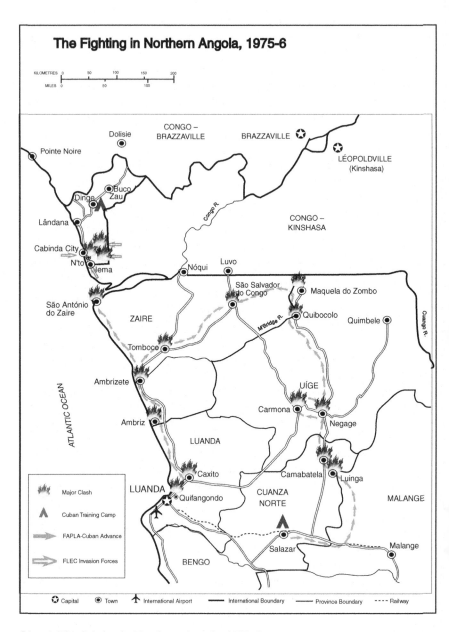

Map 4 The fighting in Northern Angola, 1975–6.

from thick forest near the villages of Talicuma and Talibeca (three miles east of Subantando). This time, the FAPLA did not turn and flee, but instead dug trenches 200 yards from Talicuma from where they fought off repeated attacks throughout the day. It was at this point that, in the words of Espinosa, 'the initiative passed to our side'.[2] That night Cuban sappers laid further minefields around Subantando to prevent night-time infiltration, and during heavy fighting the next day FLEC tried fruitlessly to break through these defences, suffering heavy casualties in the process.

As the defensive lines stabilised around Subantando, Espinosa's focus switched back to N'to where the main FLEC–Zairian force crossed into Cabinda, intending to capture the capital by the end of the day. The Cubans had been alerted to their approach following a series of clashes on patrol during the night, the last of which took place one mile inside Cabinda. Emboldened by the weak resistance they had encountered, the FLEC–Zairian troops marched complacently into the N'to valley, some of them singing as they advanced. It was a scene which was to be repeated later that day 230 miles to the south at Quifangondo, as an over-confident Zairian and Angolan force marched over open ground towards well-defended positions, appearing to the defenders 'like a parade ground drill'.[3] Once they were within range, the FAPLA–Cubans opened up with mortars and 'cuatro bocas' (14.5 mm guns), tearing swathes through their ranks. The advance quickly disintegrated, and the invaders retreated towards the border leaving more than a hundred bodies littering the N'to valley.

Espinosa was at Subantando when he heard the start of the attack, and as he raced back to N'to he was informed that yet another FLEC force – this time in launches – was preparing to land near Labe (south of Cabinda city). Anxious to get to N'to, Espinosa took a quick detour via Base Chica (a promontory overlooking the landing site) where a solitary GRAD-1P rocket-launcher had been set up. Several launches loaded with troops were already visible off the coast, and with no time to wait for them to come into range Espinosa set the rocket-launcher's elevation and left the Angolan operator (who had little experience) to open fire at the right moment. Ultimately luck was with the Cubans and the first rocket hit the leading launch, the demoralising effect of the barrage driving off the others before they reached the shore. Espinosa reached N'to in time for a second, more determined assault against the Cubans' right flank at Labe. But in a repeat of the morning's debacle, sustained machine-gun and artillery fire ensured the attackers never got within fifty yards of the Cuban trenches, and they were again driven off with heavy casualties. 'The image they offered was one of absolute defeat,' Espinosa wrote later.[4]

Having defeated two invasions from the west, Espinosa turned his attention back to the east where FLEC was still attempting to capture Subantando. Heavy fighting raged in this area throughout 10 and 11 November, but FLEC failed to break through the defences. When, on the second day, the FLEC commander was killed in the fighting, the attacks faltered. Sensing victory, Espinosa ordered a counter-attack, and at dawn on 12 November FAPLA–Cuban forces swept eastwards, driving the disintegrating FLEC–Zairian forces back towards the border. As they advanced, Cuban troops found evidence of atrocities committed by the retreating troops, including a massacre of civilians at the village of Talibeca. When they reached the border at 3 p.m. on 13 November, the invasion of Cabinda was effectively over (though sporadic fighting with FLEC would continue for decades) and the first serious threat to the MPLA's survival had been removed.

The Cubans had shown remarkable cool-headedness against simultaneous invasions from three different directions, and without any extra help from Luanda, they had succeeded in hanging onto the vitally important enclave. Over 600 casualties had been inflicted on the invading forces – including their two commanders – while FAPLA and Cuba losses probably did not exceed thirty killed and fifty wounded.[5] Fighting on three fronts simultaneously, Espinosa had used his limited forces to great effect, and in five days had secured the MPLA's future economic lifeline – Cabinda oil – which has kept it in power to this day. Espinosa would have to wait for his actions to receive official recognition, however, as he was rapidly replaced by General Joaquín Quintas Solá (on 11 December), possibly reflecting Argüelles's displeasure at Espinosa's refusal to comply with his orders. While fighting was raging in Cabinda, however, an equally crucial battle was being fought for the control of Luanda, and its outcome would decide the outcome of the struggle between the MPLA and FNLA.

Build-up to the battle of Quifangondo, early November 1975

By the time Neto and Argüelles sent their desperate request for reinforcements to Havana, the FNLA's final assault on Luanda was known to be imminent.[6] For the previous two weeks, Roberto's forces had been concentrating in Caxito and Morro do Cal, and with less than a week to go before Independence Day, the Cubans were convinced that Roberto would wait no longer. Like Neto, Roberto believed that without control of Luanda any future FNLA government would lack international legitimacy. But, since recapturing Caxito in July, the FNLA had failed to take the initiative, and by early November Roberto had no remaining option but a direct assault on Luanda from Morro do Cal (the only alternative involved a 500-mile detour). This approach into Luanda's northern suburbs would take the FNLA directly under the defences at Quifangondo, and in the fortnight since the first clashes around Morro do Cal they had grown considerably.

Quifangondo's strength was due as much to its strategic location as it was to Cuban ingenuity (see Map 5). The hills of Quifangondo dominate

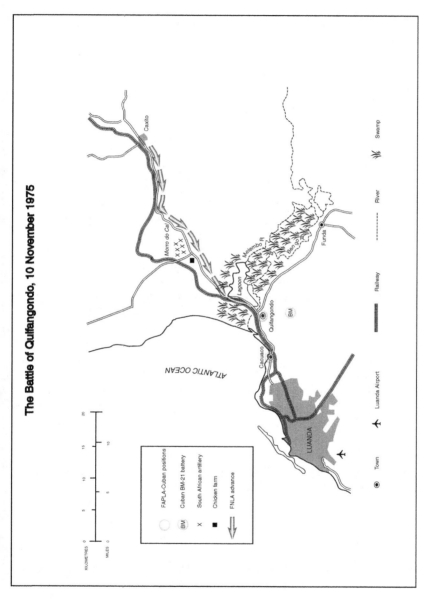

The Battle of Quifangondo, 10 November 1975

KILOMETRES 0 5 10 15 20

MILES 0 5 10

Caxito

Morro do Cal

X X X
X X X

Lagoon

Melembo R

Bengo R

Quifangondo

BM

Cacuaco

ATLANTIC OCEAN

LUANDA

Funda

Swamp

River

Railway

Town

Luanda Airport

○ FAPLA–Cuban positions

BM Cuban BM-21 battery

X South African artillery

■ Chicken farm

⇨ FNLA advance

Map 5 The Battle of Quifangondo, 10 November 1975.

the northern approaches to Luanda, overlooking the main roads towards Funda (in the east) and Morro do Cal and Caxito (in the north). West of the main road lies the Atlantic Ocean, and to the east is the Panguila Lagoon, a swampy area unsuitable for vehicles and (rumour had it) infested with poisonous snakes. This meant that the only viable approach was to march directly down the main road from Morro do Cal – across several miles of open ground – and pass directly under the Quifangondo positions, affording the defenders an unobstructed field of fire. Cuban engineers had constructed deep underground bunkers, and these were to prove highly effective at protecting their troops during the heavy bombardment which preceded each FNLA attack.

The FNLA got an inkling of the strength of these defences when it launched a second, exploratory attack on Quifangondo on 5 November. By this stage the Cubans knew that reinforcements were on their way, but until the first of these arrived – in three days at the earliest – they were effectively on their own. Despite having lost their 200 Katangese allies shortly after the 23 October battles (they were sent to defend Benguela), MMCA fielded just over 1,000 troops, backed by mortars, heavy machine-guns and light artillery. When the five armoured cars leading the FNLA attack were within range, the defenders opened up with artillery, rockets and mortars, driving off repeated assaults on their positions. Eventually, around 2 p.m., the attackers gave up, having suffered heavy casualties (there were no FAPLA–Cuban casualties). Encouraged by their improved performance, the defenders of Quifangondo drove off a third attack (possibly no more than a raid) on 8 November, and that night they received another morale boost with the arrival in Luanda of the first reinforcements from the MININT Special Forces battalion.

These MININT troops were not only exhausted by their forty-eight-hour trip (including a gruelling, mosquito-infested stopover in Bissau), but by this stage many expected that within hours of landing they would be taking part in an evacuation to Cabinda. On arrival in Luanda, however, they were heartened by the news that all three assaults on Quifangondo had been repulsed, and they immediately changed into their uniforms and marched to Cacuaco where – due to their exhaustion – they were placed in the second line of defence as a reserve. More significant than their arrival, however, were the first six BM-21 missile-launchers which were brought up to Quifangondo during the night of 9/10 November. Since 7 November, a team of twenty Cuban specialists had been working to get them operational, but they had discovered that the Soviets failed to send fuses vital for the weapon's operation. Realising it could take weeks to get replacements from Moscow, an urgent request was sent to Havana, and the fuses were flown in just before the BM-21s took up their positions. Ironically, this mix-up might have been to their advantage as it delayed the BM-21s' deployment until only a few hours before the battle started, taking the enemy by surprise.

With only twenty-four hours to go until independence, Roberto finally ordered the assault on Luanda, although there is some dispute over his motivations. Most writers blame the debacle which followed solely on his arrogance and refusal to listen to advice.[7] The SADF liaison officer appointed to advise Roberto – Brigadier Ben Roos – claims that he strongly advised against an attack, a warning which was repeated by Generals Viljoen and Malan (Chief of the SADF) who visited Roberto at Ambriz on 4 November. In their opinion, the terrain was unsuitable for a frontal assault, and privately they harboured reservations about the FNLA's competence to mount a coordinated attack. Roberto would be wiser to withdraw to his core areas of support and retrench there, they argued, saving his military strength for a later date. Roberto tells a different story, however. He claims that Viljoen and Malan asked him to hold off his attack because they were sending five battalions of commandos (3,000 men) to do the job for him. However, the following day the offer was withdrawn,[8] leaving Roberto in a dilemma. Either he could ignore South African advice and go ahead with the attack on the off-chance that it was successful, or he could withdraw and lose a crucial opportunity to crush the MPLA while it was still weak. In the end he decided to chance an attack, and the decision was to haunt him for the rest of his life.[9]

The final attack on Quifangondo, 10 November 1975

A final assault was ordered for 10 November, and at Roberto's request the SADF provided three 140 mm howitzers to support the attack (these were flown to Ambriz on 8 November) as well as a preliminary aerial bombardment by Canberra bombers. While the defences were being softened up, commandos under Colonel Santos e Castro (a former officer in the Portuguese colonial army) would capture the bridge over the Bengo river. Then, the main force would advance down the road towards Luanda, with the South African guns following them as soon as was practical. The attacking force was made up of 2,000 FNLA troops, two battalions of Zairians (1,200 men) and 120 Portuguese mercenaries, and was supported by twelve armoured cars and six jeep-mounted recoilless guns.[10] Artillery support would come from the southern ridges of Morro do Cal where a team of fifty-two South Africans were manning four howitzers alongside two North Korean 130 mm guns. Awaiting them in the hills around Quifangondo were over 1,000 FAPLA and Cuban troops, supported by field guns, mortars, light artillery and the first BM-21 battery which secretly took up position four miles behind Cuban lines that night.

Throughout the night of 9/10 November, the South African howitzers bombarded Quifangondo and Luanda (hitting the area around Grafanil, an FAPLA barracks six miles south of Luanda, killing an Angolan woman). Shortly before 6 a.m., three Canberra bombers flying from Rundu

(Namibia) bombed Quifangondo as planned. Had the assault immediately been launched – insist the South Africans – it might have overwhelmed the defenders before they emerged from their bunkers. But Roberto insisted on witnessing the advance in person, and his leisurely breakfast put this back forty minutes, a delay which proved fatal. Under strict orders to hold their fire until the entire attacking force had emerged into the small corridor between the coast and the lagoon, the defenders watched silently from their trenches as the FNLA advanced on Quifangondo. A dozen armoured cars led the attack, followed on foot by the bulk of the troops who dismounted from trucks at an abandoned chicken farm a couple of miles south of Morro do Cal. The column was allowed to advance several hundred yards before machine-gun fire from its leading armoured car hit the parapet of an FAPLA gun emplacement, unleashing a devastating response.

In one moment the entire hillside erupted in a deafening barrage of machine-gun, mortar and artillery fire, knocking out the four leading armoured cars and inflicting heavy casualties on the infantry. The advance buckled under the deluge of fire and, as reinforcements attempted to regroup at the chicken farm, the Cubans brought their secret weapon into action. Two twenty-rocket salvos from the BM-21 decimated the soldiers at the chicken farm, and then it turned its fire on the main force, raining down over 700 missiles over the next few hours. Watching the carnage from Morro do Cal, the South African guns were powerless to answer the BM-21 which outranged them by over two miles, while both North Korean guns misfired on their first shot (the first misfire killing the crew). The attack quickly disintegrated, the fleeing troops – now more a mob – failing even to blow up the bridge to cover their retreat. On the road behind them they left half-a-dozen burning vehicles and over 120 bodies.[11] The FAPLA–Cuban forces had lost only one man – an FAPLA soldier who had disobeyed orders to stay in his trench and was killed by machine-gun fire – and five wounded (two of them Cuban).

The defeat at Quifangondo was a devastating blow to Roberto's dreams of capturing Luanda before Independence Day, and cemented the MPLA's grip on the Angolan capital. Cold War military technology had arrived dramatically in Angola, and the scale of forces engaged at Quifangondo demonstrated how far foreign intervention had escalated the conflict since street-fighting broke out exactly one year before. The repercussions of this battle would far exceed the losses in men and material, however, for within days it became clear that the psychological blow inflicted on Roberto's soldiers had broken their will to fight on. In fact it is no exaggeration to say that the battle of Quifangondo destroyed the FNLA, even if fighting between them and the FAPLA–Cubans was to continue for another four months. For, as exaggerated accounts of the defeat spread among Roberto's forces – who referred to Quifangondo as '*Nshila wa Lufu*' (The Road of Death) – discipline collapsed, and what started as a military withdrawal degenerated into a scramble for the border, forcing Roberto to take desperate measures to stem the FAPLA–Cuban advance.[12]

As fighting was raging at Quifangondo, in the centre of Luanda the Portuguese High Commissioner officially granted Angola independence. The ceremony was by this stage meaningless, however, as any semblance of Portuguese authority had long since evaporated – as the missiles raining down at Quifangondo attested. Despite having displayed a marked sympathy towards the MPLA during Angola's chaotic decolonisation, the Portuguese government decided not to recognise any single movement. Instead it granted independence to 'the people of Angola', withdrawing its colonial government without leaving anything in its place. In fairness to the Portuguese, the time had long since passed (around August 1975) when they could influence events in Angola. But this did little to excuse the stark fact that, after nearly 500 years, they were washing their hands of a colony which had been the jewel in their African Empire and leaving it to a terrible fate. That evening – with fighting engulfing the country, hundreds of thousands of refugees fleeing Angola, and three foreign armies fighting it out for supremacy – Commodore Leonel Cardoso boarded a Portuguese frigate and sailed out of Luanda harbour. It is hard to imagine how Portugal could have bequeathed Angola a more cruel legacy.

In Luanda, the MPLA held delirious celebrations as midnight struck, celebrating the vanquishing not only of its oldest oppressor (Portugal) but also of its oldest rival (the FNLA). To cheering crowds, Neto declared the formation of the People's Republic of Angola (PRA), which was immediately recognised by nearly thirty countries (among them MPLA stalwarts such as Cuba, the Soviet Union and the PALOPs). Seventy-five miles away in Ambriz, a dispirited FNLA and UNITA delegation declared the Popular Democratic Republic of Angola (PDRA), which was recognised by no one. By now it was clear that FLEC's invasion of Cabinda had failed, and it was with a renewed sense of determination that MMCA's commanders turned their attention to the south where a third threat to Luanda – Zulu Force – was advancing rapidly from Lobito. Halting the South Africans would be a different experience for the Cubans, however, as the soldiers in Zulu Force were of a much higher calibre than the poorly motivated and undisciplined rabble they had seen off at N'to and Quifangondo. Not in the habit of launching suicidal attacks against well-defended positions, Zulu Force had shown great tactical originality, and the danger that it might take the Cubans by surprise would make the campaign in Cuanza Sul the most dangerous and costly of Operation Carlota.

The race to the Queve river

Following the violent clash at Catengue, the South Africans had continued their relentless advance northwards, moving quickly on Angola's commercial ports, Benguela and Lobito. Opting for its trademark pincer movement, Zulu Force moved north from Catengue to attack Benguela from the south whilst Foxbat moved in from the west towards Lobito, cutting off the only line of retreat. This put Benguela's defenders in a terrible dilemma: either they could withdraw from both ports without a fight and endanger the MPLA's already tenuous grip on Luanda, or they could make a final stand and risk being annihilated, an equally disastrous outcome. Their indecision was demonstrated the day after Catengue when reports that South African armoured cars were in the Pundo mountains above Lobito prompted the order to evacuate Benguela – an order which was rescinded once it became clear that Zulu Force had not yet launched its assault on the city.

On 5 November – after a couple of days spent recuperating and clearing FAPLA positions east of Catengue – Zulu Force set out for Benguela. Expecting only weak resistance after their hard-fought victory at Catengue, the South Africans opted for a frontal assault on the city, hoping that the defenders would melt away as they had on previous occasions. Advancing west through deserted towns, Alpha came upon the abandoned Cuban camp eight miles south of Benguela, seizing over thirty tons of petrol, ammunition and supplies which had been left behind. Alpha then continued to the airport (nine miles south of the city), and it was there that it ran into heavy resistance. FAPLA mortars in the city centre and a Katyusha rocket battery on the hills above Benguela began a noisy barrage which pinned down Alpha's troops and brought their advance to a standstill. FAPLA or Cuban commandos (accounts differ) then launched a counter-attack which briefly recaptured the airport, forcing Alpha to abandon four armoured cars and several guns.[13] Alpha nevertheless retook the airport, recovering the vehicles and guns, but the troops' confidence had been shaken and they remained pinned down until nightfall under bombardment from the 'Red Eyes' (as the South Africans called the Katyushas). That evening, Zulu Force's commanders met to discuss a change in tactics, belatedly recognising that Benguela 'would be a very tough nut to crack'.[14]

Anxious to avoid house-to-house fighting – which would be bloody and leave the city in ruins – they opted for a flanking attack through the east of the city to capture the high ground to the north, thus neutralising the Katyusha and cutting off the FAPLA's line of retreat. The change of tactics proved unnecessary, however, as by the following morning the defenders of Benguela had decided that the risk of encirclement was too great – and that they should withdraw while they still could. A second pan-icked evacuation of both cities began and the defending forces fled north towards Novo Redondo (Sumbe) – to the consternation of civilians who had returned to defend their city after the first bungled evacuation and now found themselves at the mercy of UNITA.[15] By the time Bravo assaulted the city's southern suburbs, what little resistance was left quickly melted away, and Zulu Force was able to occupy the rest of Benguela almost unopposed. Aware that Lobito had also been abandoned, Zulu Force occupied the port the next day, setting up camp seven miles to the north (so as to avoid losing its men to Lobito's infamous brothels).

Divisions intensify in the South African leadership

The capture of Lobito completed Zulu Force's conquest of southern Angola, and brought the Benguela railway line as far east as Silva Porto (Kuito-Bié) under South African control. But now there were splits opening in the South African leadership, and once it became clear that Zulu Force would not reach Luanda by Independence Day these led to the first calls to withdraw. After being told that a 1,500-man SADF force would be needed to capture Luanda (sustaining up to 40 per cent casualties in the process), many in the South African cabinet favoured immediate withdrawal while Zulu Force still had the advantage (for this purpose, 101 Task Force was set up at Rundu to prepare for the pullout).[16] Perhaps sensing the change in Pretoria's mood, on 10 November Savimbi flew there to implore Vorster to keep Zulu Force in Angola until the OAU met to discuss the war on 9 December. Insisting that many OAU members were opposed to an MPLA government in Angola (Savimbi for once was telling the truth), Savimbi urged Pretoria to keep up the military pressure, reasoning that the more Angolan territory under FNLA and UNITA control, the stronger their position would be in the OAU negotiations which followed.

Despite serious misgivings, Vorster agreed to extend the operation beyond 11 November, and instead of withdrawing Zulu Force he ordered it to capture as much territory as possible before the OAU meeting. It was a poor decision, however, for such were the divisions in the OAU that the meeting would be repeatedly postponed, putting Zulu Force's commanders in a no-win situation. For not only did it starve them of a clear military objective (such as capturing Luanda, or advancing as far as the Cuanza river), but it ensured that any gains they made would quickly be abandoned, making the remaining two months of the operation a waste of time and lives. Pretoria was belatedly trying to prevent Operation Savannah from escalating further, but with thousands of Cuban troops pouring into Angola, it was too late to turn back, and Vorster's veto of further reinforcements merely ensured that, when Foxbat did finally achieve its breakthrough, it would be unable to follow it up.

Zulu Force advances towards the Queve river

With its logistics secured through Angola's most important ports, on 11 November Zulu Force was ordered to continue its advance along the coast and attack Novo Redondo (Sumbe) and Porto Amboim, before turning inland towards Gabela and Quibala (see Map 6). Simultaneously, Foxbat would advance through the interior from Alto Hama towards Quibala, where both forces would link up for the final push on Luanda. Two new Battle-Groups – X-Ray and Orange – were also formed in Silva Porto (Kuito-Bié) to extend UNITA's influence over eastern Angola, and Orange was immediately sent northwards towards Malanje while X-Ray headed east to secure the rest of the Benguela railway-line. With this fresh commitment of South African forces, Breytenbach remarked that 'the whole campaign was beginning to look more South African than Angolan',[17] and there was little reason to think the FAPLA would be able to stop this expanded force from capturing Luanda within the week.

Alpha once more spearheaded the advance, brushing aside an FAPLA ambush at the Cuula river (forty miles north of Lobito) and continuing unchecked until the bridge over the Quicombo river, eight miles south of Novo Redondo. Surprised to find the bridge still passable (Cuban sappers had laid explosives on it earlier that day, but they had failed to destroy it completely), Alpha advanced over it and triggered a second ambush on the other side. Alpha's two leading armoured cars were quickly knocked out by RPG rounds and, as the force withdrew, one of its mortar platoons took a direct hit, killing one and wounding seventeen others. Alpha then spent the rest of the afternoon pinned down in a noisy artillery duel with the FAPLA–Cubans, unable to outflank their position as the bridge (which was the only means of crossing the river) was under heavy fire. Finally, at dusk, the FAPLA–Cubans withdrew to Novo Redondo, probably having suffered significant casualties, and the following morning Bravo occupied the town with only light resistance. Anxious to press on, Zulu Force split in two, Alpha heading inland towards Gabela while Bravo moved north to capture Porto Amboim, from where it was only two hours to Luanda. It was at this point, however, that Operation Savannah suddenly ground to a halt.

The Cubans blow up the bridges over the Queve river, 13 November

The reason for this sudden change of fortune was the arrival in Porto Amboim of the first 150 reinforcements from the Cuban Special Forces Battalion, even as Zulu Force was completing its capture of Novo Redondo only forty miles to the south.[18] Charged with halting the South Africans using any means possible, the Cubans decided to destroy the three bridges over the Queve (or Cuvo) river – the only barrier between Novo Redondo and the towns to the north – hoping this would give them breathing-space to reorganise their defences. On the night of 13 November, Cuban demolition teams raced to Gabela where they blew the bridge at Sete Pontos (twelve miles south of Gabela), deploying a Cuban

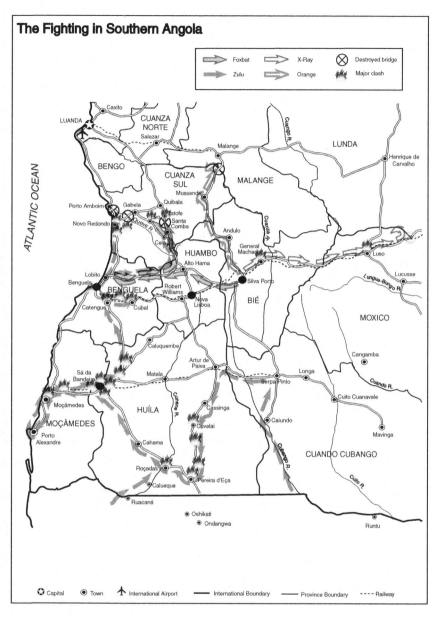

The Fighting in Southern Angola

Foxbat	X-Ray	⊗ Destroyed bridge	
Zulu	Orange	🔥 Major clash	

ATLANTIC OCEAN

LUANDA
Caxito

CUANZA NORTE
Salazar

BENGO

Malange

LUNDA

Henrique de Carvalho

CUANZA SUL
Mussende

MALANGE

Porto Amboim
Gabela
Quibala
Catofe
Santa Comba
Cela

Novo Redondo
Queve R.

Andulo

General Machado

Luso

Lucusse

Lungue-Bungo R.

HUAMBO
Alto Hama

Silva Porto

Lobito
Benguela
BENGUELA
Robert Williams
Nova Lisboa
BIÉ

MOXICO

Catengue
Cubal

Caluquembe

Cangamba

Sá da Bandeira
Matala
Artur de Paiva
Serpa Pinto
Longa

Cuando R.

Cuito Cuanavale

Moçâmedes
HUÍLA
Cassinga
Caiundo

Mavinga

MOÇÂMEDES
Porto Alexandre
Cahama
Ovelai
Carreira R.

CUANDO CUBANGO

Roçadas
Pereira d'Eça
Cubango R.
Cuito R.

Calueque

Ruacaná

Oshikati
Ondangwa

Runtu

🔀 Capital   ◉ Town   ✈ International Airport   — International Boundary   — Province Boundary   ---- Railway

Map 6 The fighting in Southern Angola.

company to warn of any South African advance into the area. They then drove west and blew the Caxoeiras bridge (thirty miles south-west of Gabela) and then the only bridge into Porto Amboim (fifteen miles south of Porto Amboim), blocking the coastal route. Having bungled previous attempts to destroy bridges in the path of Zulu Force, the Cubans had at last seized the initiative, and with the rainy season swelling the Queve into a raging torrent they could be confident that, at least for now, Zulu Force had been contained.

The significance of the Cuban move became apparent the following morning when Bravo set out from Novo Redondo for Porto Amboim, expecting to capture it by nightfall. On reaching the bridge Commandant Breytenbach found it completely destroyed, and his force was immediately drawn into a firefight with the FAPLA dug in on the other bank. Soon Cuban BM-21s (which had arrived in Porto Amboim shortly before the fall of Benguela) were firing salvos at the South Africans, and their commander – who would not withdraw without 'a defiant gesture' – brought up his 25-pounder guns to counter-bombard the BM-21s, three of which his gunners claim to have destroyed.[19] Possessing no bridge-building equipment, Bravo withdrew to Novo Redondo while a patrol checked if the Caxoeiras bridge to Gabela was still serviceable, but it returned with the news that it too had been destroyed. Attempts to find alternative crossings (the Queve is shallower east of the Caxoeiras bridge) also foundered when Bravo's men refused to ford the turbulent river.

The coastal advance of Zulu Force was thus effectively blocked, and Alpha's commander (who was posted to Novo Redondo for the remainder of the campaign) was to have a frustrating time over the next two months as he dreamed up daring schemes to get his forces across the river, none of which were successful.[20] As if to compound the South Africans' turn in fortune, the following day two foreign journalists (Reuters correspondent Fred Bridgland and Michael Nicholson of British Independent Television News) filed stories confirming that South African troops were fighting in Angola, blowing the lid off Pretoria's secret invasion.[21] The international outcry which greeted this news – especially from South Africa's neighbouring states – was a diplomatic disaster for Pretoria, and redoubled the pressure to wind up the invasion as quickly as possible. The Cubans, on the other hand, were in no hurry to take on the South Africans, and preferred to pin them down at the Queve until they were strong enough to launch a counter-offensive.

A defensive line was therefore established – running from the Porto Amboim bridge, through Gabela and Cariango, to Mussende – with the intention of blocking every possible invasion route from the south. This defensive plan – while successfully blocking a coastal advance – had one serious flaw, however. In their haste the Cuban demolition teams had failed to destroy the last bridge over the Queve at Techirimba (sixty-five miles south of Quibala), and this enabled Foxbat to advance unhindered from Alto Hama to capture Cela on 15 November. Over the following weeks, the Cubans would pay for this oversight as the area between their defensive line and the Queve became a no-man's-land through which opposing forces patrolled, raided and launched assaults. Setting up HQ in Cela, Foxbat's commander George Kruys sent a team of engineers to check if the road to the north was clear, but they reported back that the bridge over the Nhia river (designated Bridge 14) had been severely damaged, and that until it was repaired an advance on Quibala was impossible. Anxious to maintain momentum, Kruys opted for the smaller road to Gabela via Ebo (thirty miles to its south-east), reaching the tiny settlement on 18 November. After waiting five days for reinforcements, Kruys decided to press on unsupported, and just west of Ebo he led his troops into an ambush, precipitating South Africa's first setback of the campaign.

The ambush at Ebo, 23 November 1975

The Cubans had been expecting a South African advance via Ebo and had set up ambush positions along the Mabassa river.[22] Seventy Cubans were dug in along the shoreline, manning one BM-21 battery, one 76mm field gun and several anti-tank rocket batteries, while two companies of FAPLA troops (c.140 men) were dug in on the high ground to the west of them. Unaware they were being observed, Foxbat's leading elements (a company of Bushmen and a dozen armoured cars) approached the river which the infantry forded, fanning out while the armoured cars hung back on the other side. They had scarcely gone 100 yards when the Cubans 'opened up with murderous automatic, mortar and other shell fire, quickly cutting down the whole company, including the company commander'.[23] Foxbat's armoured cars tried to pull back, but they were unable to manoeuvre in the mud and at least seven of them were destroyed by anti-tank rounds, precipitating a scramble back towards Cela. Bravo (which had arrived in Cela that morning) was ordered northwards to cover Foxbat's retreat, and it quickly set up defences west of Santa Comba. But the expected counter-attack never occurred, and the battered remnants of Foxbat slowly appeared, the wounded in a very bad way. At least thirty had been killed and sixty wounded, many of those left behind on the other side of the river being summarily executed by the Cubans.[24] The Cubans had lost just one killed and five wounded, while the FAPLA (which had seen no action) suffered no casualties.

The ambush at Ebo was the South Africans' first major setback of the Angolan campaign, although it was not quite the devastating defeat depicted by the Cubans. The losses in men, equipment and armour were not catastrophic, but they did bruise Foxbat's morale, forcing the South

Africans to retrench their positions while Foxbat rebuilt itself. Bravo was sent north to occupy the high ground south of Bridge 14 to prevent a counter-offensive, and its reports that the bridge had not been completely destroyed (although it was impassable) gave Kruys an idea for a surprise attack. Determined to exact revenge for Ebo, Kruys planned to repair the bridge secretly under cover of darkness and then launch a surprise dawn attack across it. With FAPLA–Cuban forces still operating south of the Nhia river, Kruys sent out patrols to reconnoitre their positions and start driving them out of the area, while Foxbat began preparations for an attack. Next time it would be the Cubans' turn to be complacent.

The Cuban presence in Angola grows

On 25 November – two days after the ambush at Ebo – Furry flew into Luanda to take command of MMCA. MMCA's responsibilities had by now grown from the relatively simple task of organising a 500-man training mission to coordinating a military intervention dozens of times the size, and Furry's appointment was as much an acknowledgement of the new challenges ahead as it was a sign that Argüelles no longer had Havana's confidence. The logistical complexities of the operation – which involved processing the arrival of thousands of troops, issuing them with weaponry and supplies and sending them off to diverse units around Angola – were enormous, and Furry quickly became the 'lightning rod' of the operation. 'Everyone came to me to ask me what they should do,' he recalls. 'I commanded the planning and conduct of our operations myself. Every time I had to make a decision, I didn't send a cable to Cuba asking for advice, although every day at 6 p.m. I would transmit a report on how things were going.'[25]

Furry's daily report was intended for Castro who, throughout Operation Carlota, was reputed to have spent fourteen hours a day in the operations room specially built for him in the basement of MINFAR (on Havana's Plaza de la Revolución).[26] All senior Cuban veterans have since emphasised his intricate knowledge of the operations theatre – he allegedly knew the location of every Cuban unit, tank, mortar and heavy gun in Angola – and it is clear that Castro wielded a commanding influence over the Cuban operation at every stage. More independent officers – such as Arnaldo Ochoa Sánchez who later clashed with Castro during the Cuito Cuanavale campaign (see Chapter 10) – might have found Castro's interference unhelpful or even counter-productive. But in Furry, Castro had a loyal and obedient subordinate, and the relationship they developed over the following months made him Castro's preferred trouble-shooter in Angola. Castro's message-bearer would be Jorge Risquet (a veteran of the Brazzaville mission) who arrived in Luanda on 3 December, quickly becoming the official go-between with the MPLA government. These two men would play influential roles in the Angolan War over the next fifteen years, and along with other officers (such as Moracén and Rosales del Toro) would make their reputations in Angola, all but Risquet rising to prominence after the withdrawal.

The Cuban sealift to Angola

On 27 November – two days after Furry's arrival in Angola – the first Cuban troop ship docked in Luanda, and this was followed by two others on 29 November and 1 December, bearing a total of 1,253 troops with all their weapons and supplies, several troops of tanks and various artillery pieces.[27] Over the next four months these three ships would be followed by dozens of Cuban transports and cargo ships, transporting in forty-two round trips over 25,000 men and hundreds of tons of equipment and supplies. Much of the heavy equipment destined for the FAPLA – such as T-34/54 tanks, BM-21s and B-10 guns – was sent directly from the Soviet Union to Luanda (to avoid transhipment delays in Cuba). There it was handed on to Cuban personnel who then instructed the Angolans in its use, often minutes before (or even during) battles.[28] Often FAPLA cadres would accompany Cuban tank and artillery units in an apprentice role, assisting in the tank's or gun's operation until they had mastered its controls, and then taking possession of it at the end of the offensive. This mammoth injection of Soviet war material quickly had an effect as more Cuban troops joined the FAPLA and, as their numbers grew, so did their competence. So enormous was the Cuban sealift that by February 1976 – with dozens of Cuban ships anchored in the Bay of Luanda – Neto remarked: 'It's not right. If they go on like that, the Cubans will ruin themselves.'[29]

The Cuban airlift to Angola

The Cuban airlift did not go as smoothly, however. Hampered by crippling technical limitations, the Cuban Air Force had, between 7 November and 9 December, managed an impressive seventy reinforcement flights to Luanda. But this was only achieved using a less-than-ideal route (via Barbados, Bissau and Brazzaville) which pushed the ageing aircraft to the very limits of their capacity and range, and forced the limited number of pilots to fly dangerously-long hours.[30] The Cubans were prepared to take extreme measures to maximise the size and speed of forces being sent to Angola, even if this meant troops loading their weapons and removing explosives and missiles from their cases before the flight to lighten the load. The fragility of the airlift was quickly recognised by Washington and, on 9 December, Ford called a meeting with the Soviet Ambassador,

Anatoly Dobrynin, to ask the Soviets to suspend the airlift (wrongly assuming it was a Soviet-run operation).[31]

By this stage, Operation IAFeature was in serious trouble, and following the disaster at Quifangondo the Americans had adopted increasingly desperate measures to prevent a Cuban victory. By late November, Congress's investigations into CIA activity were reaching their climax, and with the FNLA disintegrating before their eyes IAFeature's chiefs had resorted to drawing up fanciful $100m military aid programmes in the full knowledge that Congress would never authorise the funding. When they went to Kissinger on 2 December in a last-ditch attempt to save the FNLA he showed no interest, leaving for Beijing without commenting on their proposal.[32] The 40 Committee decided to wait until his return before taking further action, but the truth was that it was already too late to prevent the FNLA's defeat. Three days later, the CIA's Deputy Director of Operations Bill Nelson was forced to admit to a Senate committee that the CIA was sending arms to Angola, and in reaction it endorsed an amendment proposed by Senator Dick Clark to curtail CIA involvement in Angola. The 'Clark Amendment' would restrict the CIA's covert budget (which was part of the 1976 Defense Bill being debated in Congress) and specifically ruled out any further CIA activity in Angola.

Conscious that a vote on the amendment was imminent, Ford's request to Dobrynin was an attempt to sabotage the Cuban operation and give the FNLA time to regroup. That he sought Soviet support to restrain the Cubans was a sign of how little influence the Americans had on the ground in Angola. But it appears that Ford's threats that Cuban actions in Angola could jeopardise détente persuaded the Soviets (who had not authorised the operation in the first place) to restrain their allies, because the airlift was suspended the same day.[33] It was a short-lived victory, however, as ten days later the Senate passed the Clark Amendment by a 54–22 vote, outlawing further CIA involvement in Angola. Although the Defense Appropriations Bill still had to be passed by the House of Representatives (which would not vote until January), the Senate vote convinced IAFeature's chiefs that the game was up, and after this date IAFeature assumed the character of a 'damage limitation' operation.

With few options left, Washington did the only thing in its power to hinder the Cuban airlift and used diplomatic pressure to deny Cuba landing rights along every conceivable route to Angola. Initially the Cubans tried flying via Georgetown (Guyana), but the runway proved too short for Britannias, and then, on 31 December (under pressure from Washington), Georgetown withdrew landing rights. Cuba then tried flying from its easternmost airport (Holguín, 480 miles east of Havana) via the Azores, but this caused alarm in Washington which had been operating a NATO base in Lajes since the Second World War. Lisbon's decision to let Cuban aircraft use the Azores reflected its sympathy for the MPLA, and initially the Americans had to tread carefully as the lease on their base needed to be renewed every year. But, in the end, they resorted to bullying to get their way and, on 21 January, Portugal withdrew landing rights. It was another hollow victory, however, as by this stage the Soviets had decided to give their full logistical support to the Cuban airlift.

The Soviets had refused to involve their personnel in the Cuban operation since first hearing of its existence in early November, and throughout late 1975 they continued to hold back, only continuing with previously agreed weapons shipments. Now the tide of battle was turning in Cuba's favour, however, full support for Operation Carlota began to look more attractive. Having let Cuba bear all the risks of failure, the Soviets could now to step in as Operation Carlota's benevolent overseer, gaining a new African ally at almost no risk to themselves. Soviet minds were finally decided by the passing of the Clark Amendment which signalled that America was out of the running, and in early January 1976 they agreed to provide ten charter flights using long-range Il-62s (the first of these left Havana for Bissau on 9 January).[34] One week later they signed a military protocol with Cuba, formalising their alliance in Angola.[35] Under the agreement the Soviets would supply all future weaponry for the FAPLA and Cuban troops, transporting it directly to Angola so that the Cuban airlift could concentrate on personnel. Although the promised assistance would be slow in arriving,[36] the agreement formed the basis of a new Cuban–Soviet military alliance in Africa, and would last almost until the collapse of the Soviet Union itself.

While Cuban logistical officers were battling to keep the airlift operational, on 4 December the counter-offensive against the FNLA in northern Angola was finally launched.[37] The move had been timed to coincide with the opening of the First Party Congress (17 December), Castro perhaps feeling that now military disaster had been averted he would make the most of Cuban dominance in Angola. Shortly after Furry arrived in Luanda, therefore, Castro sent orders to launch counter-offensives in the north and south as soon as possible, anxious to conclude the war before it turned into a protracted (and unpopular) struggle. MMCA opted for the northern offensive first, satisfied that the destruction of the bridges over the Queve and the ambush at Ebo had stopped the South Africans in their tracks. But the Cubans had underestimated Foxbat's determination for revenge, and before the northern offensive had advanced beyond its first objective (Caxito, captured on 4 December), the focus of the war dramatically shifted back to southern Angola where the Cuban operation was once more thrown into jeopardy.

The Battle of Bridge 14

Since the ambush at Ebo, Foxbat's commander had been preparing an attack over Bridge 14 on the Nhia river.[38] Aware of the bridge's importance to Quibala's defences, the FAPLA had set up its HQ a few miles north of the river. Considerable forces were deployed in the area (including 'cuatro bocas' and BM-21s), some of which occupied the hill overlooking the southern approach to the bridge (which the South Africans designated 'Top Hat'). The South African plan was to drive the FAPLA out of the bridge area, then occupy Top Hat and bring in engineers to repair the bridge under cover of darkness. In early December, the South Africans infiltrated the bridge area, enabling two artillery officers to set up an Observation Post (OP) on the summit of Top Hat. From there they directed artillery onto enemy positions, destroying several over the next few days. Probably in response to this, the FAPLA sent a large contingent of troops to reinforce Top Hat, but as it attempted to wade across the swollen Nhia river it was spotted by the OP which directed fire down onto it, causing devastating casualties.[39]

Although Cuban accounts fail to mention this disaster, it forced Argüelles to call off the offensive he had been planning to launch on 11 December, and he instead ordered an immediate withdrawal from Ebo and the Nhia river. This quickly turned to disaster, however, when the armoured car carrying Argüelles hit a land-mine as it was taking a short-cut, killing him instantly and seriously wounding two others. The circumstances leading to Argüelles's death remain unclear,[40] but its effect was to sew confusion in the FAPLA–Cuban camp less than twenty-four hours before Foxbat's attack. Castro's preferred man in a crisis – Furry – was immediately sent from Luanda to take command of the front (he arrived the next day), and an improvised line of defence was set up north of Ebo to protect Condé and Quibala. In the confusion, the Cubans overlooked Bridge 14, however, believing that a South African crossing of the Nhia river would be impossible, and this enabled Foxbat to occupy Top Hat and the river's southern bank the next day. On the night of 11/12 December, South African engineers repaired the bridge, and at first light the following morning the attack was launched.

Kruys planned the assault in three waves, one company in Eland armoured cars driving the main FAPLA–Cuban force back towards Cassamba (five miles to the north) while a second company attacked an artillery concentration and ammunition dump (the 'kraal'), and a third captured the hilly positions north of the river. All three companies would then link up with the armoured cars for a final push on Cassamba. Facing them on the other side of the Nhia were over 1,000 FAPLA–Cuban troops, supported by mortars, 'cuatro bocas' and BM-21s, with Sagger anti-tank missile teams covering the main road. The South African force numbered around 300 men, with a dozen armoured cars leading the attack. There was heavy mist on the morning of 12 December, and once it had cleared the South African artillery opened up, wiping out several mortar positions and ammunition trucks north of the river. At 7 a.m. the main force raced across Bridge 14, the armoured cars deploying 100 yards on either side of the road to confuse the Sagger crews who had trained their weapons on the centre of the road. Taken by surprise, the FAPLA–Cubans scrambled to make their escape, but in the confusion a Soviet truck loaded with twenty Cuban soldiers mistook one of the Elands for a Cuban armoured car, and indicated to overtake. Slowing down to let the truck pass, the Eland slammed a 90 mm shell into its rear, killing the occupants.

As the one-sided battle progressed, South African encounters with Cuban troops took on a surreal quality. One Eland commander claimed to have run into a group of Cuban soldiers smoking marijuana in an abandoned farmhouse, shooting eleven of them through the turret hatch with his pistol as they clambered recklessly over his armoured car. After occupying the 'kraal' (where large amounts of weaponry and ammunition were captured), Foxbat's two leading companies linked up and sped northwards, passing their objective of Cassamba. By now news of the military collapse south of Quibala had reached MMCA, and it was considered serious enough for Furry to drive down to Quibala immediately to take charge of the defences. A reserve Cuban tank company and two FAPLA infantry companies were sent to the Catofe river (ten miles south of Quibala) to hold the last remaining bridge between the South Africans and Quibala, and by 1 p.m. they had established a defensive line, expecting an attack at any moment.

A last stand at the Catofe river was not necessary, however, as around midday Kruys called a halt to the attack, worried that his small force would overextend itself and fall victim to a counter-attack. Kruys had some difficulty persuading his gung-ho Eland commanders who – flushed with the morning's success – wanted to go the whole way to Quibala. But they were eventually reined in, and Foxbat spent the rest of the day consolidating its gains while engineers continued repairs on Bridge 14 under sporadic mortar and Katyusha fire. During the fighting, Foxbat had lost four men killed, with perhaps a dozen wounded. In comparison several hundred Cubans had been killed, with even greater losses among the FAPLA.[41] By the end of the battle, Foxbat had come within three miles of the Catofe river bridge, the capture of which would have ensured the fall of Quibala and put Luanda under threat again. But ironically their advance northwards had been prevented not by the Cubans but by Pretoria which was reining in Foxbat even as it was at the very peak of its success.

Pressure grows on South Africa to withdraw from Angola

Since Vorster agreed to keep Zulu Force in Angola until OAU negotiations started, divisions within the South African leadership had intensified and, by mid-December, Vorster and General Viljoen had swapped positions. Arguing that the intervention in Angola had caused enormous international damage and that the tide of battle had turned against their Angolan allies, Viljoen now favoured an immediate withdrawal. With the Senate debating the Clark Amendment, he was convinced that it was only a matter of time before the Americans withdrew their support, leaving South Africa isolated in an African Vietnam.[42] Vorster, on the other hand, was now determined to stick it out in Angola, convinced that Zulu Force's presence there was essential for the FNLA and UNITA to gain equal status with the MPLA in upcoming OAU peace negotiations. This bitter debate paralysed Pretoria's decision-making process, and the resulting compromise was – unsurprisingly – counter-productive.

Postponing the decision to withdraw, Pretoria ordered Zulu Force and Foxbat to suspend all attacks and concentrate instead on consolidating their gains. The new orders were an implicit admission of the failure of Operation Savannah, for not only was Pretoria now ruling out the capture of the capital – the goal of any intervention force – but it was handing the initiative back to the Cubans, allowing them plenty of time to recover from the disaster at Bridge 14. News of the change in plan did not reach Kruys in time, however, and ironically he went ahead with the most successful attack of the campaign in violation of his superiors' orders. But the change in strategy ensured that his success was short-lived, and the window of opportunity created at Bridge 14 quickly closed as the Cubans brought in reserves to shore up their defences. The failure to capitalise on Bridge 14 was the first in a series of lost opportunities for Zulu Force, and demonstrated how a divided leadership in Pretoria with conflicting agendas could undermine success on the battlefield. Lauded after the war as the SADF's greatest victory, the 'Battle of Bridge 14' actually achieved no strategic or tactical gain whatsoever, and though it comforted Kruys's bruised ego, its only tangible result was to leave both sides eager for a second round.

Castro's triumphal First Party Congress, 17–22 December

The disaster at Bridge 14 must have caused some consternation in Havana as it came only five days before Castro was due to open the long-awaited First Party Congress. Expecting to announce the victorious advance of Cuban forces into northern Angola, Castro once again faced a military disaster involving hundreds of Cuban casualties, among them the operation's commander. His reaction was characteristically robust, and after reprimanding the commanders on the ground (the late Argüelles proving a useful scapegoat), he ordered a counter-offensive against Santa Comba – 'Operation 1st Party Congress'. Once again luck was on Castro's side, and two days after the Congress opened in Havana the Clark Amendment was passed in the Senate, curtailing CIA involvement in the Angolan War. This news – coupled with South African failure to follow up Bridge 14 – enabled Castro to close the Congress with the announcement that Cuban troops were fighting (and winning) in Angola. No mention was made of Bridge 14, however, and to this day Cuban accounts spuriously maintain that the battle occurred at the Catofe river ten miles to the north, thus avoiding reference to the heavy Cuban casualties sustained that day.[43]

With American support suspended indefinitely – and Soviet aid to the FAPLA mushrooming – the tide had turned against the FNLA and UNITA and, on 20 December, Savimbi made another visit to Pretoria to beg Vorster to postpone the withdrawal until the OAU meeting took place (now put back to 3 January). Under duress, Vorster once more agreed, and on Christmas Day General Viljoen flew to Cela to inform Savimbi and Chipenda that South African forces would start withdrawing from Angola after this date. In military terms the advance had come to a halt anyway, as all attempts by Battle-Groups Orange and X-Ray to extend the war into the interior had been forced to turn back by destroyed bridges.[44] As if to underline the cloud hanging over the South African operation, the day before Viljoen's arrival, tensions between the FNLA and UNITA erupted in Benguela, machine-gun and mortar duels leaving dozens dead. The SADF's Angolan alliance was unravelling in dramatic terms, but Vorster was determined to stick to his plan, and he resisted the final decision to withdraw against increasing opposition from within his cabinet.

Cuba launches a counter-offensive, January 1976

Following the set-back at Bridge 14, the Cubans made great efforts to rebuild their forces north of the Queve river and, after a visit to the area on 30 December, Jorge Risquet wrote optimistically to Castro that 'Operation 1st Party Congress' would shortly be underway.[45] The key to capturing the initial objectives – Santa Comba and Cela – lay in the Tongo and Medunda hills fifteen miles to the north, from where artillery could dominate the surrounding area. Recognising the hills' strategic importance, Foxbat had driven the FAPLA off them in mid-November, and over the following month they changed hands several times. On 17 December, the Cubans captured Tongo, renaming it 'Congress Hill' after the Party Congress which opened that day in Havana. Two weeks later they captured the Medunda hills in fighting which became so desperate that Cuban BM-21s were ordered to fire directly onto a Cuban artillery OP on the hills' crest after it was surrounded by South African troops (the Cubans took shelter in a nearby cave). Both sides suffered significant casualties during the fighting, in particular from the South African 122 mm guns and Cuban BM-21s. But once the Cuban presence was firmly established on the Medunda hills (on 16 January), the South Africans had little choice but to withdraw from the area.[46]

Vorster still refused to face the inevitable, however, and after hearing that the OAU meeting had been put back again (this time to 12 January), he once more postponed the withdrawal. Since arranging a truce at Mombassa in January 1975, the OAU had exerted little influence over events in Angola, and its president Idi Amin's efforts to exclude the MPLA from peace talks in September had further undermined its legitimacy. Nevertheless, the OAU vote taken on 12 January was crucial for Pretoria, for if the FNLA and UNITA could rally enough support then Zulu Force could continue in southern Angola with the OAU's implicit support. The exact split of the vote – twenty-two for and twenty-two against (with two abstentions) – confirmed that Africa was still divided over Angola. But it was not the dead heat it appeared as Ethiopia (which as the host country had abstained from the vote) recognised the PRA shortly afterwards, giving the MPLA the simple majority it needed to become an OAU member. Pretoria's last hope had gone, and on 23 January – following a vote in the OAU (which condemned the South African invasion but made no mention of Cuban or Soviet intervention) – it ordered the final withdrawal from Angola.

The South African withdrawal was the final turning point in the 'Second Liberation War', and was followed by the immediate collapse of UNITA and the FNLA. The South Africans withdrew rapidly and, by 4 February, their presence in Angola had been reduced to a rearguard (numbering between 4,000 and 5,000 troops) within thirty miles of the Namibian border.[47] The battle-hardened FNLA and Bushman soldiers of Zulu Force also withdrew to Namibia where they were housed in SADF barracks, unaware of the role they would play in the Angolan war over the following decade.[48] Deprived of their most powerful ally, the FNLA and UNITA were no match for the combined FAPLA–Cuban forces, and from late January onwards the 'Second Liberation War' became a one-sided affair, the FAPLA–Cubans rapidly advancing towards the Zairian and Namibian borders in the face of sporadic local resistance. Although the fighting on both fronts occurred simultaneously, for ease of analysis the Northern and Southern Fronts will be examined separately.

The Northern Front, December 1975–March 1976

Within days of the victory at Quifangondo, planning began for a counter-offensive against the FNLA.[49] Determined to remove the FNLA from

Angola for good, the Cubans planned a staged advance northwards, first seizing Caxito and then swinging westwards to capture the FNLA's air-bases at Camabatela and Negage, after which the remaining northern strongholds were expected to fall easily. Initially, MMCA could only commit two FAPLA battalions to the offensive, supported by *c.*150 Cubans who operated the mortars, heavy guns and armoured cars. But, as it progressed, these forces grew in size, and by mid-February totalled thirteen battalions (one Cuban and twelve FAPLA), with various companies of tanks and heavy artillery in support. On 3 December, Brigadier Víctor Schueg Colás, a veteran of Guevara's Congo campaign and one of the original members of Argüelles's team, took command of the combined force, and two days later it set out for Caxito.

The forces facing them were by now 'a demoralized, undisciplined rabble, out of control of their officers'.[50] With the withdrawal of Zairian forces only a few hundred FNLA troops were still defending Caxito, and the town was easily captured the same day, the FAPLA–Cubans taking 150 prisoners and seizing fourteen tons of weapons. It was then decided to avoid a direct advance along the main road to Carmona (Uíge) as the FNLA had destroyed numerous bridges along this route. Instead, the 1,000-strong FAPLA battalion in Lucala would launch a flanking attack from the south-east (with the support of 250–300 Cubans), while the FAPLA's Ninth Brigade (1,200 troops plus some Cubans) took the coastal route from Caxito (see Map 4, page 84). Keen to avoid further clashes with a large FNLA force located north of Lucala, Brigadier Schueg led his force east via the Calandula falls and attacked Luinga from the south. After fighting off three determined counter-attacks, the FAPLA–Cuban force captured the town on 27 December, putting Camabatela within their grasp.

Described by the Cuban commander as 'The Key to the North', Camabatela was the FNLA's main airbase in northern Angola, and its capture would cut off the logistical lifeline for the FNLA's HQ in Carmona. Around 1 January 1976, a two-pronged attack was launched from the north and east by the FAPLA's first two battalions but, after capturing the town centre, the 1st Battalion was pinned down by a counter-attack which Schueg described as 'the most difficult battle of the offensive'.[51] With ammunition running low, the situation became desperate, and the 1st Battalion was only saved by the timely arrival of the 2nd Battalion which after capturing the airport drove off the FNLA. Following the arrival of the first reinforcements – a Cuban tank company and a motorised infantry battalion – on 3 January the FAPLA–Cuban force captured Negage in a lightning attack, inflicting over 140 casualties on the FNLA and advancing to within five miles of Carmona itself. The FAPLA–Cuban forces were not strong enough to capture Carmona that day, however, and they dug in where they were for the night – fighting off an inevitable counter-attack – before moving in the following morning to occupy the FNLA's capital.

The FNLA makes a final stand with foreign mercenaries

The fall of Carmona was a devastating blow to the FNLA's international standing, and signalled its total collapse as a fighting force. Having been abandoned by his principal backers – the CIA and Zaire – Roberto turned to the only remaining source of military personnel: foreign mercenaries.[52] The decision to use mercenaries in Angola was not unprecedented – prior to Quifangondo, hundreds of former Portuguese troops who could loosely be described as mercenaries had fought alongside the FNLA – but in the highly charged atmosphere of the 'Second Liberation War' it was a major miscalculation, stirring painful memories of Mike Hoare's mercenary army in the Congo during the early 1960s. Furthermore, the mercenaries Roberto hired were poorly motivated and undisciplined, and their destructive behaviour in northern Angola would prove a propaganda gift which the MPLA exploited to the full.

In late 1975, the FNLA started recruiting British mercenaries through a bogus security company, the 'Security Advisory Service' based in Camberley, Surrey, and by late December, 128 men had been sent into northern Angola. Their commander Costas Georgiu – 'Colonel Callan' – was a Greek Cypriot who had served with the British Parachute Regiment (and had been imprisoned for armed robbery) before embarking on a career as a mercenary. Described by Roberto as a 'professional' who was 'perhaps a little headstrong', Callan was less generously summed up by Stockwell as a 'raving psychopath', and those who served with him later admitted that his mercenaries were little more than 'a loose band of bandits with a very dangerous leader'.[53] With Carmona in FAPLA hands and Ambriz under threat of attack, the FNLA moved its HQ to São Salvador do Congo (M'banza Congo) while Callan drew up a defensive plan. Mixed mercenary and FNLA forces were sent to defend the FNLA's remaining strongholds – the deep-water port of São António do Zaire (Soyo), São Salvador and Maquela do Zombo – while smaller units patrolled the area south of São Salvador, laying mines and ambushes. With less than 250 mercenaries and a few hundred dispirited FNLA soldiers at his disposal, Callan's defence plan did not stand a chance, as by now he was up against more than six battalions of FAPLA soldiers, supported by Cuban tanks and heavy artillery.

On 11 January, the FAPLA–Cubans captured Ambriz and Ambrizete (N'zeto), and from there they split into a pincer movement on São Salvador, one arm advancing north-east while the other converged on the FNLA's HQ from the south-west. On 31 January, this second column ran into a group of mercenaries near Maquela do Zombo, and in a furious battle it killed nineteen of them and wounded sixteen others. These heavy casualties undermined mercenary morale – many having had little battle experience – and that afternoon twenty-three recent arrivals refused to fight. Furious, Callan placed them under arrest while he took his main force (around seventy men) back to base camp. But with enemy forces nearby, tensions were high, and when a vehicle suddenly appeared unannounced that night, the detained mercenaries opened fire with machineguns and anti-tank rockets, fleeing northwards to São Salvador. Forcibly returned to Maquela do Zombo by an FNLA detachment, they discovered they had actually destroyed one of their own Landrovers (miraculously killing no one). Incensed by their incompetence, Callan called over the mercenary who fired the anti-tank rocket and shot him through the head, immediately ordering the execution of fourteen others.[54]

This single act made Callan the most notorious war criminal of the 'Second Liberation War', and demonstrated how desperate and crazed the fighting in northern Angola had become. Roberto was shocked by the news and flew to Maquela do Zombo to see for himself, but he was unable to locate Callan who had headed south to set up an ambush at Quibocolo (twenty miles to the south). The ambush backfired – quite literally – when Callan's bazooka round hit an ammunition truck, unleashing a devastating series of explosions which wounded him in the shoulder and leg, and killed three of his own men. Dragged to a hut by four mercenaries, Callan fled north as the surviving mercenaries were either killed or captured, but within days he had been taken prisoner by the FAPLA–Cubans who were determined to make an example of him. Keen to distance themselves from Callan, the FNLA stripped him of command and threatened a court martial, but its reputation had been irreparably tarnished and what little support remained for Roberto evaporated. Remaining FNLA and mercenary resistance quickly crumbled and, on 15 February, the FNLA's last foothold in Angola – São Salvador – fell to FAPLA–Cuban forces, ending FNLA dominance in northern Angola.

The offensive against the FNLA in northern Angola was Operation Carlota's greatest single victory, and its one irreversible success. The FNLA – which for twenty years had been the MPLA's bitterest rival and looked set to take power in Angola – had been crushingly defeated. Although sporadic FNLA activity would continue for another four years, Roberto would never again field such a large army nor obtain the backing of such powerful allies. Roberto's decision to use mercenaries was the last in a line of blunders which started with his failure to advance on Luanda in late October 1975, and what little African support he still had quickly disappeared when the extent of his mercenaries' atrocities leaked out. Most of the mercenaries had volunteered for Angola in the belief they would see only sporadic fighting against a disorganised and demoralised enemy, and when faced with professional Cuban forces they had been decisively outclassed on the battlefield.

Determined to make the most of the propaganda gift represented by the capture of thirteen mercenaries, the MPLA put them on trial in June

1976, sentencing nine of them to prison terms ranging from sixteen to thirty years, and four of them – including the infamous Callan – to death. The execution of Callan on 10 July – a man whose actions embodied the greed, moral corruption and brutality of the West – was a brutal rebuke to the FNLA, and for the Cubans was in some part revenge for Guevara's humiliating defeat in the Congo at the hands of Mike Hoare's mercenary army. With its traditional areas of support now under FAPLA–Cuban occupation – and with its remaining forces fleeing over the border into Zaire – the FNLA's bid for power was over, and Roberto would spend the next three years in a fruitless struggle to resurrect his liberation movement as the MPLA established itself in Angola.

The Southern Front, January–April 1976

Following the final order from Pretoria to pull out of Angola, South African forces withdrew rapidly towards Namibia, handing over the towns they had captured to UNITA and destroying bridges behind them to slow down the FAPLA–Cuban pursuit. The Cubans recognised the military vacuum created by Zulu Force's withdrawal, and they immediately began moving large columns of Cuban troops and armour into southern Angola in the face of sporadic and ineffective UNITA resistance. Cuban accounts have since depicted 'Operación General Antonio Maceo' – as the campaign was codenamed – as a triumphant campaign against a demoralised South African opponent. But the truth is that, in the two months which the withdrawal took to complete, there was no contact between the Cubans and South Africans, and the remainder of the 'Second Liberation War' more resembled a military manoeuvre than an intensely fought campaign.

The advance southwards nevertheless faced enormous obstacles, not least of which were the dozens of bridges destroyed in the fighting either by the Cubans themselves or by the retreating South Africans. The Queve river, which in November had proved an effective first line of defence for the Cubans, now became the main obstacle in their path. Throughout January, frantic efforts were made to repair the main crossings at Caxoeiras and Techirimba so that Cuban tanks and armoured cars could join the advance. The engineering task was formidable – eight bridges had to be rebuilt in the Ebo and Nhia river area alone – and the advance was further delayed while sappers removed South African landmines and booby-traps laid in the retreat. The first FAPLA–Cuban troops were ferried across the Queve at Massango (fifteen miles west of Santa Comba) in improvised rafts, quickly capturing Amboiva on 1 February and advancing on Cassongue. Four days later, Cuban engineers completed repairs on the Techirimba bridge, and then a general advance into southern Angola began.

The Cuban plan was to first capture the main towns along the Benguela railway line, consolidate a defensive position there, and then move in to southern Huíla and Cuando Cubango. While two FAPLA–Cuban columns cleared pockets of UNITA resistance south of the Queve river, a third advanced south from Mussende, capturing Teixeira de Silva (Bailundo) before moving on UNITA's capital – Nova Lisboa – which fell on 8 February after heavy fighting. The fall of Nova Lisboa was a devastating blow for UNITA which lost over 600 troops in the battle, and signalled its collapse as a military force in Angola. Bereft of the crucial support of Zulu Force, Foxbat and Orange, UNITA put up only token resistance against the overwhelming forces ranged against it, and over the next fortnight its remaining strongholds fell in quick succession to the Cubans' relentless advance.

With Nova Lisboa now under their control, the FAPLA–Cubans advanced east and west simultaneously, easily capturing the ports of Lobito and Benguela on 10 February, and UNITA's main base on the Benguela railway at Silva Porto two days later. Sá da Bandeira and Moçamedes (UNITA's last remaining port) fell shortly afterwards and, with the capture of Luso on 14 February, the Cubans' Eastern and Southern Fronts were able to link up, cementing their control of the Benguela railway line. Having vowed during his last meeting with a CIA officer on 1 February never to leave the Angolan bush alive, Savimbi fled with the few hundred men left under his control to his last remote outpost – Gago Coutinho (Lumbala-N'Guimbo) in southern Moxico – and made preparations for a protracted guerrilla war.

At this point, however, the FAPLA–Cuban advance came to an abrupt halt. For the next month the Cubans remained behind their defensive line – which ran from Moçâmedes (Namibe) through to Serpa Pinto (Menongue) – making no attempt to advance into southern Huíla. Moves were made to extend the FAPLA's control eastwards, both into Cuando Cubango and Moxico. But no advance south was made either from Lubango or Matala, despite the availability of forces for such a push. The reason for Cuban reticence was that they had come within range of the South African rearguard, and the Cubans – who still had painful memories of the disaster at Bridge 14 – were keen to avoid a confrontation with the SADF unless absolutely necessary. Although Cuban accounts have since claimed that the South Africans were forcibly driven back towards the Namibian border, the reality was that the rapid Cuban advance – which covered nearly 400 miles in a little over three weeks – was only possible because of a total absence of South African forces in the area. Once within range, the Cubans chose to hold back, waiting for the South Africans to complete their withdrawal before advancing any further.

The advance on Gago Coutinho nevertheless continued and, on 17 February, two columns set out from Luso, destroyed bridges delaying their arrival until 13 March. Cuban MiG-21s – on their first combat appearance in Angola – bombed the airfield prior to the assault, destroying an F-27 which the CIA had borrowed from Mobutu, and this convinced Savimbi that he was not only outnumbered but also outgunned. Before abandoning Gago Coutinho, however, Savimbi ordered the execution of seventeen Cubans who had been captured by UNITA during the previous five months of fighting. Accusing five of rape, the rest of murder, they were shot by an all-woman firing squad only hours before their comrades captured the town, this callous act calculated to demoralise the Cubans who found the bodies.[55] It was by no means UNITA's first atrocity – the MPLA later alleged that UNITA had massacred hundreds of MPLA sympathisers in Silva Porto, Lobito and Porto Alexandre – but it contributed to the ruthless reputation which the 'kwacha' earned over the following years.[56] Gathering his remaining forces together, Savimbi headed off into the Angolan bush, vowing to continue his seemingly hopeless struggle against the MPLA and its powerful allies alone.

In early March the FAPLA–Cubans made timid moves south from Lubango – occupying Tchibemba and Virei – but they held back from entering southern Huíla where the bulk of the 5,000-man South African rearguard was stationed. The reason Pretoria refused to withdraw its remaining men – despite an obvious desire to bring an end to its intervention – was the same that had motivated its incursion into Cunene the previous August: the Calueque hydroelectric scheme. Paranoid that a hostile MPLA government would shut down (or even demolish) Calueque, Pretoria refused to withdraw until it had cast-iron assurances that Calueque would continue to operate as it had under the Portuguese. Finally, on 18 March, the MPLA guaranteed to the UN that it would not damage the installations, and offered to negotiate their operation with Pretoria. This move quelled remaining South African reservations and, on 27 March, the last elements of Zulu Force withdrew across the border into Namibia.[57] Cuban forces immediately moved to capture the last remaining provincial capital outside the MPLA's control – Pereira d'Eça – and, with the occupation of the frontier post at Santa Clara a few days later, the 'Second Liberation War' was officially over.

Aftermath of the 'Second Liberation War'

News of the withdrawal of South African forces was greeted with elation by the MPLA which designated the date a national holiday, naming Luanda's annual Carnaval da Vitória (Victory Carnival) in its honour. After fifteen years of fighting, the MPLA was at last triumphant and, with the help of its Cuban allies, it had not only vanquished its bitterest rivals – the FNLA and UNITA – but in the process it had seen off the CIA and humbled the mighty Pretoria war machine. Overnight Neto became a hero of the Third World, and in the final weeks of the 'Second Liberation War' the PRA obtained recognition not only from the OAU (which admitted it as a member on 10 February 1976), but also from the EEC (on 17 February) and Portugal (22 February). The Americans were the one notable exception, stubbornly refusing to recognise the government they had sought to keep out of power. But their moves to deny Angola a seat in the UN General Assembly could not be sustained and, on 22 November, the PRA was admitted as the UN's one-hundred-and-forty-sixth member.[58] It was a dramatic change in the MPLA's fortunes from the dark days of factional splits and military collapse, and with thousands of Cuban troops bolstering its military forces, the MPLA's power base looked secure. Neto's confidence was dangerously misplaced, however, as the fighting had only briefly submerged the MPLA's chronic disunity, and when it next surfaced it was to have bloody consequences (see Chapter 6).

For Castro, the Cuban-led victory represented the peak of his political career, and gave him his first unequivocal internationalist victory. His daring, even reckless decision to send thousands of troops into Angola could have backfired disastrously. But through a combination of cold determination and pure luck he had once again turned potential defeat into overwhelming victory, dramatically thrusting himself back onto the international stage. It had been a nail-bitingly close contest – Cuban reinforcements arriving only hours before crucial battles occurred – but the gamble had paid off, and Havana was presented with a propaganda victory the completeness of which it could scarcely have imagined when it took the fateful decision to launch Operation Carlota. For not only had it saved an internationally recognised African government from annihilation, but in the process the regional pariah – South Africa – had been humbled in no uncertain terms, and (at least for the time-being) its presumed invincibility quashed. The American government, still licking its wounds from Vietnam, had watched its ill-chosen allies trounced on the battlefield, and was barred from helping them by the humiliating Clark Amendment which would keep the CIA out of Angola for almost a decade. And almost incredibly, all of this – not least the insertion of a massive military force into a region previously bereft of Cuban troops – had been achieved without the censure of either the OAU or the UN, an outstanding feat of diplomacy.[59]

Cuba's stunning victory against the forces of imperialism was the ideal climax to Institutionalisation, and confirmed Castro's position as one of the Soviet Union's most important allies. Having spent the early 1970s engulfed in the Soviet bear-hug, Castro had gone ahead with Operation Carlota against his patron's wishes, and his gamble had paid off spectacularly. Following victory in Angola, Castro would be allowed a degree of independence unlike any other Soviet ally, extending Soviet influence into countries outside their grasp. Delighted at the acquisition of a new African ally, Moscow was more than happy to bankroll the Cuban operation, and the generous Five Year Agreement it signed with Cuba on 14 April 1976 (which increased aid by over 250 per cent and rescheduled Cuba's massive foreign debt) must in some way have been a payoff. From now on the Soviet Union – which only a few months before had refused to escalate its involvement in Angola – would be the benevolent overseer of the Cuban operation, supplying or underwriting the vast majority of the military hardware. What neither Cuba nor the Soviet Union had any inkling of at the time was just how long this operation would last.

For Pretoria, the failure of Operation Savannah left it 'without a single crumb of comfort'.[60] Not only had it failed to install the FNLA and UNITA in power but, by invading Angola, it had triggered Cuba's military intervention and catapulted the MPLA to power. South African attempts to keep the invasion secret were hopelessly bungled, and once news that its troops were fighting in Angola leaked out in late November 1975, the international outcry it caused gave Cuba all the justification it needed to send in an intervention force ten times the size. For a while, Pretoria blamed the Americans, accusing Washington of losing its nerve and abandoning South Africa at the critical moment.[61] But there was little escaping the reality that before it invaded there were fewer than 1,000 Cuban troops in Angola, and that by the end of Operation Savannah that force had grown to over 36,000. Whatever monstrous chimera Pretoria imagined it was facing in October 1975, it now had a very real hostile force up against its borders – and only itself to blame for it being there. The internal repercussions of the Angolan debacle were felt quickly when, on 16 June 1976 – emboldened by the FAPLA–Cuban victory – the Soweto Uprising began, inaugurating a period of civil unrest which was to continue up until and beyond the collapse of apartheid. With SWAPO and ANC training camps springing up across southern Angola and their insurgency on the rise, the regime braced itself for a war for its very survival.

Yet despite Cuba's overwhelming victory on the ground, the war in Angola was far from over. For, although the FNLA, UNITA and FLEC had suffered crushing defeats, they were to prove more resilient than the either the MPLA or Cubans anticipated. The FNLA would threaten northern Angola from its bases in Zaire for the next three years, and UNITA – which by March 1976 had effectively been written off as a threat – would confound everyone's expectations and rebuild itself into a military force which would eventually challenge the MPLA. More significantly, neither Cuba nor the MPLA appreciated that the failure of Operation Savannah was a political rather than a military one, and that the SADF (which fought impressively throughout the campaign) was far from defeated. It had been Pretoria's weak political leadership which compromised Zulu Force's chances of success in Angola, its constant changes to the operation's objectives and withdrawal schedule (which was postponed three times) preventing its ground forces from exploiting their break-throughs (such as the attack across Bridge 14).

In the words of Operation Savannah's commander, it had been a 'war of lost opportunities',[62] and other SADF officers believed – rightly or wrongly – that they had been robbed of victory. They had unquestionably got the better of their opponents in all but one of their engagements (the ambush at Ebo), and many were convinced that had they been given proper technical support – bridge-building equipment, for example – nothing could have prevented them taking Luanda. The failure of Operation Savannah thus left the SADF hungry for a second round, and bitterly determined to exact revenge for its most humiliating defeat of the Cold War. In the short-term, the SADF would need to retrench and brace itself for an onslaught on Namibia from the dozens of SWAPO bases springing up across southern Angola. But in the long-term, Pretoria could not allow SWAPO to operate with impunity so close to the Namibian border, and it was thus only a matter of time before it sought authorisation to launch cross-border raids against its Angolan camps. Renewed SADF interest in southern Angola would also re-ignite its alliance with UNITA, only this time the partnership would prove to be more durable.

For the Cubans, therefore, victory in the 'Second War of Liberation' proved illusory, and fostered a false sense of security. Believing his huge gamble had paid off, in March 1976 Castro started withdrawing troops from Angola, anxious to avoid them becoming bogged down in a lengthy internal counter-insurgency. What Castro failed to grasp, however, was that the tangled web of conflicts consuming southern Africa – among them SWAPO's war in Namibia, ZANU's war in Southern Rhodesia, and the Katangese war in Shaba – ruled out any Cuban withdrawal if the MPLA government was not to face immediate collapse. For the reality was that as a result of over a dozen countries' intervention, the Angolan War had become entangled with its neighbouring conflicts, all of which would need to be resolved before peace could return to the region. To his growing dismay, Castro would discover that the short-term intervention he had envisioned in November 1975 had in fact committed Cuba to Angola indefinitely, and had inadvertently initiated Cuba's fifteen-year occupation.

6

THE FAILED WITHDRAWAL FROM ANGOLA, 1976–81

Cuba's victory in the 'Second Liberation War' did not bring peace to Angola. Instead, the five years which followed were a time of growing instability and great frustration for Havana whose efforts to curtail the Cuban operation were continually thwarted. As Angola's security steadily deteriorated – with two invasions of Zaire's Shaba province by Katangese gendarmes, an attempted coup against Neto and the relentless growth of UNITA – Cuba's short-term intervention force evolved into a long-term army of occupation, committing Cuban troops to Angola indefinitely. Very quickly the delirious optimism which had accompanied the South African withdrawal gave way to a bleak realisation that the fighting was far from over, and eventually both Havana and Luanda would be forced to recognise that, in Savimbi, they had a far more persistent and intractable enemy. Having won the ground war with great speed and drama, the Cubans would spend the next five years fruitlessly trying to win the peace. But their attempts to hand over the defence of Angola to the newly-trained FAPLA would prove unsuccessful, and by the end of this period the Cubans would have become locked into a full-scale counter-insurgency against UNITA.

Cuban attempts to withdraw from Angola

Even before South Africa completed its withdrawal, Cuba had begun discussing ways of reducing its 36,000-man contingent in Angola, with the aim of withdrawing it altogether within a few years. From the outset Castro envisaged Operation Carlota as a short-term operation with the simple objective of securing the MPLA in power. Now this had been achieved, he was keen to start withdrawing his troops before they became committed indefinitely. Cuban casualties had been light (less than 300 had been killed by this stage),[1] and Castro was only too aware how quickly his dramatic victory could degenerate into a Vietnam scenario if the operation were not reined in. Furthermore, Cuba's overwhelming regional support was in danger of ebbing away if its military presence in Angola continued

116

indefinitely, exposing it to accusations of being a foreign occupying army. By March 1976, there were around 36,000 Cuban troops in Angola (supported by over 300 tanks) and, if only to ensure Cuba's own defences were not prejudiced, the bulk of these needed to be withdrawn quickly before they became bogged down in 'mopping-up' operations.

Accordingly, on 14 March 1976 – nearly a fortnight before the South Africans completed their withdrawal – Castro met with Neto in Conakry and outlined a plan to withdraw Cuban troops at a rate of 200 per week. Neto agreed to Castro's proposals, and on 22 April both governments announced that the Cuban withdrawal had begun. Four days later, Raúl Castro flew into Luanda for a seven-week visit to hammer out the details. Raúl Castro was keen for 15,000 troops to be withdrawn by October 1976, and he instructed the Chiefs of MMCA's Rearguard to draw up a detailed withdrawal programme which they presented to Fidel Castro on 7 May.[2] Castro was not happy with the plan, however, for despite being anxious to withdraw his troops rapidly he was also keen to conceal the size of Cuban forces from foreign observers. He suggested that instead of returning in one large convoy, the troops should be spread among different ships and aircraft over a period of months. Some troops would be transferred to other Cuban missions in the region (such as Brazzaville) where they formed an emergency reserve. In the end Raúl Castro's estimates were shown to have been wildly optimistic as, by August, only 2,000 Cuban troops had returned to Cuba, and for the next year the withdrawal continued at no more than a trickle. By the time Fidel Castro visited Luanda in March 1977, he would have become sufficiently concerned by its slow pace to propose ambitious new withdrawal plans to Neto.

Cuban 'mopping-up' operations against FLEC and the FNLA

With the completion of the offensives on the Northern and Southern Fronts (April 1976), the Cuban military set about crushing the remaining pockets of FNLA, FLEC and UNITA resistance. Having survived a military disaster in Cuba two decades previously, Castro was only too aware how illusory a victory Angola could prove if the guerrillas were given time to regroup, and he ordered 'mopping-up' operations to be launched as soon as was practicable. Despite its military collapse in northern Angola, the FNLA was particularly difficult to stamp out as it continued to operate from bases along the Zairian border. In an effort to isolate Roberto, on 29 February 1976 Neto met Mobutu in Brazzaville and signed a non-aggression pact. In return for Neto's pledge to disarm and repatriate the FAPLA's 6,000 Katangese allies, Mobutu promised to expel all remaining FNLA and UNITA personnel from Zaire, and to curtail FLEC operations in Kinshasa. It was a bold attempt to defuse tensions between Neto and

117

Mobutu, but the mistrust between them was simply too great – and the regional situation too volatile – for the deal to stick, and it would take the invasion of Zaire's Shaba province to bring them back to the table (see pp. 125–6).

In Cabinda, FLEC still posed a threat, and fighting continued throughout 1976 and 1977, the Cubans suffering heavy casualties as they struggled to crush the persistent insurgency.[3] The small FAPLA–Cuban force under Espinosa had defeated FLEC's invasion in November 1975, but it was not strong enough to take control of the rest of the enclave until reinforcements were sent from Cuba. These duly arrived on 3 December when the *Sierra Maestra* docked at Pointe-Noire, unloading over 1,000 troops, tanks and artillery. By February 1976, the Cuban contingent in Cabinda had grown to over 5,000.[4] FLEC activity stepped up in late December with a series of ambushes, one of which – on 27 December – destroyed two supply trucks en route from Lândana to Massabi. In February 1976, the Cubans struck back with Operación Pañuelo Blanco (White Handkerchief), a large-scale operation to surround and destroy the remaining 700 FLEC guerrillas operating in the Necuto area (sixty miles north-east of Cabinda city). The guerrillas broke out of the encirclement, however, and laid minefields which caused the Cubans some casualties as they pursued them into the jungle. Further skirmishing continued throughout the month, but when, in late March, FLEC attacks left five Cubans dead (including the Cuban Political Commissar for Cabinda) it was decided to liquidate the guerrillas once and for all.

In early April, the entire Cuban contingent was deployed in a horse-shoe encirclement east of the guerrillas, cutting off their supply lines and driving them back to the sea. This time the Cuban cordon held, and nearly 100 FLEC guerrillas were killed over two nights as they tried to break out of their encirclement. A further 100 guerrillas died and 300 were taken prisoner when the Cubans moved in for the kill the next day. The annihilation of the column was a serious setback for FLEC but did not herald its collapse – as Espinosa (who was re-appointed Chief of the Cabinda mission in March) discovered to his personal cost. On 8 May, as he was leading a small Cuban column along the eastern frontier with Zaire between Tando Zinze and Chiobo, his armoured car hit an anti-tank mine, overturning the vehicle in a massive explosion.[5] One Cuban officer was killed, and four were seriously wounded, among them Espinosa who was trapped in agony underneath the BTR while his soldiers tried to lift it off him. The Cuban Political Commissar took command of the column and guided it as far as Chiobo, before Furry ordered its return to Cabinda city. Espinosa required a lengthy hospitalisation and was eventually flown back to Cuba for specialist treatment, but his active military career was at an end.[6]

News of Espinosa's misfortune drew sharp criticism from Castro who was hosting a dinner for senior Cuban commanders. One of his guests – Cabinda's former commander Divisional-General Joaquin Quintas Solá – sprang to Espinosa's defence, however, and he was duly re-appointed commander of the Cabinda operation. Following his return to Cabinda in May, the Cubans launched a series of operations against the remaining pockets of FLEC resistance, including naval and helicopter landings behind enemy lines. The jungle made conditions extremely difficult and the Cubans suffered heavy losses in ambushes but, by the end of 1976, they had broken FLEC's grip on the enclave and for the next decade its activities never exceeded nuisance value. The MPLA's most precious assets – the rich oil fields off Cabinda – were now secure, and a Cuban garrison was installed at Malembo to protect against attempts to sabotage oil production. It would be nearly a decade before a raid by South African commandos would once again threaten the enclave's security (see Chapter 8).

Attempts to crush UNITA – the *Luta Contra Bandidos* (LCB)

Attempts to crush UNITA were not as successful. In part this was because the Cubans and Angolans underestimated Savimbi's tenacity and determination to fight on. By far the weakest military force during the 'Second Liberation War', UNITA was (perhaps understandably) viewed as a minor threat, and following the capture of its last base in March 1976, the Cubans expected to mop up remaining pockets of UNITA resistance without great difficulty. To assist in this operation, Cuban specialists in counter-insurgency were called in to plan an Angolan '*Luta Contra Bandidos*' (LCB, literally 'Fight against Bandits').[7] Given their extensive experience in fighting counter-insurgency campaigns, Cuban troops were the obvious choice to oversee the first LCB operations, and between April and November 1976 they launched four successive operations to drive UNITA out of Mexico, southern Cuando Cubango and Cunene. UNITA held out tenaciously, however, and as the fighting dragged on resentment grew among the Cuban troops who were bearing the brunt of it while the FAPLA were mostly assigned to garrison duties.[8] Criticism of the Angolan LCB steadily increased among the Cuban commanders in Luanda, and by March 1977 it was serious enough for Castro to raise the matter in his talks with Neto (see p. 125).

Location and size of Cuban forces in Angola (1976 onwards)

The vast majority of Cuban forces were not involved in the LCB, however, and following the South African withdrawal they were assigned to garrison duties in Angola's main cities. Adopting a pattern which continued for most of Cuba's occupation, the bulk of Cuban forces were located in or around Luanda, protecting the political and economic capital and the operation's principal supply port. The LCB training camp – containing between 3,000 and 4,000 Cuban troops – was located in the Funda suburb, with naval units in the port itself and a large aerial contingent which included jets (MiG-21s and MiG-23s), helicopters (Mi-8 and Mi-24) and fighter-bombers (Su-22s). As the operation extended into the 1980s, each of Angola's seventeen provincial capitals was also garrisoned with at least one Cuban regiment. One of the largest, in Huambo, had its own MiG-21/23 regiment and a brigade of tanks (c.100 in total) stationed to the south in Caála. The largest single concentration of Cuban troops outside Luanda – initially around 10,000 men – was located along the 400-mile defensive line (Agrupación de Tropas del Sur, Southern Troop Grouping) which ran from Namibe along the railway line to Menongue (see Map 7).[9] As the war intensified in southern Angola, the Cuban HQ at Lubango grew into the single largest garrison in Angola – Batallón 2 – with nearly 5,000 troops, tanks, artillery and sophisticated radar and air defences. Some Cuban bases were located south of this line – for example at Tchibemba, Tchamutete and Jamba (Huíla) – but the official policy was for Cuban troops not to operate in Cunene or southern Cuando Cubango.

The precise number of Cuban troops in Angola is still hotly disputed and has been scrupulously covered up by the FAR which – given the sensitivity of this information – did not wish to reveal the size of its military forces. However, it is clear that American estimates in late 1977 that there were between 12,000 and 15,000 Cuban troops in Angola were woefully inaccurate; by that stage there were around three times that number.[10] As Angola's instability worsened, the Cuban contingent swelled, and by 1983 there were no fewer than twenty-six Cuban regiments in Angola – each numbering 2,000–3,000 men, bringing the grand total to as many as 80,000 troops.[11] This figure would start to decrease in the late 1980s, as the Soviets took over the running of the FAPLA's operations. But Havana's inability to scale back its operation nevertheless demonstrated how foreign powers – first Portugal, then Cuba and South Africa – could get sucked into Angola's conflict even when they were actively trying to disengage. Throughout Cuba's fifteen-year occupation of Angola, however, Havana never admitted to having more than 40,000 troops in Angola (prior to 1987), and the debate over the size of the Cuban contingent would prove one of the major sticking points of the peace negotiations (see Chapter 11).

The decision to assign the majority of Cuban troops to garrison duty while the inexperienced FAPLA struggled to stamp out what was left of the FNLA and UNITA was adopted for two reasons. First, Havana was anxious to keep Cuban casualties (which up to that point had been

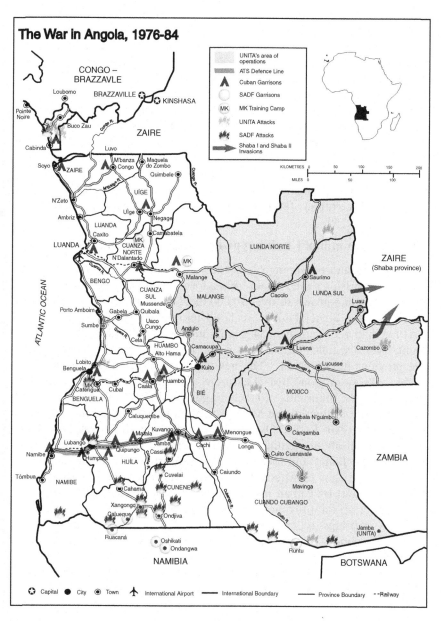

The War in Angola, 1976-84

UNITA's area of operations
ATS Defence Line
Cuban Garrisons
SADF Garrisons
MK **MK Training Camp**
UNITA Attacks
SADF Attacks
Shaba I and Shaba II Invasions

KILOMETRES 0   50   100   150   200
MILES 0   50   100

CONGO – BRAZZAVLE

Louborno
BRAZZAVILLE
KINSHASA
Pointe Noire
Buco Zau
ZAIRE
Cabinda
Soyo
ZAIRE
N'Zeto
Ambriz
LUANDA
Caxito
LUANDA
BENGO
Porto Amboim
Gabela
Sumbe
Cela
Lobito
Benguela
BENGUELA
Catengue
Cubal
Caala
Namibe
Lubango
Humpata
HUÍLA
Tômbua
NAMIBE
Ruacaná
Xangongo
Calueque
Luvo
M'banza Congo
Maquela do Zombo
Quimbele
UÍGE
Ulge
Negage
Carmabatela
CUANZA NORTE
N'Dalantado
Malange
CUANZA SUL
Mussende
Quibala
Uaco Cungo
Andulo
HUAMBO
Alto Hama
Camacupa
Kuito
Huambo
BIÉ
Caluquembe
Kuvango
Matala
Jamba
Cassinga
Quipungo
Menongue
Chichi
Longa
Cuvelai
CUNENE
Cahama
Ondjiva
Oshikati
Ondangwa

LUNDA NORTE
Saurimo
Cacolo
LUNDA SUL
Luau
Luena
Lucusse
Lunge-Bungo R
MOXICO
Lumbala N'guimbo
Cangamba
Cuito Cuanavale
Mavinga
CUANDO CUBANGO
Jamba (UNITA)
Runtu
Caiundo

ZAIRE (Shaba province)
Cazombo

ZAMBIA
BOTSWANA
NAMIBIA

ATLANTIC OCEAN

MALANGE

⊕ Capital   ● City   ⊚ Town   ✈ International Airport   — International Boundary   — Province Boundary   --Railway

Map 7 The war in Angola, 1876–84.

remarkably light) to an absolute minimum, conscious that the 'body bag factor' could sap public support for the Angolan adventure. But, second, by keeping Cuban troops out of the firing line, Havana reinforced the impression that it was not crushing internal dissent in Angola, but rather protecting the MPLA from external enemies.[12] Castro envisioned a short-term intervention, and following the ejection of foreign forces from Angola he planned to scale back the Cuban contingent to a modest garrison – perhaps 5,000 troops, with a large military instruction force for the FAPLA and the various liberation movements based in Angola – while greatly expanding the civilian contingent. Eventually – it was hoped – Cuban troops would hand over their duties to the FAPLA, enabling them to withdraw from Angola with a strong professional army in their place which could see off any future threat, both from within and without.

Cuban military training programmes in Angola, 1976–7

The training and equipping of the new FAPLA army therefore became the Cuban mission's other main task, a formidable one given that, by 1977, the FAPLA had grown to over 70,000 men. By March 1976 – exactly one year since the Soviet Union escalated its military aid programme – the FAPLA had received over $400 million worth of Soviet military equipment, over five times the amount it had received from the Soviets during the previous fifteen years.[13] The new equipment included at least 120 T-34/54 tanks, twenty-one BM-21s, dozens of armed helicopters, hundreds of armoured cars, thousands of machine-guns and pistols, and the FAPLA's first aircraft – a squadron of MiG-21 fighters which formed the nucleus of the Angolan Air Force. Over the next five years, Cuban and Soviet instructors set about creating a FAPLA army of twenty-three brigades – nineteen of infantry and four of anti-aircraft artillery – which could deter any future invasion of Angola and crush UNITA. The bulk of the training was carried out by Cuban instructors in camps across Angola (including the four set up the previous September), although a contingent of Soviet advisors (perhaps 100 officers) maintained a presence in the FAPLA High Command – overseeing the planning of operations and weapons deliveries.

As the mission to train the FAPLA progressed, it evolved into the blueprint for Soviet–Cuban operations in Africa – the Cubans providing the instructors while the Soviets provided the hardware – and in many ways resembled the embryonic partnership that developed during the Brazzaville mission (1965–7). This alliance of interests proved particularly successful as it drew on each partner's comparative strength. The Soviet strength was its colossal military industrial complex which provided the raw material for building the FAPLA into a sub-Saharan superpower. Cuba's strength was its manpower, in particular its supply of specialist officers who were familiar with the sophisticated weaponry supplied by the Soviets to the FAPLA, and who often had combat experience. The MPLA preferred Cuban instructors because their training went beyond the basics and included ideological and political instruction, a bonus for even the more experienced FAPLA cadres who, in general, lacked political training. The Cubans emphasised discipline and loyalty to the regime as much as they did the technical aspects of weaponry and tactics, and this proved a powerful combination in a region where army mutinies were a regular occurrence.[14]

The Cubans were also involved in a massive covert programme to run dozens of training camps for the MPLA's allies – SWAPO, the ANC and ZAPU – all of which were still engaged in independence struggles with southern Africa's last colonial powers, South Africa and Southern Rhodesia. By June 1976, all three movements had opened offices in Luanda's renamed *Rua da Libertação*, and over the following year Cuban and Soviet specialists helped them set up training camps across Angola. The main camp of the ANC's military wing – Umkhonto weSizwe (Spear of the Nation) or 'MK' – was located in the Portuguese barracks at Novo Catengue (near the site of the clash with Zulu Force in November 1975).[15] The camp was run by a contingent of Cuban instructors and weapons specialists who oversaw six-month training programmes for groups of up to 500 MK recruits. Between late 1976 and the camp's destruction in March 1979, over 1,000 MK cadres were trained there and – in recognition of Cuba's solidarity with the ANC – the third contingent to graduate in November 1977 was named the 'Moncada Detachment' in their honour. MK also operated many smaller camps in Angola using its own instructors – including 'Camp Thirteen' at Quibaxe (100 miles east of Caxito) where MK recruits underwent induction courses – but the Cubans nevertheless maintained contacts with them, and occasionally helped out with supplies.

Cuban and Soviet instructors also helped to run a number of SWAPO training camps in Angola, although Cuban garrisons in Cunene and Malange were housed separately from their allies throughout the war. SWAPO had been operating in southern Angola since the mid-1960s, and had switched sides to the MPLA in August 1975 after news of Savimbi's alliance with the SADF leaked out. Following the South African withdrawal, SWAPO started to receive Soviet military aid and, by February 1977, it was strong enough to begin infiltrating northern Namibia and Caprivi from bases in Cunene and Zambia. Cuban instructors were also involved in training ZAPU troops at a camp in Cuculama (forty miles east of Malange) and, by early 1977, there were nearly 6,000 ZAPU troops training across Angola, representing a genuine threat to Ian Smith's regime in Southern Rhodesia.[16] Cuban instructors may also have been involved in training the MPLA's Katangese allies in eastern Angola, although the evidence is still sketchy (see 'Shaba I invasion', pp. 125–6).

As a result of Cuba's many clandestine training programmes, by early 1977 Angola had become what Guevara had originally envisioned for eastern Zaire back in 1965: a vast training ground for Africa's leading liberation movements (SWAPO, the ANC and ZAPU), with almost limitless possibilities for infiltrating enemy territory and concealing the presence of training camps within Angola itself. The subsequent increase in MK activity within South Africa and SWAPO infiltration into Namibia did not go unnoticed by Pretoria, however, and it was only a matter of time before the SADF sought authorisation to launch cross-border raids against SWAPO and MK camps in Angola.

Fidel Castro's African tour, March 1977

In March 1977, Fidel Castro set out on a triumphal tour of Africa, not only celebrating Cuba's victory in Angola but also confirming his role as chief spokesman for the Third World.[17] Castro was keen to play the role of mediator in African affairs, and during his tour he visited Libya, South Yemen and Somalia to discuss proposals for a Socialist Federation between the latter two and Ethiopia. The proposal was doomed, however, and Castro was instead drawn into the territorial dispute between Ethiopia and Somalia over the former's eastern border area (the Ogaden). At the time the recipient of substantial Soviet military aid, Somalia pressed for Cuban support, but Castro kept his distance, urging the Federation as the answer while he waited to see how Mengistu's revolutionary government (which overthrew Haile Selassie on 2 February) turned out. Castro's opportunistic involvement in the Ogaden dispute would place him in a position of great influence when the Somalis invaded the Ogaden the following July.

On 23 March 1977, Castro arrived in Angola for his first official visit, and over the next nine days he was fêted by the MPLA which had him to thank for its survival. The visit by the Cuban Head of State was a follow-up to Neto's visit to Havana the previous July (his first for a decade), and symbolised the revitalisation of the Cuban–MPLA alliance. During his visit, Castro and Neto unveiled a plaque at Quifangondo, scene of Cuba's greatest victory in the 'Second Liberation War', and on 27 March Castro spoke at a triumphant rally in Luanda to rapturous crowds. Beneath the veneer of triumphalism, however, Castro was keen to curtail the Cuban operation. Indeed, his decision to emphasise that Cuban troops had only intervened in Angola to save Luanda from capture may have been intended as a hint that the Cuban operation had achieved its goal – and that it was time to wind it up. In particular, Castro must have been alarmed by Neto's public revelations of an alleged FNLA–SADF plot to invade Cabinda and destabilise central Angola – 'Operation Cobra 77'.[18] For even if the rumours were false, they implied a painful truth: that the FNLA and the SADF still posed a threat to Angola. This not only made a Cuban withdrawal unfeasible, but it could necessitate further reinforcements, an outcome Castro was determined to avoid.

At the start of his talks with Neto, therefore, Castro presented an ambitious timetable which envisioned reducing the Cuban contingent to only 15,000 men by the end of 1977, and 7,000 by 1978. It was a bold initiative, but as Pretoria discovered in 1975, the escalation of the war in Angola was beyond any one party's control, and Castro's dreams of reining in the Cuban operation were unrealistic. For not only were the original threats to the MPLA still present – UNITA, the FNLA and the SADF – but by 1977 the Angolan conflict had become entangled with several other conflicts in the region. It is thus strange that Castro doggedly clung onto the delusion that a Cuban withdrawal was still possible, confidently informing Eric Honecker a month later that it was going ahead. Perhaps Castro's grasp of southern African politics was far weaker than his supporters have consistently boasted, and this might explain why it took him more than five years to accept that a uni-lateral withdrawal of Cuban forces from Angola was out of the question while the rest of the region remained consumed by conflict.

During the talks, Castro also raised his concerns about the LCB, criticising the FAPLA for failing to take UNITA seriously, and com-plaining that Cuban troops were bearing the brunt of the fighting. Castro was anxious to avoid the negative publicity which would result from Cuban troops participating in counter-insurgency operations in which Angolan civilians were killed, an all-too-common occurrence during the Angolan War. Castro insisted that the FAPLA needed to be playing a more prominent role in the LCB, but when Neto suggested that the Cubans simply take over command of the FAPLA, Castro resisted, fearful of upsetting his Soviet patrons who were not only sup-plying the weaponry for the Cuban operation, but who were also involved in strategic planning at the FAPLA's highest levels. As Castro saw it, the Soviets would not take kindly to Cuba taking control of the army they were bankrolling, and he did little more than admonish Neto to take the UNITA threat more seriously. Castro's warnings were not heeded, however, and they would come back to haunt the MPLA as the movement they had written off mounted a challenge to its power.

The 'Shaba I' invasion, March 1977

The other main issue on the agenda was the news that Katangese gen-darmes had invaded Zaire's Shaba province from Angola. The Katangese force, numbering between 3,000 and 6,500 troops (estimates vary wildly), was a leftover from the Katanga Secession (1960–3) and had fled into

Angola following the fall of Moïse Tshombe. Once established in Angola, the Katangese were co-opted by the Portuguese who used their presence on the Zairian border to deter Mobutu from increasing support for FLEC and the FNLA. With the collapse of Portuguese rule in early 1975, the Katangese threw in their lot with the MPLA, and many gendarmes saw action at Quifangondo, Luso (Luena) and Benguela. Under the terms of the pact signed in February 1976, Neto promised to disband and repatriate the Katangese force. But with the FNLA still operating from bases inside Zaire, Neto decided they were too useful a bargaining chip to give away, and throughout 1976 the FAPLA (and possibly some Cubans) continued to arm and train the Katangese in eastern Angola. The revelation of 'Cobra 77' was the catalyst for the invasion, although the possibility that the MPLA fabricated it as a cover story cannot be ruled out. By early April, the Katangese were approaching Kolwesi, a mining town 250 miles east of Luau, and they were only prevented from capturing it by France and Belgium which airlifted in 1,500 Moroccan troops. After three weeks of bloody fighting, the Katangese were driven back across the Angola border, bringing 'Shaba I' to an end.

The invasion caused an international crisis, and Zaire and the USA immediately accused Cuba of masterminding it, an accusation Castro vehemently denied. In an interview two months later, Castro insisted that Cuba had 'refused and avoided every form of commitment to and collaboration with the Katangese'.[19] On balance, Cuban denials seem genuine, as the timing of the invasion was acutely embarrassing for Castro (who was in the middle of his African tour) and threatened to undermine his legitimacy as a mediator in the Ogaden dispute. Given that he was trying to speed up the Cuban withdrawal, it is unlikely he would have authorised the invasion as it could only destabilise Angola's border region and necessitate even more Cuban reinforcements – the diametrical opposite of what he was trying to achieve. The MPLA, on the other hand, immediately gave its support to the Katangese and, from the available evidence, it is likely that they backed the invasion as a means of striking back at Mobutu. The underlying dispute between Luanda and Kinshasa remained, however, and it would take a second invasion of Shaba the following year to bring both sides to their senses.

The return of factionalism and the rise of Nito Alves

During his talks with Castro, Neto touched on an issue which had plagued the MPLA since its foundation: factionalism. As President of the MPLA, Neto had seen off numerous challenges to his authority – from Viriato da Cruz in 1963 to the Eastern and Active Revolt factions in 1974 – but he had intended his re-election in September 1974 to heal divisions in the party and bury factionalism for good. When the fighting in Angola developed into a struggle for MPLA's very survival, underlying enmities were briefly forgotten, but once the 'Second Liberation War' drew to a close they surfaced again, threatening to shatter party unity. Castro was sympathetic to Neto's plight – having seen off many challenges to his power over the years – but neither man realised how serious a threat this final bout of factionalism would pose to Neto's leadership, or how profoundly it would affect the future of the party as a whole.[20]

The figurehead of the new faction was Nito Alves, MPLA Minister of Internal Administration and ironically the man credited with suppressing the previous two challenges to Neto's power: the Eastern and Active Revolt factions.[21] Originally from the Dembos, Alves joined the MPLA in October 1966, infiltrating the 1st Military Region where he joined the guerrillas from the recently arrived Camilo Cienfuegos Column. Enduring desperate conditions in the Dembos – which was cut off from Brazzaville and Lusaka for years at a time – these men developed a strong sense of independence from the MPLA leadership in Lusaka, and a fierce loyalty to each other. Alves rose quickly through the MPLA's ranks and following the Carnation Revolution he came into contact with the man who became his co-conspirator, Jose Van Dúnem.[22] By the time they were both elected to the MPLA's Central Committee in September 1974, they had become a separate clique, and it was only a matter of time before they mounted a challenge to Neto's power.

The main grievance of the 'Nitistas' (as they were called) was straightforward – they were angry that their years of struggle in the Dembos had not been recognised, and they felt (with some justification) that they were being passed over for senior party appointments. Deep down, however, there was a virulent strand of racism in Alves' speeches, and it is clear that he disliked the presence of so many whites, *mestiços* and former *assimilados* in the MPLA leadership.[23] The product of the brutal conflict in the Dembos, Alves was a different man from Neto – lacking his intellectual acumen, foreign education and links with African leaders – and his radical vision for economic and social development clashed head-on with Neto's more pragmatic approach to governing Angola. According to some sources, Alves was also striving to align Angola more closely with the Soviets – in opposition to Neto's policy of maintaining economic links with the West (for the export of oil).

Alves first found a voice in the discussion groups which sprang up following the Carnation Revolution, among them the radical Cabral and Henda Committees. He then expanded his influence through mass organisations (such as the DOM which he founded in late 1975), his control of Angola's regional newspapers and radio, and even ownership of the Sambizanga football team. By December 1975 – as fighting was raging on all fronts – Neto was so concerned that he spoke out against factionalism in the MPLA, and moved quickly to crush the more radical elements before they created another split. Initially Alves led Neto's purge, closing down the Cabral and Henda Committees and arresting the remaining members of Active Revolt. But Neto soon realised that the real threat came from Alves himself and following his return from the Soviet Union in October 1976 (where he signed a generous treaty with Brezhnev) Neto moved to purge the Nitistas from the party's inner circle.

Calling a plenum meeting of the Central Committee, Neto announced a radical reorganisation of the party (formally adopting Marxist–Leninism) and a purge of the Nitistas. Alves' Ministry and the DOM were abolished, his control of the media curbed and – in an effort to remove him from the party – a Commission of Enquiry was set up to investigate factionalism within the MPLA, with particular focus on the Nitistas. It was a bold move by Neto, but by ordering the Commission to report back at the end of March he was setting a time-bomb under his leadership, giving the Nitistas five months to plan their response. By the time Castro arrived in Angola, Neto was anxiously awaiting the Commission's report, and Castro picked up on the political tension in Luanda. While in Luanda, Castro was even approached by Nitistas who were seeking Cuban and Soviet support, a sure sign that Neto's grip on power was faltering.[24] Castro rejected these advances out of hand – staunchly maintaining his support for Neto (as he had during earlier leadership crises) – but the fact that the Nitistas dared break ranks and seek his support should have alerted him to the fact that a coup was imminent.

In fact, Alves and Van Dúnem had been planning a coup for over a year. With tensions mounting in Luanda after a series of heavy-handed searches in Sambizanga (the Nitista heartland), they decided to strike before the Commission published its report. Their plans to arrest Neto and his supporters before a meeting of the Central Committee were undone, however, by a last-minute change of venue, and it went ahead as planned with the Commission accusing Alves and Van Dúnem of forming a faction. Alves fought his corner, accusing Neto of not being pro-Soviet, but the Central Committee was against him, and after twelve hours of heated debate it voted 26–6 to expel Alves and Van Dúnem from the party. Neto expected a strong response from the Nitistas, but he refused to believe they would launch a coup and never imagined the bloodbath they were planning. Following the report's publication, Alves and Van Dúnem went into hiding, and as Birmingham puts it: 'The stage was set for a *coup d'etat* which unrolled with incredible slowness, callous brutality and farcical incompetence over the next six days.'[25]

The coup conspirators were all former comrades from the 1st Military Region, and stood to gain positions in the new government.[26] Within Luanda, the Nitistas could count on the support of the FAPLA's 8th Brigade, and they planned to bring their own supporters out into the streets once the coup was launched. The coup would start with a dawn raid on the São Paulo prison to free Nitistas detainees, then they would seize the radio station and announce Neto's overthrow, calling for a public demonstration in support of Alves. Nitista death squads would round up and eliminate specific members of the government (Neto was initially to be spared) and, as crowds gathered at the Government Palace, Monstro Imortal and Bakalof would proclaim Alves the new president. With eleven Nitistas already under arrest, Alves knew time was running out, and on the morning of 27 May (after twice rescheduling the date) the Nitistas struck.

The coup, 27 May 1977

The coup began at 4 a.m. when a detachment of ten armoured cars from the FAPLA's 8th Brigade under Monstro Imortal attacked the São Paulo prison in Luanda, killing the prison warder and releasing over 150 prisoners, among them their eleven comrades arrested the previous week. The force then moved on to the radio station which it captured around 7 a.m., immediately broadcasting that the government had been overthrown by the 'MPLA Action Committee', and ordering all citizens to the Presidential Palace for a demonstration in support of Alves. Neto was no longer there, however, as several days previously, Moracén – who had heard rumours that a coup was imminent – had persuaded him to move to the Ministry of Defence, a decision Neto only accepted under duress. This building became Neto's de facto HQ, but in the rush to call in reinforcements, three FAPLA generals did not realise that the 8th Brigade was under Nitista control, and two of them – Bula and Dangereux – were captured as they entered the barracks. By 10 a.m. crowds of Alves supporters were converging on the Presidential Palace and, at Neto's insistence, Moracén sent a Cuban unit based in Vidrul (on the outskirts of Luanda) to protect the Palace. Moracén led the force in himself from the edge of the city (leaving a company of four Cuban and fifteen FAPLA tanks in Sambizanga as a reserve), and once the Palace was reinforced he set out to recapture the radio station.

By the time his force arrived at the radio station, nearly 300 civilians had gathered at the front entrance which was being guarded by a large group of Nitista soldiers and a lone armoured car. There was confusion over which soldiers were Nitistas and which were pro-government (both sides wore the same uniform), but eventually a firefight broke out which lasted for twenty minutes, Moracén leading a platoon of fifteen Cubans through the back gate to capture the building and disarm the defenders inside. Fighting off a brief counter-attack, Moracén called in the Cuban tank company, and its arrival half-an-hour later secured the radio station for the government. Striding into the recording studio at the head of his troops, Moracén grabbed the microphone from the presenter (who was in the middle of reading a biography of Alves) and forced him to say '*Viva*

Neto!' But the presenter was too terrified to say anything further, and Moracén ended up making the announcement that the radio station was back in government hands himself in faltering '*Portuñol*'. Shortly after the tank company arrived, a detachment was sent to recapture the barracks of the mutinous 8th Brigade, and this was completed without much bloodshed by 1:30p.m., officially ending the coup.

Moracén's decisive action had been pivotal in crushing the coup, and once the radio started transmitting pro-Neto announcements, the conspirators realised the coup had failed, and began making their escape. The failed coup had a nasty sting in its tail, however, as during the siege of the 8th Brigade the Nitistas had smuggled out seven senior MPLA and FAPLA members (who were captured in the early hours of the coup) and spirited them to a safe house in Sambizanga.[27] All seven were tied up, taken to an outhouse and machine-gunned, the seventh man – Comandante Gato – miraculously surviving the hail of bullets and crawling to the port where Cuban workers came to his aid. News of the killings shocked Neto, as it did the Cubans who knew many of those killed, and as the extent of the blood-letting planned by the Nitistas became apparent, Neto ordered a full-scale round-up, promising swift retribution against those involved in the killings.

The aftermath of the coup

The Alves coup attempt was the most serious challenge to Neto's authority in his fifteen years as MPLA President, and once he had retaken power he determined to eradicate Nitista influence right down to its grass roots. In the weeks following the coup, tens of thousands of Angolans were arrested – many from Alves' heartland of Sambizanga – and a nation-wide manhunt was launched to capture the coup leaders.[28] Most of the conspirators went into hiding in the Dembos, but by November they had all been apprehended.[29] They were tried in secret by the Minister of Defence, 'Iko' Carreira, and executed by firing squad, although the MPLA has still not revealed when the executions took place, or where the bodies were buried. A wide-ranging purge of the political establishment followed, the net effect of the coup murders, subsequent executions and suspensions reducing the Central Committee by a third. To purge the military, the FAPLA convened a special court martial, and thirteen officers were stripped of their ranks – among them Monstro Imortal, Bakalof and Alves.

The Cuban government reacted to the coup with a characteristic show of solidarity, Raúl Castro flying to Luanda on 12 June to demonstrate his support. Recognising Neto's weakness – and the danger that disaffected elements in the FAPLA could take advantage of this to launch a second coup (at the time the coup leaders were still at large) – he promised a further 4,000 Cuban reinforcements.[30] Raúl's offer put paid to his brother's withdrawal plans, but it was intended (as at every stage) only as a temporary measure, undertaken with the proviso that the withdrawal programme would resume once security had improved. In thanks for the Cuban help which once more had saved his government (and was continuing to prop it up), in August Neto made a private visit to Cuba, accompanied by Raúl Castro who was returning from his own African tour. Neto's visit demonstrated the closeness of the Cuban–MPLA alliance, which made dealing with the thorniest issue raised by the coup all the more difficult: namely the possibility of Soviet involvement.

Alleged Soviet complicity in the Alves coup

Alves had maintained close links with the Soviets since before the Lisbon coup – he was a frequent visitor to their Embassy in Luanda and was well-known for seeking to align the MPLA more closely with Moscow. The Soviets had shown an ambivalent attitude towards Neto's leadership over the years, and they were quite happy to flirt with challengers to Neto who seemed more amenable to their viewpoint (such as Chipenda). Uneasy in their relationship with Neto – who was fiercely protective of Angola's independence and clashed violently with the Soviets in his determination to maintain it – the Soviets looked on Alves as a man who might better serve their interests.[31] What is less clear is whether Alves told the Soviets of his plans to overthrow Neto, or, if he did, whether these plans received their blessing. On the available evidence, however, it appears that the Soviets did not intervene and simply let matters run their course, anxious not to upset the Cubans whose loyalty to Neto was constantly emphasised in their meetings with the Soviets.

Soviet inaction during the coup contrasted sharply with the Cubans, whose rapid intervention was crucial in crushing it. Moracén's insistence that Neto move out of the Presidential Palace prevented his capture (and probable death) at the hands of the Nitistas, and the Cubans' recapture of the radio station convinced the local population that the government was back in control, and triggered the flight of the conspirators. The possibility that Neto's Soviet patrons had been aware that a coup was imminent (and had done nothing to warn him) was alarming, and the cooling-off in Angolan–Soviet relations over the following months reflected Luanda's deep mistrust of Soviet motivations. Despite attempts by both the Angolan and Soviet governments to quash any suggestion of Soviet complicity in the coup,[32] privately Neto and his colleagues were convinced that the Soviets had been involved, and this meant that Cuban and Soviet policies in Angola were dangerously at odds.

Neto's First Party Congress (4–10 December 1977)

Neto's leadership of the MPLA had been shaken to the core, and in recognition of the divisions within the party he initiated a programme of radical reform which, over the next six months, transformed the MPLA into a model Communist party. By now diagnosed with cancer, Neto was determined before his death to reform the party he had led for fifteen years and resolve its chronic divisions. Modelling his approach on Cuba's Institutionalisation, Neto adopted the standard Communist party structure and ideology, replacing the old guard with a new generation of MPLA cadres headed by José Eduardo dos Santos. Anxious to repair Angola's relationship with the Soviet Union, in September Neto visited Moscow for talks with Brezhnev and Kosygin where he was awarded the Lenin Peace Prize, signalling their renewed support. By the time the First Party Congress opened on 4 December, the old MPLA – with its diversity of ideologies – had been transformed into the MPLA–Partido Trabalhador (MPLA–Workers Party), ushering in a new era of Angolan politics. During the Congress, Cuba and the Soviet Union were represented by Raúl Castro and Andrei Kirilenko respectively, the presence of the second-highest-ranking members of both governments symbolising the renewed Cuban–Soviet alliance in support of Neto.

The Cuban intervention in Ethiopia, December 1977

Raúl Castro's presence in Angola masked another purpose, as by late 1977 Cuba had been drawn into the conflict over Ethiopia's Ogaden region.[33] Since Fidel Castro's mediation between Somalia and Ethiopia in March, relations between the two countries had deteriorated. Finally, on 17 July, Somalia invaded the Ogaden with 40,000 troops and 250 tanks, hoping to capitalise on the weakness of the new regime in Addis Ababa. Denouncing Somali aggression, Cuba sent a team of military instructors to Ethiopia, and by September there were 200 Cubans operating there. In reaction to Cuban and Soviet support for Mengistu, on 13 November Mogadishu expelled all Cuban and Soviet personnel from Somalia. This produced one of the strangest moments in the Cold War when – overnight – Somalia and Ethiopia swapped sides, Soviet and Cuban personnel in Mogadishu changing places with their American counterparts in Addis Ababa. Nine days later, Somalia launched a new offensive in the Ogaden which overwhelmed the Ethiopian army, and after receiving desperate requests for help, on 21 December Castro finally agreed to send troops. Unlike Operation Carlota, however, the intervention in Ethiopia was a joint Cuban–Soviet operation from the start, the Soviets handling the transport of the troops and heavy equipment to Ethiopia while the Cubans carried out the fighting on the ground.

To assemble the Cuban force (which numbered 16,000 men), troops were drawn not only from Cuba but also from the Cuban missions in Congo-Brazzaville and Angola. Angola – which had the lion's share of Cuban personnel in Africa – would provide around 5,000 men, but this was a risky strategy as it was rumoured that the Katangese were planning a second invasion of Shaba, and this would further destabilise Angola and necessitate more Cuban reinforcements. By late February 1978 – with the fighting in the Ogaden reaching a critical phase – Castro was sufficiently concerned to send Jorge Risquet to Luanda to ask Neto to curtail Katangese activities in Angola, at least until the Ethiopian campaign was over.[34] That the Cubans should have asked the MPLA to restrain the Katangese suggests not only how little influence they had over them, but also that Luanda had the final say over when the invasion would go ahead. Risquet's request appears to have been granted, for it was not until May that 'Shaba II' finally occurred, by which time the Somalis had been driven out of the Ogaden. On 5 March, the Cuban–Ethiopian force – commanded by the popular General Arnaldo Ochoa Sánchez – captured the Jijiga and Marda Passages on the Somali border, and three days later the Somalis were forced to withdraw from the Ogaden.

Cuba's resounding success in Ethiopia – its second major intervention in Africa in only three years – further boosted Castro's prestige in Africa, and raised alarm in the new Carter administration, which feared it would be followed by a rash of other interventions across Africa. The Americans need not have worried, however, as Havana immediately reined in its military operation. With the Somalis expelled from the Ogaden, Castro refused to let Cuban forces get involved in the internal war against Eritrean secessionists, despite a visit by Mengistu to Havana. Castro was not prepared to wage war against the very guerrillas his Cuban instructors had been training during Haile Selassie's reign, and instead he tried to persuade Mengistu to find a political solution to the Eritrean insurgency, whilst reducing the Cuban military contingent from 16,000 to around 4,000 by the mid-1980s.[35] Castro's decision to keep Cuba out of the Eritrean war proved canny as Ethiopia was sucked into bloody fighting in the border area, finally losing control of Eritrea in 1993.

The 'Cassinga Raid', May 1978

Any fears Washington had that Cuba would extend its military power into other parts of Africa were allayed when, in May 1978, the SADF launched a dramatic raid into Angola, throwing its security into chaos again. South African incursions into southern Angola had been on the increase since early 1977 when SWAPO – revitalised by dozens of new training camps – had stepped up its operations in Namibia. Following a major skirmish between SWAPO and the SADF in late October 1977 (which ended fourteen miles inside Angola's borders), the SADF requested permission to launch a raid against SWAPO's southern Angolan camps. Aware of the military infrastructure SWAPO was constructing – which enabled it to infiltrate northern Namibia along a border 1,000 miles long – the SADF was keen to target SWAPO's main camps at Cassinga and Chetequera (200 miles and 17 miles north of the Namibian border respectively). In December 1977, President Vorster begrudgingly authorised the raid which was code-named 'Operation Reindeer' and, throughout early 1978, the SADF made preparations for what would be its most controversial Angolan operation.[36]

Operation Reindeer involved a simultaneous assault on both SWAPO bases. One force of 257 paratroopers (under Combat-Group Bravo's former commander Jan Breytenbach) would be dropped on 'Moscow' (the Cassinga camp) which they would destroy before withdrawing by helicopter. A second mechanised force would attack 'Vietnam' (the Chetequera camp) overland from Namibia, before withdrawing in the evening (see Map 7, page 121).[37] According to South African accounts, aerial reconnaissance revealed that both camps were well-defended – with trench networks, bunkers and AA defences – and were being used for training guerrillas (Cassinga) and as a transit camp (Chetequera) for those waiting to be infiltrated into Namibia. In the weeks following the attack, SWAPO would fiercely deny this, insisting that Cassinga was a refugee camp full of unarmed refugees, old people and children. The South Africans planned a swift attack, the element of surprise giving the paratroopers the advantage over the defenders who would outnumber them at least five-to-one, but they would have to be careful not to draw in a nearby Cuban battalion (less than ten miles to the south at Tchamutete) which could hinder their withdrawal.

At 8 a.m. on 4 May 1978, the assault began with an air strike against Cassinga by SAAF bombers. Timed to coincide with the morning parade, the air raid with 1,000 lb bombs caused devastating casualties among the hundreds of people gathered in the central square, paralysing the camp's defences. SADF paratroopers (who had accidentally been dropped over a mile from the camp) then assaulted the camp from the south, killing many of the shocked survivors. Around 2 p.m., the withdrawal by helicopter began, but at this point the Cuban garrison in Tchamutete – which had been hit by stray bombs – launched a counter-attack down the main road, threatening to cut off the South African withdrawal. Buccaneers and Mirages were called in to bomb the Cuban column, and at least sixty Cubans were killed when their vehicles – which were exposed in the middle of the road – were hit by air-to-ground missiles, bombs and small arms fire.[38] The Cuban attack disintegrated and the SADF withdrew in good order, the last paratroopers reaching Namibia by early evening. The attacking force had sustained three killed, eleven wounded and one MIA (who was never seen again). Behind them they left over 600 dead and at least 340 wounded. The attack against 'Vietnam' was also a walkover, the SADF losing just two killed and sixteen wounded before it withdrew, taking over 200 prisoners and leaving behind 250 SWAPO dead. Operation Reindeer was the SADF's single most successful operation against SWAPO, and inflicted losses in personnel and material from which SWAPO never recovered. In pure military terms the attacks were a resounding success, shattering SWAPO's Angolan infrastructure and delivering a devastating psychological blow. But in the political arena the 'Cassinga raid' (as it became known) was a disaster, sparking international outrage. Five days after the attacks, SWAPO flew in a team of Western journalists who photographed two mass graves containing a total of 582 men, women and children who had been killed in the attack. Rejecting accusations that it had committed a war crime, the SADF insisted that the defenders of Cassinga were armed and in uniform. Furthermore, the fighting had been so intense that its troops stayed for two hours longer than expected, withdrawing with some parts of the camp still under SWAPO control. Opponents of the apartheid regime maintain the opposite, describing the attack as a 'massacre at bayonet-point of unarmed women, children and old people'.[39] The SADF's admission that some of those killed may have been women and children (who were caught in the cross-fire or were combatants themselves) has only reinforced this impression. Nevertheless, the failure of any of the paratroopers to speak out in twenty-five years is puzzling, and suggests that many (though not all) of those killed were defending the camp.[40] Ultimately, opinion is still fiercely divided, and to this day even South African writers who support the SADF version of events admit that the whole story has yet to come out.

The international outrage which followed the 'Cassinga raid' was seized on by SWAPO, the MPLA and Cuba which were only too happy to side-step the more embarrassing question of how the SADF had wiped out two of SWAPO's most important camps with almost complete impunity. Cuban defensive reactions to the attack had been woefully inadequate, and the damage done to SWAPO's offensive capability and its reputation would take years to rebuild. More ominously, however, the raid demonstrated that South Africa would no longer tolerate SWAPO and MK camps in Angola, and was prepared to strike at them directly. The prospect of a prolonged cross-border campaign could only have one impli-cation for the Cubans in Angola, ruling out any reduction in the Cuban contingent for the foreseeable future. Fanciful withdrawal plans were nev-ertheless drawn up by the Cubans in 1979, but the truth was that the 'Cassinga raid' had exposed the fragility of Angola's defences, and while the South African threat remained, the Cubans would have to stay put.

The 'Shaba II' invasion, May–June 1978

Less than a fortnight after the 'Cassinga raid' the world's attention swung back to southern Zaire where, on 17 May, a force of 6,500 Katangese gendarmes invaded Shaba, quickly capturing Kolwesi and threatening to take control of the copper-rich province.[41] Several foreign-owned copper mines were damaged in the fighting, and then, in a rerun of the previous year's invasion, the rapid intervention of a French and Belgian military force drove the Katangese out of Kolwesi (with much bloodshed) and back across the Angolan border. Though quashed as quickly as Shaba I, Shaba II had more serious repercussions, not only for the Katangese but for Angola itself. The timing of the invasion could not have been worse for Castro, as it diverted attention away from the 'Cassinga raid' and focused it instead on Havana for supposedly masterminding the invasion. On 25 May, President Carter – whose administration had offered only a muted reaction to both Shaba I and the intervention in Ethiopia – accused Cuba of direct involvement, an allegation the Cuban leader denied. Not for the first time, Castro was discovering the limitations of his influence over the MPLA which was prepared to pursue its own goals irrespective of the damage they did to his regional strategy. Having twice been caught off-guard, Castro would not allow a 'Shaba III', and he admonished Neto to resolve the issue once and for all.

Katangese motivations for launching a second invasion are unclear, but it is likely that the incursion of a large FNLA force into the Cazombo salient (Moxico) the previous March goaded the MPLA into action.[42] Determined to step up the pressure on Mobutu to curtail FNLA and FLEC activities, Luanda probably authorised a second invasion of Shaba without anticipating the negative reaction it would provoke. Accusations of Cuban involvement appear to be without foundation, however, although rumours continue to circulate that Cuban officers helped plan the invasion, and even accompanied the Katangese into Shaba.[43] Under pressure from Cuba and the USA, Angola and Zaire were coaxed to the negotiating table, and in July 1978 – scarcely a month after the last Katangese withdrew into Angola – Neto and Mobutu signed a second non-aggression pact. In a simple *quid pro quo*, Neto pledged to disarm and repatriate the Katangese if Mobutu pulled back FNLA, FLEC and UNITA bases from the border, and cut off military aid to them.[44] This time the deal stuck and the Katangese were disarmed and repatriated (with the assistance from Cuban troops) while FNLA, FLEC and UNITA bases along the Angolan–Zairian border were shut down.[45] The deal was the end of the line for the FNLA, and Roberto would spend a little over a year trying to hold out in Kinshasa before he was expelled for good.

UN Security Council Resolution 435

With the FNLA threat to northern Angola eradicated, Havana and Luanda received a further boost on 29 September 1978 when the UN Security Council passed Resolution 435, demanding South Africa's withdrawal from Namibia, to be followed by its independence and free elections.[46] The passing of Resolution 435 – fuelled by revulsion at the carnage of the 'Cassinga raid' – was a major diplomatic victory for SWAPO, and gave its war against South Africa international legitimacy. From 1978 onwards, Resolution 435 formed the keystone of SWAPO, MPLA and Cuban policy in the region, and all three parties would use every opportunity to demand its implementation, determined to capitalise on the advantage they had gained over the South Africans. Unfortunately for SWAPO and the Cubans, however, far from forcing the South Africans to pull out of Namibia, Resolution 435 became the principal obstacle to their withdrawal, locking the negotiations in an impasse which was to last for nearly a decade.

For the reality was that South Africa would not withdraw from Namibia while SWAPO and MK were still operating from bases across Angola. In Pretoria's eyes the struggle against these two movements was the struggle for the survival of apartheid, and though there was general consensus in South Africa that Namibia should be granted independence, Pretoria would not allow this if it meant handing over the country to a hostile SWAPO government which could position MK forces up against South Africa's borders. Indeed, the 'Cassinga raid' had been launched specifically to counter SWAPO's growing threat to Namibian security, and unless this threat was addressed Pretoria would never accept any form of withdrawal. Pretoria's opponents saw no reason to compromise, however, and doggedly insisted on the implementation of Resolution 435 as the only acceptable resolution to the Namibia question. It would take a new approach under the new American Secretary of State for African Affairs – 'linkage' – to break the logjam, and lay the groundwork for a lasting regional settlement (see Chapter 8).

Neto's last year

One month after the passing of Resolution 435, the MPLA imposed a curfew in Huambo and Kuito-Bié – UNITA's core areas of support – finally acknowledging the seriousness of its insurgency. Unbowed by seven offensives launched against it since April 1976, UNITA had emerged as a highly effective guerrilla army, and by late 1978 it was expanding its operations from bases in Cuando Cubango into Moxico and Bié.[47] Simultaneously the SADF stepped up its cross-border campaign, on 7 March 1979 launching dual operations – Rekstok and Saffraan – against SWAPO and

MK camps in Angola and Zambia. Although these operations were inconclusive, the SAAF did destroy MK's main training camp at Novo
Catengue, killing two MK guerrillas and one Cuban officer in the air-
strike. With Angola's security steadily deteriorating, Neto entered into
secret ceasefire talks with Savimbi, determined to end the insurgency and
incorporate UNITA into the government before his death.[48] But these
talks came to nothing as, in September 1979 – with his health deteriorating
– Neto left Angola for cancer treatment in the Soviet Union. The Soviet
doctors could do little for him as, by this stage his liver and pancreas
cancer were far advanced, and on 10 September Neto died in a Moscow
clinic.[49]

News of Neto's death was greeted with an emotional outpouring in
Angola, the MPLA's Central Committee declaring forty-five days of
national mourning. Viewed by many Angolans as their greatest national
hero, Neto's premature death was a blow to party unity which threatened
to reopen the damaging factional splits of the past, and moves were immediately made to elect a new leader with a broad consensus of support.
Brushing aside the more controversial candidates – including die-hard veterans Lúcio Lara and Lopo do Nascimento – on 21 September the MPLA
chose the lesser-known José Eduardo dos Santos, at the time only thirty-
seven years old.[50] The decision to elect Dos Santos was taken because he
was the consensus choice, and few at the time had any inkling of how successfully he would entrench his position as President of Angola. Described
as 'perhaps Africa's most frightened Marxist',[51] Dos Santos would prove a
far less reliable ally for Cuba and the Soviet Union than Neto, and would
oversee the MPLA's transformation from an ostensibly Marxist–Leninist
party into the venal cryptocracy it is today.

In an ironic coincidence, Neto's demise was followed almost immediately by the eclipse of his main rival, Holden Roberto. Having struggled to
maintain Mobutu's favour in the wake of the 'Shaba II' invasion, Roberto
was finally expelled from Zaire in November 1979 (while he was in Paris
receiving medical treatment), effectively ending his involvement in the
Angolan War. Disaffected FNLA elements nevertheless fought on under
new leadership – forming the FNLA–COMIRA (Angolan Military Resistance Committee) – but they proved ineffective, and by late 1983 had
ceased to play any part in the conflict. Roberto's removal from international affairs contrasted sharply with his rival Savimbi who visited
Washington the same month, meeting with Henry Kissinger and Alexander Haig. Although constrained by the Clark Amendment, Washington
was determined to cultivate its relationship with Savimbi who it viewed as
a bulwark against Communist expansion into southern Africa. Informal
contacts with UNITA would continue throughout the early 1980s until the
repeal of the Clark Amendment cleared the way for a programme of military aid (see Chapter 9).

The 'Second Cold War' erupts, renewing superpower interest in Angola

Renewed American interest in Savimbi was the result of a sea-change in international politics between 1979 and 1981 which unleashed the 'Second Cold War', drawing Angola back into the epicentre of superpower confrontation. Throughout 1979, a series of revolutions and military coups brought down several Western-backed regimes – most notably in Iran and Nicaragua – causing alarm in Washington which feared the spread of Soviet influence into these areas. When Soviet troops invaded Afghanistan on Christmas Day, the Carter administration abandoned détente and condemned the invasion, discarding the SALT II Treaty recently signed by both parties. As a new generation of Western leaders emerged – headed by Margaret Thatcher and Ronald Reagan – Western governments adopted a more confrontational approach towards the Soviet bloc, sparking a series of proxy wars across the globe.[52] Already the victim of reckless foreign intervention, Angola would once more be drawn into the Cold War, encouraging the Soviets to increase their involvement, and eventually leading to their complete take over of the FAPLA's operations (see Chapter 8).

South Africa adopts 'Total Onslaught'

The catalyst which unleashed Angola's second round of conflict did not come from outside Africa, however, but from Zimbabwe which gained independence in April 1980. Since the mid-1960s, an intermittent guerrilla war had raged in Southern Rhodesia between the white minority government and African nationalist forces (ZANU and ZAPU) but, by late 1979, it had reached a stalemate. On 5 December all parties agreed to a ceasefire and negotiations brokered by the former colonial power Britain. In elections held in February 1980, Robert Mugabe (leader of ZANU) was elected President. The election of a declared Marxist–Leninist and outspoken opponent of apartheid confirmed Pretoria's worst nightmare, and sent shock waves through the government. Having steadily lost its regional allies in the fight against African nationalism,[53] South Africa now faced the prospect of fighting alone against a hostile continent, and with its back to the wall it adopted the 'Total Onslaught' policy. Convinced that the forces of Communism (and implicitly African nationalism) were ranged in a 'total onslaught' against the apartheid regime, Pretoria vowed to strike back at any neighbouring states which harboured anti-apartheid forces.

Almost immediately the SADF stepped up its cross-border campaign against SWAPO and MK bases in Angola, Mozambique and Zambia. On 10 June 1980, the SADF launched its largest operation since the Second World War – Operation Sceptic – against a SWAPO command-and-control centre at Chifufua (110 miles north of the Namibian border).[54]

During heavy fighting, 360 SWAPO guerrillas were killed (versus seventeen SADF) and the camp destroyed, but as the SADF was withdrawing it was attacked by the FAPLA, the first engagement between the two forces since the cross-border campaign began. This was a worrying development for the SADF which had waged its war against SWAPO in isolation, and it marked the start of eight years of violent clashes with the FAPLA in southern Angola. Sceptic was followed on 30 July by a lightning raid by eighty SADF paratroopers on a SWAPO base at Chitado (just over the border near Ruacaná), but attempts to keep FAPLA troops out of the fighting again failed, and several were among the twenty-seven defenders killed in the attack. South African assistance in UNITA's capture of Mavinga in September further cemented the alliance with Savimbi, and by the end of the year the SADF was considering the permanent occupation of parts of southern Angola.

Talks between Angola, SWAPO and South Africa had been underway at the UN since 1979 on the setting-up of a demilitarised zone in southern Angola, but by 1981 they had lost all meaning as UNITA had taken control of the area under discussion. With SWAPO intensifying its insurgency and the SADF's alliance with UNITA growing ever closer, Pretoria decided to create a 'buffer zone' in southern Angola which could be placed under joint SADF–UNITA control, and plans were drawn up for a full-scale invasion. Operation Protea (named after South Africa's national flower) would involve 5,000 troops, supported by Centurion tanks, Ratel armoured cars and Mirage fighters. It was intended not only to destroy SWAPO's presence along the border, but also the FAPLA's which had grown over the previous five years and now posed a threat to Namibia. Its principal objectives were Xangongo and N'Giva (where there were large FAPLA–SWAPO concentrations), the destruction of the air-defence installations at Cahama (which the Cubans had helped the FAPLA set up) and the annihilation of all SWAPO–FAPLA forces encountered en route.

Operation Protea (August 1981)

Operation Protea began on 23 August 1981 with an air-strike on the FAPLA's air defence and radar installations in Cahama and Chilemba, completely destroying them.[55] Simultaneously, a mechanised SADF force crossed into Angola and occupied Humbe, cutting off Xangongo from reinforcements in Cahama. The following day Xangongo was captured by a second SADF column after a brief fight, and the combined force moved on to N'Giva, brushing aside an FAPLA holding position at Môngua. The defenders of N'Giva – FAPLA and SWAPO troops advised by Soviet officers and probably some Cubans too – were better prepared and put up a brave defence, fighting off three assaults before abandoning the town after their artillery was destroyed. The South Africans then moved on to their final objective, Cahama, but twelve miles south of the town they ran into heavy defences, and were forced to pull back to Uia. By the end of August, the SADF had captured 15,000 square miles of Angolan territory, and seized over 3,000 tons of Soviet weaponry, armour and supplies (most of which was handed on to UNITA).[56] Over 1,000 casualties had been inflicted on the FAPLA–SWAPO forces for the loss of ten SADF killed and several dozen wounded. Most significantly of all, however, before withdrawing, the SADF installed two garrisons at Xangongo and N'Giva, enforcing its occupation of southern Cunene.

Cuban reaction to Operation Protea

The Cuban reaction to Operation Protea was uncharacteristically muted. Aside from predictable protests at the UN and OAS, no military action was taken by Cuban troops in Angola. Despite the fact that MMCA had over 10,000 men dug in along the ATS Defence Line, Cuban forces remained in their positions, while the garrisons in Xangongo and N'Giva were wiped out. Possibly the Cubans ruled out an immediate counter-attack in case Lubango turned out to be one of Operation Protea's object-ives, but once the South Africans stopped short of Cahama it is puzzling that Cuban forces made no effort to recapture Xangongo or N'Giva. Cuban troops were, after all, in Angola for the specific (and oft-stated) purpose of repelling foreign aggression, and Operation Protea was a blatant violation of Angola's territorial integrity. In November 1975, the invasion of South African troops had been sufficient for Cuba to launch the largest military intervention in its history, yet only six years later – with thousands of Cuban troops less than 150 miles from the fighting – the Cubans held back from any contact with the invaders.

Clearly something fundamental had changed in the running of the Cuban operation, and the reckless adventurism of Operation Carlota had given way to a more defensive strategy. The root of this change appears to have been in Cuba itself, where the government was still recovering from the worst domestic crisis in the Revolution's twenty-one years – the April 1980 Mariel boatlift. Following the panicked departure of nearly 125,000 Cubans from the port of Mariel to Florida, domestic support for the Cuban Revolution had been severely shaken, and a great deal of effort was made by the Cuban government to improve basic living conditions, including some modest economic reforms. When South African troops invaded Angola less than a year after the boatlift, therefore, it appears that Havana was unwilling to escalate its military operations in Angola for fear of the domestic backlash.

141

The end of Cuban plans to withdraw from Angola

The result of Cuban reticence was to hand South Africa a permanent foothold in southern Angola from which it could operate against SWAPO and MK bases with greater ease and mobility. The FAPLA–SWAPO forces in southern Angola had been decidedly outclassed by the SADF, and although Cahama was saved they were in no position to launch a counter-attack against the two SADF garrisons based in Cunene. Both the FAPLA and SWAPO would require re-training and re-equipping before they could contemplate such a move, and in the meantime the defence of southern Angola depended on the Cuban-manned ATS Defence Line. South Africa's occupation of southern Cunene thus turned the ATS into the front-line of the Angolan war, and this ruled out any talk of a Cuban withdrawal for the foreseeable future. Indeed, within five months of Operation Protea, Cuba would commit itself to sending a further 7,000 troops to bolster the Cuban contingent as part of a new Soviet military programme for the FAPLA (see Chapter 8). Against all expectations, Cuba's intervention force had become a permanent army of occupation, and over the next four years Castro would struggle in vain to prevent his troops getting sucked into Cuba's Vietnam.

7

'THE PEOPLE'S WAR'

Cuban internationalists in Angola, 1975–91

The Cuban people have endured many ideological and political experiments during more than forty years of revolution, but few have affected as many Cubans quite so directly as the sixteen-year intervention in Angola. Between 1975 and 1991, over 430,000 Cubans served on internationalist missions in Angola, in the military and as part of a civilian programme involving doctors, teachers, technicians and construction workers.[1] For a generation of Cubans, internationalist service in Angola represented the highest ideal of the Cuban Revolution, and by the end of the 1980s Angola had become (in García Márquez's phrase) a 'People's War',[2] involving as much as 5 per cent of the Cuban population.[3] With the withdrawal of Cuban forces from Angola constantly being postponed, the FAR looked to the civilian population for manpower, and with the humanitarian programme expanding in tandem, a vast logistical operation evolved, processing tens of thousands of internationalists each year. By the mid-1980s, Angola had become the standard 'tour of duty' for Cuban youth, resurrecting (and once more remoulding) Guevara's model of internationalism, and radicalising a generation of Cubans who grew up under the Revolution and who were eager to prove their revolutionary credentials.[4]

Expanding the Cuban operation in Angola

Although the internationalist mission in Angola was not Cuba's first foreign intervention – there were at least half a dozen before November 1975 – it dwarfed its predecessors and placed enormous strain on the FAR's manpower.[5] Prior to 1975, the FAR drew internationalist volunteers from its professional ranks, favouring MININT and FAR artillery officers whose skills were of most use to guerrillas recruits. Given the small size of the Cuban contingents, these missions were heavily oversubscribed. With the launch of Operation Carlota, however, the FAR turned to the national reserve for reinforcements, and with constant extensions to the mission's deadline it was only a matter of time before this expanded to include conscripts on military service.[6] The FAR quickly discovered that

143

servicemen fresh out of school were preferable to reservists who tended to have dependants in Cuba and were costly to replace in the workplace and, by the early 1980s, national servicemen formed the bulk of troops serving in Angola.[7] Thus very quickly Cuban civilians were drawn into the Angolan operation, and within two years of its launch MMCA had evolved from a small training mission manned by elite officers into a huge occupying army made up of Cuban civilians (although command of the operation remained within the professional ranks of the FAR).

The Cubans who served in Angola were part of a new generation born during the Revolution who were keen for adventure and anxious to prove their credentials. The Cuban regime – which at first fought to curtail the operation in Angola – discovered that service abroad was the ideal vehicle for politicising Cuban youth, and by the early 1980s internationalist service (principally in Angola) had become part of a broader political programme which included voluntary work (such as cane-cutting) and political rallies. The Cuban regime was keen to channel the vitality of this younger generation into activities which would radicalise them and ensure their future support, and in the aftermath of Operation Carlota a highly effective propaganda campaign was launched to promote the ideals of internationalism, not only giving the ideology a sense of historical mission, but also emphasising the ties linking Cuba and Angola which (it claimed) made Cuban support for the MPLA inevitable.

The Cuban government also had pragmatic reasons for maintaining a contingent of 5,000 civilians and up to 65,000 troops in Angola as, by the late 1970s, Cuba was experiencing the dual effects of long-term overemployment and the coming of age of the 'Baby Boom' generation. In 1959, Cuba had suffered the same catastrophic exodus of skilled talent that Angola did sixteen years later but, thanks to an ambitious training programme, by the early 1970s Cuba had produced a surplus of doctors, teachers and engineers for whom it was doubtful there would be enough postings. Government institutions and businesses were chronically overstaffed (they remain so to this day), and it is no surprise that both were able to send their most experienced workers to Angola – often for years at a time – without effecting productivity (if such a concept can be applied to the Cuban economy). The ever-increasing demand for troops in Cuba's expanding African operations also proved ideal for absorbing the thousands of Cuban 'babyboomers' who were about to enter the job market, and to some extent alleviated Cuba's overstaffing problems.

The rebirth and remoulding of 'Cuban internationalism'

The involvement of Cuba's civilian population in Angola called for an ideological overhaul, and shortly after the launch of Operation Carlota, Guevara's model of internationalism was resurrected and re-moulded to fit the new agenda. Anxious to recapture the idealism that motivated Cuba's first revolutionaries in the 1960s, a sustained propaganda drive was launched to highlight the historical precedents of internationalism in Cuba, much of it of dubious validity. Conscious of Cubans' strong sense of patriotism, internationalism was declared 'a sentiment higher than patriotism', while fighting for the freedom of Angola was 'more noble than fighting for the independence of one's own land'.[8] A path for internationalism was traced through Cuban history, stretching from the sixteenth-century Indian chief Hatuey through to the 10,000 Cubans who fought during the Spanish Civil War. Although, to judge from the first Cuban internationalists sent to Africa in the 1960s, this ideology was a creation of the Revolution rather than a genuine Cuban tradition.[9]

The bedrock of the Revolution's new ideology rested on the ethnic and cultural ties between Africa and Cuba's Afro-Cuban population, and on this issue it was on firmer ground. The slave trade lasted longer in Cuba than in any other part of the Caribbean (from 1521 until the late 1870s), and during this period 1.3 million African slaves passed through Cuba, representing nearly one tenth of all slaves sent to the Americas.[10] Around one-third of these slaves came from the Bantu ethnic group – which includes the Bakongo and Abudu from northern Angola and southern Zaire – and their cultural influence can still be seen in the '*palo monte*' religion practised in Cuba today. Exhaustive research even unearthed an Angolan slave – Aquilino Amézaga from Soyo – who escaped from his Cuban plantation during the War for Independence and joined Serafín Sánchez's troops, rising to the rank of captain.[11]

Where the argument starts to falls apart, however, is in the assertion that Havana's status as the principal slave entrepôt of the Americas engendered a 'historical debt' which ordinary Cubans were duty bound to repay through internationalist service in Africa.[12] For not only was the Revolution's survival the result of a pragmatic and often opportunistic foreign policy which took no account of 'historical debts' but, prior to Operation Carlota, Cuban involvement in Africa had been chaotic, switching from Algeria to Brazzaville and then to Conakry in the search for reliable allies. If Cuba had been concerned about its historical debt to the Yorubas (one-fifth of slaves sent to Cuba) then it would have intervened in the Biafra War (1967–70) rather than concentrating its efforts on the PAIGC in Guiné. By the same token, Havana's lack of support for the MPLA in its most desperate hours (in 1961, 1972 and 1974) suggests that political priorities rather than historical guilt drove its involvement in Angola.

The threat that Argüelles's mission and his Angolan allies would be wiped out was the trigger for Operation Carlota, not the desire to repay a historical debt, and Cuba's resulting occupation of Angola was one of its unintended consequences, forcing the army to draw on Cuba's civilian population for manpower. Of course, this does not mean that the majority of Cubans who served in Angola did not passionately believe in internationalism and Cuba's 'historical debt' to Africa. But the weakness of Cuba's 'unbreakable' ties with Angola and the ideology which inspired internationalists to risk their lives there has been confirmed by the complete disappearance of Angola from the political agenda in the decade since Cuba completed its withdrawal.

Personal motivations for serving in Angola

Aside from strong ideological beliefs, the more than 400,000 Cubans who accepted internationalist missions to Angola were motivated by selfless and selfish reasons, some of which went hand-in-hand.[13] The vast majority of young Cubans were keen to emulate Che Guevara whose idealised image they had been raised on, and many hoped to match the feats of their fathers during the Revolution. Some had more mundane motivations for going, however. Nearly all the younger veterans agreed to go to Angola in part out of curiosity – to see what Africa was really like and to confirm if the exaggerated stories they had heard of cannibals, man-eating snakes and zombies were true.[14] Some agreed to an internationalist mission to reduce their military service by one year (missions in Angola lasted two years whereas military service in Cuba was a minimum of three), and many saw the opportunity to travel to Angola as a way of escaping the boredom of life in Cuba – or in some cases family problems. Nevertheless – except in the rarest of cases – it is clear that all those who served in Angola were motivated by strong ideological beliefs, even if today some feel they were rather young and impressionable at the time.

Selection procedure for internationalist military service in Angola

The call-up procedure for reservists and national servicemen was similar to that used in November 1975, although the FAR made sure it did not repeat the chaotic scenes which accompanied Operation Carlota when thousands of reservists fought to get a place on ships bound for Angola. The selection of internationalists was dealt with by Military Committees (*Comités Militares*) in each Cuban municipality. When the FAR required a new unit for Angola, the Provincial Army Staff contacted the Military Committees under its jurisdiction and requested a percentage of men from each, leaving the selection procedure to the Committees.[15] Reserves and those about to start military service were called to their local Military Committee for an interview by a panel of up to a dozen officers and doctors. After a medical examination they were asked the same carefully-worded question: 'Are you prepared to carry out an internationalist mission abroad?' The country was never specified (volunteers learned where they were going only days beforehand). They were told only that the mission would last a minimum of eighteen months, although this might be extended by a further six.[16] During this time their salary would be paid to their families (reservists were guaranteed their jobs back), and they received room and board in Angola plus a small stipend which varied according to rank. Service on internationalist missions was strictly voluntary, and should a candidate decline his decision was – at least in theory – without prejudice.

In practice, however, the candidate's decision was not as voluntary as the Cuban regime has depicted it. For Castro, it was essential that all internationalists went to Angola voluntarily, not only to refute accusations that Cuba was using its citizens as unwilling pawns in its international adventures, but more importantly to prevent a 'Vietnam scenario' developing, with mass protests against conscription and draft-dodging. As a result, all Cubans were asked if they were prepared to volunteer for the mission, and no internationalist left Cuba without first signing a form declaring their free participation. Every Cuban veteran I interviewed stated explicitly that they went to Angola voluntarily (those who initially refused were given several opportunities to change their mind), but several admitted that they felt they had little choice but to accept for fear of the repercussions if they refused. At the time it was feared that if you refused you would be assigned to the toughest units in Cuba for military service (in Oriente or Pinar del Río), or that you would prejudice your chances of getting a place at university or your future career (both of which were controlled by the government). Several veterans recall that those who refused were criticised and ridiculed in public, and this might explain why very few Cubans turned down the offer.[17] Ultimately the evidence is contradictory, and while on paper all Cubans went voluntarily to Angola, many did so under psychological coercion.

Anomalies in the selection procedure

Several anomalies in the selection procedure stand out, however, in particular the small proportion of *habaneros* (Cubans from Havana) who served in Angola. Despite containing at least 20 per cent of the Cuban population, fewer than 1 per cent of internationalists sent to Angola were from Havana.[18] The reason for this disparity is not immediately clear – indeed, the Cuban government has never even acknowledged it – but it would appear to be ideological. Since the mid-1950s, Havana has resisted revolutionary change, having been the centre of the entertainment industry, various corrupt dictatorships (backed by the mafia) and Cuba's middle class. This is reflected to this day by the disproportionately high level of policing compared to the provinces.[19] When seeking volunteers for

Angola, therefore, the Cuban government appears to have drawn on its core regions of support – in particular Oriente (where Castro and the Revolutionary Army were born) and other parts of Cuba which have experienced some improvement in their standard of living since Castro came to power – and took only a handful from Havana, anxious to avoid exacerbating social tensions in the city.

Even thornier an issue is whether black Cubans were sent to Angola in disproportionately large numbers while whites avoided the worst of the fighting, an accusation made by several veterans and foreign governments. This contentious issue will probably never be resolved as the question of race in Cuba is extremely emotional and overwrought, many Cubans refusing to be classified as 'mulattos' or 'negros' despite their ethnic origin.[20] The Cuban government is acutely sensitive to accusations of racism as it has depicted its regime as a champion of racial rights. But its case is undermined by the fact that, prior to 1975, all Cubans sent on internationalist missions to Africa were black, a policy adopted in the belief that black Cubans would blend more easily with the local population. Ironically, many black Cubans in the FAR may have looked on Angola as an opportunity to gain promotion otherwise denied to them in Cuba. Indeed by the end of the war several black officers – including Kindelán, Schueg, Moracén and 'Pombo' – had achieved top ranks in the FAR thanks to internationalist service. However, until verifiable data on the ethnic make-up of the internationalist brigades comes to light, no useful conclusions can be drawn on this issue.

Equally contentious a question is whether – as subsequent defectors from the regime have claimed – senior members of the FAR and PCC used their influence to control where they or their family and friends were posted in Angola, and what role they were assigned. Castro's most outspoken critic – Brigadier-General Rafael del Pino who defected to the USA in May 1987 (see Chapter 9) – claimed that the sons of Politburo members 'not only do not go to Angola, but they do not even do their military service', and that the few who did were posted to Luanda or Lubango 'where the worst that can happen to [them] is to get bitten by a mosquito carrying malaria'.[21] Other sources have claimed that senior Cuban officers used their influence to take their lovers to Angola as 'internationalist workers', where they would be kept in a luxurious lifestyle but nevertheless received the usual diplomas and medals when they returned to Cuba.[22] One case involved the highly decorated General Arnaldo Ochoa, and was the first of several accusations of moral corruption levelled at him on his return from Angola (see Chapter 12). Like all of the above accusations of corruption, this also requires further investigation.

Procedure for travelling to Angola

Once the quota of internationalists had been selected, they were assigned to their units, the reservists taking up specialist roles in their old units while the servicemen made up the bulk of the soldiers. Volunteers received forty-five days of basic training (those assigned specialised tasks took longer – for example, a tank driver took around six months to train), although this was sometimes reduced when there was an emergency in Angola. Internationalists were not allowed to reveal their destination to anyone (few knew themselves), and it was only once the Cuban operation in Angola became firmly established (around 1980) that internationalists could talk more openly about their missions.[23] Internationalist soldiers were issued with uniforms and weaponry before leaving Cuba, while the heavy equipment (such as tanks, BM-21s and armoured cars) was sent directly from the Soviet Union to Angola to be operated by the Cubans before it was handed on to the FAPLA. The bulk of the troops went by ship in contingents of around 1,000 men, and the transports *Leonid Sovinov*, *Vietnam*, *Trece de marzo* and *Habano* made dozens of crossings throughout the war, the *Habano* being sunk in a raid on Namibe in June 1986 (see Chapter 9). Units were seen off from Havana or Mariel by senior officers – often by Fidel or Raúl Castro themselves – and after a crossing of around fourteen days (usually via Cape Verde) they were separated into their units and posted to wherever they were needed in Angola.

The majority of officers, weapons specialists and civilian internationalists went by air, using a different procedure. They were first called to concentration points around Havana (for example, at Lomba Blanca) where they were issued with civilian clothes (such as *guayaberas*), a suitcase and a passport before boarding the aircraft for Angola. It was essential that all internationalists were issued with passports – a deliberately time-consuming and expensive procedure in Cuba – in case an incident arose en route (such as an aircraft breaking down) which required them to disembark and go through customs in a third country. On arrival in Luanda, however, all internationalists (including those who came by ship) had to surrender their passports, a measure adopted to prevent Cubans defecting to the West.[24] This measure caused some resentment, for not only did it effectively imprison internationalists in Angola until Havana decided to recall them, but it did not apply to PCC members or senior officers, a clear abuse of privilege. Only when they were due to leave Angola would non-Party internationalists get their passports back, ensuring the government maintained as much control over its citizens' movements abroad as it did in Cuba.

Charges for the Cuban internationalist mission

The issue of who paid for Cuba's military and civilian operation in Angola is still hotly disputed. According to the Cuban government, all military aid was given to Angola free of charge, the Cubans providing the manpower while the Soviets supplied all the weaponry, supplies and equipment for the FAPLA and the Cuban troops posted there.[25] Humanitarian aid was initially free too but, in 1977, Luanda committed to paying the living expenses of the civilian contingent (around 5,000 strong) with an additional increase scheduled for 1978.[26] The decision to charge the MPLA was taken because Angola was an oil-exporting country, but the exact amount of money paid to Cuba is still contested.[27] In 1989, Castro declared that Angola paid Cuba $20 million per year for its humanitarian operation, a 'modest fee' given that any other country would have charged four to five times that amount.[28] Other sources, however, allege that Cuba was making between $300m and $700m per year from the difference between the fee paid by Angola and the salary paid to internationalists back in Cuba.[29] But whatever the financial arrangement between Luanda and Havana, it was short-lived as, by the early 1980s – with the Angolan economy imploding under UNITA's onslaught and a mushrooming foreign debt – the MPLA was unable to meet its commitments. After a visit to Havana by Dos Santos in March 1984, Havana agreed that Angola would no longer have to pay for humanitarian assistance, and it was provided free of charge for the remainder of the Cuban operation.[30]

Cuban internationalist soldiers in Angola, 1975–91

The experience of Cuban soldiers serving in Angola varied greatly, depending on where they were posted, and what role they were assigned. For those garrisoning the main cities – Luanda, Benguela and Lubango – the living conditions were, on the whole, good. Although they were housed in separate camps from the FAPLA and forbidden all contact with the local population (unless authorised), there was enough food and entertainment in the camps – including bars and even a cinema – to keep the troops happy. Like the civilian internationalists, senior and specialist officers (such as pilots and weapons experts) were housed in their own buildings in the city centre where they ate, slept and socialised. Most had additional privileges, such as being able to visit the officers' club at the Quinta Rosa Linda (near the Futungo de Belas palace in Luanda). Soldiers based in remote outposts in Huíla, Moxico and Cuando Cubango endured far worse conditions, however, with infrequent deliveries of supplies and the vast emptiness of the Angolan interior contributing to their boredom and frustration.[31] One veteran recalled eating nothing but tinned ham for six months, and then corned beef for the next six. Ironically the

Cuban policy of keeping its troops out of the firing-line enhanced the monotony of life in the interior, and with supplies in chronic shortage it was only a matter of time before Cubans sneaked out of camp to scavenge for what they could find. With the growth of UNITA in southern and eastern Angola, this became a dangerous exercise, and Cubans soon turned to the only other source of goods, the *candonga* (black market).

The *candonga* in Angola

As one would expect for a country ravaged by over a decade of warfare and in the grip of a guerrilla insurgency, by the late 1970s Angola had developed a vibrant black market supplying everything from basic food-stuffs to weaponry and medications, much of its stolen from the docks in Luanda or Benguela.[32] Each town had its own *candonga* (literally, a mar-ketplace), some of which were enormous (throughout the 1980s, Luanda's Roque Santeiro was the single largest marketplace in the world).[33] Although off-limits to Cubans, the *candonga* was a hub of commercial activity between the Angolans and the internationalists. Black market deals between foreign soldiers and local populations are common in warfare – they have occurred during every military confrontation in history – but the Cubans were particularly adept at dealing on the *candonga* having had years of experience surviving in Cuba's equally corrupt and starved economy.[34] Despite severe penalties for being caught in the *candonga*, Cubans regularly sneaked out of camp to buy supplies there, to trade goods and occasionally to negotiate large deals. Cubans also traded with SWAPO, and a trade network developed between the Cubans, SWAPO and the *candonga* – on occasion involving UNITA too.

One controversial scam was the trading of used AK-47s, and involved most of the forces fighting in southern Angola. The AK-47 (or its modified version, the AKM) was the most common weapon issued to the FAPLA during the Angolan War (it is the most produced weapon in history). Many ended up in UNITA hands, either seized from dead or captured FAPLA soldiers, or traded with them in secret. Cubans would then capture the AK-47s from UNITA during clashes on patrol, bury them in crates until the time was right, and then sell them to SWAPO who were mostly issued with outdated Yugoslav rifles. Occasionally SWAPO would trade old AK-47s for newer ones issued to the FAPLA, and the trade cycle was complete. On occasion – when they had nothing to trade – some Cubans would resort to theatrical diversions (such as starting a bogus fight or firing an AK-47 in the air) to distract attention while they grabbed what they could from the nearest stalls and made their escape. But all *candon-gas* near Cuban units were patrolled by FAPLA and Cuban military police (the 'green berets'), and Cubans caught in the *candonga* faced five days in the hole.

The *candonga* was not out of bounds to officers, however, and they regularly visited it under the pretext of looking for Cuban soldiers who were AWOL. Although officers were officially forbidden to trade on the *candonga*, the difficulty of getting even the most basic supplies to Cuban troops in the Angolan interior led to a number of exemptions – most notably the bartering of Cuban sugar and salt for basic supplies. This loophole gradually widened to include trade in all sorts of luxury items and weaponry, and by the late 1980s the commander of the Cuban mission – General Ochoa – was trading ivory, diamonds and rare woods, while even considering expanding into Cuban cigars, works of art and fighting cockerels.[35] The heavy involvement of Cuba's officer class in the *candonga* would have serious repercussions for Ochoa and his subordinates when they returned to Cuba in early 1989, and was a further incentive for Havana to set up its own subsidised shops in Angola itself (see p. 157).

The *caravanas* (supply convoys)

The only other relief from boredom for Cubans based outside the cities were the *caravanas* – convoys carrying supplies overland from Lobito, Namibe and Huambo to garrisons stationed between Lubango and Menongue, and occasionally into Cunene and Cuando Cubango.[36] Every Cuban soldier based in the south was obliged to carry out a minimum of five *caravanas*, but by the war's end some Cubans had been on five times as many, more often than not to escape the tedium of camp life. *Caravanas* were made up of a mixture of FAPLA, Cuban and occasionally SWAPO troops, and the more regular routes acquired (rather predictable) nicknames, such as Che Guevara, Antonio Maceo and Camilo Cienfuegos. Supplying FAPLA units in Cuito Cuanavale was the responsibility of the FAPLA's 8th Brigade (based in Menongue), but once the fighting intensified in late 1987, Cubans started accompanying these convoys, experiencing some of the heaviest fighting of the war. *Caravanas* were crucial for the maintenance of the ATS Defence Line and for the survival of smaller Cuban units dotted across southern Angola, and UNITA realised that by attacking them it could weaken the FAPLA's grip on the whole region. With UNITA expanding its operations northwards, the *caravanas* increasingly passed through territory it controlled, and both sides developed sophisticated tactics to outwit each other.

Caravanas faced three principal dangers from UNITA – landmines, ambush and air attack (provided by the SAAF) – all of which shaped the make-up of a column. A typical convoy would be led by a bulldozer driving down the middle of the road with its pincers down, each subsequent vehicle following in its tracks.[37] Should the bulldozer detonate a mine, the damage would be minimal and the convoy could restart quickly.

Next came the BTR-60 (a large armoured car with top-mounted machine-guns, carrying up to a dozen men) which was ideal for fighting off ambushes, then a BMP-1 (a small tank with wire-guided missiles) for use against other armoured vehicles, and then the AA-defences.[38] Only after these vehicles had passed would the five-to-ten supply trucks appear, protected from behind by a similar succession of military vehicles in reverse order. *Caravanas* were usually around twenty vehicles in length, but some became so clogged that they stretched for over five miles, allowing UNITA to attack both ends without the other knowing about it. Ambushes were frequent, and by the end of the war the route from Menongue to Cuito Cuanavale was littered with the wrecks of over 160 vehicles, one ambush destroying thirty-six petrol tankers en route to re-supply the faltering 1987 offensive (see Chapter 10).[39]

UNITA was adept at laying mines and adopted sophisticated tactics for drawing the convoys into their minefields. As each *caravana* had at least half-a-dozen sappers who were called to the front if anything suspicious appeared on the road, UNITA often laid decoy mines (which could easily be detected) to draw attention away from mines laid further down the road. UNITA often set anti-tank mines with a twenty-second delay, calculating that this would be the exact moment when the command vehicle passed over them, the death (or incapacitation) of the commander spreading confusion just as the ambush was launched. The combined effect of searching for landmines and fighting off ambushes slowed down the *caravanas*, and it was common for the 115-mile journey between Menongue and Cuito Cuanavale to take ten days, and up to a month to complete the round-trip.[40] *Caravanas* nevertheless operated throughout the heaviest of the fighting, and in recognition of their feat the Cuban regime made a Rambo-style film celebrating their exploits – called simply *Caravana* (1989) – during the Cuban withdrawal.

Patrolling and the Search-And-Destroy (SAD) missions

Throughout the war, Cuban units in southern and eastern Angola patrolled aggressively in the areas surrounding their camps, laying ambushes and clashing frequently with UNITA. Cuban units needed to show great vigilance on patrol and they constantly varied their routine as UNITA was known to be observing them and would often lay mines along their return route to base. Cuban patrols also faced danger from the local wildlife, although not from being attacked but rather from the confusion caused by animals moving about in a tense war zone. One veteran serving on a *caravana* recalled a monkey setting off a string of eight Claymore anti-personnel mines just as the *caravana* was passing (injuring several Cubans), while a Cuban commander managed to drive his tank into an elephant trap at the height of battle, causing him some embarrassment.[41]

153

The most controversial aspect of the joint Cuban–FAPLA operations in southern Angola were the Search-And-Destroy (SAD) missions aimed at rooting out UNITA sympathisers. Mixed FAPLA–Cuban units regularly carried out SAD raids on UNITA villages in southern Angola, much as American units raided Vietcong villages during the Vietnam War. Suspected *kimbos* (villages) were surrounded and the inhabitants driven out with machine-gun fire which was directed over the roofs of the huts to avoid civilian casualties (but which inevitably caused some). The *kimbo* was then searched for hidden supplies, ammunition and any valuables, all of which were confiscated (and a great deal looted by the troops) before the *kimbo* was set alight and the troops withdrew. Although no evidence has come to light of any My Lai-style massacres,[42] it is likely that some unarmed Angolan civilians were killed during these SAD missions, and many Cubans who took part are scarred by the experience.[43]

Aside from the *caravanas*, patrols and occasional SAD missions, most Cuban units posted in Angola saw very little action, and the monotony of life in the remote interior drove some over the edge. Officers received one month's leave for every six they spent in Angola and they usually took this in Cuba. But this perk did not apply to ordinary soldiers, and many Cubans spent over two years in Africa without seeing their families or friends. Reservists suffered especially as – unlike the younger servicemen – most had left ageing parents, spouses and children in Cuba, often in difficult financial straits. The strain of being apart for years at a time broke up many marriages and families, and for this reason there is some bitterness among reservist veterans who feel that their personal sacrifice in Angola has been forgotten. There were occasional suicides (an event not uncommon in war) and isolated violent confrontations between Cuban soldiers, at least one resulting in a duel.[44]

Generally, however, discipline in the Cuban camps was good (bar the occasional trip to the *candonga*), and during Cuba's sixteen-year occupation of Angola, there were very few reported rapes, murders and robberies considering the size of the forces posted there.[45] As the Cuban operation dragged on into the late 1980s, there was nevertheless a noticeable drop in the enthusiasm of the Cubans serving in Angola, and though a strong sense of camaraderie remained among the men in the field, many lacked the ideological conviction of their predecessors. This change in attitude was inevitable as the Cuban occupation extended itself indefinitely, and once the opportunity of travelling to Africa lost its exotic appeal and merely became a 'tour of duty' the Cuban regime would turn to material incentives to encourage volunteers.

Cuban relations with the Angolans

For two allied armies fighting a common enemy, Cuban relations with the FAPLA were troubled. The majority of Cuban troops garrisoning the cities north of the ATS Defence Line lived in separate camps from the FAPLA, and what little contact did occur (for example, between Cuban instructors and FAPLA recruits) was amicable and professional.[46] The situation for Cuban units in southern Angola was quite different, however. These Cubans regularly fought alongside the FAPLA in joint operations against UNITA, and their working relationship was far from the harmonious portrait painted by the Cuban regime.[47] Since the first LCB operations started in 1977, the Cubans had complained about the incompetence and indiscipline of the FAPLA troops, but despite the Soviet–Cuban training programme their quality had improved little.[48] This was primarily due to the FAPLA's brutal recruiting methods which often involved surrounding *candongas* and cinemas with trucks, rounding up all able-bodied males inside and flying them down to the southern front for combat.[49] Such methods ensured that most front-line troops were demoralised, inexperienced and motivated only by a desire to get through the war alive, and this contributed to their high desertion rate to UNITA. The realisation that the FAPLA was regularly informing UNITA on operations and trading weaponry with its guerrillas bred in the Cubans a deep mistrust of the Angolans, and this pushed them into closer alliance with their other ally, SWAPO.[50]

In many ways, SWAPO was in a similar position to the Cubans: both were foreigners fighting another country's war against an enemy (UNITA) which was not technically their own. But, critically, both saw the Angolan War as an extension of their own struggles: for SWAPO against South Africa, for Cuba against the USA and (more contentiously) imperialism. As the conflict intensified, however, they discovered that their ideological commitment was far stronger than their Angolan allies, and that some of their so-called allies were UNITA sympathisers. Uncertain of Angolan loyalties, Cuban and SWAPO troops looked out for each other during joint operations, and as confrontations with UNITA and the SADF increased, a strange dynamic evolved on the battlefield. The Cubans, SWAPO and MK guerrillas would fight tenaciously (and often to the death) while Angolan units crumbled around them. Gradually resentment grew among the FAPLA's allies at the way they were being used to fight a proxy war, and this erupted in mutiny at an MK training camp in May 1984.[51]

Cuban military relations with Angola's civilians were exactly what one would expect from an occupying military power. The presence of thousands of Cuban troops aroused excitement at the prospect of commerce, but also resentment that a foreign power was bringing war into remote regions. Unlike the Cuban civilians who worked on a daily basis with Angolans and occasionally socialised with them, Cuban soldiers were forbidden to fraternise with the locals and their only contact was, by its very nature, illegal and clandestine. Cuban contacts with Angolan men were strained as they usually involved the *candonga* which generated a lot of distrust and ill-feeling. Relations with Angolan women were much warmer, if veterans' memories are anything to go by. Despite restrictions many Cuban–Angolan romances flourished during the war, and though few Cubans brought Angolan wives back with them, it is probable that these relationships produced the war's first Cuban–Angolan babies. Since the withdrawal in 1991, however, Angola has been in too much chaos for any of these children to be identified, and it is possible that, once peace returns, dozens – possibly hundreds – of children will appear looking for their Cuban fathers.[52]

Salaries, stipends and bonuses

Salaries for soldiers serving in Angola were calculated, processed and paid out by a secret unit in the FAR – the *Departamento de Abastecimiento* (Supply Department) – set up in Havana's Nuevo Vedado district in December 1972.[53] With responsibility for coordinating the monetary activities of all Cuban internationalists serving abroad, this department employed thirty staff who dealt with the payment of salaries to the military, and pensions to war widows and the wounded. Much sensitive information – including casualty figures and numbers of personnel posted abroad – passed through the department, and the operation was cloaked in secrecy. The selection process was tough, complex mental and psychological tests accompanying the usual medical examination, and candidates' private lives were vetted by G-2 (Cuba's secret police) before they were cleared to work there. As the Cuban operation in Angola expanded in the early 1980s, the Department employed a 'money ship' – the Soviet cruise liner *Leonid Sovinov* – to sail to Angolan territorial waters and process the paperwork of thousands of Cubans before they returned to Cuba.[54] This meant cutting down on the chaos which ensued when large groups of Cubans from different provinces arrived at the same time demanding their salaries. The ship was heavily protected (it often carried huge amounts of Cuban pesos) and it regularly anchored off the Angolan coast for three days at a time, although on one occasion it remained for over a month.

Cuban soldiers received their salary partly in Cuban pesos and partly in Angolan kwanzas. The pesos were paid on a monthly basis to the soldiers' families (or, in the case of some officers, directly into their bank accounts) while the kwanzas were kept 'on account' for collection when the soldier completed his service. The amounts were small, however, and by the end of a two-year mission a soldier could expect to have received his basic living requirements for free but to have earned less than US$200 (officers fared comparatively better at around US$1,000).[55] In an effort to compensate for this paltry salary, Cubans could purchase clothes, electrical goods and other luxuries unavailable in Cuba in subsidised shops in Luanda, for example at Cacuaco. Shortly before leaving Angola, Cuban troops could visit these shops and buy items up to the value of their kwanza stipend which was calculated on the spot. Throughout the 1980s this bonus system was increasingly used as a sweetener for internationalists whose missions grew ever longer, and it is no exaggeration to say that, by the end of the war, every internationalist soldier believed he had a right to a *ventilador* (electric fan) after serving in Angola.[56]

The humanitarian mission in Angola, 1976–91

The humanitarian mission in Angola started shortly after the end of the 'Second Liberation War', and though it ran in tandem with the military mission it was organised separately. The selection of civilians was carried out by Cubatécnica (renamed Logitécnica in the 1980s), which ran humanitarian missions in over two dozen Third World countries, Angola receiving over 70 per cent of the internationalists sent to Africa each year.[57] Angola's infrastructure (which had improved in the five-year boom preceding the Portuguese withdrawal) had been severely damaged in the war (at least 130 bridges were destroyed), and what few social services existed before 1976 had broken down completely. The SADF invasion alone caused an estimated $6.7 billion worth of damage, and during the panic and looting which accompanied the flight of 90 per cent of the Portuguese settlers, over 200,000 vehicles were destroyed or stolen, and many factories and businesses left in ruins.[58] More serious in the long-term was the flight of Angola's skilled workforce – in particular doctors, teachers, engineers and construction workers – creating a shortage which Cuba was well-equipped to fill.

The selection of internationalists for the humanitarian mission in Angola was different from the army as Cubans were chosen specifically for their skills. Civilians were singled out by their hospital or factory managers both for their proficiency and ideological beliefs. Nearly all of those selected were members of the PCC or UJC (Communist Youth) – a fact denied by the Cuban regime but supported by those who served in Angola – and most considered their selection a sign of recognition by the regime. On paper, civilian missions were shorter (only nine months), but in practice most internationalists extended their mission once they were in Angola, spending around eighteen months there before returning.[59] The term 'civilian' was misleading, however, as all Cubans received basic military training, a wise precaution given Angola's volatility but one which led to accusations that they were part of the military reserve. Castro did not deny this, declaring that internationalists must be workers and soldiers at the same time, promising that they would not only rebuild bridges but also defend them against attack. Internationalists were 'civic soldiers', dedicated to civilian tasks but ready to defend themselves and their allies if necessary, and often the 'line between civilians and military personnel was blurred'.[60] Despite this disparity, the Cuban regime insisted that the humanitarian mission in Angola was its overriding priority, when in reality civilians made up little more than 7 per cent of the Cuban contingent in Angola, the rest being military.[61]

Civilian internationalists were involved in thirty-five areas of activity, divided into three branches – medical, teaching and technical (in particular construction). In the big cities – Luanda, Benguela and Huambo – each branch was housed in its own building. Although Cubans mixed with Angolans during the day, most lived in hermetic communities, being driven to and from work in their own bus, and eating and socialising with each other in their own buildings.[62] Cuban civilians had better living conditions than soldiers posted outside the main cities, but they rarely went out at night as there was a curfew in Luanda from 10 p.m. and the streets were dangerous after dark. The long working-hours and cloistered existence bred a strong sense of camaraderie among the Cubans, and many look back on their time in Angola as one of the best experiences in their life. Thanks to their hard work, the humanitarian mission was the most successful facet of the Cuban intervention, laying the foundations for Angola's social services. This success was reflected in the rapid expansion of the humanitarian mission – which grew at a rate of 2.7 per cent in its first five years[63] – until by the early 1980s there were around 5,000 Cuban civilians working in Angola, a level which remained more or less consistent for the rest of the Cuban occupation.

The medical brigades

The first Cuban civilians to arrive in Angola were the medical brigades, and they faced an enormous task.[64] Following independence, there was only one doctor per 100,000 Angolans, and the few hospitals were understaffed, lacked medicines and overflowed with the sick and wounded. Large medical teams were posted to Luanda's University and Prenda hospitals, and clinics were opened across Angola to provide basic treatment to people living in remote areas. Working conditions were difficult for the Cubans who not only had to cope with Portuguese systems but also had great trouble communicating. This may seem surprising as Spanish and Portuguese are – at least on paper – similar languages. But the reality is that Cuban Spanish (which is notoriously difficult for foreigners to understand) and Angolan Portuguese are far from mutually intelligible, and though some Cubans could muddle through with 'Portuñol', communication problems were to dog relations between the Cubans and Angolans throughout the mission. Many patients spoke no Portuguese at all, and consultations often required three separate translations for the doctor, nurse and patient. Many Angolans put their faith in traditional medicine (which often involved black magic) and waited until their health deteriorated seriously before visiting a doctor. But given the high standard of medical treatment they received from the Cubans, most Angolans made miraculous recoveries, greatly enhancing the reputation of Cuban doctors' in Africa.

Cuban medical teams worked very hard during their missions, as is reflected by the thousands of consultations, vaccinations and operations they carried out in Angola.[65] Outside working hours many nurses ran clinics to cope with demand, and Cuban–Angolan working relations were reportedly very good. The MPLA was keen to employ Cuban as opposed to Western doctors for several reasons, not least because the average Cuban cost only a quarter of a similarly qualified doctor from the World Health Organisation (WHO).[66] But Cubans were also prepared to endure more basic living conditions – medical teams often shared apartments and were happy to eat meals as a group – and were more sociable, easy-going and more racially tolerant than their Soviet and East German comrades. Most Cubans could communicate in faltering '*Portuñol*', and their innate ability to improvise when equipment or supplies were lacking (a skill learned in Cuba) was a major bonus in Angola where blackouts and shortages were a daily occurrence. While it is true that Cuban doctors were in Angola to look after thousands of Cuban soldiers, their contribution to Angola's fledgling health service should not be understated. By 1978, three-quarters of all doctors working in Angola were Cuban, and by 1982 they represented 30 per cent of all Cuban medical personnel posted abroad.[67]

The educational programme

The task facing the Cuban teaching brigades was equally daunting as, at independence, over 90 per cent of the Angolan population was illiterate. However, it was not until Raúl Castro's visit to Angola in June 1977 that the first steps were taken to set up an educational programme for Angola. The reason for this delay is not clear, as Cuba had been providing educational assistance to developing countries since 1971 when it opened an educational complex for foreign students on the Isle of Pines (to the south of Cuba). Renamed '*Isla de la Juventud*' (the Isle of Youth) in their honour, the complex eventually boasted over sixty schools and 18,000 students from Africa, the Americas and Asia, the students receiving their travel, board and education in return for seasonal work on the island's citrus plantations.[68] Speaking at a rally in Luanda, Raúl Castro corrected this oversight, offering 2,000 scholarships for Angolan students to study on the Isle of Youth (an offer he later extended to Mozambique). Over the next decade the programme steadily grew until, by 1987, there were 4,000 Angolans studying there, representing one-quarter of all foreign students.

Angola also desperately needed teachers and, in March 1978, the first secondary school teacher brigade – the *Destacamento Pedagógico Internacionalista* (DPI) 'Che Guevara' – arrived in Angola. The delay in sending this brigade to Angola – two years after the end of the 'Second Liberation War' – is puzzling, and was probably due to a lack of qualified volunteers (a sign that internationalist service may not have been popular in the teaching profession). The 732-strong contingent started teaching the following month, and they were joined a year later by 500 primary school teachers who were dispersed across Angola.[69] Like the medical teams, the teachers had great difficulty breaking through the language barrier as few had studied Portuguese before going to Angola. Although most made do with '*Portuñol*', it took an average of two months before the majority of their students fully understood them. For this reason teaching missions were extended from one to two years, as most teachers had overcome any communication difficulties by the end of their first year.[70] In the early 1980s, the programme was extended with the opening of schools in remote areas and the provision of 60 Cuban professors for Luanda's Agostinho Neto University, and for the rest of the decade there were around 2,000 Cuban teachers (of all levels) in Angola.

The technical aid programme

The third and largest branch of Cuba's humanitarian mission was the technical programme which began shortly after Cuba and Angola signed their first economic and technical agreement in July 1976. Following the 'Second Liberation War', Angola was desperately short of technicians to oversee the reconstruction of the dozens of bridges, roads and buildings damaged in the fighting, and to build thousands of new houses for the refugee populations swelling Angola's cities. In January 1977, the first construction teams arrived in Angola, and over the next five years they built fifty new bridges and 2,000 houses in Luanda (many in the deprived Golfe *musseque*).[71] They also reopened several thousand miles of road and partially reconnected the electricity and telephone networks. Encouraged by their success, Havana planned to expand the programme threefold, but due to a lack of funding or qualified volunteers the plans were never realised, and around 2,000 Cuban construction workers remained in Angola for the rest of the 1980s. The quality of their workmanship is still disputed, however, and although Cuban rates were competitive with the West there were reports of shoddy, late and over-budget projects, undercutting the success of the programme.

Cuban specialists also tried to rehabilitate Angola's coffee plantations which only four years before had made Angola the world's fourth largest coffee exporter. But with the spread of UNITA their efforts were doomed, as were initially successful attempts to resurrect Angola's sugar plantations.[72] More controversial were Cuban logging operations in Cabinda's vast Mayombe forest. The Mayombe had already been exploited by Portuguese loggers prior to independence, and once the threat from FLEC receded the MPLA was keen to resume logging. Cuba responded by sending a massive contingent to Cabinda – over 500 men supported by 100 Angolans – to work on Cuba's single largest civilian project in Angola. The *Contingente Forestal Arnaldo Milián* set up its main camp in Buco Zau (eighty-five miles north-east of Cabinda city) with six smaller camps inside the forest. In only three months it cut down 14,000 cubic metres of wood, a feat which would normally have taken two years.[73] The success of this project led to accusations that the Cubans had ravaged the Mayombe, destroying large swathes of virgin rain forest. Indeed many locals viewed the Cubans in the same light as the Portuguese – as foreigners who came to plunder to Cabinda's wealth. The Cuban government has vehemently denied these accusations, but the controversy remains, as does a great deal of bad feeling among the local population.

Other foreign workers in Angola

Although Cuban internationalists were assisted by foreign nationals – mostly from the socialist bloc – their numbers were small and they worked only in a few areas. Cuba's medical brigades received some assistance from Czech, East German, Bulgarian, Portuguese and English doctors (although not in great numbers), while the technical teams occasionally worked alongside Brazilian and Lusophone African technicians. On the whole, however, civilian internationalists had little contact with the Soviets who were exclusively involved in the military side of the operation – as planners, pilots and advisors – and who lived in their own complexes. As paymasters of the Angolan operation, the Soviets reportedly behaved like colonial rulers, avoiding the local population, cordoning off sections of beach to create 'Soviet only' areas, and even demanding that swimming pools which had been used by Angolans be drained and refilled before they would use them.[74] The racism of East European personnel contrasted sharply with the Cubans and, as a result of their easy-going and flexible attitude (and their willingness to communicate in '*Portuñol*'), the Cuban civilians built good working relationships with the Angolans, who relied on their innate ability to improvise when machinery or vehicles broke down.

Internationalist casualties in Angola, 1975–91

The question of how many casualties the Cubans suffered in Angola is the single most contentious issue of the Angolan operation, and will be discussed in the last chapter. What is clear, however, is that as a result of confining Cuban troops to barracks (with occasional sorties on patrols and *caravanas*), most casualties were the result of accident and disease. Few reliable figures are available, but probably only one-third of Cuban casualties were suffered in combat, and many of those from landmines, booby-traps and ambushes.[75] Official statistics state that one-third of fatalities were caused by accidents, but judging from veterans' accounts it was probably more like half. The most common causes were guns going off accidentally and dangerous (or drunken) driving.[76] Most accidents were caused by a failure to follow procedure, and there were numerous aircraft and helicopter crashes throughout the Cuban occupation, many subsequently claimed by UNITA as 'kills'. Disease – in particular malaria and tropical fever – took hundreds of Cuban lives (one-quarter of fatalities), and the Cuban medical brigades initially struggled to treat some diseases which were unknown in Cuba. Civilian casualties were likewise light, although there were occasions when Cuban civilians were killed (such as the UNITA truck bomb in Huambo in April 1984 which caused nearly 200 casualties). However, the impression veterans give is that casualties did occur but not in great numbers, and that they only started to rise once Cuban troops were drawn back into the fighting in late 1987.[77]

Return procedure at the end of internationalist missions

On completion of their mission, Cuban internationalists were gathered in Luanda where they filled out the relevant paperwork (often aboard the *Leonid Sovinov*), shopped at subsidised shops in Cacuaco, and underwent a medical examination. Most civilians and officers flew back to Cuba while the bulk of the soldiers returned by ship. On arrival in Cuba they were transferred to military camps for two to three days of more rigorous medical tests, in particular for malaria and tropical diseases. Only once they got the all-clear were they allowed to return home. The number of Cubans affected by disease is not known (the Cuban government has released no figures), but it is likely that several thousand Cubans returned from Angola with debilitating diseases (most commonly malaria), and some possibly with HIV.[78]

The debate over whether Cuban troops brought AIDS into Cuba from Angola has been ruthlessly suppressed by the Cuban government which claims that the disease was first introduced into Cuba by foreign tourists. However, the appearance of HIV in the Cuban population only five years after the intervention in Angola began – along with the death from AIDS of the Cuban artists Carlos Alfonso and Reinaldo Arenas who fled to Florida during the Mariel boatlift – fuelled rumours that it had been introduced into Cuba from Africa. As exaggerated reports about AIDS swept the world in the early 1980s, the Cuban government took draconian measures to prevent the spread of the disease. From the mid-1980s onwards, HIV testing was introduced for all internationalists before they left Angola, and anyone diagnosed with the virus was transferred on arrival in Cuba to a special hospital (Los Cocos) where they were interned indefinitely.[79] The story of the Los Cocos inmates – and the tragic collapse of the care provided to them – remains a scandal which has yet to be uncovered.[80]

The vast majority of Cubans cleared their medical tests, however, and returned home to rejoin civilian life. Reservists and civilians took up their old jobs (which had been kept for them in their absence), while those completing military service either went to university or entered the job market. All internationalists received certificates and medals for their missions, those who had seen combat (including some civilians) receiving the '1st Class' medal. Occasionally veterans were singled out for Party recognition, but it was not until the latter stages of the Cuban operation in Angola that the regime celebrated the return of its internationalists with ceremonies and marches. The most elaborate ceremony of them all – at the Cacahual military monument on 7 December 1989 – would mark the end of the internationalist phase of the Cuban Revolution (see Chapter 12). The experience of Cuba's internationalists since their return to Cuba – and their thoughts and feelings about their experience of serving in Angola – will be discussed in the conclusion.

8

ABORTIVE PEACE NEGOTIATIONS AND THE PATH TO FULL-SCALE WAR, 1981–5

South Africa's occupation of southern Cunene in late 1981 initiated a period of instability and deepening conflict in Angola. With garrisons in Xangongo and N'Giva, the SADF had the springboard it needed to step up its campaign against SWAPO, and this provided cover for UNITA to expand its insurgency in tandem into central and eastern Angola. Inevitably Cuban troops (and some civilians) who had so far stayed out of the fighting were drawn into fierce clashes – at Cangamba (August 1983) and Sumbe (March 1984) – threatening to escalate Cuban casualties seriously. With a potential Vietnam scenario developing, Havana and Moscow concentrated their efforts on building up the FAPLA into a formidable army which could crush UNITA, and between 1981 and 1985 bolstered it with a further $3 billion worth of Soviet hardware.[1] By the summer of 1985, it would be in a position to launch the first in a series of offensives against UNITA's bases in Cuando Cubango – Mavinga and Jamba – which Havana and Moscow hoped would deliver the death blow to the insurgency.

Against this background of intensifying conflict in Angola there were sporadic and inconclusive negotiations between the MPLA and South African governments – brokered by the UN Contact Group, the British Commonwealth and the USA – but the few successes achieved were short-lived. Of all the negotiating strategies in this period, however, Chester Crocker's 'linkage' would prove to be the most durable, quite simply because it addressed head-on the genuine security concerns of each of the warring parties. But in the confrontational atmosphere of the 'Second Cold War' all negotiating strategies had to operate under the shadow of the war in Angola, and by 1985 a combination of factors would derail them altogether, plunging Angola back into bloody fighting.

The explosion of UNITA's insurgency, 1981–3

Prior to Operation Protea, UNITA posed only a localised threat to the MPLA, operating exclusively in its core regions of support (Huambo and Bié) or in the remote interior (Moxico and Cuando Cubango). Significant economic damage was caused by attacks on the Benguela railway line (averaging three per week during 1981),[2] but UNITA's few military successes – such as the capture of Mavinga in September 1980 – did little to loosen the FAPLA's grip on the country. Following the delivery of thousands of tons of captured Soviet weaponry, however, UNITA drew up ambitious plans to extend its operations across the whole country. Given SWAPO's intimate alliance with FAPLA and Cuban forces in Angola and the escalation of its insurgency, the SADF inevitably rekindled its alliance with UNITA and, by the early 1980s, it was operating three UNITA training camps in Namibia. In addition, a permanent liaison officer was appointed to help Savimbi coordinate the delivery of supplies to Jamba (Cuando Cubango), UNITA's secret HQ twenty miles north of the Caprivi Strip.[3] The campaign against SWAPO provided ideal cover for UNITA to build up its strength, and in the six months following Operation Protea, SWAPO and the FAPLA were distracted by a series of SADF operations in Cunene which killed over 600 guerrillas and captured vast quantities of military equipment which was handed on to UNITA.[4]

Conscious of the growing threat in Angola's borderlands, in November 1981 Dos Santos made a secret request to UNITA (through the Senegalese President Abdou Diouf) for a ceasefire to be followed by negotiations.[5] Having been president for a little over two years, Dos Santos was staving off a power struggle within the MPLA over the conduct of the war, and he was desperate to end the fighting quickly. But his approach (and a second by Paulo Jorge in January 1982) did not bear fruit and, instead, Dos Santos opted for beefing up the FAPLA, negotiating a further $2 billion of Soviet aid at the annual tripartite meeting in Moscow in January 1982.[6] UNITA continued its relentless expansion and, on 10 November 1982, it captured Lumbala-N'Guimbo, threatening the FAPLA's remaining garrisons in Moxico – Cangamba and Luena – and further intensifying the power struggle in Luanda. Ironically, the same day, the Angolan Defence Minister 'Pedalé' met Raúl Castro in Havana to review the deteriorating situation in Angola, and they discussed the FAPLA's collapse in Moxico and Cunene. Both were concerned about the rise of UNITA but felt that little could be done until the re-equipment programme got underway, and in the meantime FAPLA and Cuban units would have to make do with what they had.

During 1983, UNITA experienced its greatest expansion of the war, launching every type of operation from small-scale raids to full-scale assaults on FAPLA–Cuban garrisons.[7] These included sabotage operations against the Lomaum dam (January) and the Cuema power station (June), kidnappings, indiscriminate mine-laying, terrorist bombings and even shooting down civilian aircraft.[8] Bolstered with captured Soviet war booty, in late 1982 UNITA expanded its conventional warfare operations with a campaign to capture Moxico's capital, Luena. UNITA started with a series of attacks along the Benguela railway line which, by July 1983, had effectively cut it in two, threatening to outflank the ATS Defence Line 150 miles to the south. This was followed by two full-scale assaults on FAPLA garrisons, the first of which captured Mussende (Cuanza Norte) on 26 July, threatening the nearby Cambambe Dam which supplied Luanda with water and electricity. The second attack 500 miles away in the remote savannahs of Moxico was to prove far more harrowing, however, as an assault by at least 3,000 UNITA troops against the stranded Cangamba garrison developed into a gruelling nine-day siege, the outcome of which is still hotly disputed.

The siege of Cangamba, late July–14 August 1983

The nine-day siege of Cangamba was the first major battle between FAPLA–Cuban forces and UNITA since the end of the 'Second Liberation War', and provided a foretaste of the bloody and inconclusive confrontations which were to come over the next five years.[9] Lauded by both sides as one of their hardest-fought victories, the battle for Cangamba was actually the Angolan War's most inconclusive (and costly) stand-off, drawing attention not only to the FAPLA's vulnerability but also to UNITA's weakness in fighting conventional operations. The Cuban military machine – and a handful of instructors on the ground – would once more be called on to rescue the FAPLA from disaster (just as they had in November 1975), opening the way for ever greater levels of Cuban involvement in the war against UNITA. By far the bloodiest confrontation of UNITA's insurgency (with as many as 2,000 killed and twice as many wounded), the battle of Cangamba would force both sides to step back and take stock of their strategic and tactical deficiencies.

The town of Cangamba was of dubious strategic importance, situated in the remote west of Moxico (see Map 7). It was over 150 miles from the nearest garrisons at Luena and Cuito Cuanavale (which could only be reached by poor roads) and was dependent on supply from the air base at Menongue, over 150 miles to the south-west. The tiny settlement had no value other than to exert FAPLA authority in the area, and by 1983 it had long since lost its civilian population, leaving a small garrison made up of the FAPLA's 32 Infantry Brigade, a team of forty-to-sixty Cuban instructors and perhaps thirty Angolans from the militia.[10] After capturing Lumbala-N'Giumbo in November 1982, UNITA looked on Cangamba (100 miles to the north-west) as the next logical step towards Luena, but the FAPLA failed to spot this obvious move. Despite a raid on Cangamba in late July, no steps were taken to reinforce the garrison, and thus it was easily encircled when a larger UNITA force – numbering between 3,000 and 6,000 troops[11] – returned to Cangamba on 1 August.

Desperate requests for reinforcements were sent to Luena and Menongue, and the next day (as UNITA started shelling Cangamba) Luanda responded. Four detachments were hastily assembled from units closest to Cangamba – two from Huambo, one from Menongue and a fourth from Lubango (which became the reserve) – and the first three immediately set off on the hazardous 250-mile journey to Cangamba, much of it across UNITA territory. These columns would take nearly a week to reach Cangamba, however, and in the meantime its small garrison was desperately outnumbered. But with an absence of Cuban military personnel nearby, the best Luanda could do was to fly in a thirty-man team by helicopter which arrived shortly before UNITA's bombardment closed the airstrip for good. Aside from air support (see p. 168) the defenders were on their own, placing the fifty-odd Cuban trainers in the same situation facing their predecessors eight years earlier at Catengue.

Accepting that they could not defend the town from the UNITA onslaught, the Cubans concentrated on protecting the FAPLA camp and airstrip on the town's edge. The camp's perimeter was divided into four sectors (south, east, west and north), the Cubans commanding the first three while the FAPLA covered the north of the camp (which backed onto their HQ). The limited artillery at their disposal – seven mortars, five B-10 guns and four GRAD-1P missile-launchers – was positioned around the camp's perimeter, while a mobile force carried around three RPG-7s for use wherever they were needed. Uncertain how long the siege would last, ammunition was carefully husbanded – each Cuban receiving only 300 rounds – and a large reserve was kept in bunkers under the camp (most of this was used up during the fighting). Due to the suddenness of the encirclement, however, the defenders failed to bring adequate water into the camp, and this would have series implications as the siege wore on.

The Cuban defence plan would be tested to its limits as UNITA had opted to change tactics. Abandoning costly full-frontal attacks which stood little chance of breaking through, UNITA switched to a strategy of creeping encroachment (much in the style of the Western Front during the First World War). Guerrillas would dig trenches east of Cangamba and then edge them towards the camp's outer defences, steadily reducing the perimeter whilst bringing UNITA's heavy artillery into range. Deceptive tactics would also be employed to wear down the defenders' morale – including false bombardments (which drove troops out of safe trenches into areas targeted by UNITA's artillery) and the simulation of reinforcements arriving (which were actually UNITA guerrillas in stolen uniforms). It is even rumoured that UNITA drugged its troops to ensure they held their nerve when the fighting got thickest. As a result of intense tribal rivalry, however, the UNITA force was very disorganised, leading at times to a complete breakdown in command.

The attack started on 2 August with a three-day bombardment using captured Soviet guns which failed to cause the defenders any casualties as they took shelter in their bunkers. UNITA slowly began infiltrating the town and, by 6 August, it had secured a perimeter around the camp, directly bombarding it and causing the first casualties. Conditions inside the camp deteriorated under the relentless bombardment and assaults, and were made worse by the lack of drinking water after the camp's well was destroyed by a direct hit on the second day. Within a couple of days, troops were desperately searching for water wherever they could find it – from vehicle radiators and muddy puddles, some even chewing banana skins and toothpaste to alleviate their thirst. By 7 August the situation was so grave that Castro stepped in, declaring Cangamba 'an immortal symbol of Cuban and Angolan valour', and urging the defenders to hold on until reinforcements – which he promised would include the entire Cuban army if necessary – came to their rescue.

But with enemy trenches now less than fifty feet from the camp, the artillery destroyed and over 170 bombs falling on the camp each day, the situation looked hopeless, and the defenders looked to air power for salvation. Recognising its importance, the FAPLA–Cuban air force had been relocated to Menongue on the first day of UNITA's attack, and within hours its pilots were flying missions over Cangamba. Despite Menongue's distance from Cangamba, Cuban and Angolan pilots clocked up over 400 missions during the nine-day siege. Most were reconnaissance flights over the battle area, although Cuban MiG-21s and Mi-17s (attack helicopters) also carried out bombing and strafing runs against UNITA which inflicted heavy casualties. Supply aircraft took great risks – one An-26 flying through heavy UNITA fire to drop desperately needed supplies on Cangamba – and they did much to lift the defenders' morale which, by the last days, was drooping as they lost all radio contact and their defensive perimeter shrank to the size of a football pitch.

Unknown to the defenders, however, around 6 August the two reinforcement columns reached a point 150 miles west of Cangamba and held their positions until aerial reconnaissance had confirmed the camp was still under FAPLA–Cuban control. By 10 August both the Cubans and UNITA were ready to make their final move, and as UNITA launched its final assault the relief columns moved on Cangamba under cover of a lightening strike by Cuban MiGs and BM-21s. According to Cuban accounts, the Cuban MiGs came in low over the camp and caught the UNITA troops swarming out of their trenches, the MiG rockets and BM-21 missiles tearing swathes through the densely packed ranks.[12] As the survivors stumbled back to their trenches, the reinforcement columns moved in to relieve the camp, seizing on a lull in the fighting to fly out the surviving Cubans. This move was controversial, however, as no such VIP treatment was offered to the Angolans, fuelling accusations that the Cubans had abandoned them in their most desperate hour.

The decision to abandon Cangamba after so much bloodshed was by now inevitable as, two days after the relief columns arrived, UNITA called in its secret weapon – the South African Air Force (SAAF). Although South African troops had played no part in the attack on Cangamba, several SADF officers had been present during the siege, and they no doubt supported UNITA's request for air support after witnessing the devastating casualties it sustained. Worried that the FAPLA would refortify the camp and retake the town, UNITA asked the SAAF to destroy Cangamba completely. On 12 August, Canberra bombers and Impalas began an intensive bombardment which, within two days, reduced what little was left of the town to rubble. The battle of Cangamba thus ended as it began – with a tremendous display of firepower – having achieved very little for either side. During the fighting, as many as 1,100 UNITA soldiers had been killed (with at least as many wounded)[13] while the defenders had lost several hundred men (at least twenty of them Cuban), with many more wounded and captured.[14] So fierce was the artillery duel that, by the end of nine days, the Cubans had fired off 2,700 C-5 rockets, 2,700 shells and 400 mortars, leaving the debris of nearly 1,500 bombs littering the camp's tiny perimeter. Having made the area uninhabitable with tons of unexploded ordinance, both sides had little choice but to withdraw.

The myth and reality of Cangamba

Within days of the withdrawal from Cangamba, however, both sides were claiming victory. Each issued doctored and contradictory accounts of what had happened while side-stepping the more embarrassing issues – namely how UNITA failed to capture the camp, or why the FAPLA failed to withdraw the garrison long before it became encircled. In Cuba, the regime elevated the desperate defence of Cangamba to a major victory against the forces of imperialism, and claimed that UNITA had been forced to withdraw by the arrival of the Cuban relief columns. UNITA claimed the opposite, insisting that its troops had breached the camp's defences on 11 August, sparking the flight of the Cubans by helicopter and enabling UNITA to capture the camp three days later. The truth probably lies somewhere in between. For, after nine days of heavy fighting, neither side could hold on to the town, the FAPLA–Cuban withdrawal being followed almost immediately by Cangamba's complete destruction by South African bombers, after which UNITA withdrew from the area.

In the cold light of day, therefore, the siege of Cangamba gave both sides little to crow about, and behind the triumphant rhetoric the Cubans had cause for concern. The intensity of the fighting at Cangamba – the fiercest the Cubans had encountered since the 'Second Liberation War' – presaged far greater Cuban casualties in the upcoming months, and once again it was Cuban troops who were paying the price for FAPLA incompetence. In a scenario which was to be repeated several times over the next five years, a FAPLA garrison (supported by a small Cuban presence) had been encircled in an assault which it should have been expecting, prompting the by-now well-rehearsed Cuban response to prevent it being wiped out. The FAPLA had singularly failed to address what to do with the stranded Cangamba garrison in the eight months following UNITA's capture of Lumbala N'Guimbo, and when they had turned to Cuba for assistance it was almost too late. Not for the first time, Cuba was extricating its personnel from a disaster created by the FAPLA, although in fairness to the Angolans the Cubans also bore part of the blame, having also failed to withdraw their personnel in time. Communication between these allies would continue to be poor as the fighting intensified in Angola, and would be a major factor in the military disasters which befell the FAPLA in the late 1980s.

The withdrawal from Cangamba further weakened the FAPLA's faltering grip on Moxico, and in response Cuba sent a further 5,000 troops to Angola (many of them transferred from Ethiopia).[15] Cuban reinforcements were matched by the Soviets who sent at least ten shiploads of military supplies and ordered an aircraft carrier to sail to Luanda as a show of support.[16] Having failed to take the initiative throughout 1983, the FAPLA launched a fresh offensive against UNITA in September, killing over 500 guerrillas in its capture of Mussende the following month. But its success was again short-lived, and a second offensive in November got bogged down, enabling UNITA to retake the initiative, capturing Cazombo (Moxico) and Andulo (Bié). With the countryside sinking into chaos, the FAPLA was then thrown into disarray in December by yet another South African invasion of Angola – Operation Askari. The outcome of South Africa's twelfth incursion would confound everyone's expectations, however, and instead of resulting in another crushing victory for the SADF would turn into a tense and bitter confrontation, forcing Luanda and Pretoria into peace talks (see p. 182).

Background to the 'linkage' negotiations, 1978–81

Against this background of deepening crisis in Angola, the first serious negotiations to end the conflict took place, adding a further dimension to the complex confrontations consuming southern Africa. Previous peace initiatives in the months preceding Angolan independence had long been overtaken by events, and the UN Contact Group's one tangible success – Resolution 435 – had signally failed to advance peace in the region (see

Chapter 6).[17] Indeed, by 1980, Resolution 435 had become the main obstacle to a settlement, the Cubans, MPLA and SWAPO repeatedly demanding its implementation in the face of Pretoria's outright refusal. Ironically South Africa did not oppose Namibian independence – indeed the idea had been under discussion in the South African parliament for over a decade. But it rejected Resolution 435 because it failed to address the main cause of South African instability: namely SWAPO and MK bases in Angola and the support they were receiving from the Cuban garrison. However unpleasant the apartheid regime – and however illegal its occupation of Namibia – the reality was that it would not withdraw from Namibia if this put SWAPO in power and placed MK forces on its borders.

Neither the Cubans nor the Angolans saw any reason to compromise, however, and they insisted on Resolution 435 at every opportunity. Their stance was encouraged by Zimbabwe which became independent in April 1980 under the Marxist Robert Mugabe, an outcome Pretoria had vociferously opposed but had been forced to accept. Convinced that South African power was on the wane, Luanda and Havana believed that Namibian independence could likewise be forced on Pretoria without discussing Cuban troop withdrawal. This strategy they believed would lead to SWAPO's victory in Namibia, expanded MK operations in South Africa and the eventual collapse of apartheid. What they failed to grasp, however, was that Pretoria had drawn a line under the loss of Southern Rhodesia and had adopted the apocalyptic 'Total Onslaught Strategy'. In Pretoria's eyes this elevated apartheid's struggle for survival against the forces of reform to a messianic crusade against Communist imperialism in Africa. Convinced that it had nothing to lose, South Africa steadily escalated its incursions into neighbouring states, until, by the time the Americans re-entered the fray, Angola's warring parties had become locked into a bitterly fought struggle from which there was no end in sight.

Chester Crocker proposes 'Constructive Engagement' and 'Linkage', April 1981

Determined to break the deadlock, in April 1981 the new American Assistant Secretary of State for African Affairs, Chester Crocker, embarked on a new and radical strategy which embraced the conflicting agendas of the main parties involved in the fighting. On the one hand, there would be 'Constructive Engagement' with Pretoria, whilst on the other – even more controversially – Namibian independence would be linked to the withdrawal of Cuban troops from Angola (the notorious 'linkage' policy). In late 1980, Crocker (who had yet to be appointed to Reagan's administration) first proposed the idea of 'constructively engaging' the South African government in an article in *Foreign Affairs*. Crocker argued that

171

Washington was forfeiting what little influence it had by ostracising Pretoria, and in the process was damaging their common interests. By re-engaging Pretoria, the USA could use its influence to bring the South Africans to the negotiating table, and 'linkage' was the carrot needed to secure their participation. Eager to stem the spread of Soviet influence into southern Africa, Crocker believed that both policies could not only secure Namibian independence (he rather optimistically predicted it would take only eighteen months to achieve), but they could also rein in Cuban and Soviet intervention in the region, a major policy objective.

Formally adopted by Reagan's administration in March 1981, 'Constructive Engagement' and 'linkage' were immediately condemned by the Cubans, Angolans and Soviets who accused Crocker of introducing extraneous issues into a debate which had already been resolved with Resolution 435. Despite its poor reception, however, there was an underlying logic to Crocker's analysis of the conflict in southern Africa which was compelling. For the undeniable truth was that the SADF–SWAPO conflict in Namibia had become entangled with the FAPLA–UNITA conflict in Angola, both politically and militarily (through the FAPLA–SWAPO alliance on the one hand and the SADF–UNITA alliance on the other). One only had to look at the fighting in southern Angola – with SWAPO and MK troops fighting UNITA, whilst SADF troops (in their pursuit of SWAPO) clashed with FAPLA and Cuban units – to see that the two conflicts were entwined. Thus it followed that a regional settlement could only work if both conflicts were resolved simultaneously and – perhaps most difficult of all – interdependently. No matter how often the Cubans and Angolans brandished Resolution 435 at South Africa, there was no escaping the stark fact that without a settlement based on the concept of 'linkage' – which addressed the security needs of all the parties involved – the prospects for a lasting peace in the region were bleak.

Limitations of and challenges to Crocker's strategy

Persuading the Angolans, South Africans and Cubans of the validity of his approach was quite a different matter. For, despite the compelling logic of 'linkage' there was enormous mistrust of the Americans, undermining Crocker's status as a mediator. Crocker had little credibility with the Angolans and Cubans in whose eyes he was anything but impartial, and the gains he stood to make from a 'linked' settlement – including the eclipse of Cuban influence in the region and the incorporation of UNITA into the Angolan government – reinforced the impression that 'linkage' was a thinly disguised attempt to pursue American goals to Havana and Luanda's detriment. Cuban and Angolan mistrust was further exacerbated by Washington's refusal to recognise either government – despite having been Angola's principal trading partner for over a decade. Thus, however hard Crocker argued that 'linkage' offered gains for Angola and Cuba – including Namibian independence and an end to SADF aggression – he could not shake the impression that he was trying to unseat the MPLA and remove the Cubans from the region. As a result, his approach received a cold reception from Angola, Cuba and their allies.

American relations with South Africa were equally troubled, after suffering almost irreparable damage during Operation Savannah. Convinced that Washington was responsible for South Africa's precarious security, Pretoria viewed any American initiative with suspicion. Regarding Resolution 435 as a non-starter, Pretoria required much persuasion to join Crocker's process, and the early phase of the negotiations was dominated by American attempts to rebuild confidence with the South Africans. Ironically, Crocker's approach to mediation fostered mistrust. For, by demanding opening bids from each side without revealing their opponents', Crocker fuelled suspicion that he was working in cahoots with the enemy on a secret agenda. In fairness to Crocker, given the complexity of the issues at stake his method of mediation was the most logical. It was only by gaining an intimate knowledge of both sides' demands in isolation that he could draw up a proposal based on the common ground between the two. But the effect of this 'collusion with everyone against everyone' (as he later put it)[18] undermined his credibility and, as a result, it took him over three years to extract the first official bids from Luanda and Pretoria.

One startling anomaly in the 'linkage' negotiations was the exclusion of Cuba. In retrospect, given the volume of Cuban manpower posted to Angola and the strength of Cuban–MPLA ties, it seems incredible that Cuba was not invited to join the talks. After all, its withdrawal from southern Africa was one of the essential components of 'linkage' – Pretoria's quid pro quo for pulling out of Angola and Namibia. It is hard to imagine how any deal on Cuban troop withdrawal could have been reached without a Cuban signature, and there is little doubt that Cuba's absence from the talks contributed to their interminable length. Crocker's reasons for excluding the Cubans were political. By 1981, Washington's relations with Cuba were acutely strained by the Mariel crisis, and Crocker was not prepared to offer Havana a seat at the talks without a sizeable concession in return. By excluding the Cubans, however, Crocker allowed Castro to act like a loose cannon whenever the negotiations moved in an unfavourable direction, and on several occasions enabled him to derail the process. In the long-run, Crocker knew the Cubans would have to be brought on board, but few imagined that this would take seven years to achieve.

The exclusion of SWAPO and UNITA from the negotiations (other than behind the scenes) was, on balance, more sensible, as both Pretoria's and Luanda's relationship with them was complicated by nearly two decades of bitter rivalry. Given that South Africa and Angola were supporting one guerrilla movement whilst engaging in war with the other, any decision to involve SWAPO or UNITA could have further fuelled mistrust between the negotiating parties, and might have raised questions about their future relationship with the guerrilla movements to which there were no easy answers. Washington's relationship with UNITA was a further complication, and Crocker's efforts throughout the 1980s to get the Clark Amendment repealed caused great anger in Cuba and Angola – and eventually led to Luanda's withdrawal from the talks in July 1985. Crocker believed that, until Washington could provide covert assistance to UNITA, its leverage over the Angolans would be severely restricted, but his administration's ambiguous relationship with the MPLA's nemesis generated resentment and mistrust in Luanda, and called into question Crocker's impartiality as a mediator.

Crocker's attempts to promote dialogue between Luanda and Pretoria were further hampered by fierce (if concealed) disagreements within the opposing camps. As discussed in Chapter 7, Cuban–Angolan relations were far from harmonious (both on the ground and at the highest echelons of government), and Castro's relationship with Dos Santos was cool when compared to the loyal friendship he shared with Neto. Dos Santos was the consensus choice for president – attempting to balance conflicting interests within the MPLA whilst simultaneously advancing his own – and throughout the early 1980s he would keep Castro at arm's length from the negotiations, only partially informing him of their progress and on occasion forcing him to step in to impose Cuban conditions. Incapable of stamping his authority on the MPLA with the same confidence as his predecessor, Dos Santos would exasperate Castro with his ambiguous negotiating position and (as Crocker put it) his habit of never 'miss[ing] an opportunity to miss an opportunity'.[19] Pretoria set no better example, fierce divisions over Namibia causing periodic paralysis in the South African delegation, and occasionally bringing the negotiations to a halt at their most critical juncture.[20] Getting the opposing parties on-side simultaneously would be one of Crocker's greatest challenges, and he would require phenomenal patience to push the process forward when years of progress were swept aside on the whim of Luanda or Pretoria.

Ultimately, the negotiating process operated under the shadow of the war on the ground, and its success depended on Crocker's team taking advantage of military developments – which alternately put pressure on Luanda and Pretoria – to coax both sides towards a settlement. The problem was that the war in Angola and Namibia acted as both a spur and an impediment to the negotiations. For, while a reverse on the battlefield could prompt a vital concession from one of the negotiating parties, conversely a military victory (perceived or otherwise) could give it the impression that it had the upper hand in the war – and make it less likely to compromise. The trick would be to probe the areas of agreement while the fighting was heaviest, and then exploit both sides' desire for compromise when it ended (as it usually did) in a bloody stalemate. It was a matter of bringing the Angolan and South African orbits into alignment, and then holding them there long enough for substantial progress to be made on the thorniest issues.[21] When alignment was achieved, significant progress could be made, for example the first Lusaka Accord (February 1984). But when external events pushed both parties away from talks (as they did in mid-1985), the negotiations could be put back to square one.

When drawing up his strategy in April 1981, therefore, Crocker opted for a staged approach which aimed to bring the opposing parties together, identify their key demands and then – somehow – form these into a coherent proposal. Crocker first needed to get the South Africans on board and extract from them a firm commitment to implement Resolution 435 under the 'linkage' formula. Then Crocker could dangle the carrot of conditional South African compliance in front of the Angolans, in the hope of persuading them to discuss Cuban troop withdrawal. The irony was that all the parties involved were not opposed to seeing an end to the fighting in Angola and Namibia – indeed, both Cuba and South Africa had been trying unsuccessfully to disengage from Angola for nearly five years. But the combined effect of deep-seated mistrust and the increasingly bitter fighting had driven them away from the negotiating table, and onto the path of all-out confrontation.

The challenge for Crocker's team would be to tease out the very real concerns each party had about entering into negotiations with its sworn enemy, and then make sure that not only were these concerns addressed in the upcoming settlement, but also that both sides understood them and accepted their validity. If trust could not be built between the warring factions, then making them recognise their common interest in resolving the conflict – the very essence of 'linkage' – would push the peace process forward and make a definitive settlement a possibility. In early 1981 it was an incredibly ambitious strategy to undertake. But, convinced that 'linkage' was the only approach which could provide the key to a settlement, Crocker pushed ahead with it, sweeping aside initially unanimous opposition. Few could have imagined – least of all Crocker himself – that it would require seven-and-a-half years of torturous negotiations to achieve his goal.

Phase 1: April 1981–March 1983

The first phase in the 'linkage' negotiations ran in parallel with the UN Contact Group's efforts to secure South African acceptance of Resolution 435, and to an extent operated in its shadow. Since September 1978, the UN Contact Group had watched in frustration as South Africa refused to implement Resolution 435 whilst stepping up its incursions into southern

Angola. Following Operation Protea, the Contact Group mounted a mission to Pretoria, Windhoek and the capitals of the six Front-Line States.[22] After lengthy discussions, on 24 September 1982 the Contact Group reported to the UN Secretary General that it had finally obtained South African acceptance of an expanded Resolution 435 – with the full backing of the Front-Line States and SWAPO. This was to prove the Contact Group's final success, however. For, although it had ironed out some technical details it once again failed to address the issue of Cuban troops and SWAPO/MK bases in Angola, ensuring Pretoria would never implement the new procedures it had just accepted. When the Contact Group then rejected 'linkage' in October, it could offer nothing in its place to satisfy South African security concerns, and it made no further useful contribution to the peace process before its break-up in December 1983.

Crocker's attempts to launch 'linkage' during his first tour of Africa in April 1981 got a hostile reception, and shortly after his return to Washington, the Front-Line States convened a summit in Luanda to denounce 'linkage', demanding the implementation of Resolution 435 in an atmosphere hardly conducive to negotiations. Behind the combative rhetoric, however, Havana was worried by the implications of 'linkage' – which spelled an end to its Angolan adventure – and it launched an energetic campaign to discredit the American strategy. Crocker's talks with Pretoria were more successful, however and, following an exchange of letters in July between Alexander Haig (US Secretary of State) and 'Pik' Botha (South African Foreign Minister), an 'understanding' was reached which signalled South Africa's albeit reticent acceptance of Crocker's role as mediator. One month later, the SADF launched its surprise invasion of southern Angola (Operation Protea), and this turn of events – coupled with Crocker's rapprochement with the South Africans – goaded Havana into action.

For Castro, the success of Operation Protea was a humiliating blow, in one month reversing Cuba's victory in the 'Second Liberation War' and sinking all hopes of a Cuban withdrawal. South Africa's occupation of southern Cunene gave the SADF a direct stake in the Angolan War, and ironically strengthened the arguments in favour of 'linkage'. Still smarting from the Mariel boatlift (which had cast the Cuban regime in a negative light), Castro was not happy that the Americans were muscling in on his area of influence, and as the Third World's self-appointed spokesman he was determined to hit back at Crocker – and to be seen to be hitting back. Privately Castro may also have been alarmed by Dos Santos' conciliatory gestures towards UNITA and South Africa in the months following Operation Protea, which presaged a very Angolan compromise over which Cuba would have little control.[23] Dos Santos was keeping his cards close to his chest, and Castro needed to act before Crocker and Dos Santos took the fate of the Angolan mission out of his hands altogether.

The first 'Joint Statement of Principles', 4 February 1982

The 'Joint Statement of Principles' issued on 4 February 1982 was the Cuban and Angolan governments' reply to 'linkage', and laid down their vision for a regional settlement.[24] Accusing Crocker of using 'linkage' to block the implementation of Resolution 435, the 'Joint Statement' detailed Cuba's justification for its troops' continued presence in Angola, and laid down the conditions under which they would be withdrawn. Perversely inverting 'linkage', Havana and Luanda declared they would reconsider restarting the withdrawal of Cuban troops once three conditions had been met: Namibian independence according to Resolution 435, the election of an independent government and the withdrawal of all South African troops beyond the Orange river (Namibia's southern border with South Africa). There was one proviso, however, which pointed to the true motivations behind the statement: any treaty on Cuban troop withdrawal would be between the Cuban and Angolan governments. The inclusion of this proviso was probably at Cuban insistence and was to let Washington know that Havana alone would determine the fate of its intervention.

The bizarre thing about the 'Joint Statement', however, was that, despite its categorical rejection of 'linkage', this was precisely what Havana and Luanda were proposing. The only difference in their approach was that they demanded the fruits of victory – Namibian independence and South African withdrawal – in advance before discussing the issue which was holding Pretoria back, namely Cuban troop withdrawal. Cuba and Angola's negotiating position over the next few years was therefore rather absurd, as they decried an American strategy which they were proposing themselves under a different name. Possibly Castro issued the 'Joint Statement' as a way of signalling to the Americans that he wanted a seat at the negotiating table. But it is more likely he was pulling his unreliable Angolan ally into line, worried the Americans might force Dos Santos into an agreement which damaged Cuban interests. Only too aware how his integrity as supreme leader of the Cuban Revolution could be damaged if Cuba were forced to withdraw from Angola under duress, Castro pressed for the 'Joint Statement' to protect his domestic and international interests, and he probably dragged Dos Santos along with him against his will. Crocker's strategy had rattled the Cubans, and he could take some comfort from the fact that he had forced Castro to reveal his hand, suggesting that the Cuban leader took 'linkage' and its consequences very seriously indeed.

Castro's action was a powerful demonstration of the dangers of excluding Cuba from the negotiations, but Crocker's team pressed on regardless, holding regular talks with the MPLA throughout 1982. Crocker's initial marathon meetings with the Foreign Minister Paulo Jorge in January and March 1982 (the first lasted twelve hours) failed to make any progress, probably as a result of poor chemistry between the two men who, by their own accounts, couldn't stand each other. In June, Crocker changed tack by sending two subordinates – Vernon Walters and Frank Wisner – to Luanda for further talks.[25] But they quickly discovered that Dos Santos had no mandate to negotiate until he had resolved the power struggle brewing in Luanda.[26] Finally, in December, Dos Santos persuaded the Central Committee to grant him special powers, and he then purged the politburo and FAPLA of his detractors, reorganising the government to put it on a war footing. Strengthened by the purge, Dos Santos appointed a new negotiator – Manuel Alexandre Rodrigues ('Kito')[27] – and this move was warmly welcomed by Crocker's team which quickly established a good working relationship with him.

Phase 2: the 'Kito phase' in the negotiations, March 1983–July 1985

The 'Kito phase' of negotiations (as Crocker termed it) was the most turbulent and inconclusive of the 'linkage' process, and was punctuated by periods of deadlock followed by sudden breakthroughs. Dos Santos' grip on power continued to falter throughout this period, undermining Kito's genuine attempts to move the peace process forward, but significant foundations were nevertheless laid which were to prove crucial to the negotiations' future success. The Americans' first talks with Kito were encouraging, and in March 1983 he headed a four-man delegation to the USA during which he met senior American figures (George Shultz and George Bush Sr. among them) and discussed draft proposals for a settlement. Kito's willingness to negotiate raised false expectations, however, as Dos Santos was under pressure from established party stalwarts – such as Foreign Minister Paulo Jorge – to abandon the negotiations altogether. In August, after the near-disaster at Cangamba, Dos Santos was unable to prevent the politburo voting to suspend Angolan participation in the negotiations. Hoping to coax the Angolans back in, Crocker briefly flirted with the idea of granting Angola diplomatic recognition in return for an opening bid, but the idea was rejected by his superiors, and as UNITA's campaign continued to expand, Luanda's position hardened noticeably.

Meanwhile the UN's negotiating strategy reached a dead-end with the publication of a report by Pérez de Cuellar in late August 1983. In it he confirmed Pretoria's readiness to implement Resolution 435 and implied that the issue of Cuban troop withdrawal was the only thing holding it back. The report caused a storm of protest in the UN General Assembly and, after furious lobbying by Angola's allies, a new resolution was passed against South Africa on 28 October. Condemning attempts to link Namibian independence to 'irrelevant and extraneous issues' (i.e. Cuban troop withdrawal) – and reasserting Resolution 435 as the 'sole and exclusive basis' for a Namibian settlement – Resolution 538 reconfirmed the status quo, and once again deadlocked the negotiations. Convinced that Crocker's peace initiative had failed, the Soviets immediately moved in to capitalise on their diplomatic victory. On 18 November, two Soviet officials met with their South African counterparts in New York and informed them that, now 'linkage' was off the agenda, Moscow would no longer tolerate an SADF presence in southern Angola. Sinisterly insisting that their message should not be viewed as a threat but rather as a means of making South Africa aware of the 'logical and reasonable consequences' of its military action in southern Angola, the Soviets added that they would give the FAPLA all the military assistance it needed to defend itself.[28]

But if the Soviets were seeking to intimidate the South Africans into withdrawing, then their veiled threats had the opposite effect, goading the SADF into launching its twelfth incursion into Angola since independence. Pretoria failed to inform Crocker of this decision, however – despite holding its first meeting with him in over a year the day before the invasion was launched – and when in protest France suspended its participation in the UN Contact Group, the peace process seemed to be well and truly dead.[29] Operation Askari – as the South African invasion was codenamed – would confound everybody's expectations, however. And within a few weeks an invasion which should have sunk the negotiations for good had instead created a window of opportunity for Crocker's team, enabling them to pull off their first success of the 'linkage' negotiations.

Background to Operation Askari

Since gaining its foothold in southern Cunene in late 1981, the SADF had stepped up operations against SWAPO and, in a series of attacks, had inflicted devastating casualties on the guerrilla movement, severely disrupting its efforts to infiltrate Namibia. By the time the SADF launched Operation Phoenix in February 1983,[30] incursions deep into Angola in pursuit of SWAPO had become routine, and the lack of reaction from the FAPLA or Cubans had bred in the South Africans a false sense of security. When, in late 1983, the SADF learned that SWAPO was planning to infiltrate up to 1,000 guerrillas into Namibia once the rainy season was underway, plans were drawn up for another pre-emptive strike.[31] Modelled on Operation Protea, Askari had three objectives: to disrupt SWAPO's logistical infrastructure in Angola, to prevent its guerrillas from infiltrating Namibia and to capture or destroy as much military equipment as possible.

Initially planned as a small-scale raid, the operation expanded to involve four 500-man mechanised units which would cross into Angola to attack SWAPO concentrations (identified during aerial reconnaissance), while smaller units patrolled the border to intercept any guerrillas infiltrating Namibia. Ground forces would be supported by Mirage and Impala fighter-bombers, although reports that the SADF was testing out its answer to the Soviet BM-21 – the newly developed G-5 155 mm gun – appear to be unfounded.[32] According to some sources, Operation Askari also had the objective of taking pressure off UNITA's insurgency in the east by inflicting as much damage as possible on the FAPLA's growing military power in southern Angola.[33] It seems unlikely, however, that the SADF intended to take on the entire FAPLA army in southern Angola with no more than 2,500 men, and throughout the operation South African troops were under strict orders not to engage FAPLA–Cuban forces unless it was unavoidable.[34]

But if the South Africans thought they were in for an easy ride against the FAPLA, then they were in for a nasty shock. By late 1983, the FAPLA had completed its two-year training and re-equipment programme, and had greatly increased in size, technical capability and (to a certain extent) competence. By 1983 Luanda was spending 35 per cent of its budget on the armed forces and, thanks to the Soviet–Cuban training programme, the FAPLA was starting to resemble a professional army, deploying tanks in mobile formation, flying attack missions against Mirages, and operating the elaborate air defence system installed by the Soviets and Cubans in Cahama. Unlike the isolated garrisons in Moxico and Cuando Cubango, the FAPLA–Cuban forces in Cunene and Huíla were well supplied and competently organised and, crucially, they were under orders to protect SWAPO if the situation became desperate. Humiliated by the ease with which the SADF had occupied southern Angola during Operation Protea, the Cuban and Soviet commanders were determined the South Africans would not have another free run in Angola.

Operation Askari

The first SADF units crossed into Cunene on 6 December 1983, the main battle-group heading for a large SWAPO camp at Mulondo (Huíla) which it attacked six days later, drawing in a nearby FAPLA unit. Across southern Angola, other FAPLA units quickly joined the fighting, sending reinforcements to SWAPO and laying several ambushes, one of which caught a South African unit near Caiundo, killing five and capturing their Unimog truck. Less than a week into the fighting, President Botha made a surprise peace gesture, offering in an open letter to the UN Secretary General to withdraw South African forces from Angola if Luanda reciprocated the gesture. Botha's offer seemed inconsistent at the time, but he appears to have been capitalising on the renewed military pressure to force Luanda into a deal which would remove SWAPO from southern Angola for good. Angola's allies responded with five days of lobbying at the UN, and on 20 December the Security Council passed Resolution 546, demanding South Africa's withdrawal from Angola and reparations, and this once more deadlocked the negotiations. Crocker nevertheless sensed an opportunity, and as the fighting intensified, his team worked furiously behind the scenes to broker a deal.

The attack on Cuvelai, 3–7 January 1984

When planning Operation Askari, the SADF had selected a large SWAPO training camp three miles north-east of Cuvelai (northern Cunene) as one of its principal objectives, confident that neither the FAPLA's 11th Brigade garrisoning the town nor two nearby Cuban battalions would come to SWAPO's aid. The camp was heavily defended – with sixteen minefields around its perimeter and artillery firing air-burst shells (which were lethal against infantry) – but the going was made tougher by the heaviest rains in living memory, which turned the battlefield into a quagmire. Within hours of the South Africans launching their attack, FAPLA units had come to SWAPO's aid, using Soviet T-55 tanks for the first time in a mobile role. One of them destroyed a South African Ratel which got bogged down in a minefield, killing its five crew. Two Cuban battalions then joined the fray, and a ferocious battle ensued over the next four days as the SADF attempted to push the FAPLA and Cubans back towards Cuvelai, eventually taking what was left of the town on 7 January.

The fighting at Cuvelai was the SADF's costliest single engagement in Angola to date, accounting for twenty-one of Operation Askari's twenty-four South African fatalities. The battle was by no means one-sided, however, as the South Africans claim to have killed 324 SWAPO, FAPLA and Cuban soldiers, destroying eleven T-55s and fourteen armoured cars, and capturing intact a SAM-6 missile defence system. Despite the high enemy body count, the South Africans were as shocked as their adversaries by the ferocity of the fighting, and it is no coincidence that, within days of Cuvelai, peace talks had restarted between Luanda and Pretoria. Following the capture of Cuvelai, the South Africans started withdrawing from Angola (the last elements crossed into Namibia on 15 January), leaving behind small garrisons at Calueque, N'Giva and Xangongo as their only permanent presence in southern Angola.

The South African withdrawal from Angola more than two weeks before a ceasefire was signed therefore gave the negotiating process a certain absurdity, as the Angolans demanded the withdrawal of forces which Pretoria knew were no longer there.[35] Peace overtures began on 5 January when SWAPO's president Sam Nujoma asked the UN Secretary General to arrange ceasefire negotiations with the South Africans. Five days later, Kito met with the American Ambassador to Maputo and proposed talks with Crocker in ten days' time, offering a thirty-day 'truce' and an agenda which included restrictions on SWAPO and the basic 'linkage' formula.[36] Alarmed at Luanda's sudden change of heart, Castro put pressure on the Angolans to exclude Cuban troop withdrawal from the negotiations and, on 18 January, Dos Santos acquiesced, publicly insisting that his government would only enter into ceasefire talks if they excluded any reference to 'linkage'. Castro was once more nervous at the revitalisation of Crocker's peace process, and the Americans pressed home their advantage, convinced that a ceasefire in southern Angola would encourage Luanda to make a proposal on Cuban troop withdrawal.

The first 'Lusaka Accord', 16 February 1984

With the fighting around Cuvelai now causing grave concern, the negotiations progressed rapidly and, on 31 January, Angola and South Africa signed a ceasefire brokered by Crocker's team – the first treaty between their two governments. With hostilities suspended, on 6 February Botha proposed further talks to establish a framework for a South African withdrawal, and these led to the setting up of a Joint Monitoring Commission (JMC) – made up of FAPLA and SADF officers – to oversee the withdrawal process, and to monitor any violations of the agreement.[37] Crucially the agreement included an understanding that the JMC was a first step towards a regional peace settlement, thus incorporating what had been a unilateral South African proposal into the wider peace process. Three days later, the delegations met in Lusaka to hammer out the details of the JMC, and the accord signed on 16 February – the 'Lusaka Accord' – was the first significant victory in Crocker's peace process, creating (as he put it) 'a balanced context for South African withdrawal and Angolan reassertion of sovereignty'.[38]

The JMC fell far short of expectations, however, and within days of its formation, it was bogged down in procedural disagreements and recriminations. Deadlines were repeatedly re-set and re-broken, and by the time the JMC's HQ was set up in N'Giva on 3 May (over five weeks behind schedule) all progress on withdrawing the remaining South African contingents from Angola was deadlocked. The main reason for the JMC's failure was the Lusaka Accord itself. For, although it admonished the MPLA to restrain SWAPO while the South Africans completed their withdrawal, SWAPO was not a signatory of the accord and was therefore not bound by its conditions, giving it a free rein to step up its Namibian insurgency. Inevitably the SADF was drawn back into the fighting, and as its confrontations with SWAPO escalated outside the JMC's area of operations, the JMC lost all legitimacy. Indeed, by late 1984, it had become an obstacle to the peace process, giving each side plenty of opportunity to bicker with the other over alleged violations of the agreement, while removing any incentive for them to advance on substantive issues.

The Soviets take over in Angola

News that South African forces had again invaded Angola elicited a robust response from Luanda's Cuban and Soviet allies, and at an emergency meeting in Moscow on 12 January 1984, they authorised a further increase in military aid for the FAPLA, their third in only two years. Over the next fourteen months, the Soviets would provide the FAPLA with upgraded SAM-8 missile-launchers, MiG-23s, T-62 tanks and Mi-24 assault helicopters, as well as a radar network covering the whole of southern Angola.[39] The launch of this new programme marked the start of the Soviet take-over of the operation in Angola, and within eighteen months the FAPLA's strategic and tactical decision-making had come under the complete control of the dozen or so Soviet officers in Luanda. Seizing on the opportunity to test out the military capability it had amassed over the previous decade – and keen to extend its influence into what was becoming a Cold War hot-spot – the Soviet military began planning a full-scale offensive against UNITA along standard Soviet lines.

Castro's reaction to this take-over was never revealed in public, but he cannot have been happy about it after struggling to keep control of the Angolan operation for nearly a decade. He could hardly confront the Soviets on this issue, however, as his political survival depended on their good will, and if they decided to increase their role in Angola there was little he could do about it. Besides there was never any question of the command of Cuban forces being wrested from his control, and provided the bulk of them remained on garrison duty, the risk of increased casualties (and the popular backlash this might cause) was minimal. Castro therefore did not oppose the Soviets taking over the planning of the FAPLA's operations, little suspecting the bitter disagreements this would provoke between the Cuban and Soviet commanders in Angola. Of more immediate concern to Castro, however, was the Lusaka Accord which once more threatened to resurrect the 'linkage' negotiations, and less than a month later Dos Santos was summoned to Havana to explain himself.

The second 'Joint Statement of Principles', 19 March 1984

By the time Dos Santos arrived in Havana on 17 March – four years to the day since his last (and only) visit to Cuba – Cuban forces were fully engaged in the fighting in Angola, losing as many as 100 men at Cangamba and Cuvelai. Alarmed at the revival of Crocker's peace process – which threatened to reopen dialogue between Pretoria and the Front-Line States (with unpredictable results)[40] – Castro moved quickly to restrain Dos Santos before he made concessions on the crucial question of Cuban withdrawal. A second, more belligerent 'Statement of Principles' was issued, declaring that the two years which had passed since its predecessor had reconfirmed the justice of its demands, and vehemently denouncing the Americans and South Africa for 'stubbornly clinging for years to the pernicious formula of so-called linkage'.[41] The conditions for a Cuban withdrawal were emphatically laid down – the unilateral withdrawal of SADF forces from Angola, the strict implementation of Resolution 435 and the cessation of South African aggression against Angola (including aid to UNITA) – all under the proviso that any Cuban withdrawal would take place under a bilateral agreement between the Cuban and Angolan governments.

Reading between the lines, however, the statement contained a concession which few picked up at the time. For, in what was a significant climb-down, the Cubans and Angolans conceded that the conditions laid down in the 1982 Statement should not be considered as demands but rather as 'a basis of principles for any negotiating process'. Implying that they were prepared to make concessions on the final agreement, this softening of stance may have been at the insistence of Dos Santos whose political survival depended on ending the fighting in Angola as quickly as possible, and who (according to one source) was pressured into the statement against his will.[42] Perhaps Castro's decision during Dos Santos' visit to waive the $20 million annual fee for Cuba's humanitarian mission in Angola was intended as a sweetener for agreeing to such a belligerent statement. But whatever Dos Santos' motivations, the incident was a powerful illustration of how competing agendas in Havana and Luanda could strain relations between the allies.

The second Joint Statement elicited an angry response from Pik Botha, who declared that the MPLA's support for SWAPO and the ANC – which were praised in the closing paragraph – had undermined the legitimacy of the JMC. Once more unilateral action by Castro threatened to derail the 'linkage' peace process, and by now Crocker suspected that the Cuban leader was using the statements to put in a bid for a seat at the negotiating table. But the political climate dictated against Crocker offering the Cubans a role in the negotiations, and in the meantime his team had to press on regardless in their attempts to coax an opening bid from the South African and Angolan governments. Speed would be essential as less than a week after the publication of the Joint Statement, UNITA launched the first in a series of attacks on Cuban targets in Angola, bringing the war deep into MPLA territory, and putting Cuban civilians in the line of fire for the first time.

The Sumbe raid, 25 March 1984

Following the bloody siege of Cangamba, UNITA had returned to unconventional tactics with a wave of attacks against civilian targets. Shying away from frontal assaults on well-defended garrisons, UNITA opted for a campaign of indiscriminate mine-laying (which caused hundreds of civilian casualties), truck-bombs, missile attacks on passenger aircraft and (especially in 1984) hostage-taking.[43] Taking foreign hostages was an effective tactic, for not only did it cause Luanda great embarrassment (and put it under pressure to get foreign nationals released), but it gave UNITA large amounts of publicity quite out of proportion to the scale of the raids. UNITA took its first foreign hostages – sixty-four Czechs and twenty Portuguese – during an attack on Alto Catumbela (Benguela) in March 1983. This was followed in February 1984 by a raid on the Cafunfo diamond mines (Lunda Norte) which netted more foreign nationals.[44] The Lundas were too remote to threaten Luanda, however, and in an attempt to bring the war onto MPLA turf, UNITA planned a raid on Cuanza Sul's provincial capital – Sumbe (formerly Novo Redondo) – where there were known to be 300 foreign aid workers, two-thirds of whom were Cuban internationalists.[45]

In early March 1984, UNITA scouts reconnoitred Sumbe, pinpointing the buildings housing Cuban, Soviet, Bulgarian, Italian and Portuguese civilians, and they discovered that there were fewer than eighty soldiers defending the town. Assembling a force of 1,500 guerrillas – supported by mortars and RPGs – UNITA planned a three-pronged attack. First, Sumbe would be surrounded from the north and south to cut off all possible escape routes. Then the guerrillas would sweep into the town centre where hostage-taking units would snatch as many foreign workers and senior MPLA officials as possible, after which they would withdraw. UNITA wanted the raid to demonstrate its ability to strike at the MPLA deep behind enemy lines and, according to Cuban accounts, there were plans to call a public meeting after the town was captured to show popular support for UNITA. On 22 March, the raiding force was spotted by the FAPLA near Vila Nova do Seles (Uku, forty miles south-east of Sumbe), potentially jeopardising the operation. But strangely no effort was made to reinforce Sumbe (the Cubans later claimed they were unsure if the town was UNITA's intended target). As a result, when the attack came three days later, they had no choice but to call on their civilian – and in particular Cuban – contingents to defend the town.

Given Sumbe's location, over 250 miles north of the ATS Defence Line, the town had seen no guerrilla activity since its recapture in January 1976. Viewing it as beyond UNITA's range of operations, Luanda saw no reason to garrison the town with conventional units and instead entrusted its defence to a handful of soldiers, the police and militia. Once it was clear that an attack was imminent, a joint FAPLA–Cuban command was set up which worked furiously in the hours leading up to the attack to prepare a defence plan. Drawing on one company each of MINSE (State Security), MININT (Ministry of Interior) and ODP (militia) troops, it mustered 230 men, to which were added 206 Cuban civilian internationalists.[46] Every

Cuban had received basic military training, but few had combat experience, and they were poorly armed, supported by only a single mortar and four RPGs. Fearing their defences would be overwhelmed, all foreign civilians (unless, like most of the Cubans, they were involved in the defence of Sumbe) were evacuated from their buildings and moved to securer parts of the city, while the bulk of the FAPLA–Cuban force was deployed in a single ring around the city centre, protecting the government buildings.

At dawn on 25 March, the UNITA force stopped just south of Sumbe and split into three groups, one heading north towards the airport while the other two cut off the southern approaches to the town. At around 5 a.m., all three forces launched their attack simultaneously. The northern force quickly captured the airport while the other two swept through the MINSE training camp (on the road to Vila Nova do Seles) and advanced on the town centre. Having blown up the runway and the militia's warehouse, UNITA occupied the Antenas heights overlooking the town centre, and from there it unleashed a bombardment which continued for most of the day. By 7 a.m., Luanda had been informed of the attack and it immediately organised air support, although given Sumbe's distance from Luanda it offered no more reinforcements than a detachment of armoured cars which was dispatched from Lobito. By then bitter street-fighting had broken out as UNITA infiltrated the town centre, capturing the MINSE and militia HQs before getting bogged down in an assault on the MPLA HQ. UNITA's northern assault was also briefly halted by a force of fifty Cubans and Angolans at the Provincial Commissary. But after eleven had been killed and twenty wounded, they too were forced to withdraw, taking up positions at the UNECA building (where the Italians were still hiding) for a last stand.

At this point, the tide of battle turned, however, and a spirited counter-attack drove UNITA back through the town centre and out through the northern suburbs. By now, FAPLA–Cuban aircraft were flying over the scene, and their bombing runs on the airport and city outskirts did much to lift the defenders' morale, forcing UNITA to call off its assault. At 3 p.m., a company of Cuban commandos was airlifted into Sumbe by helicopter, and in a bloody two-hour battle they recaptured the Antenas heights. By this time UNITA had been driven out of the town centre, and its guerrillas melted back into the hilly interior. That evening, helicopters flew out twenty Cuban and three Angolan wounded, and over the following days FAPLA–Cuban aircraft repeatedly tried to hit UNITA as it withdrew eastwards, having little success in the dense jungle terrain. By the end of the fighting, as many as 100 UNITA guerrillas had been killed, forty-five of them in the close-quarter battle in the town centre. The defenders lost at least eleven killed and twenty-three wounded (although losses on both sides may have been much higher). Thanks to the measures taken to protect foreign workers, UNITA had only captured one small group of Portuguese who had ignored Cuban orders to evacuate their building (their fate is not recorded).

The brave defence put up by the Cuban civilians at Sumbe powerfully demonstrated the strength of the 'civic soldier' programme and, in recognition of the fierceness of the fighting, the 206 Cubans who fought at Sumbe were awarded the Internationalist Combatant Medal (First Class), a decoration usually reserved for front-line troops. Behind the triumphant propaganda, however, genuine concerns were growing that Cuban personnel – in particular civilians – were being drawn into the fighting, threatening to escalate casualties alarmingly. Fears that Sumbe was merely the first in a series of attacks against civilian targets were confirmed a month later when UNITA planted a car-bomb outside a building housing Cuban internationalists in Huambo, killing fourteen and wounding sixty-six others.[47] Although the Cuban regime channelled popular outcry into a massive recruitment drive for internationalist missions, privately the leadership feared the effect a dramatic rise in casualties could have on public opinion. But with UNITA intensifying its insurgency – with attacks on the Benguela railway line and on the Cabinda oil installations[48] – the prospects for keeping Cubans out of the firing line steadily diminished, and Castro struggled in vain to keep a lid on the fighting as his Soviet patrons sought to escalate the war to ever greater heights.

Elusive progress in the negotiations, July 1984–March 1985

Against this background of deepening conflict in Angola, the American peace process edged forward. Boosted by the Lusaka Accord, Crocker's team spent the rest of 1984 coaxing opening bids out of the Angolan and South African governments as an essential step in creating a workable basis for negotiation. But the window of opportunity was rapidly closing, and the threat of hostilities escalating into full-scale war acted as both a spur and a brake to progress. Attempts to bring Pretoria and SWAPO together for talks in July 1984 failed dismally (the meeting broke up within hours), but separate talks between the Cape Verdean government and Castro later that month proved more significant, Castro confirming that Cuba was ready to withdraw from Angola 'under the right conditions'.[49] This was not the U-turn it appeared, however, as the 'right conditions' were those laid down in the previous March's Joint Statement. But it did pave the way for a visit by Kito to Cuba in August, and following his talks with Castro, Kito finally presented the Angolan government's opening bid to Crocker on 7 September – over a year after it had been promised.[50]

Unsurprisingly, the bid fell short of Crocker's expectations and on the crucial issue of Cuban withdrawal introduced a new set of conditions which were to dog the peace process until its end. While the four essential demands had not changed,[51] it now became clear that Luanda was not offering to withdraw *all* Cuban forces from Angola, but only those based in the south (the ATS). The 10,000 Cubans in the 'Northern Troop Grouping' (or ATN) – which protected Luanda, Malanje and Cabinda – would be excluded from the negotiations, and would remain in Angola until Havana and Luanda agreed to withdraw them. Furthermore, the Angolans envisioned a four-year timetable for the withdrawal (rather than one year, as Crocker had suggested). For Castro and Dos Santos, the rate at which Cuban troops were withdrawn from Angola was fundamental to their political futures, and both were seeking as lengthy a timetable as possible. For Castro, the Cuban withdrawal was above all a matter of honour, and needed to be carried out (and to be seen to be carried out) in an orderly manner to dispel any impression that Cuba was scrambling out of Angola just as it had scrambled in during Operation Carlota. For Dos Santos, it was a matter of pure survival: the lengthier the withdrawal timetable, the less likely the FAPLA would collapse in the face of UNITA's insurgency.

From his talks in Pretoria only a week earlier, however, Crocker knew that the South Africans were proposing a *seven month* period during which *all* Cuban forces would be withdrawn, presenting him with a forty-one month gap to bridge. Realising the Angolan proposal was a non-starter, Crocker urged Kito to work on the two-year timetable. One month later – after two more rounds of talks in Luanda and much wrangling with the Cubans – Angola presented a revised bid which, though far from ideal, was recognised by the Americans as the best they were likely to get. Not only did it 'enshrine linkage in all but name', but it had 'Cuban fingerprints all over it', making it less susceptible to unexpected changes.[52] In late October, Crocker discussed the Angolan bid with the South Africans in Cape Verde, and on 15 November Pretoria replied with it own bid. It had taken Crocker three-and-a-half years to extract the opening bids and, although they were miles apart (South Africa was now suggesting the Cuban withdrawal be reduced to only *twelve weeks*), his team could at last start drawing up a 'basis for negotiation'. Time was running out for the peace process, however, with South Africa's internal crisis worsening by the day and the sanctions debate heating up in Congress. Crocker's team nevertheless worked as quickly as it could to produce a workable document, and this was finally presented to the Angolan and South African governments in March 1985.

Crocker presents the 'basis for negotiation', March 1985

Melding together the many proposals, joint statements and bids he had received over the previous four years, Crocker's 'basis for negotiation' was an attempt not only to find common ground between the two parties, but also to focus their attention on the outstanding issues and – Crocker hoped – encourage them to start making concessions in the horse-trading which was bound to follow.[53] While the 'basis for negotiation' contained elements already agreed by both parties – the commitment to implement Resolution 435 and to respect each other's territorial integrity – the meat of the proposal was in the withdrawal conditions which Crocker knew would be seen as a sell-out by both sides. Sticking to his original proposal, Crocker proposed a two-year timetable which would start as soon as South Africa started implementing Resolution 435. In the first year, 80 per cent of Cuban forces would withdraw, while a residual of no more than 6,000 troops would remain north of the 13th parallel for up to one additional year. To quell South African fears, Cuban troops would promise not to carry out offensive action during this period, and to satisfy the Angolans, SWAPO and the Front-Line States, the UN Security Council would adopt a resolution guaranteeing the commitments made by both parties.

Unfortunately for Crocker, the very boldness of his 'basis for negotiation' was to be its undoing. For once the Angolan and South African governments (which had never taken the American peace process entirely seriously) had taken time to consider its implications, they balked at the prospect of negotiating any further. Both sides had been attracted to the Lusaka Accord specifically because it avoided the major issues in the southern African dispute. But faced with the prospect of negotiating these issues with their arch enemies, they did not feel ready to make the many crucial and politically painful concessions which would be demanded. Both parties therefore backed off from the negotiations, and over the next four months they took up belligerent positions as a series of events in Angola and South Africa pushed them away from talks and back onto the path of military confrontation.

As if to augur the impending collapse of the peace process, the day Crocker arrived in Pretoria to present his proposal to Pik Botha – 21 March 1985 – South African police killed nineteen blacks at Uitenhage (near Port Elizabeth) who were marching on the twenty-fifth anniversary of the Sharpeville massacre, rekindling civil unrest and sparking international outcry. The timing for Crocker was acutely embarrassing, and to compound the blow, the next day Savimbi rejected the 'basis for negotiation', refusing to back a process which would cut off all his external aid.[54] Hopes were briefly raised a month later when – in an apparent gesture of goodwill – Pretoria announced that it would withdraw all its remaining forces from Angola within one week. But the true meaning of this gesture became clear the day after the last South African troops crossed into Namibia (17 April) when Pretoria set up an 'Interim Government' in Namibia. This move was in direct contravention of Resolution 435 (which entrusted any political changes in Namibia to the UN) and provoked immediate condemnation from SWAPO and its allies who complained – with justification – that South Africa had violated the spirit of the negotiations.

The South African raid on Cabinda, 20/21 May 1985

One month later, their complaints turned to outrage when two SADF commandos were captured carrying out a sabotage attack on the Gulf Oil installations in Malongo (Cabinda).[55] The nine-man unit was intercepted while laying sixteen mines on oil storage tanks and pipelines in the complex, and during a fiercely-fought withdrawal, one commando was killed and two captured, the remaining six escaping in dinghies to a waiting South African submarine. News of the attack caused an international scandal which intensified when the head of the team – Captain Wynand du Toit – admitted in a press conference that the attack on Malongo was the fourth sabotage mission his unit had carried out in Angola since 1980.[56] More controversially, the South African team had been carrying bags of UNITA leaflets which were to be left behind (to give the impression UNITA carried out the attack), sparking speculation that many UNITA attacks over the previous five years had been carried out by the South Africans. The realisation that the SADF had been conducting a clandestine campaign to destabilise Angola throughout the negotiating process caused outrage in Luanda, and not a little embarrassment that it had taken a full five years to uncover.[57]

The raid also highlighted, however, Washington's paradoxical relationship with Luanda, and demonstrated how tangled and absurd the alliances of the Angolan War had become. For, while Washington had spent the decade since Angola gained independence isolating Luanda – refusing to grant it the diplomatic recognition it craved – the American-run Malongo installations (which produced 65 per cent of Angola's petroleum) had simultaneously provided the MPLA with an economic lifeline, generating most of Angola's hard currency revenue and making Angola the USA's largest trading partner in sub-Saharan Africa. The absurdity of this situation was compounded by the fact that Luanda – which recognised the importance of Cabinda oil to its future survival – had posted an elite garrison of around 5,000 Cuban troops in Cabinda to protect the installations from guerrilla attacks. Thus the Cuban forces which Washington was decrying as instruments of Soviet imperialism in Africa were actually responsible for protecting the assets of one of the largest American companies there.[58] Once it became clear that South African units had carried out the attack on Malongo, Crocker's strategy of 'Constructive Engagement' lost all credibility and, with the sanctions debate reaching a climax in Congress, the Cabinda raid strengthened the argument for breaking off ties with Pretoria. When SADF commandos launched another raid on 14 June – this time against ANC offices in Gaborone (Botswana's capital) –

the American administration withdrew its Ambassador from Pretoria, rupturing the alliance with South Africa.

The negotiations collapse

The final blow to the peace process did not come from the South Africans, however, but from the Reagan administration which – after four years of lobbying – finally succeeded in getting the Clark Amendment repealed on 10 July 1985. The amendment had been a thorn in the side of American policy for nearly a decade, and Crocker had energetically advocated its repeal since his first days in office, arguing that, until Washington was free to intervene militarily in Angola (on however small a scale), it lacked the leverage to force Luanda into making serious concessions. But Crocker did not appreciate that Luanda could only interpret the amendment's repeal as an outright provocation – indeed almost a declaration of war – and with the mediator about to start arming UNITA, Luanda predictably declared that the negotiating process had lost all legitimacy. Three days later, Luanda withdrew from the negotiations, ironically citing the repeal of the Clark Amendment as proof of complicity between Washington and Pretoria to overthrow it, when in reality relations between the two were at their lowest ebb in years.[59] With the warring parties now looking to settle their dispute militarily – and Crocker's 'linkage' strategy under departmental review – the peace process which had promised so much at Lusaka was dead in the water.

Scarcely a fortnight after Luanda's withdrawal from the negotiations, the FAPLA launched a massive Soviet-style offensive against UNITA's strongholds in Moxico and Cuando Cubango. The offensive dwarfed all previous FAPLA operations and was intended to deliver the definitive blow to Savimbi's guerrillas in time for the MPLA's Second Party Congress scheduled for December. Using over 20,000 troops and sophisticated Soviet technology, the offensive would plunge UNITA into its deepest crisis for a decade, and rekindle its alliance with the SADF. Having declared a State of Emergency one week after the negotiations collapsed, Pretoria was fighting for its very survival against internal unrest and international sanctions. But with MK and SWAPO operations on the increase, it could ill afford to let its erstwhile Angolan ally be crushed by a resurgent FAPLA. And so, as FAPLA forces started to advance on Mavinga, a fresh SADF intervention in Angola grew ever more likely, drawing the battle lines for the largest military confrontation in southern African history.

9

THE BIG OFFENSIVES, 1985–7

The collapse of the 'linkage' negotiations and the launch of the FAPLA offensive against Mavinga initiated the most violent phase of the Angolan War, with Soviet military influence at its peak. Bolstered by over $4 billion of military hardware, the Soviets confidently predicted that 'Operation Congresso II' (as the offensive was code-named) would deliver a crushing blow to UNITA's remote bases in Moxico and Cuando Cubango. But, as happened so often in the Angolan War, outright victory eluded the FAPLA, and 'Congresso II' spawned a succession of equally inconclusive 'final offensives'. As casualties mounted for the FAPLA and its allies, relations between them grew severely strained, sparking fierce disagreements over the military strategy and further fuelling the discontent brewing in the Cuban contingent. Against this background, Crocker's team stubbornly refused to give up on 'linkage', and persistently pushed for a resumption of talks during periodic lulls in the fighting. But with all sides set on a military solution there was no mood for compromise, and it would take a full three years of bloody fighting before the warring parties could be brought back to the negotiating table.

Background to Operation Congresso II

Following the Soviet take-over of the FAPLA's operations in the early 1980s, ambitious plans were drawn up to destroy UNITA's growing presence in the remote east and south-east of Angola. The FAPLA's first full-scale offensive against UNITA's bases in Cazombo and Lumbala-N'Guimbo in the summer of 1984 was a disappointing failure, however, with the 15,000-man force failing to reach either objective. Undaunted, in early 1985 the Soviets began planning a more ambitious two-pronged offensive against Cazombo and Mavinga (Cuando Cubango) on a scale which dwarfed previous FAPLA operations.[1] The plan was to drive UNITA out of Moxico and back into the south-east of Angola, paving the way for a final push against Jamba once Mavinga was in FAPLA hands. Convinced that nearly a decade of Soviet and Cuban training had created a FAPLA army capable of carrying out such a complex operation, the Soviets predicted that Cazombo and Mavinga would fall in time for the MPLA's Second Party Congress that December (hence the offensive's codename). The ambitious Soviet plan immediately met with objections from the FAPLA and Cuban commanders, however. The FAPLA commanders opposed splitting their forces between two fronts, arguing that a single assault on Mavinga would be sufficient to defeat UNITA (although it is also likely that many of them privately harboured doubts that the FAPLA could carry out an offensive on such a scale). More ominously, the Cubans raised the possibility of a South African intervention in support of UNITA, and warned that the offensive could quickly turn into a disaster unless precautions were taken to prevent this. The Soviets overruled their objections, however, confident that the vast amount of hardware at their disposal would see off any UNITA resistance. The conventional nature of the offensive was to be its undoing, however. For, although the Soviets were experienced in planning large-scale operations, none of them appreciated the logistical difficulties presented by south-east Angola's terrain, nor UNITA's effectiveness in harassing the advancing armies. But, as the senior partner in Angola, the Soviets overrode their allies' objections and set about assembling the largest FAPLA force to date.

Totalling as many as twenty brigades (at least 20,000 men), the FAPLA force was supported by upgraded MiG-23s, Su-22 fighter-bombers, Mi-24/25 helicopter gun-ships (in combat for the first time in Angola) and T-62 tanks. For the first time, Soviet personnel would be involved on the ground – a dozen officers accompanying each battalion – and logistical support was provided by the Soviet bases at Lobito, Luanda (naval base) and Lubango. Despite denials by Havana, it is also likely that Cuban officers accompanied the FAPLA throughout the offensive, operating their artillery and air defence systems, and providing air support. The plan called for both forces to set off simultaneously, the smaller force moving from Luena along the Benguela railway line towards Cazombo, while the larger force headed south from Cuito Cuanavale towards Mavinga. Confidence was high, and the Soviets expected the first objective – Cazombo – to be in their hands by the time the NAM Ministerial Conference opened in Luanda that September.

Operation Congresso II, July–October 1985

In late July 1985, the two FAPLA forces began moving out from Luena and Cuito Cuanavale, and within days UNITA's operations had been thrown into chaos. Although UNITA had as many as 30,000 guerrillas, most were lightly armed and trained for unconventional warfare, and it quickly became clear that without armour and artillery they would be unable to defend Cazombo and Mavinga from the double assault. UNITA guerrillas did slow down the advancing columns with ambushes, mine-laying and raids but when, in early September, the FAPLA reached both towns' outer defences, the situation became critical. Facing the impossible task of fighting on two fronts over 300 miles apart, UNITA requested South African assistance. In mid-September the SADF launched Operation Magneto, providing artillery officers, medical personnel and air transports to fly hundreds of guerrillas from Mavinga to Cazombo. Nevertheless, the situation on both fronts continued to deteriorate and, on 19 September, Savimbi ordered his troops to abandon Cazombo and withdraw for a last-ditch defence of Mavinga.

Facing annihilation, Savimbi urged the SADF to step up its assistance, and in late September it responded with Operation Wallpaper, providing UNITA with the crucial support it needed to save Mavinga. By then, the FAPLA had crossed the last remaining obstacle in its path (the Lomba river) and was less than twenty miles from the town, while Cuban MiGs were pounding the tiny runway on which UNITA depended for supplies and reinforcements. If Mavinga were allowed to fall, then UNITA would probably have to abandon Jamba, threatening the security of the Caprivi Strip and inevitably leading to a resurgence in SWAPO activity. The top priority, therefore, was to get UNITA's guerrillas to Mavinga as quickly as possible – a formidable task given its remote location and UNITA's lack of aircraft – and SAAF transports were provided to fly thousands of guerrillas from Cazombo back to Mavinga. UNITA also lacked firepower to respond to the BM-21s and heavy guns, and to counter this threat, the SADF dispatched a troop of MRLs (multiple rocket-launchers), and provided air cover with Mirage and Impala fighter-bombers.

The South African MRLs took up position south of the Lomba river on 27 September, and over the following week the combined effect of UNITA's ground attacks, South African artillery and air strikes broke the back of the offensive, inflicting punishing casualties on the FAPLA whose limited air defences were no match for South African air power. In an effort to rescue Congresso II from disaster, ten Soviet officers were flown to Cuito Cuanavale to plan a resumption of the offensive, but when their aircraft was shot down by a Mirage as it came in to land (killing all on board), Luanda decided to cut its losses. Fearing its forces might get stranded hundreds of miles from their nearest base if the offensive dragged on into the rainy season, in early October the Soviets ordered the withdrawal from Mavinga. Although sporadic clashes continued until the end of the year, Congresso II had effectively ended at the Lomba river.

While, publicly, both sides declared victory, the carnage of the confrontation was a sobering experience and demonstrated how costly the Angolan War had become. The FAPLA sustained nearly 2,500 casualties, losing more than a dozen aircraft, thirty-two armoured vehicles and over 100 trucks, many of those who died succumbing to thirst in the gruelling retreat to Cuito Cuanavale.[2] The FAPLA's allies also suffered casualties, the Soviets losing ten killed and nine wounded while the Cubans – who still officially deny any involvement in the offensive – suffered fifty-six fatalities and sixty wounded, their heaviest loss since the 'Cassinga raid' seven years before.[3] UNITA lost over 500 killed and 1,500 wounded, severely weakening its military strength, and only just managed to hold onto Mavinga thanks to the last-minute South African intervention.[4] Recognising how close UNITA had come to defeat, Savimbi drew up plans with the South Africans to disrupt FAPLA operations in south-east Angola, determined to prevent a fresh offensive against Mavinga.

For the Soviets, the failure of Congresso II was a major embarrassment. Having repeatedly ignored Cuban warnings of a South African intervention, they had been forced into a humiliating retreat when they were within twenty miles of Mavinga. Millions of dollars of military equipment – including helicopter gun-ships and tanks which had only recently been supplied to the FAPLA – had been destroyed or abandoned, and the FAPLA had suffered heavy casualties, necessitating yet another re-training and re-equipping programme before a fresh offensive could get underway. Congresso II's failure was a frustrating setback for the Cubans who had argued against it and then watched their worst predictions come true, and their strained relationship with the Soviets added to their growing feeling that the war in Angola was becoming a waste of time and Cuban lives. The offensive nevertheless captured Cazombo and, having come within touching distance of Mavinga, the Soviets were eager for a second round, prompting immediate preparations for an even larger offensive the following summer.

Soviet preparations for the 1986 offensive

In December 1985, General Konstantin Shagnovitch flew in to Luanda to take command of the upcoming offensive, heading a team of the most senior Soviet officers ever posted beyond the periphery of the Soviet Union. Many of them were experienced veterans of the Soviet intervention in Afghanistan. The arrival of more than 1,000 Soviet instructors to train the FAPLA was matched by over $1 billion of Soviet military equipment to replace that lost the previous year, including high-altitude AA missiles and even aircraft which were part of the European strategic reserve.[5] Once again there was serious disagreement over the proposed strategy, the FAPLA opposing Soviet plans to concentrate its forces for a move against Mavinga, preferring an all-out effort to destroy UNITA in central and northern Angola before finishing it off in the south-east. Again the Soviets overruled them, however, and this time the Cubans backed them, agreeing to provide technical and air support just as they had during the 1985 offensive.[6]

The growing dispute between Castro and Gorbachev

Castro's close alliance with the Soviet military in Angola masked a dispute brewing with the new Soviet General Secretary Mikhail Gorbachev, and this came to a head at the CPSU Party Congress in Moscow in late February 1986. Since becoming Soviet leader in March 1985, Gorbachev had struggled to push ahead with radical reforms to the Soviet economic and political system – his so-called 'New Thinking' – proposing a major restructuring of the Soviet economy (*perestroika*), increased democracy and political openness (*glasnost*). While Castro acknowledged the gross inefficiency of the Communist economic system (and launched his own version of *perestroika* – the 'Rectification of Errors and Negative Tendencies' campaign – on his return to Cuba), he fiercely opposed calls for political reform. During the Congress, Gorbachev's reforms came under heavy criticism – in particular from the two men whose support had been crucial in his bid for power the previous year, Igor Ligachev and Andrei Gromyko. Castro used his speech at the Congress to declare that Cuban troops would remain in Angola for thirty more years if necessary, linking their withdrawal to the end of apartheid, and his belligerent statement contrasted sharply with Gorbachev's conciliatory message to the West which called for a collective effort to end conflicts across the globe.

When the two leaders met for talks on 2 March 1986, the divisions between them on political reform and the Angolan War were apparent. For Castro, it was essential that Soviet support for the Angolan operation continued until there was either a clear-cut victory on the battlefield (a remote possibility) or an honourable negotiated withdrawal (the more likely outcome). Gorbachev, on the other hand, was eager to rein in the Soviet military in order to use the massive resources being poured into the Angolan War (over $4 billion by 1986) to improve the dismal economic situation of the average Soviet citizen. Although Gorbachev publicly declared his support for the MPLA during Dos Santos' visit to Moscow two months later, he and his supporters favoured a rapid conclusion to the war, and Castro knew that his survival as Cuban leader was unlikely to be one of Gorbachev's overriding objectives. It is thus no coincidence that, only four days after first meeting Gorbachev, Castro held talks with his two most outspoken opponents – Nikolai Rizkhov and Igor Ligachev – signalling his opposition to 'New Thinking'. The battle-lines were being drawn for an acrimonious struggle between Castro and Gorbachev over the next three years, as Castro fought to end the Cuban intervention on his terms in the face of Gorbachev's attempts to cut off the Soviet support upon which it depended.

Crocker attempts to revive the negotiations, March–May 1986

Even as Castro was meeting with Rizhkov and Ligachev in Moscow, in Geneva Crocker was holding talks with Vladillen Vasev (the Soviet interlocutor in the negotiations). Vasev was a strong advocate of 'New Thinking', and he stressed to Crocker Gorbachev's willingness to cooperate with the West in bringing an end to the southern Africa dispute. Crocker had continued to pursue 'linkage' despite Luanda's withdrawal and growing opposition within Congress, but his success in re-engaging the Angolans in late October had been torpedoed by Castro, who summoned Dos Santos to Havana two days after his meeting with Crocker and persuaded him to harden his position. By the time Crocker visited Luanda and Cape Town to present a revised 'basis for negotiation' in January 1986, the brief window of opportunity had closed, and both sides once again rejected the American proposals. Crocker's talks with Vasev were nevertheless significant, and convinced him that the Soviets could be useful partners in the negotiating process. However, it would be over two years before they officially joined the negotiations and, in the meantime, the few breakthroughs achieved – such as the South African offer on 4 March to withdraw from Angola within six months – were sunk by assertive action from the Angolans, the Front-Line States and Castro himself.

The 1986 offensive, May–August 1986

Throughout the first half of 1986, preparations had been underway for a second offensive against UNITA in Moxico and Cuando Cubango.[7] By May, over 20,000 FAPLA troops had been concentrated in Luena and Cuito Cuanavale – supported once more by 7,000 SWAPO and 900 MK guerrillas – in readiness for what the Soviets promised would be the final push against UNITA. UNITA was determined to avoid a repeat of the previous year, however, and in conjunction with the SADF had prepared operations to prevent the FAPLA build-up and to disrupt its logistics. By mid-1986 UNITA was receiving its first American military aid which, although tiny compared to the FAPLA's, included the first surface-to-air Stinger missiles and TOW anti-tank missiles, boosting UNITA's defensive capability and removing the FAPLA's air superiority.[8] In late May the offensive began, two armoured columns moving out from Luena towards Munhango (on the Benguela railway line) and Lumbala-N'Guimbo, while a third waited in Cuito Cuanavale for supplies (in particular petrol). In early June, the FAPLA captured Cangumbe, but this success was overshadowed by a surprise raid on Namibe which threw the offensive's logistics into chaos.

Namibe was a natural target as it was not only the principal port in southern Angola supplying the ATS Defence Line, but it was also the main logistical depot for the offensive against Mavinga. Although Pretoria subsequently denied involvement in the raid which took place on the night of 5/6 June, it is likely that it was carried out by Special Forces from the South African Navy. Small teams infiltrated the harbour in rapid strike crafts and fired Skerpioen missiles at the main oil depot, destroying two storage tanks (which were full of fuel) and damaging one other. South African frogmen also planted mines on three ships in the harbour, sinking the Cuban freighter *Habano* and severely damaging the Russian *Kapitan Visblokov* and *Kapitan Chirkov*. The loss of so much fuel (which was destined for the advance on Mavinga), coupled with continuing UNITA attacks on the *caravanas* plying the route from Namibe to Cuito Cuanavale, delayed the move-out from Cuito Cuanavale until the end of the month, by which time the offensive in Moxico had became bogged down. Eager to rescue the offensive from its predecessor's fate, the Soviets began moving their forces across the Cuito river in late July, but on 9 August a surprise raid on Cuito Cuanavale destroyed the only bridge across the river, bringing the offensive to a standstill.

The raid, carried out by up to 4,000 UNITA guerrillas (with c.200 SADF troops operating their artillery), was intended to cause maximum disruption to the offensive. Over two nights of fierce bombardment, severe damage was inflicted on Cuito Cuanavale's radar and AA installations, temporarily closing the runway and destroying several ammunition dumps which had been stockpiled for the assault on Mavinga. During the night of 9/10 August, a four-man SADF team laid explosive charges on the Cuito river bridge, partially destroying it and threatening to cut off the FAPLA forces gathered on the river's eastern bank.[9] Frantic efforts were made to re-open the bridge to heavy vehicles, but these were frustrated by another sabotage raid four days later, this time by UNITA. These raids set a pattern for the war around Cuito Cuanavale over the next two years, with constant attacks on the bridge being followed by improvised attempts to repair it, reducing the crossing to a cannibalised collection of steel girders and timber logs.[10] Recognising how exposed the FAPLA was east of the Cuito river, the Soviets begrudgingly called off the offensive. Dozens of MiGs and helicopter gun-ships were sent to cover the withdrawal, and sappers laid minefields to the south and east of Cuito Cuanavale to prevent a counter-attack. The two FAPLA forces in Moxico (whose advance was also bogged down) were withdrawn to Lucusse and Munhango and, by late August, the offensive was over before it had even begun.

The failure of the 1986 offensive was a further embarrassment to the Soviets who had been posted to Angola specifically to ensure its success, and once again left them frustrated. Eager for a third round against UNITA and the South Africans – and now in total control of the military operation – the Soviets sanctioned a further escalation in military aid.

Following a brief offensive in December by two FAPLA brigades which briefly captured Lupire (Cuando Cubango), planning started for what would be the deciding offensive of the Angolan War: Operation 'Saludando Octubre' (see p. 200). Flushed with UNITA's success, Savimbi miscalculated his next move, believing the FAPLA was too weak to launch offensive operations until 1988 at the earliest, and he let his contacts with the SADF lapse, handing the initiative back to the Soviets. For the Cubans, the failure of a second consecutive offensive was deeply demoralising, and the mounting Cuban casualties aggravated the discontent brewing in the army, leading several senior officers to conclude that the war in Angola was a lost cause.

Castro strikes back

Determined to dispel the defeatism creeping into the Soviet–Cuban camp, Castro gave a robust response to the failed FAPLA offensive in a speech to the 8th NAM Summit in Harare on 2 September, boldly declaring that Cuban forces would remain in Angola until the end of apartheid if necessary. Intending to send a strong message to his adversaries that Cuba's commitment to Angola was as strong as ever, Castro's declaration turned out to be a major faux pas, alarming his African allies who had no desire to see Cuba's occupation of Angola extended indefinitely. For, no matter how hard Castro draped his Angolan operation in rhetoric, there was no escaping the fact that, by 1986, Cuban troops had been occupying Angola for over a decade, and that the prospect of their presence continuing for perhaps another ten years presaged further instability in the region. Castro's declaration was his second major gaffe of the year,[11] and led to furious back-pedalling by his spokesmen who argued rather unconvincingly that his comments had been misinterpreted.

Any doubts over his determination to see the war through to the bitter end were dispelled by his subsequent visit to Angola from 7–9 September, during which he declared to a crowd of Cuban internationalists that their mission would continue in Angola for 'one hundred times eleven years' if necessary. The contrast with Castro's previous visit a decade before – during which he had hinted that it was time to wind up the Cuban operation – was striking, and illustrated how his political future now depended on the successful outcome of the Angolan operation. If an honourable withdrawal settlement could not be reached with the South Africans, then nothing short of a military victory was essential if Castro's regime were to maintain public support in the difficult times ahead. Cuban personnel were therefore authorised to become involved in the 1987 offensive, providing air support, specialist officers to operate the heavy artillery and even tanks for the front-lines. On 13 February 1987, Castro met MPLA Defence Minister N'Dalu in Havana to discuss the upcoming offensive, and following annual tripartite talks in Moscow one month later, Raúl Castro secretly visited Luanda to oversee massive arms deliveries to the FAPLA.[12]

Planning for 'Operation Saludando Octubre'

The new offensive – code-named Operação Saludando Octubre (Operation Saluting October, in reference to the seventieth anniversary of the October Revolution) – was to be the Soviets' last throw in the Angolan War. Employing at least 10,000 troops and an additional $1.5 billion of Soviet equipment – including 150 T-55 and T-62 tanks, Hind helicopter gun-ships (upgraded Mi-24s), and M-46 and D-30 guns – the offensive aimed once more to capture UNITA's forward base at Mavinga prior to a final assault on Jamba. Once again, however, the Soviets failed to make contingency plans for a South African intervention, despite being warned in May 1987 by Ronnie Kasrils (one of MK's most senior commanders in Angola) that an SADF invasion from Namibia was imminent.[13] Given the Soviets' painful experience over the previous two years with the South Africans, it seems incredible that they dismissed these warnings. But it appears that they were confident that the colossal military force concentrating in Cuito Cuanavale would see off any opposition and, dismissing Cuban and Angolan warnings, they went ahead with their greatest gamble of the war.[14]

The SADF re-ignites its alliance with UNITA

As early as March 1987, the SADF had warned UNITA that the FAPLA was preparing another offensive in Cuando Cubango, but it was not until April – when the FAPLA launched a diversionary attack from Lucusse – that UNITA took the South Africans seriously. Following a meeting between the SADF and UNITA on 1 May, Operação Chuva (Operation Rain) was launched, UNITA opting for the previous year's tactics with attacks on the supply lines to disrupt the build-up around Cuito Cuanavale. With national elections only weeks away, however, Pretoria was not prepared for another intervention in Angola, and initially the SADF sent only two small liaison teams to advise UNITA. Once evidence of the massive build-up in Cuando Cubango began to mount, it became clear that UNITA needed more assistance and, on 15 June, Pretoria authorised a limited programme of covert support, including anti-tank and rocket teams, and aircraft to transport guerrillas to the front-lines.[15] At this stage, Pretoria envisioned a short-term operation which it hoped to keep small and (if possible) clandestine. But, just as in late 1975, the fighting in Angola would quickly escalate beyond all expectations, forcing Pretoria into a full-scale intervention (see pp. 207–10).

The defection of Del Pino

With only a couple of months until the launch of the FAPLA offensive, the Cuban military was plunged into crisis by a surprise defection. On 28 May 1987, the Deputy Commander of the Cuban Air Force (DAAFAR) Brigadier-General Rafael del Pino flew to an American naval base in Florida, denouncing Castro and Cuba's involvement in Angola.[16] Although Del Pino's defection probably resulted from personal disputes with the Cuban High Command, his detailed criticism of the Cuban operation in Angola revealed a deeper malaise in the armed forces.[17] In particular, Del Pino criticised the Cuban commanders' handling of military operations, citing examples of their alleged incompetence which resulted in heavy casualties. More controversially, he accused them of covering up each other's blunders and then misleading the relatives of those killed into thinking they had died heroically in combat.[18] Bleakly concluding that Cuban forces in Angola were 'a mercenary army' in 'Cuba's Vietnam', Del Pino claimed that senior Cuban officers were openly declaring that the war in Angola was lost – a disturbing revelation in the run-up to the most ambitious offensive to date.

Del Pino's defection was an alarming development for Castro. For although he could be publicly dismissed as a lone and disaffected traitor, his accusations of discontent in the officer class had a ring of truth to them which Castro could not easily ignore. Already aware that time was running out for his Angolan adventure – with Gorbachev seeking to pull the plug on Soviet aid and support from Cuba's African allies on the wane – the prospect that his own military had lost their stomach for the war was disastrous. Furthermore, Del Pino's association with the 'New Thinkers' was clear evidence that there were senior officers who supported Gorbachev's reforms and whose loyalty to Castro was in question. Havana reacted swiftly, responding to Del Pino's accusations of corruption by arresting the General Secretary of the UJC, and then launching a national campaign to vilify both men's reputations.[19] Having seen off the domestic threat, Castro then turned his attention back to Angola and, in an effort to seize back the initiative, on 27 July he sent a message to Crocker proposing that Cuba join the negotiations.

Castro's bid to join Crocker's negotiations

By the time Crocker received Castro's message, the 'linkage' negotiations had been deadlocked for over a year. The Americans' first meeting with the Angolans in nearly fourteen months, on 5 April 1987, had brought little progress, and any hopes of a breakthrough were dashed when Kito was replaced with Mbinda, a man Crocker did not believe took the negotiations seriously. Meetings in July with Soviet officials – including Vasev and Soviet Deputy Foreign Minister Adamishin – confirmed only that they believed the American negotiations to be irremediably deadlocked and, following his first talks with Mbinda a fortnight later, Crocker publicly declared that any hopes of a breakthrough had evaporated.[20] Thus Castro's message only five days later suggesting that Cuba join the negotiating process came as a complete surprise.[21] And it was all the more perplexing in Castro's demand for a reply within forty-eight hours, a bizarre request after he had spent the previous six years rejecting all association with 'linkage'. Typically Castro's message contained a threat – warning that, if the negotiations failed, Cuba would fight on another ten years if necessary – but Cuban willingness to engage in the 'linkage' negotiations was nevertheless significant, and revealed how eager Havana was to curtail its Angolan operation.

Castro's motivations for making the request are unclear, but it was clearly his initiative – hence his demand for a reply before Dos Santos arrived for an official visit to Cuba on 30 July. No longer able to influence the negotiations from Havana, Castro was seeking direct involvement now that the character and shape of the Cuban withdrawal was under discussion, and there was a real danger his Angolan ally would let slip politically disastrous concessions. Keen to bring an end to his Angolan adventure, Castro viewed the 'linkage' negotiations as much more likely to deliver an acceptable peace settlement than the elusive victory the Soviets were seeking on the battlefield. But with a new offensive already underway, Castro was playing a double strategy – on the one hand going along (albeit grudgingly) with the Soviet offensive, whilst on the other attempting to join the 'linkage' negotiations and using the renewed military pressure to extract concessions from the South Africans.

Castro's demand for a reply within 48 hours was unrealistic, however, as the issue of Cuban involvement in the negotiations was still politically sensitive for Reagan's administration. Fearing that Castro might use the opportunity to introduce extraneous issues into an already torturous agenda, Crocker dodged the request, replying that it was up to the MPLA to decide if they wanted the Cubans as their negotiating partners. The Angolans responded well to Crocker's suggestion, but he was not prepared to let the Cubans join the talks without a sizeable quid pro quo, and over the following months the Cubans and Angolans would repeatedly press the Americans to include the Cubans, eventually agreeing to concessions on the crucial issue of the Cuban contingent in northern Angola (see Chapter 10).

The Soviets struggle to launch the offensive

From late April 1987, FAPLA forces had started building up around Cuito Cuanavale. Determined to dispel any sense of defeatism, dozens of Soviet officers accompanied the troops on the ground while General Shagnovitch made regular visits to Menongue to oversee the operation. By early July, eight FAPLA brigades had assembled at Cuito Cuanavale, four of which (16, 21, 47 and 59) would spearhead the assault on Mavinga while the others provided logistical support and protected the rear from attack.[22] The Soviets opted to split their forces in two for a pincer move on the Lomba river (only twenty miles north of Mavinga). 47 and 59 Brigades would first secure its southern banks to allow 16 and 21 Brigades to cross, then the combined force would make the final assault on Mavinga itself (see Map 8). Within days of the offensive's launch, however, the leading brigades were bogged down fighting UNITA around the source of the Chambinga river (twenty miles east of Cuito Cuanavale). Determined to avoid a repeat of the previous year's stillborn offensive, the Soviets halted the advance – ordering the FAPLA to retrench its positions while further supplies, equipment and troops poured into Cuito Cuanavale – and fresh plans were drawn up to resume the offensive in August, prompting the now inevitable South African response.

The SADF responds with Operation Moduler

Recognising that UNITA could not face the renewed FAPLA threat on its own, on 4 August the SADF launched what was to prove its most controversial intervention of the war: Operation Moduler.[23] By now it was clear that a major offensive was underway against Mavinga, and as its fall could only lead to a resurgence in SWAPO activity in the Caprivi Strip, it was decided to send a South African force to UNITA's aid. The 700-man force – designated 20 Brigade – was assembled from the SADF's 32 'Buffalo' Battalion (formed in the aftermath of Operation Savannah from Battle-Group Bravo), and comprised five motorised infantry companies (with one extra in support), three reconnaissance teams, one battery each of MRLs and mortars, and two troops of AA artillery. In late August, 20 Brigade was bolstered by 61 Mechanised Battalion Group (61 Mech), two infantry companies of 101 Battalion in Casspirs, and one battery each of G-5 155m howitzers and 120mm mortars.[24] But even with this reinforcement, the South African force in Angola never exceeded 3,000 men.

20 Brigade's small size (initially fewer than 1,000 men against at least 6,000 FAPLA troops) is illustrative of the constraints Pretoria put on the SADF in its attempt to keep Operation Moduler clandestine, an unlikely outcome when all previous South African interventions had been uncovered within weeks. Ignoring the painful lessons of Operation Savannah – when a small, secret intervention had, against all expectations, escalated into a full-scale war of intervention – Pretoria again opted for a day-to-day strategy. The crucial question of when South African forces should withdraw (or whether they should advance and capture Cuito Cuanavale) was

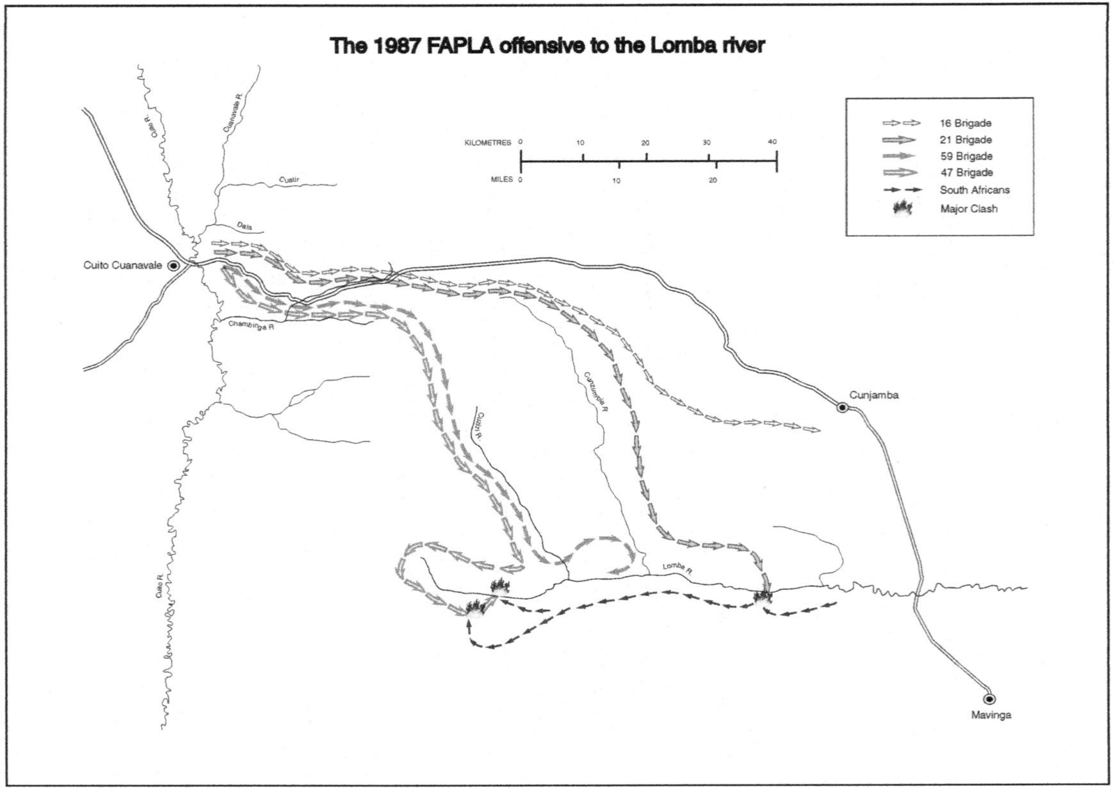

Map 8 The 1987 FAPLA offensive to the Lomba river.

left undecided, and this encouraged the sort of 'mission creep' which had blighted Operation Savannah.[25] Once again failing to appreciate the weakness of its Angolan allies or the difficulty of the terrain, Pretoria launched its tiny intervention force into what would prove to be the SADF's hardest fought campaign of the Angolan War.

The FAPLA fights its way to the Lomba river

Operation Moduler began on 4 August 1987 when the first elements of 32 Battalion crossed from Namibia into Cuando Cubango. Nine days later, South African mortars fired the first shots of the campaign against 47 and 59 Brigades as they advanced on the Lomba river. At this stage the SADF was under orders to minimise its involvement in the fighting and, at a meeting on 14 August, it was agreed that its armoured cars and anti-tank squadron would only be deployed if Mavinga were in danger of capture. But this decision proved premature as, on the same day, all four FAPLA brigades moved out of Cuito Cuanavale, forcing the SADF and UNITA to move their command post six miles to the south. On 19 August, South African MRLs were deployed to slow down 47 and 59 Brigades' advance – hitting them continually over the next eight days – and, in an effort to cut off reinforcements, a six-man Special Forces team carried out a sabotage raid on the Cuito river bridge.[26] The raid was not as successful as the previous year, however, and although it did briefly close the bridge to traffic, it was quickly repaired by Cuban engineers, prompting sporadic bombing raids by the SAAF over the next two months.

Despite the disruption caused by the raid, the FAPLA continued its advance on the Lomba, and by 28 August, 47 and 59 Brigades were only two miles north of the river, the last significant obstacle before Mavinga. At this point, the western force split in two, 47 Brigade looping west around the source of the Lomba to secure a bridgehead on its southern banks, while 59 Brigade moved east to link up with 21 Brigade (see Map 8, page 204). Once the three brigades had completed their crossing of the Lomba, they intended to join 16 Brigade (which was approaching Mavinga from the north) for the final assault. The decision to split the attacking force proved a fatal blunder, however, exposing each brigade to attack as it struggled to link up with other FAPLA forces in the area. On 2 September, South African MRLs and G-5 guns opened up against 47 and 21 Brigades as they moved along the northern banks of the Lomba, and four days later South African troops clashed with the FAPLA, initiating the month-long battle along the Lomba river.

The battle of the Lomba river,
9 September–7 October 1987

The 'battle of the Lomba river' proved the turning-point of the offensive, stretching the military capabilities of the FAPLA, UNITA and the small SADF force to their limits.[27] With the FAPLA brigades split into smaller components and cut off from each other by the network of rivers and marshes in the area, the opportunity was ripe for 20 Brigade to pick off each force before it could link up. But the FAPLA was a more formidable opponent than the ramshackle army which faced Zulu Force in 1975, and the South Africans would have a bitter fight on their hands when FAPLA tanks put up sterner resistance than expected, fuelling suspicions that Cuban personnel were fighting on the front-lines. By early September, the South Africans' main aim was to prevent 47 and 59 Brigades linking up, as this would provide a bridgehead for 21 Brigade to cross the Lomba, and therefore throughout September it was these three brigades which bore the brunt of the onslaught.

The confrontation began on 9 September when Combat Group Bravo attacked two battalions of 21 Brigade as they were attempting to cross the Lomba river using a mobile bridge. Several hundred FAPLA troops had already reached the southern bank when the South Africans attacked with one infantry company (in fourteen Casspirs) and one anti-tank troop (in four Ratels). The leading Ratel immediately shot out a FAPLA armoured car crossing the bridge, blocking all further attempts to cross the river. A prolonged artillery duel then broke out between the FAPLA's mortars, guns and BM-21s and the South African armour, but with the arrival of two more troops of South African armoured cars the FAPLA troops abandoned the crossing, leaving behind over 100 dead and the burning wrecks of six T-55 tanks on the river banks.[28]

Having seen off 21 Brigade, Bravo raced westwards towards 47 Brigade which had reached the southern bank of the Lomba and was setting up a bridgehead for the crossings of 59 and 21 Brigades. On 13 September, Bravo launched its attack. After considerable difficulty manoeuvring through the terrain, the South Africans caught a large mass of FAPLA infantry up against a large shona (dry river) running along the edge of the Lomba, and they raked the area with cannon and machine-gun fire, killing over 200 troops as they struggled to flee. At this point, all four South African Ratels got stuck in the FAPLA's trench system, making them easy targets for a company of FAPLA tanks which launched a sudden counter-attack. A vicious close-quarter firefight ensued until dusk, and by the time the South African commander ordered his forces to withdraw, three South African armoured cars and several FAPLA tanks were burning hulks.

The fighting against 21 Brigade had been the costliest for the South Africans so far – Bravo losing eight men killed, four wounded and three armoured cars. But they had forced 47 Brigade to give up its attempt to link up with 59 Brigade, and had destroyed five tanks and nearly all of the FAPLA's bridging vehicles. Furthermore, the South Africans had killed nearly 400 troops, leaving the brigade stranded on the southern banks of the Lomba and short of fuel, ammunition and supplies. A further attempt by 21 Brigade to cross the Lomba on 17 September was beaten off by a devastating G-5 bombardment with air-burst shells, the heavy casualties these inflicted forcing the FAPLA commander to call off the crossing the next day. This allowed the South African troops to concentrate their efforts on 47 Brigade which was still attempting to link up with other FAPLA brigades in the area.

On 16 September, South African bombers carried out their first air strikes of the campaign, bombarding 47 Brigade ahead of an attack by Combat Group Alpha. Alpha's assault did not go as planned, however, as (in a scenario which was becoming familiar) the South African armour got bogged down in the tricky terrain, withdrawing under mortar and machine-gun fire with one killed and three wounded. Despite this minor set-back, 20 Brigade continued to harass 47 Brigade over the next fort-night – preventing all attempts to find an alternative crossing of the Lomba – while the Soviet commanders in Luanda struggled to extricate the stricken brigade. Finally, on 27 September – after issuing a series of contradictory orders to 47 Brigade – the Soviet military advisers accompanying 21 Brigade were withdrawn by helicopter, leaving the FAPLA brigades along the Lomba bereft of any senior command element. The bold Soviet offensive had ended in failure for the third time, and now the Soviets on the front-line were abandoning ship, leaving 47 Brigade to the mercy of the South African forces converging on it.

South Africa extends Operation Moduler, 29 September 1987

It was at this stage that the South African leadership decided to extend Operation Moduler and, at a meeting between P.W. Botha and the SADF High Command, a more aggressive policy was adopted. Determined to prevent the FAPLA regrouping and re-launching its offensive later in the year, Botha ordered the SADF to destroy all FAPLA forces east of the Cuito river before the start of the rainy season, turning what had been a covert spoiling operation into a counter-offensive – and ensuring that it would remain clandestine no longer. Given its isolation on the southern banks of the Lomba, 47 Brigade was the natural target of the new South African strategy, and 20 Brigade immediately began planning its assault. Ironically, 47 Brigade's Angolan commander had refused Soviet orders to withdraw and was still trying to cross the Lomba under G-5 bombardment, his forces suffering heavy casualties as they struggled to construct a log pathway for the tanks and vehicles to cross. Eventually – under threat of court martial – he gave in to the Soviet order, but his forces were then pinned down by South African shelling (which destroyed the remaining mobile bridge), leaving them exposed when the attack came two days later.[29]

The destruction of 47 Brigade, 3 October 1987

The South African force comprised C Squadron (Ratel-90s) and three mechanised infantry companies (c.400 men), and was supported by mortars, AA batteries, G-5s and MRLs which kept up a steady bombardment throughout the day. South African observers had identified a large group of FAPLA troops and vehicles in a shona south of the Lomba preparing to drive onto the log pathway, and the arrival of the Ratels scattered the FAPLA troops who fled on foot to the crossing. With the mobile bridge no longer operational, the FAPLA drove several armoured cars into the river to improvise a bridge but, in the rush to escape, a T-55 and a jeep collided, blocking the crossing to all further traffic. The Ratels then pressed home their attack, shooting out five FAPLA tanks and inflicting heavy casualties on the Angolan troops before a counter-attack by (possibly Cuban-operated) T-55s forced them to withdraw.

At 2 p.m., the South Africans returned for a second attack, the leading Ratels shooting up an entire battalion of FAPLA infantry fleeing on foot towards the shona, but once again they ran into heavy resistance from FAPLA tanks (one Ratel commander being killed by a shell ricochet) and were forced to withdraw. C Squadron was sent back to recover the damaged Ratel, shooting out two T-55s in the process and, at 4 p.m., the South Africans regrouped for a final assault. By now discipline had broken down among the Angolans (their commander having fled or been killed) and troops were fleeing en masse to the crossing point which was a chaotic mess of shattered trees and burning vehicles, all under South African bombardment. The remnants of the brigade were caught huddling in a wide shona south of the Lomba, with no cover and unable to manoeuvre through the muddy terrain. In an orgy of violence, the Ratels shot out dozens of tanks, armoured cars and trucks while the MRLs mowed down the panicked FAPLA troops as they floundered in the mud.[30]

By 5 p.m., 47 Brigade had effectively been destroyed. Over 600 FAPLA troops lay dead on the southern banks of the Lomba, and a total of 127 tanks, armoured cars and other vehicles had been destroyed or captured.[31] The South Africans had lost only one killed and five wounded in the fighting – a striking statistic which underlines how one-sided the battle had been. In addition to seizing millions of dollars of Soviet hardware (much of it brand new), the South Africans captured the only fully-working SAM-8 missile-launcher system ever to fall into Western hands. (It was flown to South Africa after an ugly dispute with UNITA which had promised the system to the Americans.)[32] To add to its humiliation, the FAPLA was forced to call in Cuban MiG-23s to bomb the battlefield in an attempt to destroy the abandoned equipment before it fell into enemy hands. But this was little more than damage limitation and, on 5 October, the FAPLA began withdrawing to Cuito Cuanavale.

The failure of Operation Saludando Octubre – the Soviets' third in a row – was the final embarrassment for General Shagnovitch. Shortly after the retreat from the Lomba began he was recalled to Moscow in disgrace, marking the end of Soviet dominance in the Angolan War. The FAPLA had suffered over 4,000 casualties – some brigades losing all their weaponry and armour – and, in addition, UNITA claimed to have killed twenty Cuban and four Soviet military advisers (wounding over 100 others), raising the stakes for the intervention forces. But the fighting was far from over, and the FAPLA now faced the daunting task of withdrawing thousands of demoralised troops through 100 miles of hostile terrain, all the time under South African attack. With Cuito Cuanavale and possibly the whole of Cuando Cubango under threat of collapse, the Angolans turned to the Cubans to extricate them from the looming disaster, and over the next six weeks Cuban forces were drawn into the fighting, MiG-23s providing air cover while Cuban detachments reinforced key positions in Cuando Cubango. Nothing short of a full-scale intervention could prevent the capture of Cuito Cuanavale, however, and by mid-November the situation would be critical enough for Castro to consider committing Cuban troops to the front-line.

The South Africans extend Operation Moduler
once more

Flushed with their crushing victory over 47 Brigade, on 6 October the SADF High Command issued orders to destroy all remaining FAPLA forces east of the Cuito river, hoping to snuff out any chance of a revived offensive later in the year. The 4th South African Infantry Battalion Group (4 SAI) – including more Ratels and the first Olifant tanks and G-6 guns – was sent to bolster 20 Brigade, but the crucial question of whether it would capture Cuito Cuanavale was left undecided until the FAPLA had been driven back to the Cuito river. This would prove a fatal misjudgement because, by the time South African forces were ready to launch an attack on Cuito Cuanavale, they would find themselves facing a fully reinforced garrison. But, despite their many previous entanglements with the Cubans, the South Africans did not consider the possibility that Cuba would intervene massively in the war, and they once more set their small intervention force on a collision course with the Cuban army.

Following the order to retreat on 5 October, the remaining FAPLA forces withdrew rapidly towards the last major obstacle between them and the Cuito river – the Chambinga river (fifteen miles east) – with 20 Brigade and UNITA in hot pursuit. The difficult terrain between the Lomba and Cuito rivers made the going tough for both sides, and the South Africans – who called off several attacks due to navigational problems and poor visibility – relied on their Mirages and G-5s to keep up the pressure. Cuito Cuanavale came under siege almost immediately when, on 14 October, G-5s shelled the FAPLA's Forward Command post, killing twenty-five soldiers and initiating over seven months of bombardment. Within a fortnight they had closed the airstrip to jets and heavy air transports, weakening the town's air defences and putting further strain on the supply lines. With UNITA's Stinger missiles forcing pilots to fly at higher altitudes, Cuban MiGs lost their effectiveness, allowing the SAAF to fly dozens of sorties unmolested. When, on 30 October, South African reinforcements arrived – including the first Olifant tanks (a modified version of the British Centurion) and G-6 guns (a self-propelled, armoured version of the G-5) – they were ready to make a move on Cuito Cuanavale, pushing the situation in southern Angola to crisis point.

Castro urges the Angolans and Soviets to escalate the war

By early November, the FAPLA's predicament was gravely concerning the Cubans whose personnel were heavily involved in the fighting. On 3 November – before leaving for Moscow – Castro appointed General Arnaldo Ochoa Sanchez as the new Chief of MMCA, a move calculated to pre-empt the intervention he was already planning. In crisis talks with the Angolans and Soviets in Moscow, Castro urged them to confront the South Africans head-on at Cuito Cuanavale, and even proposed extending the war into south-west Angola to put pressure on the Namibian border. But the Soviets – still chafing from their humiliation at the Lomba – were in no mood to escalate the fighting, and they pressed for a political solution, leaving the issue unresolved when Castro left for Havana two days later.[33] Over the following week, the situation in Angola continued to deteriorate, the South Africans killing a further 500 FAPLA troops (and probably some Cuban tank operators too), and destroying or capturing thirty-three tanks and over 110 logistics vehicles.[34] Eventually, on 15 November, Dos Santos wrote Castro a desperate letter requesting urgent Cuban military assistance.[35] Faced with the opportunity to seize back control of the Angolan operation, Castro needed no further prompting, and that evening he authorised the first 3,000 troops for what would prove to be Cuba's final intervention in Angola.

Cuba launches 'Maniobra XXXI Anniversario'

The decision to re-engage in the fighting in Angola marked the final stage in Cuba's long and difficult intervention. Just as in November 1975, the stakes were high for Castro whose political future had become inextricably linked to the fortunes of the Angolan operation. With the support of his Soviet patrons, African allies and even the Cuban army weakening by the day, the prospect of Cuito Cuanavale falling to the South Africans was catastrophic for Castro, and threatened to push Luanda into negotiations with the South Africans on unfavourable terms. It was an almost identical situation to that facing Castro twelve years previously, once more presenting him with the opportunity of taking full control of the fighting while the Soviets watched from the side-lines,[36] only this time with none of the technical or logistical restraints which plagued Operation Carlota. After more than a decade, the Cuban intervention had come full circle, and Castro would ensure that having regained the initiative he would not let overall control slip from his grasp again.

The decision to launch 'Maniobra XXXI Aniversario' was taken at a joint meeting of the Politburo, FAR and MININT, and involved an initial reinforcement of 3,000 Cuban troops to bolster Cuito Cuanavale's defences.[37] It comprised one armoured brigade, several self-propelled AA missile units (including SAM-8s), one rapid response unit, and a contingent of MININT Special Forces which Castro offered personally.[38] The besieged garrison at Cuito Cuanavale would now be the focus of all Cuban efforts, and Cuba's best MiG pilots were immediately flown to Angola to bolster the air contingent. The choice of Cuito Cuanavale for a final stand against the South Africans was as much pre-emptive – to prevent the fall of Menongue – as it was symbolic. The town's location, over 100 miles from the ATS Defence Line, gave it little strategic value other than as a staging post for future offensives into southern Cuando Cubango.[39] The 'Siege of Cuito Cuanavale' would perform another essential function, however, providing Castro with the crucial showdown with the South Africans he needed before withdrawing his forces from Angola, and over the next two months he would override repeated requests from his officers in Angola to withdraw from Cuito Cuanavale.

Like its predecessor, Operation Carlota, Maniobra XXXI Aniversario also had long-term objectives beyond the defence of Cuito Cuanavale. While reinforcements raced to Cuando Cubango, Castro secretly started building up a large force in Lubango in preparation for a move into southwest Angola. The FAR's elite 50th Division – Castro's personal division which guarded the American base in Guantánamo (Cuba) – was dispatched to Angola to spearhead this manoeuvre, and by early January 1988 the first 3,500 Cuban troops had moved into Cunene. Subsequently written off by Cuba's opponents as an elaborate exercise in sabre-rattling, the move into Cunene was an integral part of Castro's double-strategy, the pressure it put on South Africa intended to extract major concessions from them in the final rounds of negotiation. But it was a major provocation to the SADF which had operated free of Cuban interference in the area for nearly eight years, and would provide both sides with an alternative theatre for the bloody climax of the war in late June (see Chapter 11).

10

THE BATTLE OF CUITO CUANAVALE, NOVEMBER 1987–MARCH 1988

The fighting which started east of Cuito Cuanavale in November 1987 was the culmination of more than a dozen years of inconclusive clashes between the Cubans and South Africans, and over five months evolved into the second largest military confrontation in African history (after El-Alamein in 1942). The Cuban and South African commanders finally had their chance to bury the ghosts of the 'Second Liberation War', and as the fighting intensified so did the military and political stakes. As during Operation Savannah, the SADF would have to operate under crippling restraints imposed by Pretoria which pursued incompatible goals – on the one hand ordering the destruction of all FAPLA forces east of the Cuito river, whilst on the other vetoing any reinforcements. This counter-productive strategy would once again provide the catalyst for a full-scale Cuban intervention, and pit the 3,000-man South African force against the might of the FAPLA and Cuban armies.

The significance of the 'Battle of Cuito Cuanavale' would go far beyond the territorial gains made on the ground, however, and would provide the crucial window of opportunity Crocker needed to restart the 'linkage' negotiations. With both sides locked into a costly stalemate, the American strategy would slowly reassert itself in the background, advancing at a remarkable pace (compared to the previous seven years of stop-start negotiations) following the inclusion of Cuba as a negotiating party. Indeed, by August it would have eclipsed the fighting on the ground, becoming the central point of confrontation (and ultimately consensus) between the warring parties. But perhaps most significantly, the 'Battle of Cuito Cuanavale' would provide Cuba with the decisive military victory that had eluded it for over a dozen years, enabling it to enter into negotiations with its armed forces visibly victorious. The reality of what occurred at Cuito Cuanavale, and the efforts of the Cuban regime to mythologise and rewrite the battle to fit its political agenda, will be discussed below.

The road to Cuito Cuanavale,
November 1987–January 1988

By the time the Cubans took over the defence of Cuito Cuanavale, the remaining FAPLA forces east of the Cuito river were in danger of total collapse, having endured daily attacks from South African aircraft, artillery and ground forces as they retreated towards the Chambinga river bridge. Keen to repeat their victory at the Lomba, the South Africans had inflicted heavy casualties on the FAPLA as it tried to cross the river. But their final attack against 21 Brigade had to be called off (due to erroneous UNITA reports that Cuban MiGs were overhead), allowing the FAPLA to complete its withdrawal by nightfall. This lost opportunity cost the South Africans dear as the terrain north of the river was ideally suited to defensive operations, and once the FAPLA had dug in they were able to beat off two days of attacks, the South African armour getting mired in the tricky terrain and minefields.[1] This rear-guard action would prove crucial for the defenders of Cuito Cuanavale, giving them time to bring in reinforcements and prepare defensive positions ahead of the final South African attacks.

As if to compound their turn of fortune, the same day South African forces were rebuffed in the Chambinga high ground (25 November), the UN Security Council passed Resolution 502, condemning South Africa's 'illegal entry' into Angola and demanding its withdrawal by 10 December. The new Resolution greatly increased the political stakes for Pretoria and, in an effort to appease international opinion, General Geldenhuys made a public statement declaring that South African forces had begun a 'tactical withdrawal under operational conditions'. This statement was misleading, however, as the South Africans spent the remainder of December tightening the noose around Cuito Cuanavale with attacks on the Tumpo logistics base, air-strikes against FAPLA–Cuban convoys, and two 'smart bomb' raids on the Cuito river bridge (both of which failed to destroy it).[2]

On 21 December, the South Africans began planning their assault, intending to pick off the remaining brigades east of the Cuito river before moving in to occupy the town if the conditions were favourable.[3] Once again, however, political constraints greatly restricted their room for manoeuvre. Following a visit by General Liebenberg on 24 December – during which he accused 20 Brigade's commander of being too aggressive and causing unacceptably high casualties (at least twenty-five South Africans had been killed by this stage) – the South African force was ordered to scale down its involvement in the fighting, entrusting the first assault to UNITA. The guerrillas predictably proved unequal to their task, however – as, by this time, the first Cuban reinforcements had arrived in Cuito Cuanavale – and this left the South Africans little choice but to start planning an attack using their own troops (see p. 218).

Serious disagreements break out between Ochoa and Castro

Following the launch of 'Maniobra XXXI Aniversario', the Cuban leadership was put on a war footing. Castro again took personal command of the operation in Angola, dedicating himself so obsessively to the task that he 'practically didn't do government work in 1988'.[4] Almost immediately, however, problems arose with the newly-appointed Chief of MMCA, General Arnaldo Ochoa Sánchez. Ochoa was one of the FAR's most experienced officers and a rising star in the Cuban hierarchy, having served on seven internationalist missions before his posting to Angola in late 1987, most notably as commander of the Ethiopian intervention.[5] But Ochoa did not respond well to Castro's attempts to impose his will from Havana, and the two men's relationship quickly grew strained while Ochoa's colleague, General Leopoldo Cintra Frías (known simply as 'Polo'), rose in Castro's estimation.[6] Ochoa was pessimistic about his posting, and his many clashes with Havana would turn him into the ideal scapegoat for Cuban failures, much like his predecessor Argüelles over a decade before.

The initial priority for the Cubans was to prevent Cuito Cuanavale falling to the South African stranglehold, and a contingent of Cuba's finest MiG pilots was flown to Angola.[7] Over the following months they flew dozens of missions to protect the *caravanas* en route to Cuito Cuanavale, and later played a prominent role in beating off UNITA's first attack on 21 Brigade. On 23 November, Raúl Castro personally saw off the first of nine ships and twenty aircraft bearing Cuban reinforcements for Angola. The following day, Jorge Risquet delivered a message from Fidel Castro to Dos Santos, detailing the makeup of the Cuban intervention force and requesting permission for Cuban troops to operate down to the Namibian border (a request Dos Santos granted a fortnight later). The first ships would not arrive in Angola until 10 December, however, and in the meantime an advance 'Operative Group' under MMCA's Chief of Operations – Lieutenant-Colonel Álvaro López Miera – was dispatched to Cuito Cuanavale to reorganise its artillery and defences in preparation for the arrival of reinforcements later that the month.[8] This forty-man unit – including four other officers, five artillery specialists and a platoon of Special Forces – was charged with assessing the situation on the ground and reporting back to Luanda within seventy-two hours. On arrival in Cuito Cuanavale, they met with the FAPLA commander who filled them in on South Africans forces in the area, and pinpointed which FAPLA units were hardest pressed (singling out 21 and 25 Brigades).

By December 1987, five FAPLA brigades remained east of the Cuito river, organised in a two-tiered defence between the Chambinga and

Cuatir rivers (see Map 9). The first tier consisted of the three brigades which had seen the most action. In the south, 25 Brigade was guarding the Chambinga river bridge, 59 Brigade just above it protecting its left flank, and 21 Brigade two miles further north near the Cuatir river. In the second tier – protecting the 'Tumpo Triangle' (the territory between the Cuito, Tumpo and Dala rivers) – were 16 and 66 Brigades, the latter guarding the Cuito river bridge. On the other side of the river, 13 Brigade, the small Cuban Operative Group and the majority of the artillery and AA defences guarded Cuito Cuanavale itself. The total force numbered nearly 4,000 troops, supported by forty-five tanks, sixty-five armoured cars and ten BM-21s.[9] Despite the defending force's considerable size, the Cubans were concerned about the morale of the Angolan troops which had been battered by six months of South African attacks.

In an effort to steady the front-lines, Cuban soldiers were dispatched to the weakest FAPLA units, 25 Brigade receiving eighty Cubans by the end of the fighting. Each brigade's outer defences were strengthened – with bunkers, trench systems and minefields – and the artillery was reorganised and replenished with more BM-21s after the FAPLA's had been located and destroyed. On 8 December, a group of Cuban officers arrived from Luanda to take photographs of the front for Castro, and two days later the first ship bearing reinforcements docked in Lobito, nearly 300 artillery and weapons specialists arriving in Cuito Cuanavale before the end of the month. Further attempts were made to repair the bridge over the Cuito river, briefly reopening it to heavy traffic on 27 December. But these were again cut short by a South African 'smart bomb' attack on 3 January 1988 which destroyed twenty yards of the bridge and closed it to traffic for over a month.[10]

While 300 Cubans were bolstering Cuito Cuanavale's defences, 400 miles away a much larger Cuban force was assembling in Lubango. Following authorisation from Dos Santos, on 14 December the first elements of Cuba's 50th Division started moving into northern Cunene. Their advance formed an essential part of Castro's double-strategy for the negotiations, but it was initially on a small scale to hide its intentions and, by the end of January 1988, only around 3,500 Cuban troops had occupied positions in Cunene.[11] Ochoa was not in step with Castro's strategy, however and, on 19 December, Castro vetoed his requests to start withdrawing from Cuito Cuanavale and Menongue to strengthen central Angola (which was under attack from UNITA), signalling Ochoa that he was 'very annoyed by the unexpected ideas which are inexplicable and run counter to our views'.[12] Castro had no doubt that the South Africans intended to capture Cuito Cuanavale, and over the following weeks, he continued to reject Ochoa's repeated requests to withdraw, urging him to strengthen his defences in preparation for an imminent South African attack. Ultimately, Castro's instincts proved correct, but his strained

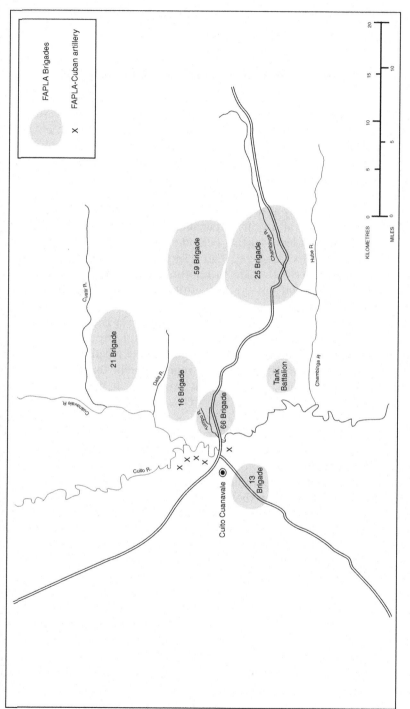

Map 9 FAPLA–Cuban forces east of the Cuito river, December 1987

relationship with Ochoa would fatally compromise his defence plan, and end up costing dozens of Cuban lives.

The first South African assault, 13/14 January 1988

The first South African attack on the FAPLA's positions east of the Cuito river began on 13 January when 21 Brigade's forward positions were bombarded G-5s, MRLs and mortars, setting off a bush-fire which engulfed them (see Map 10).[13] Spearheading the assault (with 61 Mech and UNITA in support), 4 SAI came under heavy mortar and BM-21 fire as it reached the minefields surrounding the FAPLA's forward positions, losing one Ratel to a mine. The FAPLA put up stiffer resistance than expected, one bunker firing repeatedly at the Olifants before it was destroyed by a single HESH round, killing all twenty occupants. Only after an hour's fighting did the FAPLA withdraw, leaving behind at least sixty dead. By now the commanders in Cuito Cuanavale had responded to the attack, and they sent five tanks from 16 Brigade to reinforce 21 Brigade while MiG-23s from Menongue carried out the first of dozens of air-strikes against the South Africans that day.

The South Africans continued their advance towards 21 Brigade's HQ with some difficulty, abandoning another Ratel and three Olifants which became immobilised on the slopes leading up to the position. There was a brief moment when 16 Brigade's tank reinforcement threatened to out-flank the South Africans. But when this veered north, 4 SAI was able to launch its final assault on 21 Brigade's HQ, placing 61 Mech on the high ground north of the Dala river to intercept any retreating FAPLA forces. 21 Brigade's HQ was a heavily-defended bunker complex surrounded by trenches and anti-personnel minefields, and two squadrons of South African tanks were chosen to make the difficult approach. They took heavy fire from 23 mm guns as they advanced (one Ratel was immobilised) and in fierce exchanges they shot out two T-55s, driving off four others. A lone BM-21 (firing at only 150 yards range) briefly halted attempts by the Olifants and Ratels to clear a path through the minefields, but it was destroyed by an Olifant which then became immobilised in a ditch.

Under heavy bombardment the remaining Olifants continued their attack – destroying dozens of bunkers and inflicting heavy casualties – until after about an hour's fighting resistance crumbled, the retreating forces running straight into 61 Mech. In the confusion, several FAPLA vehicles drove through the middle of 61 Mech and escaped southwards, but the remainder (including four more tanks) were either shot out by South African missile teams or abandoned by their crews who fled on foot.[14] By the time bad light brought the attack to a halt, 21 Brigade had been driven out of its positions, and these were occupied by UNITA while the FAPLA regrouped by the Tumpo under the protection of 16 Brigade.

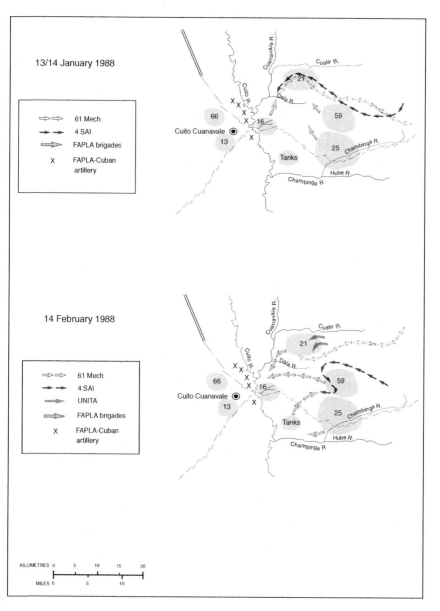

The next morning the South Africans pressed home their advantage against the FAPLA forces regrouping north of the Dala, shooting out four more tanks, two BM-21 s and two trucks, and triggering several inaccurate raids by Cuban MiG-23s (one of which was shot down by a UNITA Stinger missile).

By the end of two days fighting, the South Africans had killed more than 250 FAPLA troops and had destroyed or captured nine tanks, nine artillery pieces and eight trucks, suffering only one casualty and two damaged Ratels in the process. Despite their success in sweeping 21 Brigade back towards the river, however, the South Africans were unable to continue their attack and needed to withdraw and replenish their limited forces before taking on 66 or 59 Brigades (the next logical targets). That evening the South Africans pulled back to the Chambinga high ground, leaving UNITA to fight it out with the FAPLA over 21 Brigade's abandoned positions. The decision to withdraw effectively let the FAPLA off the hook and, as a result of delays caused by an outbreak of hepatitis, it would be a full month before the next assault was launched, giving the Cuban commanders ample breathing space to reorganise their forces east of the Cuito river.

The near disaster of 13 January caused great consternation (and not a little anger) in Havana which had spent the previous month repeatedly warning Ochoa that an attack was imminent. As an immediate measure a Cuban Tactical Group – comprising one battalion each of tanks, artillery and mechanised infantry – was sent from Menongue to Cuito Cuanavale, arriving on 21 January after twice being attacked by UNITA.[15] Overall command of Cuito Cuanavale was handed to the Cubans, although by now this was a formality as the Cubans had been overseeing the town's defences since the previous December. On 17 January, Castro ordered all FAPLA forces east of Cuito Cuanavale to withdraw to positions closer to the river (reducing their defensive perimeter and the likelihood of a breakthrough), while the bulk of the artillery was moved to the high ground west of the river where it was out of range of the South Africans and had an excellent view of the battle area.[16] Castro's plan did not go down well with the commanders in Cuito Cuanavale who feared they might trigger a panicked rush towards the river, and they instead started planning a general withdrawal to Menongue – something Castro categorically opposed.[17]

Cuba officially joins 'linkage' negotiations, 29 January 1988

Castro's inability to impose his will on Cuito Cuanavale could not have come at a worse time as Cuba was about to join the 'linkage' negotiations. Castro had been angling for a seat at the negotiating table since the previous July, but Crocker had held back until he had assurances that Cuba would not introduce extraneous issues into the agenda (such as Cuban–American relations) and that discussion of troop withdrawals would involve *all* the Cuban troops in Angola. The Cubans angled for their own concession – demanding Washington curtail support for UNITA – but Crocker held his ground, and on 29 January Jorge Risquet joined the Angolan delegation under the American conditions.[18] For Castro's double-strategy to work, however, it was essential that Cuito Cuanavale remained in Cuban hands, and the following day Ochoa was summoned to Havana where he was ordered to implement Castro's defence plan, over-ruling any opposition from the FAPLA or Soviets.[19] Despite this grilling, Ochoa appears to have resisted Castro's orders, withdrawing only 66 Brigade whilst insisting to Havana that the South Africans had started to withdraw. This left the battered FAPLA brigades east of the river exposed when a second devastating attack came a fortnight later.

The second South African assault, 14 February 1988

Following the success of its first attack in January, the South Africans had withdrawn to replenish, entrusting the next attack against 25 Brigade to UNITA. But when the guerrillas once more produced a lacklustre performance, the SADF was forced to step in and prepare its own assault. 20 Brigade's commanders were under intense pressure to complete their mission as quickly as possible, but due to an outbreak of hepatitis (during which both South African commanders were flown out for medical treatment), it was not until 11 February that plans for a second assault were finalised.[20] The principal objective would be 59 Brigade which was viewed by the South African commanders as the key to the FAPLA defensive system on the Chambinga high ground. Once it had been driven back to the river, the remaining brigades would have no choice but to also withdraw or face being surrounded. The South Africans were also keen to have another crack at 21 Brigade which had reoccupied its old positions, but given the limited forces at their disposal they entrusted this to UNITA, planning to penetrate the gap between 21 and 59 Brigades for a simultaneous assault on both positions (see Map 10, page 219).

Early on 14 February, the attack began with a fierce bombardment of both brigades, allowing 61 Mech and UNITA to manoeuvre into positions exactly between them and then launch simultaneous attacks. As a result, both brigades believed they were the objective of the attack, and throughout the day their demands for reinforcements caused great confusion in the FAPLA HQ which ordered troops back and forth between them. At 2 p.m. a squadron of Olifants swept through 59 Brigade's forward positions, and FAPLA resistance only strengthened once the South Africans reached the bunker complex protecting the Brigade's HQ. As the fighting intensified, the Ratel force (which had greater manoeuvrability and visibility) was integrated with the Olifants to pinpoint and destroy the 23 mm gun positions, and after several of these were shot out the FAPLA troops abandoned their positions and fled towards Tumpo.[21] A brief counter-attack by the brigade's tank force (which was dug in behind the HQ) descended into chaos when the South Africans jammed its communications, enabling the Olifants to shoot out at least four T-55s before they withdrew.

Cuban tanks launch a costly counter-attack

Faced with the collapse of his forces, 59 Brigade's commander urgently requested reinforcements, and 3 Tank Battalion was ordered to launch a counter-attack. Seven tanks from the Cuban Tactical Group (under Lieutenant-Colonel 'Ciro' Gómez Betancourt) spearheaded the force as it moved east towards 59 Brigade's position (one breaking down en route).[22] The FAPLA's signal was intercepted by the South Africans, however, and they sent 61 Mech to intercept the tanks, precipitating the first tank battle of the Angolan War. Visibility in the thick bush was poor and the Cuban tank force – which, according to the South Africans, arrived 'in a mob' – stumbled into a noisy point-blank firefight with the South Africans. The fighting was chaotic, and the Cuban tanks impressed the Olifant commanders with their aggressive (and often suicidal) sallies into the midst of the South African squadron in search of targets. With the range between opposing tanks down to as little as 100 yards, the Cuban commander was forced to keep his tank on the move, and by the end of the day his was the only tank still operational (although it had been hit three times). As dusk fell, both sides started to lose communication between their vehicles, and the South Africans started withdrawing. This allowed the Cuban commander (who had rammed a tree and camouflaged his tank under the foliage) to collect nine Cuban survivors scattered across the battlefield – six of them badly wounded – and withdraw to 16 Brigade's positions, arriving shortly before dawn.[23]

The attack of 14 February was another overwhelming success for the South Africans, driving the FAPLA off the Chambinga high ground and, following a weak attempt to reoccupy 59 Brigade's positions the next day, the FAPLA withdrew to its last foothold, the Tumpo triangle. The FAPLA's losses had again been heavy, with over 500 soldiers killed and seventeen tanks and eighteen other vehicles destroyed. In addition thirty-two Cubans had been killed, fourteen of them during the tank counter-attack. The Cubans claimed to have destroyed a dozen South African armoured cars and inflicted heavy casualties on UNITA, but South African figures of only four killed and seven wounded are more plausible (all of the fatalities occurred when a Ratel was hit by a single 23 mm round).[24] With the second phase of their mission complete, the South Africans immediately began planning an attack on the Tumpo triangle, intending to wind up their campaign by the end of February.

Cuban reaction to the attack of 14 February

News of the narrowly-averted catastrophe east of the Cuito river was greeted with disbelief and frustration in Havana. Castro angrily signalled Ochoa that he felt 'bitter over what happened because it was repeatedly anticipated and warned about'.[25] Had it not been for the suicidal counter-attack by Cuban tanks, the South Africans might have advanced as far as the bridge, cutting off the remaining brigades east of the river and bringing them within an inch of capturing Cuito Cuanavale itself. In Castro's mind, Ochoa was to blame, and he dispatched his most trusted subordinate, 'Polo', to Cuito Cuanavale to take personal charge of the defences, with orders to ensure that Castro's withdrawal plans – leaving only one brigade east of the river protecting the bridge – were implemented in full. The situation east of the river was now critical, and Polo would need to keep a cool head to prevent the demoralised Angolan troops – who had suffered two drubbings at the hands of the SADF and UNITA in the previous month – from abandoning their positions in a headlong scramble for the river.

Cuban attempts to cover up the disaster of 14 February

The disaster of 14 February was a major embarrassment for Havana's leadership, and following Ochoa's return to Cuba, all trace of the battle was covered up in the official account of the war which appeared in January 1989.[26] In the chapter on the 'Battle of Cuito Cuanavale' (which was ghost-written by General Harry Villegas Tamayo 'Pombo' who was not actually there), the date of the second South African attack is changed to exactly one month earlier – 14 *January* 1988 – to give the impression that one attack immediately followed the other.[27] This radical alteration to the chronology had two purposes: it absolved Ochoa from failing to reorganise the defences in the month between the two South African attacks, and it obviated the need to mention the heavy Cuban casualties sustained that day. The decision to alter the official account was probably taken to protect military reputations in the aftermath of the loudly-trumpeted victory at Cuito Cuanavale, but the re-write was clearly done at short notice. For not only do other chapters in the same book refer to the heavy fighting that day,[28] but on the map for the second attack the date '14.2' is marked eight times.

Subsequent to the book's publication, however, the priorities of the

Cuban leadership changed dramatically. Following Ochoa's fall from grace in July 1989 (see Chapter 12), Castro saw fit to reintroduce the near-disaster of 14 February to rubbish Ochoa's military reputation. Using his closing speech to the Council of State to list numerous examples of Ochoa's alleged moral and professional laxity, Castro brought up the costly Cuban tank counter-attack, blaming Ochoa for the loss of five tanks and fourteen Cuban lives. Having found a suitable scapegoat for the disaster, Castro then elevated Polo to the status of 'saviour of Cuando Cubango', his dispatch to reorganise Cuito Cuanavale's defences securing it against further South African attack.[29] The re-writing of the battle of 14 February is not the only example of the Cuban regime's tendency to alter or re-edit sections of history to fit the political agenda, but it is perhaps one of the most striking, and illustrates how quickly leading figures in the Cuban political and military elite can fall from grace.

Castro's defence plan is implemented

Following the near disaster of 14 February, remaining FAPLA forces were withdrawn to the Tumpo triangle under the supervision of Polo who arrived in Cuito Cuanavale in late February. Castro's plan involved withdrawing all forces across the river with the exception of 25 Brigade and 3 Tank Battalion which would guard the bridge and the Tumpo triangle. In anticipation of the inevitable South African attack, 25 Brigade's defences were strengthened with bunkers, trench systems and tank obstructions, and Cuban sappers laid a network of minefields east of the Tumpo covering every conceivable approach. The minefields served a double purpose, stalling the South African advance as engineers cleared a path for the armour, whilst also pinpointing their exact position for the dozens of BM-21s, M-46 and D-30 guns positioned on the high ground west of the river.

With the fighting concentrated into a small area ideally suited to defence – and with Cuban air power now fully deployed – the military advantage had swung in the FAPLA's favour, presenting the South Africans with their greatest challenge yet. By this stage, the small South African force was feeling the strain of six months of intense fighting, with over half the armoured cars experiencing technical problems and many of the troops succumbing to malaria and hepatitis. Its commanders were under acute pressure to wind up the campaign before the end of the month (when the bulk of the ground forces were due to complete their military service), but before withdrawing they were determined to crush the Tumpo triangle. A simulated crossing of the Cuito on 17/18 February failed to bluff the Cubans out of their positions, however, and the South Africans reluctantly began planning a full-scale attack, once more relying on UNITA to provide the bulk of the ground forces.

The South Africans got a foretaste of the FAPLA's new defences on 19

February when 4 SAI was sent to dislodge a battalion of 59 Brigade north of the Dala river.[30] The attack was preceded by the usual bombardment, but when the South African Ratels and Olifants launched their assault they ran into minefields south of the FAPLA's positions, losing a Ratel and an Olifant to anti-tank mines. The explosions immediately drew heavy artillery fire and, with MiGs flying over thirty air-strikes against them, the South Africans were forced to withdraw without even having reached the FAPLA's forward positions. The failure of this attack – the first set-back for nearly three months – was a demoralising development for the South Africans, and raised the prospect of far heavier casualties as they struggled to complete their mission before the end of the month.

Ironically the attack actually came close to success as 59 Brigade had fled its positions as dusk fell, but the troops were forcibly sent back in the night with orders to resist at all costs. The near collapse of 59 Brigade prompted another impatient cable from Castro demanding that the withdrawal be accelerated and, on the night of 24 February, the brigade got its marching orders, leaving only 25 Brigade protecting a bridgehead less than one square mile in area. By pure coincidence, however, the South Africans were due to launch an attack against 59 Brigade that same evening, and in the chaotic battle which ensued Castro's defence plan would undergo its first serious test, as the FAPLA struggled to maintain an orderly withdrawal under intense bombardment and attack. The confused and inconclusive fighting that night would come to characterise the final battles east of Cuito Cuanavale, and create the military stalemate which was to breathe life back into the peace process.

The third South African assault, 25 February 1988

In the days preceding the attack, South African casualties started to mount as Cuban MiGs stepped up their operations, shooting down their first Mirage on 19 February and two days later bombing a South African column east of the Cuito river, killing three South Africans and wounding one other. Painfully aware that further casualties would be politically unacceptable, the SADF Chief again imposed restrictions on the South Africans, ordering the over-stretched Olifants to support the main assault, and insisting that the destruction of the FAPLA's 23 mm guns (which had caused the heaviest casualties) be their first objective. On 22 February, 61 Mech was chosen to spearhead the assault, with 4 SAI and a small flanking force acting as its reserve.[31] The assault would be preceded by dummy attacks by 32 Battalion and UNITA to confuse the defenders, and once 59 Brigade's positions had been captured all forces would converge on 21 Brigade and possibly even the bridge itself (see Map 11, page 228). The FAPLA troops were known to be demoralised, and it was hoped that an attack on their final positions would break their will to fight on.

As South African forces were moving into position late on 24 February, 59 Brigade received its orders to withdraw across the Cuito river. This triggered a frantic meeting between the brigade's Angolan and Cuban commanders who realised that a South African attack was imminent. Fearing the withdrawal could degenerate into a disorderly scramble for the river, they ordered one battalion of 59 Brigade to remain in its positions to cover the rest of the brigade. Shortly after the South African G-5s opened up their bombardment, the first FAPLA troops started pulling back to the river, and they were followed by 25 Brigade at 4 a.m. the next morning. Two hours later, the South African's launched their attack. Almost immediately, however, 61 Mech ran into minefields east of 59 Brigade's positions. The commander's tank was the first to set off an anti-tank mine, and a further two tanks were lost to mines as they struggled to manoeuvre out of the minefield.

With the South African position announced to the defenders, Cuban M-46s and BM-21s laid down a heavy barrage while Cuban MiGs carried out the first of sixty air-strikes that day, killing a South African AA-missile operator who attempted to engage them. Difficulties with deploying the Plofadder mine-clearing equipment and the large number of anti-personnel mines greatly hindered attempts by South African engineers to clear a path for the armour. But once this was achieved, both tank squadrons passed through the minefield and linked up with 32 Battalion and UNITA for the main attack. By the time UNITA reached the FAPLA's forward trenches, however, they had already been abandoned, and the South Africans then stumbled into a second minefield, the continuous artillery fire and air-strikes destroying another Olifant and a Ratel, and causing several casualties. Cuban tanks in the bridge area deployed for a counter-attack, but with the front-lines in great disorder, the situation was considered too chaotic for it to succeed. Instead the defenders relied on their artillery which kept up a continuous bombardment of the South Africans, the Cuban loaders becoming blackened with soot by the end of the day's fighting.

By the time the South Africans reached the FAPLA's main positions, the sun was setting behind Cuito Cuanavale – shining directly into the gunners' eyes – and, with casualties mounting, the South African commander requested permission to withdraw. Determined not to give up the day's hard-fought gains, 61 Mech was ordered to withdraw only a short distance and hold its positions for a night attack. But with no let-up in the bombardment (which destroyed a further three vehicles) and technical problems with the tanks, it was decided to withdraw completely, and by dark the last South African troops had returned to their positions east of the Tumpo. Boosted by their success in repelling the South African attack, 59 Brigade completed its withdrawal across the Cuito river the following morning, by which time 25 Brigade had dug into new positions east of the bridge.

The failure of the third South African attack proved the turning point of the battle of Cuito Cuanavale, boosting the FAPLA's flagging morale and bringing the South African advance to a standstill. Although the FAPLA had again suffered heavy losses – with 172 FAPLA and ten Cubans killed, and at least seven tanks destroyed – the withdrawal to the Tumpo triangle had been completed, and the troops had simultaneously beaten off a South African assault, their first success after nearly five months of disaster. Two days later, Castro sent a congratulatory message to the men of 59 and 25 Brigades – praising them for the orderly manner of their withdrawal under fire (and reminding them that it had been his idea all along).[32] The FAPLA–Cuban defences had now reached their final positions with four brigades (plus the Cuban regiment) protecting the town on the western banks of the river, and 25 Brigade and 3 Tank Battalion defending the Tumpo bridgehead.

The South Africans rush to launch a fourth attack before the end of the month

For the South Africans, the aborted attack of 25 February was not viewed as a total failure, as all remaining FAPLA forces east of the Cuito river bar 25 Brigade had withdrawn shortly afterwards. However, the significant casualties sustained during twelve hours of fighting – two men killed, dozens wounded, four tanks and one Ratel severely damaged, and four other vehicles destroyed – alarmed the SADF, and led to several tactical changes. More engineers were brought in to deal with the minefields east of Tumpo, although the unreliability of their equipment would hamper their efforts, as would the South African habit of marking approach routes which enabled Cuban sappers to identify the direction of the attack and lay mines in its path.[33] By now the South African armour was experiencing technical difficulties (only seventeen out of twenty-eight tanks were still operational), but with less than a week before 20 Brigade was due to demobilise, its commanders had little choice but to press ahead with another attack.

On 28 February, the commanders finalised the plan of attack, encouraged by reconnaissance reports that there were only 800 FAPLA troops left east of the Cuito river, supported by only seven tanks and three BM-21s.[34] 61 Mech was again selected to spearhead the attack, with one tank squadron, 32 Battalion and UNITA in support, and 61 Mech in reserve. The plan was to assault 25 Brigade from the north and push through into the bridgehead area where a UNITA team would blow up the bridge, completing the South African mission (see Map 11, page 228). At 5:30 p.m. on 29 February, 61 Mech started assembling for the attack, but its tanks and mine-rollers had great difficulty manoeuvring through the tricky terrain, and by the time they moved off, only ten tanks and seventeen Ratels were still operational. The advance was frustratingly slow due to

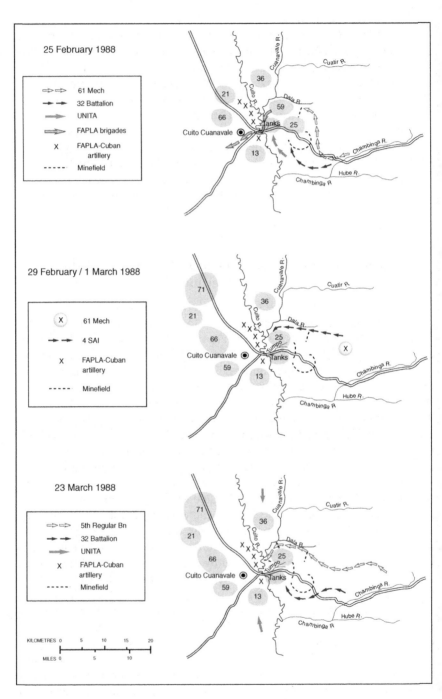

Map 11 The last three South African attacks east of Cuito Cuanavale.

heavy rain and faulty night periscopes on five of the Olifants, and the mine-rollers (which had overheated earlier) lagged far behind the advance. Eventually the attack was called off until first light while the decoy force went ahead with its diversionary raid, drawing heavy fire from the FAPLA artillery.

Aware that a fresh attack was underway, the chief Cuban adviser to 25 Brigade sent sappers to re-mine the South Africans' expected approach, and almost at once they ran into a South African forward patrol which (according to the Cubans) turned tail and fled. In the space of twenty minutes, an extra 150 mines were laid, adding to the 15,000 explosive obstacles littering the area east of the Tumpo bridgehead. Having lost its way slightly, at 9 a.m. 61 Mech reached 25 Brigade's forward positions to find them deserted. It continued its unsteady advance under ineffective BM-21 fire and several air-strikes, hitting a Cuban MiG which subsequently crashed near Longa.[35] Two miles short of the bridge, a South African mine-roller detonated several anti-personnel mines, and this unleashed a devastating barrage from the artillery on the west bank. A further four tanks set off anti-tank mines in quick succession as they struggled to manoeuvre out of the minefield.

Caught in the sights of the Cuban and Angolan gunners, the South Africans engaged in a fierce artillery and missile duel, their tanks and Ratels lobbing over 500 bombs into the FAPLA's gun positions over the next hour. Inevitably they took more casualties, with several Ratels being damaged while an Olifant had the machine-gun blown off its roof, killing the UNITA infantry huddled on its back. With eighteen FAPLA guns concentrated on the minefield, the South African commander pulled his force back a little over a mile, hoping to regroup out of range of the artillery. But by now there were reports that the Cuban tank battalion was preparing a counter-attack, and, with the South African armour experiencing mechanical problems (only five tanks were still operational), it was decided to pull back even further to escape the FAPLA's 23 mm guns which continued to lay down heavy fire. The Cuban counter-attack never materialised, but with the Ratels now developing problems, the South African commander rejected orders for a night attack and began withdrawing, darkly concluding that 'the enemy is strong and clever'.[36]

The South Africans' second consecutive defeat was a major morale boost for the defenders of Cuito Cuanavale, and conclusively proved the effectiveness of Castro's defence plan. Once again the FAPLA had sustained heavy casualties, in particular among the 23 mm gun and mortar positions. But the bridgehead had held firm, and the South Africans were again forced into a humiliating withdrawal without even having cleared the FAPLA's forward positions. It was the end of the line for 20 Brigade, and two days later it started to demobilise with the withdrawal of the Quebec Battery (which had been in action since the previous August).

Like its predecessor Zulu Force, 20 Brigade had swept aside all opposition until it found itself up against an insurmountable obstacle, and with insufficient strength to launch a further attack it was forced to hand the job to its relief, 82 Brigade. However, due to some of the worst flooding in South Africa's history, the new troops took a fortnight to arrive, giving the defenders breathing-space in which to strengthen their defences even further.

Castro escalates war into south-west Angola

The reversal of fortune at Cuito Cuanavale could not have come at a better moment for Havana, as Cuban representatives were due to meet with the Americans to begin the first round of 'linkage' negotiations. With Cuito Cuanavale's defences secure, Castro's double-strategy of 'war and talks' – which looked as if it had backfired disastrously in late January – appeared to be paying off. It is thus no coincidence that, three days before the talks were due to start, Castro ordered the Cuban contingent in Lubango to begin moving into Cunene, dramatically turning up the pressure on the South Africans on the eve of their first high-level talks with the Americans for two years. Castro's preferred subordinate, Polo, was appointed to command the operation, while the defence of Cuito Cuanavale was entrusted to Divisional-General Miguel Lorente León who was promised more troops and tanks.[37] The move into south-west Angola was intended to force concessions from the South Africans in the negotiations, but it was a strategy fraught with danger, and set the Cubans and the SADF on the path towards their final confrontations (see Chapter 11).

Crocker's team hold the first tripartite talks, March 1988

Since Cuba joined the negotiations in late January, Crocker's team had been trying to re-engage the South Africans after nearly two years of low-level and inconclusive contacts.[38] Pretoria's relationship with Washington had been soured by the imposition of sanctions in September 1986 (both Crocker and Reagan had argued against them), and the South African leadership was uneasy that its most intractable enemy (Cuba) had been given a seat at the talks. Pik Botha nevertheless agreed to meet Crocker on 14 March, and in an effort to tie down a proposal beforehand, Crocker sent a two-man team to Luanda on 9 March for three days of talks with the Cubans and Angolans. During the talks the Americans pressed for a broad agreement with the specifics left for a later date, but they were prevented by the Angolans who demanded an American commitment to stop aiding UNITA, a concession Crocker was not willing to grant. Eventually the Angolans presented a four-year withdrawal proposal, under which all Cuban forces would deploy north of the 13th parallel in the first year,

20,000 would be withdrawn in the second, and the remainder between months 30 and 48. Although the Americans knew that four years was too long, the proposal was a significant breakthrough – representing Havana and Luanda's first withdrawal timetable – and demonstrated that an agreement was at least feasible, even if there were sizeable differences between the warring parties.

But when Crocker flew to Geneva three days later to meet Pik Botha he found him unwilling to commit to the revived peace process, rejecting the Cuban proposal out of hand. By this stage, Pretoria's strategy in Angola was unravelling – with its forces bogged down east of Cuito Cuanavale and public criticism of the campaign (which had cost fifty South African lives) growing daily – and it was in no mood for making concessions while Cuba escalated the war into south-west Angola. Crocker urged Botha to seize the opportunity to make a deal, but until the timetable could be reduced, Pretoria refused to bite and so, two days later, Crocker sent his team back to Luanda to extract a lower bid. The Cuban–Angolan delegation rebuffed the American move, demanding South Africa respond to their first proposal before making further concessions, and with the fighting in Angola deadlocked, Crocker pressed the South Africans for another meeting at the earliest opportunity.

Sensing the time was now right, on the last day of the talks, *Granma* published a communiqué revealing that Cuban troops had been fighting in Cuito Cuanavale since early December, and declaring that their stand against apartheid was 'an international symbol for the peoples of the world'. The decision to acknowledge a battle while it was still going on was an unusual departure for Havana. The interventions in Algeria (1963), Congo (1965), Venezuela (1967), Syria (1973), Ethiopia (1978) and even Operation Carlota itself had not been revealed to the public until several weeks (or even years) after their completion,[39] and with the fighting in Angola not yet over, it was quite a gamble. Possibly Havana felt it could no longer keep secret its involvement in both the fighting and the 'linkage' negotiations, and reasoned that with the military situation tilting in its favour, now was as good a time as any to go public. But the announcement was also the first step in creating the myth of Cuito Cuanavale, converting what had been a military stalemate into a crushing victory over the South Africans (see pp. 234–5). The Cuban defences still had to pass one final test, however, as within a week 82 Brigade was ready to launch the attack which would decide the outcome of the 'Battle of Cuito Cuanavale'.

Build-up to the final South African assault, March 1988

Following their second failure to capture the Tumpo bridgehead, the South Africans were absorbed by the hand-over to 82 Brigade, and it was not until 12 March that a new commander formally initiated Operation Packer. 82 Brigade bore a strong resemblance to its predecessor – with two mechanised infantry battalions, two squadrons of Olifants and one of Ratels, one battery of G-5s, G-2s, mortars and MRLs, and various AA, engineer and reconnaissance platoons in support.[40] Heavy flooding severely delayed planning, however, and after much wrangling with the SADF HQ, the date of 23 March was set for the attack. The main assault against 25 Brigade would be preceded by a decoy attack from the south, after which the main force – consisting of the infantry, all of the armour and UNITA's 5th Battalion – would attack from the north (see Map 11, page 228). Once 25 Brigade had been driven from its positions, UNITA would occupy the bridgehead and destroy the bridge, completing the South African mission and enabling 82 Brigade to start its withdrawal.

By late March the defences facing the South Africans had become almost impregnable, however, and the defenders were more confident and aggressive than ever. Four days after 20 Brigade's last attack, the first FAPLA–Cuban patrols had been sent into no-man's-land, clashing repeatedly with UNITA and, on 9 March, Cuban MiGs carried out their first attack on the South Africans' supply lines, bombing a convoy near the Lomba. East of the Cuito river, the Cubans strengthened the minefield cordon, extending it from the Cuanavale to the Tumpo to cover every conceivable approach for an attack. The Cubans deliberately left gaps between the minefields and trained fifteen heavy guns on them, with a further nine behind the main positions and dozens on the opposite bank. Fifteen tanks guarded 25 Brigade's central position, with at least fourteen others in the bridge area.[41] West of the river, 13 Brigade and the small Cuban regiment guarded Cuito Cuanavale, while dozens of smaller units dotted the 110-mile supply route to Menongue. They were the most formidable defences the South Africans had faced to date, and presented 82 Brigade with a daunting task for its first attack of the campaign.

The final South African assault, 23 March 1988

In the days preceding the final attack, the South Africans carried out deceptive operations to confuse the FAPLA, simulating a crossing of the Cuito river and softening up 25 Brigade's defences with two days of airstrikes.[42] On the night of 20 March, a South African artillery observer was infiltrated into the area north of the Cuito Cuanavale confluence, and over the next two days UNITA distracted the nearby FAPLA battalion with repeated attacks. A signals intercept on 22 March revealed that the FAPLA was planning to retake the Chambinga high ground, but with 82 Brigade already forming up for the attack it was decided to go ahead anyway. At 4 a.m. on 23 March, South African G-5s began bombarding 25 Brigade, catching a platoon of Cuban officers (who had only arrived the previous day) repairing the forward trenches. As on previous occasions, the South Africans had great difficulty advancing through the rough terrain – one truck burning out its clutch en route – and it was not until 8:15 a.m. that the attack was launched, the leading elements having to readjust their positions after drifting too far to the west.

Within minutes of crossing the start-line, the leading Olifant hit an anti-tank mine, disabling the tank and drawing an immediate reaction from the FAPLA–Cuban artillery. For the next three hours, the South African engineers struggled under heavy bombardment to clear a lane through the minefield, but their efforts were hampered by the failure of their equipment to detonate properly. In reaction to the new attack, the FAPLA moved up eight tanks and a BM-21 to support 25 Brigade, and these were soon engaging the Olifants from the western bank of the river, one T-55 being destroyed by a direct G-5 hit. North of the rivers' confluence, UNITA launched a fresh attack against the lone battalion of 36 Brigade, but after struggling for several hours it was driven off with heavy casualties, forcing the artillery observer to abandon his position. With a thick mist descending on the battlefield, the South African artillery lost all observation of the fighting, and the remainder of the battle was a confused and noisy affair. Shortly before midday, South African engineers cleared a path through the first minefield, and the two squadrons of Olifants then restarted the assault on 25 Brigade.

Almost immediately they drew heavy fire from the western banks of the Cuito and were forced to pull back into dead ground, the accompanying UNITA troops taking heavy casualties. Two attempts were made to resume the advance but each time they drew crippling fire, forcing the South Africans to pull back and take cover. With the cloud briefly lifting, Cuban MiGs carried out their first bombing runs of the day, and when the South Africans tried a different approach they ran into another minefield, losing two tanks in quick succession. Several of the mines had been boosted with 122 mm missile rounds, and the South African commander was 'treated to the sight of a complete Olifant suspension unit sailing through the air', to be followed a few minutes later by the rear suspension of a mine-roller.[43] With the remaining Olifants low on fuel (having spent the day manoeuvring back and forth between the minefields) and the battlefield obscured with smoke and dust, the South African commander requested permission to withdraw his force. This was duly granted, but during the withdrawal three of the tanks which were being towed had to be abandoned in the sand, the last troops reaching their positions under artillery fire which lasted until dark.

Aftermath of the final South African assault

The failure of the final South African attack brought the 'Battle of Cuito Cuanavale' to a close, and convinced the SADF that the FAPLA could not be dislodged from its Tumpo positions without unacceptably high casualties. As on previous occasions, South African armour had been halted in the minefields east of the bridgehead, and three immobilised tanks had been left behind when it withdrew. The scale of the artillery duel demonstrated how far the fighting had escalated over the previous eight months, the Cubans and South Africans firing over 4,000 shells and rockets at each other during the attack. The high number of UNITA casualties (perhaps several hundred) prompted accusations that the guerrillas had been used as cannon fodder, forced at gun-point to clear a path through the minefields and then abandoned when the attack ran into difficulties, the South African armour driving over the dead and wounded in its haste to escape.[44] While Cuban accounts might be exaggerated, UNITA sappers *were* sent ahead to clear the minefields – and UNITA *did* bear all of the casualties that day – and doubts still remain over their use in this attack.[45]

With the Tumpo defences too strong to be overwhelmed from the east – and with operations west of the Cuito river ruled out by Pretoria – the South Africans had little choice but to withdraw, and within a few days 82 Brigade had started to demobilise. Not all South African forces would withdraw from the area, however, as there was still a danger the FAPLA might re-launch its offensive later in the year. In an effort to contain it within the Tumpo triangle, the South Africans constructed a minefield cordon of their own. A 1,500-man holding force – designated Combat Group 20 – was formed to support the mine-laying operation, with orders to carry out deceptive operations to give the impression that there were still considerable South African forces in the area.[46] Over the following months South African sappers laid a chain of minefields from the Dala to the Tumpo rivers, blocking all crossing sites along the Cuito and Cuanavale rivers and, by late 1988, turning the area east of the Cuito river into one of the most heavily mined areas in the world.[47]

Cuba constructs the myth of Cuito Cuanavale

Following the final repulse of the South Africans, the Cuban propaganda machine went into overdrive, eager to capitalise on the SADF's first defeat since Operation Savannah. On the day of the final attack, *Granma* announced the institution of the 'Medal of Merit for the Defence of Cuito Cuanavale', by personal order of Castro. Scarcely a week later the first eighty-two newly-minted medals were presented to Cuban and Angolan troops in Luanda. The same day (ironically April Fool's Day) Cuban journalists flew into Cuito Cuanavale for a publicity splurge, crossing the Cuito river to 25 Brigade's positions where they were shown the FAPLA's first captured Olifant tank (which had been retrieved with great difficulty).[48] The 'victory' at Cuito Cuanavale was an essential part of Castro's strategy – granting the FAPLA and Cubans their first tangible success against the South Africans for more than a decade – and over the coming months he would repeatedly return to the battle in his speeches, inflating its importance from a successful operation to halt the South African advance to nothing short of a turning-point in African history.

The reality was not quite as clear-cut, however, and after the war the South Africans and Americans would dismiss Castro's claims as an elaborate piece of propaganda, insisting that both sides had fought each other to a standstill.[49] At the time, they claimed, they refrained from responding to Castro's boasts because they knew he was seeking an honourable exit from Angola, and they did not want to do anything that might jeopardise the negotiations. But this strategy played directly into Castro's hands, and allowed him to set the propagandistic agenda in the crucial months leading up to the peace accords. Thus despite proving more than a match for the FAPLA–Cubans on the battlefield, in the upcoming 'battle of perceptions' the South Africans would be utterly outclassed by the Cuban leader who used his decades of political savvy to devastating effect. Ultimately, however, Castro's bravado kept the South Africans engaged in Angola, stirring up the military tensions and egging on both sides towards their final bloody clashes.

11

THE FIGHTING IN SOUTH-WEST ANGOLA AND THE NEGOTIATING END-GAME, MARCH–DECEMBER 1988

As far back as the crisis talks held in Moscow in November 1987, Castro had been preparing a move into south-west Angola. The Western Front (as the Cubans termed it) formed an essential part of Castro's double-strategy, the escalation of the war into Namibia's backyard putting pressure on the South Africans as the negotiations reached their climax. While the defence of Cuito Cuanavale hung in the balance, the move had been delayed, but following the failure of two South African attacks on the Tumpo bridgehead (which proved that Cuito Cuanavale's defences were secure), Castro ordered Polo to move his forces into south-west Angola. By 11 March, the powerful 40 Tank Brigade had reached Tchibemba (seventy-five miles to the south).[1] The Cuban strategy (which resembled the closing stages of 'The Second Liberation War') involved reinforcing the main FAPLA and SWAPO garrisons in Cunene – at Cahama, Xangongo, Mupa and Cuvelai – before moving on the Namibian border. Almost immediately the Cubans clashed with the South Africans – ambushing a patrol near Calueque on 15 March – and this sparked off three months of clashes between the two sides as the Cubans extended their influence into south-west Angola.

Construction of new airbases at Cahama and Xangongo

For Castro's strategy to work, it was essential that Cuban air power – which had proved so effective east of the Cuito river – be extended up to the Namibian border. Accordingly, on 22 March, Castro ordered Ochoa to extend the airstrip at Cahama to take fighter aircraft, all of which had to operate from Lubango and Matala, 115 miles to the north.[2] Cahama was already an important base – with two FAPLA battalions, a growing Cuban presence and elaborate radar and AA defences – and the extension of its airstrip turned it into Cuba's principal airbase in Cunene. It quickly became clear that the new airstrip would not meet the demands of the

236

operation and, in early April, Castro ordered Ochoa to extend the airstrip in Xangongo too. The funds to complete both air bases (roughly half-a-million dollars) were not made available by the FAR's Finance Department, however, and Ochoa was forced to improvise to meet Castro's deadline. Turning to the most readily available source of cash – the *candonga* – Ochoa's aides exchanged over one hundred tons of Cuban sugar stockpiled in Luanda for Angolan kwanzas, and then used the cash to buy building materials for both airports, little suspecting the consequences these actions would have.[3]

Mixed Cuban and Angolan construction teams worked around the clock to get the airstrips operational and, by early June, the first asphalt runway at Cahama (over a mile-and-a-half long) had been completed. This was followed three weeks later by Xangongo, and in July a second longer runway was constructed at Cahama.[4] A radar network covering the whole of southern Angola was also installed, linking together 150 SAM-8 missile batteries and effectively bringing South African air superiority to an end.[5] Ultimately Cahama and Xangongo were constructed so that Cuban air power could be projected into Namibia itself, and shortly before the advance into south-west Angola began, Castro ordered Ochoa to prepare an air-strike against SAAF bases in Namibia should Cuban forces fall victim to a surprise attack. It was a highly provocative strategy, and was bound to elicit an aggressive response from the South Africans who had been operating freely in the region for years, and who had economic interests there (the Calueque hydroelectric installations).

The first Cuban–South African clashes in Cunene, April 1988

The South Africans immediately detected Cuba's increased military presence in Cunene, and with the campaign against SWAPO continuing in earnest it was only a matter of time before they clashed with the Cubans. The first major clash occurred on 18 April when a SWATF unit in pursuit of SWAPO was ambushed by over 200 Cubans near Chipeque (twenty miles south of Xangongo).[6] A Cuban RPG opened the firing with a direct hit on the leading armoured car – wounding most of its occupants – and a noisy firefight ensued which lasted until the early morning. By its end, one South African major was dead and eleven other South Africans wounded. (The medic disappeared and his body was discovered six weeks later in a shallow grave.) The Cuban ambush was a striking demonstration of their growing presence in the region, and over the following weeks they became increasingly bold in their patrolling and mine-laying, extending their control south from Xangongo towards the sixty-man garrison in Calueque.

On 2 May – following a Mirage air-strike on FAPLA positions south of Tchipa – the Cuban commander of 40 Tank Brigade sent out a mixed

FAPLA–Cuban company with orders to set up another ambush.[7] The eighty-one-man force was well armed – with two grenade launchers, six heavy machine-guns, eighteen RPGs and a SAM system – and carried six anti-tank mines to be laid along the expected approach route. Shortly after midnight on 4 May, the ambush was set up one mile south of Donguena, two platoons digging trenches on the west side of the road while a third dug in behind them with six of the RPGs. They remained there throughout the day until at 4p.m. tank engines were heard approaching from the south-west. The South African force – travelling in twenty Casspirs and two trucks – had been sent from Calueque to occupy Donguena, but its commander, 'Snakes' Snyman (who was eager for some action), had ignored warnings of ambushes in the area, and in his haste to reach Donguena he drove his force right into the middle of the Cubans.

Cuban RPGs opened fire, disabling the leading Casspir and scattering the South Africans who took cover from the hail of bullets and shrapnel. Two more Casspirs were shot out in quick succession, and the South Africans pulled back to regroup, their commander (who had been wounded by shrapnel) radioing Calueque for assistance. Desperate attempts were made to recover the abandoned Casspirs, and in vicious close-quarter fighting a fourth Casspir was disabled by a point-blank RPG round, while several Cubans were crushed under the South African armour as it manoeuvred through the shallow trench system. Only at dusk did the South Africans withdraw, setting up their own ambush to catch any pursuing forces (which never came). That night, three companies from 201 and 101 Battalions were sent to occupy Donguena, but when they ran into suspected tank positions south of the town their commander called off the attack, allowing the Cubans to withdraw in the night.

The ambush of 4 May greatly increased the stakes in the south-west, and though hailed by the Cubans as a victory, had caused both sides significant losses. Fifty-four Cubans had died, many of them crushed under the Casspirs during savage close-quarter fighting. In the process they had shot out three Casspirs (which were later destroyed by the SADF), captured a fourth one and killed seven men from 101 Battalion, seizing in the process a large amount of weaponry and equipment. More importantly, the Cubans captured their first South African prisoner since 1976 – Sergeant-Major Papenfus, who was severely wounded. (In a well-choreographed propaganda coup, they flew him to Havana for medical treatment, allowing his family to visit him there five weeks later.) The clash south of Donguena could not have come at a more critical time as the first round of tripartite negotiations had only just started in London. With highly-sensitive issues under discussion, Castro's double-strategy of 'war and talks' was reaching its dangerous climax, and Crocker would struggle to keep all parties focused on negotiation as the threat of bloodier clashes threatened to sink them at any moment.

Round one of the tripartite negotiations in London, 3–4 May 1988

Following Crocker's inconclusive meeting with Pik Botha, on 28 March a three-man South African delegation arrived in Washington for three days of talks. Having suffered their final defeat east of the Cuito river less than a week before, the South Africans were extremely defensive, and Crocker urged them to seize the opportunity for a settlement before other factors – in particular the American presidential election (due in November) – derailed the process. A fortnight later the South Africans agreed to take part in negotiations including the Cubans, and on 3 May delegations from South Africa, Angola and Cuba met at the Durrants Hotel in London for the first round of tripartite talks.[8] With the fighting escalating in Cunene, the atmosphere was tense, and though the talks were deemed a success, little was achieved beyond opening statements, the discussion degenerating into 'a mini-test of wills' over where the next meeting would be held.[9]

More ominous, however, were the private conversations between the Cuban and South African military representatives which reflected the tensions brewing in south-west Angola. One meeting on the evening of 4 May degenerated into open threats when Rosales warned Geldenhuys that, if the South Africans did not accept the Cuban proposal, then nothing would stop the Cubans invading Namibia itself. Rosales was probably acting under instructions from Castro who wanted to impress on the South Africans his determination to escalate the south-west campaign to full-scale war if necessary. But if this message was intended to cow them into submission, then it had the opposite effect, Geldenhuys responding that if the Cubans dared 'to set one foot across the border ... it would be the blackest day in Cuban military history'.[10] Although the meeting ended cordially – Geldenhuys making light of their mutual threats and urging them to concentrate on the negotiations – the gauntlet had been thrown down, and following the meeting, both sides steeled themselves for the final showdown in south-west Angola.

The Cubans and South Africans reinforce Cunene, May 1988

Following the Donguena ambush, MMCA reinforced Cunene, and by the end of May there were two full Cuban divisions in south-west Angola – around 12,000 men, supported by 200 tanks and five types of AA missile defences. These were spread along a new defensive line running from Namibe through Lubango, Cahama, Xangongo, Cuvelai and Cassinga (see Map 12).[11] Three 500-man SWAPO–Cuban battalions were also formed at the main airbases, enabling SWAPO to operate in areas of Cunene denied to it since the early 1980s. With South African activity north of Calueque

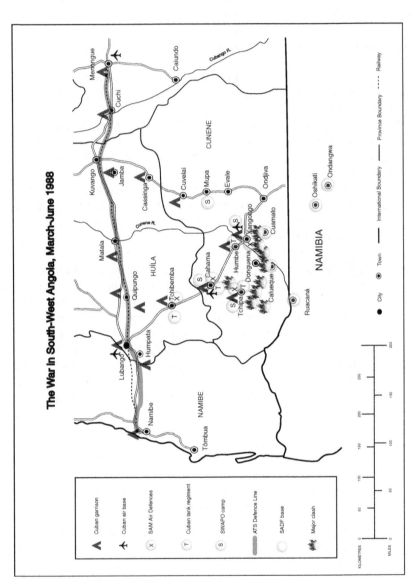

The War in South-West Angola, March–June 1988

Legend:
- Cuban garrison
- Cuban air base
- SAM Air Defences (X)
- Cuban tank regiment (T)
- SWAPO camp (S)
- ATS Defence Line
- SADF base
- Major clash

City ●   Town ◉   International Boundary   Province Boundary

Railway ----

Map 12 The war in south-west Angola, March–June 1988.

on the increase, it was further decided to reinforce the SWAPO training camp at Tchipa (fifty miles south of Cahama), as much to deter the South Africans from extending their operations northwards as to create a concentration point for an advance on the Namibian border. The camp at Tchipa – containing one battalion of SWAPO special forces – had already been reinforced earlier in the year with a company of troops from Cahama and several AA units, and over the next six weeks it received more Cuban armour, infantry and artillery, boosting the garrison to over 1,000 troops and at least thirty tanks.

The build-up in Tchipa did not go unnoticed by the sixty-man South African garrison at Calueque only thirty miles away and, on 17 May, two three-man teams from 32 Battalion were sent to reconnoitre the area south of Tchipa. They reported back on trench systems south of the camp, aggressive patrols and the first evidence of a Cuban tank force – all of which suggested a move towards the border was being prepared. The news was disconcerting for the SADF which was scaling down its operations in south-east Angola and had no desire to launch a fresh campaign in the south-west. But with no available South African force strong enough to take on Tchipa, the best it could do was dispatch three companies from 32 Battalion to act as a screening force north of Calueque. These were only an intermediate measure, however, and a few days later a new task force was set up (code-named Zulu as in 1975), which would eventually comprise one battle group from 32 Battalion, three companies from 101 Battalion, 61 Mech, one battery each of MRLs, G-5s and G-2s, and one troop of mortars.[12]

The South African ambush south of Tchipa, 22 May 1988

Zulu Force would not be deployed until early June, however, and in the meantime the three companies from 32 Battalion operated unsupported south of Tchipa. They clashed repeatedly with SWAPO until, on 21 May, they discovered two Cuban outposts ten miles south of Tchipa. Keen to gauge the strength of Cuban forces, the South Africans decided to shell these outposts in an attempt to draw out and then ambush any Cuban reinforcements sent from Tchipa.[13] Their plan backfired, however, when they failed to notice a third Cuban outpost hidden between the other two, and inadvertently set up their positions only a few hundred yards from it. The fighting started prematurely when they spotted five Cubans walking down the road towards them, and they quickly shot them down along with several FAPLA troops behind them. Four BRDMs then appeared, only to withdraw when the leading vehicle's commander was shot by a South African sniper, but they soon returned with Cuban tanks, forcing the South Africans into a hasty retreat. Mortars were called in to slow down the Cuban attack, but in the confusion one Unimog was hit and set on fire

– while two others collided with each other – and all three had to be abandoned as the South Africans withdrew under BM-21 fire.

The bungled ambush of 22 May was another costly encounter – the Cubans losing at least six men, the South Africans three Unimogs and a large amount of ammunition (although they suffered no casualties) – and it convinced both sides that their adversaries were preparing an offensive. Fearing the fighting could spill into Namibia, on 8 June General Geldenhuys announced the mobilisation of the 140,000-man Citizen Force, hoping to send a strong message to the Cubans that South Africa would respond in force to any invasion of its territory. North of the border, Task Force Zulu was also bolstered with a company of tanks from Combat Group 20 (which was still operating east of the Cuito river), but Pretoria ruled out any pre-emptive strike on Tchipa because of the projected casualties (up to 300).

The Cubans prepare to advance on Calueque, June 1988

From their study of documents recovered from the captured Unimogs, the Cubans concluded that the SADF was planning a major assault on Tchipa itself (in fact Pretoria had ruled this out), and in response they reinforced further. A second Tactical Group was dispatched to Tchipa with orders to patrol as far south as possible, while the Cuban 'Pechora regiment' in Matala (Huíla) was moved south into Cunene. By 12 June, four SWAPO–FAPLA units were operating within a twenty-mile radius of Tchipa, determining the location and intentions of South African forces in the area. Cuban engineers meanwhile constructed minefields, bunkers and tank obstructions around Tchipa, employing the same tactics they had used so successfully east of the Cuito river. A two-pronged offensive towards Namibia was drawn up, with an initial force moving south from Xangongo to capture Cuamato (fifty miles east of Calueque) after which three other columns would sweep down from Tchipa on Calueque itself. Having heard rumours that an air-strike on Tchipa was imminent, Castro also ordered the Cuban aviation to be ready for a retaliatory strike against Ruacaná (and even airfields in Namibia itself), and he informed Luanda and Moscow that clashes could occur in southern Cunene over the following weeks.[14]

On 18 June, two Cuban missile groups arrived in Namibe to reinforce Tchipa, and these were joined the same day by a third Tactical Group and the General Staff from 80 Tank Brigade which would oversee the advance southwards. The Cubans stepped up their patrols south of Tchipa, and on 22 June they clashed with a company of 32 Battalion. The South Africans shot three Cubans from a forward patrol before they were driven off by Cuban armour, abandoning a burning Buffel which had taken a direct hit.[15] Two days later, the first prong of the offensive set out from Xangongo to capture Cuamato, but the South Africans were expecting this move and had placed a screening force in the area (backed by Ratels and mortars). This clashed head-on with the Cubans, and after a noisy fight it was driven off with the loss of two more Buffels. But its stand was sufficient to halt the advance, and the South Africans were able to occupy Cuamato while the Cubans withdrew to Xangongo.[16] With Cuamato secure, the focus of the fighting switched back to Tchipa, and the timing was critical as, on the same day, the second round of negotiations was due to start in Cairo. The decision to launch the offensive to coincide with these talks was a deliberate ploy by Havana – representing the climax of Castro's 'war and talks' strategy – and even as the Cuban and South African delegations began their first day of bitter exchanges, their military forces were hours away from the final clash of the war.

Round two of the negotiations in Cairo, 24–25 June 1988

Since the first round of talks in early May, Crocker had struggled to tie down a second round. Secret talks between the Angolans and South Africans in Brazzaville in mid-May had achieved no progress, and at a meeting with Adamishin a few days later, Crocker ruefully remarked that 'African diplomacy ... was like a resort hotel with many rooms and no locks on the doors'. A summit between Gorbachev and Reagan at the end of May provided the necessary fillip – both leaders agreeing that a peace plan should be drawn up by the tenth anniversary of Resolution 435 (29 September) – and when Egypt offered to host the negotiations, Crocker set up two days of talks in Cairo. The first day was tense, both delegations engaging in 'provocative verbal fireworks' which mirrored the real fireworks occurring three-and-a-half-thousand miles away in Cunene.[17] But discreet lobbying by the Soviets and Americans persuaded them to take a more positive approach and, on the second day, they saluted the 'spirit of London' and declared that 'linkage' offered the only opportunity for a lasting settlement.[18] The talks went no further than confidence-building between the delegations, however, and it would take the final bloody clashes in Cunene to spur them into tackling the issues which had blocked a settlement for nearly seven years.

The final clashes in Cunene, 27/28 June 1988

Following the clash at Cuamato, the South Africans were keen to test the strength of Cuban forces in Tchipa, unaware that they were within hours of launching an advance on Calueque.[19] 'Operation Excite' was a carbon copy of the South Africans' previous bungled ambush, and involved bombarding Tchipa in an attempt to draw out the Cuban armour into an ambush. By 6 p.m. on 26 June, twenty-four Ratels were in position twenty miles south of Tchipa, and the South African artillery then released mete-orological balloons as radar decoys, enabling them to plot the positions of Tchipa's air defences which fired six SA-6 missiles at them. South African G-5s then opened up on the Tchipa camp – the first salvo destroying the artillery command post – and, by the end of four hours nearly 200 shells had silenced the camp's artillery. The expected counter-attack did not occur, however, and Polo – who arrived in Tchipa only a few hours before the shelling began – merely sent out a lone armoured car to locate the South Africans, its Cuban commander clashing briefly with a South African patrol before withdrawing. Satisfied with the damage inflicted (though disappointed they had failed to draw out the Cuban armour), the Ratels withdrew towards Calueque, anxious not to be caught in daylight by the Cuban MiGs.

Unknown to the South Africans, however, the bombardment *had* gal-vanised the Cubans into action. Within hours, Castro ordered an air-strike to be launched against 'the South African camps, military installations and personnel in Calueque and the surrounding area'.[20] Simultaneously, three armoured forces – each comprising 600 men with dozens of tanks in support – were ordered to advance on Calueque, their arrival timed to coincide with the air-strike. An advance group of thirty SWAPO and Cuban troops was sent ahead in the early morning of 27 June to set up an ambush south of Tchipa, and it had scarcely prepared its positions when South African armour was heard approaching over the hill. The South African force – including Ratels, mechanised infantry and a squadron of Olifants – was searching for positions for its own ambush, and as the leading Ratel cleared the crest of the hill, it was hit by an RPG round, setting off a series of internal explosions which crippled the vehicle. South African G-5s and mortars were called in to bombard the Cubans, but in fierce exchanges at least four more Ratels were damaged, one taking a direct hit which killed its commander and wounded three of his crew. Cuban reinforcements soon arrived, and in close-quarter fighting the South Africans shot out a tank, a BTR-60 and several trucks, driving off the infantry with heavy casualties.

Seizing on a lull in the fighting, the South Africans withdrew slightly – picking up the crews of the abandoned Ratels – and then sent in their squadron of Olifants to attack the gathering Cuban armour. The two leading Olifants immediately shot out another tank – killing its crew and a platoon of infantry perched on its back – and, after destroying another BTR-60 and several more trucks, they forced the Cubans to withdraw. The fighting had lasted a little over an hour, but with reports coming in that a large Cuban tank force was now en route from Tchipa, the South Africans decided to pull back before they were overwhelmed. They immediately withdrew towards Calueque under bombardment from Cuban MiG-23s, and by late afternoon their artillery and tanks had crossed the Cunene into Namibia.

With FAPLA–Cuban forces withdrawing towards Tchipa, it appeared as if the advance on Calueque had been abandoned. But the fighting that day had a nasty sting in its tail, as a dozen Cuban MiG-23s were already en route to Calueque from airbases in Lubango and Cahama, skimming the tops of trees at over 600 miles per hour.[21] Shortly before 1 p.m., they were spotted by a South African patrol on the hills above Ruacaná, but given the speed of their attack it was unable to warn Calueque in time. The first wave flew in over the dam, one pair of MiGs providing cover for a second which dropped six parachute-retarded bombs, severely damaging the bridge and nearby sluice-gates (wounding one South African). A second pair bombed the power plant and engine rooms, while a seventh MiG veered off from the main group and dropped eight bombs on the fresh-water pipeline to Ovambo, blowing it to pieces and setting its adjacent electricity plant on fire. More significantly, the last bomb landed between a parked Buffel and Eland-90, killing eleven South African conscripts who had gathered there to watch the attack.

With the hydroelectric installations engulfed in flames and smoke, the Cuban MiGs flew back over Calueque – one pilot rolling his aircraft and flying inverted over the dam – and two were hit by 32 Battalion's 20 mm guns, one subsequently crashing before it reached Lubango. The air-strike on Calueque brought the fighting to a dramatic conclusion and wound up a day of bitter confrontations which, for both sides, had been one of the bloodiest of the Angolan War. The FAPLA–Cuban force south of Tchipa had suffered heavy losses – including two tanks, two BTR-60s and eight trucks – with as many as 300 killed, at least ten of them Cubans.[22] The South Africans came off lightly in the first clash, losing only two Ratels (with many others damaged) and one killed. But, in less than five minutes, a further eleven men were killed and many injured at Calueque, while the hydroelectric installations were severely damaged and the vital bridge over the Cunene river was destroyed.[23]

Aftermath of the clashes on 27 June

The bloody clashes on 27 June proved the turning-point of the south-west campaign, and persuaded both sides to pull back from the brink of all-out war. For Pretoria, the heavy loss of life at Calueque was disastrous – sparking outrage among conservative whites who questioned the morality of South Africa's involvement in Angola – and it ordered an immediate retrenchment. Only five days later, Combat Group 20 (which was still operating east of the Cuito river) was ordered to scale back its operations, with explicit instructions that there be no further South African casualties or prisoners, and that no South African equipment fall into FAPLA hands. Worried that the Cubans might attempt an invasion of Namibia, on 13 July the SADF set up a defensive force – 10 Division – which was deployed along the border until the end of the year.[24] Although there were still isolated clashes with SWAPO in Cunene, the South Africans had effectively withdrawn from the fighting and, for the next two months, they did little more than monitor the build-up of Cuban forces in the region, avoiding contact with them wherever possible.

For the Cubans, the air-strike on Calueque gave them the 'victory' over the South Africans they had been seeking since late 1987, and Havana was quick to celebrate the attack as one of its greatest successes, grossly inflating its importance.[25] Behind the rhetoric, however, Havana was shocked by the heavy casualties – which threatened far greater Cuban losses over the coming weeks – and Cuban forces in south-west Angola were put on a maximum state of alert, expecting a robust South African response at any moment. Plans were drawn up for air-strikes against Ruacaná, air-bases in Namibia and (it is rumoured) a land invasion of Namibia itself.[26] But as the days passed with no further action from the South Africans, the plans were shelved and, in the meantime, the Cubans built up their forces in Angola to over 65,000 men while avoiding all contact with the South Africans. The fighting on 27 June had thus dissuaded the warring parties from seeking further military confrontations, and over the coming weeks they would dedicate their energies to negotiating a settlement, leading to the first breakthrough a little over a fortnight later.

The final phase of the 'linkage' negotiations, July–December 1988

Following the de facto cessation of hostilities after 27 June, the peace process entered its final phase, the remaining rounds of talks advancing rapidly (when compared to the previous seven years of stop–start negotiations) towards a final settlement.[27] Given the many interlinking issues being negotiated simultaneously by the three parties, Crocker broke down the negotiations into stages – each providing the building block for the next to commence – which enabled him to identify the sticking-points whilst picking off the minor issues. The final phase of the negotiations fell into four periods, each with its own significant breakthrough:

1   May–July 1988: Negotiating parties define the settlement framework, and obtain reciprocal commitments in principle.
    –   13 July: 'New York Principles' signed.
2   July–August 1988: Cross-border war ended, cessation of hostilities between the SADF, SWAPO, FAPLA and Cubans.
    –   5 August: 'Geneva Protocol' signed.
3   August–November 1988: Withdrawal timetable and associated trilateral agreement negotiated.
    –   15 November: Agreement on Cuban withdrawal timetable.

4 November–December 1988: Verification protocol, Joint Monitoring Commission set up, dates for signature and implementation agreed on.
   – 22 December: New York Peace Accords signed.

During this final phase, the negotiations advanced at a hectic pace, touching on many issues which had defied consensus for over a decade. As always, the threat of hostilities re-igniting in Angola hung over the talks, and added to their already tense atmosphere. The driving force behind the negotiations came from the Cuban delegation – controlled obsessively by Castro from his bunker in Havana – and their determination to close a deal dragged along their Angolan allies who were initially keen to maintain the new status quo in Angola.[28] The South African delegation had great difficulty selling the compromises it negotiated to the South African cabinet, and several mini-crises temporarily paralysed its decision-making process, often at critical moments (see p. 254). Nevertheless, from mid-July onwards the 'linkage' negotiations attained a momentum which proved unstoppable, finally bridging the gulf between the warring parties.

Round three in New York, 10–13 July 1988

Following the clashes at Tchipa and Calueque, Crocker pushed for a fresh round of talks before the fighting in Cunene escalated any further. After his team brokered six hours of secret talks between the Cuban and South African military representatives, it was agreed to hold a third round in New York on 10 July. The three days of talks which followed laid the groundwork for the first breakthrough of the peace process, and perhaps surprisingly – given their aggressive posture in Angola over the previous months – the Cubans were the first to offer the olive branch. Following the Cairo talks the Americans had complained to the Soviets and Angolans about the head of the Cuban delegation – Jorge Risquet – whose belligerent attitude was hindering progress and, in a surprise move, he was replaced by Carlos Aldana Escalante (PCC Secretary for Ideology). Aldana's conciliatory approach was recognised immediately by Crocker, and he suggested Aldana make a unilateral gesture towards the South Africans to defuse the tension.

Aldana duly approached the South Africans and declared that they should search jointly for a settlement which reflected 'the legitimate interests of all' and which could be seen as 'a peace without losers'. Promising that Cuba would leave rhetoric aside, he acknowledged that linkage between the Namibian and Angolan conflicts did exist, and concluded that nothing could be more honourable for Cuba than a withdrawal 'of our own free will and in the context of Resolution 435'. Aldana's speech stunned the South Africans – who could scarcely believe the Cubans were accepting 'linkage' after seven years of vociferous rejection – and it convinced them that a workable peace settlement was within their grasp. Over the next three days a basic set of negotiating principles was hammered out – the details being wrapped up at an informal session on the last day – and this resulted in the first publicly visible document of the negotiation, the New York Principles.[29]

The agreement was a triumph for Crocker, laying down the 'linkage' formula in its first three points – the implementation of Resolution 435, Namibian independence and Cuban troop withdrawal – whilst also committing both sides to end their support for UNITA and SWAPO. By publicly committing the warring parties to resolve their differences through negotiation (the document was published one week later), the New York Principles rubberstamped the American peace process as the principal means of conflict resolution in Angola, and put further pressure on the Cubans and South Africans to rein in their military forces. The devil – as always – was in the detail, and immediate moves were made to start discussions on the first steps towards winding up the conflict in Angola: the ceasefire and the South African withdrawal.

Round four in Cape Verde, 22–23 July 1988

The next round of talks – chaired by Jim Woods in Sal (Cape Verde) – was a 'tense and inconclusive exchange'[30] which was undermined by a lack of candour from both sides. Discussions on the size and location of military forces in Angola were always going to be strained (no military commander likes revealing this information). But they were made all the more tense by the unannounced arrival of General Ochoa half way through the talks, dressed in military fatigues with a pistol by his side. The Angolans doggedly insisted that the SADF still had at least 3,000 troops in Angola (the actual number was about half as many), and Geldenhuys was happy to maintain this misconception if he could use it to extract more concessions from the Angolans. In the end, no real progress was made – bar a commitment to set up a Joint Monitoring Commission (JMC) to oversee the South African and Cuban withdrawals – and the talks broke up without an agreement. Castro was nevertheless keen to press ahead, and in his Moncada speech three days later he took a conciliatory line, declaring that 'Cuba only seeks a just solution, not a humiliating, destructive defeat of South Africa', and offering to withdraw all Cuban forces from Angola under a negotiated agreement. Castro's speech was well received by the Americans, and they were hopeful that the next round of talks would provide the elusive breakthrough.

Round five of the tripartite talks in Geneva, 2–5 August 1988

Crocker knew that the Geneva talks would be crucial and, sensing that American and Soviet priorities had now converged, he met with Vasev two days before they started and encouraged his more active participation. Vasev readily accepted his increased role and, following the success of Geneva, he would be appointed an official observer, formalising Soviet involvement in the negotiating process.[31] The talks began (as usual) shakily, the South Africans catching their opponents off-guard with their own ambitious peace proposal. This included specific dates for a ceasefire (10 August), the re-deployment of Cuban and South African forces in Angola (1 September), the implementation of Resolution 435 (1 November) and the complete withdrawal of all forces from Angola (1 June 1989).[32] Intending to present its own forty-two-month proposal, the Cuban–Angolan delegation denounced the South African ploy – even rejecting 'linkage' at one point. Once tempers had cooled, however it was decided to leave discussion of the Cuban withdrawal timetable for later and concentrate instead on the solid dates offered by the South Africans for a ceasefire and SADF troop withdrawal.

Over the next three days a military protocol was thrashed out – Vasev interceding at Crocker's request to secure Cuban and Angolan compliance – and, on 5 August, the three parties signed the Geneva Protocol, initiating a de-escalation of the Angolan conflict which was to prove irreversible.[33] The Geneva Protocol defined what Crocker described as a 'procedural blueprint (a "road-map") for building the peace', and laid out an ambitious set of target dates and commitments:

- 10 August: South African withdrawal to start
- 1 September: South African withdrawal to be completed
                 Bilateral Cuban–Angolan agreement on Cuban troop
                 withdrawal to be agreed
- 10 September: Tripartite peace settlement to be signed
- 1 November: Implementation of Resolution 435

A ceasefire immediately came into effect. As South African forces withdrew to their bases, Cuban and SWAPO forces would move northwards, the Cubans promising not to carry out offensive operations unless provoked. Violations of the ceasefire would be investigated by the JMC in Ruacaná (with representative from all three parties), and points 'E' and 'G' of the New York Principles (forbidding support for UNITA and SWAPO) were reaffirmed. It was a victory for both sides, locking the warring parties into a clearly defined and speedy process of de-escalation and withdrawal, whilst simultaneously guaranteeing their basic inviolable conditions

(Resolution 435 and Cuban/South African withdrawal). This left one issue to be resolved which was to dog the peace process until its very end – the Cuban troop withdrawal timetable (see below).

The South African withdrawal from Angola, 10–29 August 1988

On 10 August 1988 – in accordance with the Geneva Protocol – Pretoria announced that it was withdrawing its forces from Angola, and that day Task Force Zulu and Combat Group 20 started moving towards the Namibian border. Six days later, the Joint Monitoring Commission (JMC) – made up of representatives from the SADF, FAR and FAPLA, with American military observers – held its first meeting in Ruacaná. On 22 August, General Meyer and General Polo signed an agreement covering the withdrawal of all remaining South African forces. For Polo there must have been a strong sense of déjà vu (he had signed a similar accord with the South Africans at the end of the 'Second Liberation War'), and the irony cannot have escaped both sides that, after thirteen years of bloody fighting, they were withdrawing from Angola with the underlying dispute more bitter and intractable than ever. Four days later there was a long-overdue prisoner exchange in Abidjan (Ivory Coast) – UNITA swapping two Cuban pilots captured in late 1987 for Sergeant-Major Papenfus (captured on 4 May) – and, more significantly, UNITA and the Cubans secretly agreed not to attack each other during the withdrawal, tying up a dangerous loophole in the Geneva Protocol. On 30 August, the JMC confirmed that South African forces had completed their withdrawal, bringing to a close twenty-five years of military involvement in Angola.

The final sticking-point: the Cuban withdrawal timetable

During the Geneva talks Aldana admitted to Crocker that Cuba was prepared to reduce its four-year timetable, but that it was restrained by its alliance with the FAPLA which would require several years to retrain and re-deploy its forces. The South Africans, on the other hand, wanted as short a withdrawal timetable as possible, reasoning that, once they pulled out of Angola, there was little to stop the Cubans reoccupying the south, and even invading Namibia itself. Their aim was to secure a withdrawal settlement which was irreversible, hence their proposal which envisioned both sides withdrawing from southern Angola in clearly-defined stages. Ultimately the argument boiled down to whether the Cuban withdrawal would be 'front-' or 'back-loaded' – i.e. whether the bulk of Cuban troops would leave Angola in the first half of the withdrawal period, or in the second – and confusion over the size of Cuban forces in Angola (anywhere between 40,000 and 65,000) made the discussion only more heated. The compromise suggested by the Americans – which involved Cuban forces withdrawing from southern Angola quickly, with the residual withdrawing from northern Angola under a longer timetable – would provide the key to unlock this final dispute. But with a forty-one month gap between both sides' proposals, it was a daunting hurdle to clear, and few imagined that it would take another three months before an agreement was reached.

Rounds six to nine, August–October 1988

The next five rounds of talks were dominated by the search for a Cuban withdrawal formula, and while South African forces completed their withdrawal as planned, the negotiations got bogged down in haggling over detail. Having arrived at what was essentially the most important issue, it was inevitable that both sides – neither of which believed it had lost the fighting – sought to extract the maximum concessions. Furthermore, there was much room for disagreement over the many complex and time-consuming details in the withdrawal schedule.[34] Both sides had adopted extreme positions over its length – Cuba proposing forty-eight months, South Africa only seven – and both were only prepared to cede a few months at a time, stringing out the negotiations interminably. As the weeks passed, and the deadlines set by the Geneva Protocol came and went, tensions increased between the delegations who feared the achievements of New York and Geneva might go the way of the 1984 Lusaka Accord. Extraneous issues – in particular a new FAPLA offensive against UNITA and the American Presidential election – started to impinge on the peace process, and it would take great determination and focus from Crocker's team to weather the storm and push the warring parties towards a final agreement.

A little over a week before round six was due to start, a two-man South African delegation met with Crocker in Lake George (New York state) and expressed its surprise at Cuban enthusiasm for withdrawing from Angola. The 'irreversibility' of the settlement still obsessed the South Africans, however, and they were unwilling to make further concessions until they had cleared up doubts over the size of the Cuban contingent (which by their calculations had grown by nearly two-thirds since 1985). On the opening day of round six in Brazzaville, therefore, Van Heerden proposed that Cuba make a 'gesture' before 1 November – i.e. a symbolic withdrawal of forces from southern Angola – to compensate for the extra 15,000 troops which had arrived over the previous year. He further suggested that the withdrawal should continue uninterrupted until all Cuban forces left Angola. The Cubans countered with the forty-two-month timetable they had prepared for Geneva, and when this failed to impress the South Africans they presented a modified thirty-six-month timetable the next day, with 15,000 Cuban troops leaving in the first year, and all Cuban forces to be north of the 13th parallel by the end of that period. Neither proposal snared the South Africans, however and, on 26 August, the talks broke up without an agreement.

Hopes that some progress could be made in round seven a fortnight later were dashed by press reports that 5,000 Cuban troops had arrived in Angola to take part in the FAPLA offensive against UNITA (a violation of the Geneva Protocol), and a great deal of time was taken up by both delegations to refute these claims. Attempts by the South Africans to edge closer to the Cuban timetable – with a twelve-month withdrawal period, and 7,000 Cubans leaving each month – failed to satisfy the Cubans and Angolans. Crocker's compromise – a two-year timetable, with 3,500 Cubans leaving each month and 75 per cent of the entire contingent in the first year – was likewise unable to break the deadlock. By round eight (26–29 September), the deadlines laid down by the Geneva Protocol were looming and, in an attempt to keep the peace process on course, Crocker persuaded the South Africans to propose his two-year timetable – although with the proviso that the bulk of the withdrawal be front-loaded. Twenty-four months was still too short for the Cubans and Angolans, however, and they once more rejected the proposal, arriving at round nine in New York one week later with what they insisted was their final offer – a thirty-month withdrawal. By this stage it was clear that a Cuban with-drawal would have to last at least two years (given the logistical difficulties in Angola), and with the gulf between the parties reduced from forty-one to only six months – and South African compliance with 'front-loading' – a deal seemed within Crocker's grasp.

Tantalisingly, however, round nine again resulted in an impasse. The main reason for its failure was the issue which Crocker had warned could derail the peace process: the Presidential election. With less than a month to go before polling day, both sides were unwilling to commit to a deal which might instantly be abandoned by an incoming Democratic adminis-tration, and they backed off until the outcome of the Bush–Dukakis contest was known. The shutdown in the negotiations could not have come at a more dangerous time as the FAPLA's offensive against UNITA was reaching its climax, and the collapse of UNITA threatened a fresh South African intervention in Angola. Indeed, so convinced was Castro of this that the day after the New York talks broke up he sent an urgent cable to Ochoa and Polo, warning them of an imminent SAAF air-strike and ordering them to blow up the Calueque and Ruacaná dams if Cuban detachments were attacked.[35] In the end, the South Africans refrained from anything more than guarded threats – unwilling to torpedo the nego-tiations when they were within a hair's breadth of success – and when George Bush (Sr.) was duly elected on 8 November, the future of the peace process was secured. Three days later, Crocker convened round ten in Geneva, determined to close a deal before the end of the Reagan administration (20 January 1989).

Round ten of the tripartite negotiations in Geneva, 11–15 November 1988

By the time round ten began, the negotiating climate had improved significantly and, with the Presidential election resolved, both sides were at last prepared to make their final concessions.[36] The fine detail of the Cuban withdrawal timetable proved mind-boggling, however – Crocker later compared it to a Rubik's Cube – and for four days the American mediators shuttled between the two delegations in Geneva's Inter-Continental Hotel, cajoling them towards an agreement. Ultimately the argument boiled down to how many Cuban troops would withdraw during the first twelve months, the South Africans demanding five times as many as the Cubans, but after much haggling a compromise was agreed on the last day.[37] The trade-off would be additional front-loading during the first seven months (to please Pretoria) in return for a pre-implementation withdrawal of only 3,000 troops, and heavy back-loading of the residual (to please Havana and Luanda). With this compromise agreed, the two delegations split the difference and agreed on a twenty-seven-month timetable, with a series of benchmarks defining Cuban redeployment northwards and withdrawal from Angola:[38]

- 4 months: All Cuban forces to be north of 15th parallel
- 7 months: All Cuban forces to be north of 13th parallel
             50 per cent of Cuban troops (25,000) to have been withdrawn
- 12 months: 66 per cent of Cuban troops (33,000) to have been withdrawn
- 18 months: 76 per cent of Cuban troops (38,000) to have been withdrawn
- 27 months: Last 12,000 Cuban troops to have been withdrawn

As Crocker later put it: 'We had cracked the toughest nut.'[39] From this moment onwards, the negotiations raced to a rapid conclusion, the remaining rounds focusing on outstanding issues and drawing up the treaties for signature. Ironically, the twenty-seven-month timetable agreed in Geneva was the exact midpoint between the original South African and Cuban proposals, and suggested that rounds six to ten had been little more than a grudge match. Following the Geneva talks, a working group met in New York on 22 November to finalise the accords, splitting them into three parts. There would be a new Protocol (reaffirming all previous agreements and setting a date for the signature of the treaties), a tripartite agreement (covering the implementation of Resolution 435 and the de-escalation of the Angolan conflict) and a bilateral accord between Cuba and Angola (covering the Cuban troop withdrawal). A further round of negotiations was needed to finalise these documents, and round eleven was duly called for 1 December in Brazzaville, the Americans pushing for a signing in New York before the year was out.

Rounds eleven and twelve in Brazzaville, 1–3 and 11–13 December 1988

With the most intractable issue blocking a settlement resolved, the Americans could be forgiven for thinking that the final round of talks would be little more than a formality. But, to everyone's surprise, the South African delegation withdrew from the talks on the third day, leaving for Pretoria to resolve a minor political crisis. For two days the fate of the 'linkage' negotiations hung in the balance as the South African delegations struggled to persuade P.W. Botha to accept the concessions they had made. But, on 5 December, Van Heerden phoned Crocker to inform him that they were ready to sign and, on 11 December, the South Africans returned to Brazzaville for the last round of talks. On 13 December, all three parties signed the Brazzaville Protocol, which set the dates for the New York signing (22 December) and the implementation of Resolution 435 (1 April 1989), confirmed the deadline for the UN-sponsored verification agreement, and created the JMC to oversee the process.[40] The Cubans and Angolans had still not drafted their bilateral treaty covering the withdrawal, however, and despite a visit by Dos Santos to Havana in mid-December, they failed to produce one by the time they arrived in New York for the signing. This gave the Americans little choice but to engage in a 'mini-round thirteen' in the lobby of the UN's Plaza Hotel, drafting the details of the bilateral accord on top of the piano.

The signing of the New York Accords, 22 December 1988

The signing ceremony held in the chamber of the UN's Economic and Social Council was a bizarre spectacle – all three parties using the occasion to vilify each other in public – and demonstrated what a remarkable achievement it had been for Crocker to bring together such bitterly-divided foes.[41] Large delegations attended for Cuba, Angola and South Africa, the fifty-five-man Cuban delegation including nine generals, all veterans of Angola.[42] US Secretary of State George Shultz opened the proceedings with a speech that avoided reference to any controversial issues (in particular the sorry state of Cuban–American relations). He was followed by Afonso Van Dúnem (for Angola) who praised the Cuban internationalists for their contribution to Angola's freedom. When the

Cuban Foreign Minister got up to speak, however, he denounced Reagan's recent speech to the General Assembly, smarting at his calls for an end to 'Cuban military imperialism' in Africa. Pik Botha replied with an equally provocative speech, declaring (rather undiplomatically) that many African leaders had asked South Africa to keep its troops in Namibia until Cuba withdrew from Angola, and challenging Cuba to a debate on human rights. Keen to prevent a shouting match Shultz ushered the speeches on and, at 10:15, the Tripartite Accords were signed, the Cubans and Angolans initialing their Bilateral Agreement less than an hour later.[43]

Under the terms of the accords, the implementation of Resolution 435 and the Cuban withdrawal would take place under the following timetable:

- Prior to 1 April 1989: 3,000 Cuban troops withdrawn
- 1 April 1989: Implementation of Resolution 435
  Start of twenty-seven-month withdrawal time-table
- 1 August 1989: All Cuban troops to be north of 15th parallel
- 31 October 1989: All Cuban troops to be north of 13th parallel
- 1 November 1989: 50 per cent of Cuban contingent withdrawn
  Namibia to hold free elections
- 1 April 1990: 66 per cent of Cuban contingent withdrawn
- 1 October 1990: 76 per cent of Cuban contingent withdrawn
- 1 July 1991: Cuban withdrawal completed

Ironically, the final agreement bore a striking resemblance to the two-year proposal the Americans had made to the Angolans back in April 1983, and underlined how wasteful in lives, time and effort the previous five years of bitter fighting had been. Although the New York Accords side-stepped the underlying dispute which led South Africa and Cuba to inter-vene in Angola in the first place (the war between the MPLA and UNITA), they nevertheless created the conditions for a ceasefire. Indeed, less than a month before Cuba completed its withdrawal, both sides would sign a peace accord, promising to bring an end to more than thirty years of continuous conflict (see Chapter 12). For all involved, the 'linkage' settle-ment was a victory – offering each side a tangible gain in return for with-drawing from the conflict – and enabled the Cubans to initiate the pull-out that had eluded them for nearly a dozen years. But the Angolan drama had not quite played itself out and, within months of the signing, a fresh crisis would break, involving one of the most respected veterans of Angola – General Ochoa – bringing the Cuban intervention to its controversial conclusion.

12

THE STING IN THE TAIL

The Ochoa scandal, the death of
internationalism and the start of the
'Special Period', 1989–91

The Cuban withdrawal from Angola took place against a backdrop of profound global change, with the collapse of the Soviet bloc, the end of the Cold War and – for Cuba – a return to the isolation of the early 1960s. With its allies disappearing in Eastern Europe, Africa and the Caribbean, Cuba attempted to complete its withdrawal from Angola, only too aware that the imminent cessation of Soviet aid could trigger an economic meltdown. Almost inevitably the regime focused on internal dissent and, in the wake of the controversial trial of General Ochoa, a purge of MININT was launched, its apparatus being taken over by a new generation of officers who had earned their military reputations in Angola. Within months, internationalism – and the half million Cubans who had served in its cause – had disappeared from the political agenda, to be replaced by a relentless campaign of propaganda and popular mobilisation in the face of the Revolution's most serious challenge to date – the 'Special Period'. By the end of the withdrawal, Cuba would be in a desperate position, with pundits predicting Castro's downfall. But, not for the first time, they had underestimated Castro's remarkable staying-power and, through a combination of political skill, luck and naked opportunism, he would weather the storm, emerging in the late 1990s with a stronger grip than ever on the reins of power.

Start of the Cuban withdrawal from Angola,
January 1989

On 10 January 1989 – less than a month after the signing of the New York Accords – the first 450 Cuban troops landed at Havana's José Martí airport, initiating the withdrawal from Angola. Over the next twenty-nine months, Cuban forces pulled back from bases in the interior to Luanda and Lobito for shipment to Cuba, leaving the bulk of their heavy equip-

ment (armoured cars, tanks and BM-21s) with the FAPLA for its continuing war against UNITA. The long withdrawal period was necessary for
several reasons. First, it allowed an orderly hand-over of bases and
weaponry to the FAPLA; second, it enabled Cuban engineers to clear the
minefields they had laid over the previous fourteen years; and, third, it
gave MK and SWAPO time to move their bases to Uganda. In response to
a widely-held grievance, the withdrawal mission was also charged with
returning to Cuba the bodies of all internationalists killed in Angola, an
enormous task given the country's size and the dispersal of Cuban units
across it. In early 1989, a commission was set up under Divisional-General
Sixto Batista Santana to oversee this operation and, in March, a team of
forensic experts arrived in Angola to begin the process of locating, exhum-
ing and embalming the bodies for return to Cuba while pantheons were
prepared in each of Cuba's municipalities.

In recognition of the Angolan mission's changing priorities, General
Ochoa was recalled to Cuba and replaced by his subordinate Polo, a man
in whose abilities Castro had greater faith. From an operational point of
view, Ochoa's recall was logical as he had completed his mission to halt
the South African counter-offensive, but it was also a sign that he had
fallen from favour. Thus, while Ochoa received no further accolades for
his eighth internationalist mission, four of his colleagues – Generals Polo,
Rosales, Espinosa and Moracén – were made 'Heroes of the Cuban
Republic', the FAR's highest honour.[1] On his return to Cuba, Ochoa was
due to take up command of the Western Army (one of the most senior
positions in the FAR) but, as suspicions grew about his conduct in Angola,
his appointment began to look doubtful (see pp. 260–3). The first stage of
the withdrawal nevertheless continued without Ochoa, and was completed
ahead of schedule in preparation for the implementation of Resolution
435 on 1 April. What Havana did not realise, however, was that SWAPO
was planning one final infiltration into Namibia, sparking a crisis which
threatened to destroy the peace accords.

The SWAPO incursion into Namibia, April 1989

Following the signing of the Geneva Protocol, the South Africans had
carried out a staged withdrawal from Angola and Namibia in preparation
for its independence in late 1989.[2] Even before the New York Accords
were signed, however, Geldenhuys complained that SWAPO was not
withdrawing northwards and, by late March 1989, the SADF representatives on the JMC were warning that SWAPO was reinforcing southern
Angola. Finally, on 30 March – only two days before Resolution 435 was
due to start implementation – the SADF reported that SWAPO guerrillas
were within 600 yards of the border (they should have been ninety miles to
the north). Two days later a force of 1,500–1,800 guerrillas crossed into

Namibia, SWAPO's largest incursion in its twenty-three-year insurgency. This unexpected move was probably a ploy to boost SWAPO's presence in Namibia in the run-up to the November elections. But it backfired disastrously, provoking outrage not only from South Africa and the USA, but also from its allies in Havana and Luanda who feared that this reckless move could precipitate a fresh South African intervention.

An emergency summit was called at Mount Ejo (near Windhoek) which was chaired by Crocker who, only days before, had been drafting his resignation. Castro – who like Dos Santos was reportedly furious at the incursion – sent his most trusted negotiator, Carlos Aldana, to ensure the settlement was saved, while the Soviets dispatched Adamishin to Luanda to berate Dos Santos for his failure to restrain SWAPO. The two days of talks which followed on 8/9 April proved the value of the JMC in resolving violations of the agreements, and produced the 'Mount Ejo Declaration'. This provided for the safe passage of all SWAPO guerrillas in Namibia to designated UNTAG points, from where they would be escorted to bases north of the 16th parallel in accordance with the Geneva Protocol. The revelation that SWAPO had violated its commitments did irreparable damage to its reputation, and forced the UN into the embarrassing decision of authorising the SADF to hunt down and destroy rogue SWAPO units, leading to the deaths of more than 250 guerrillas.[3] By May SWAPO had withdrawn into Angola and, with the return of the SADF to its bases, Namibia's independence process was able to restart on 19 May.

The fifty-day crisis had come close to sinking the New York Accords, but its successful resolution demonstrated how far the negotiating parties had come in the year since Cuba joined the peace process. Where, on previous occasions, a serious violation of a peace accord would have led to a resumption of hostilities, by April 1989 all the signatory parties were determined to see the New York Accords work, and, thanks to the JMC, the Namibian peace process was quickly put back on track. Serious damage had been done to SWAPO, however, which not only lost 250 cadres but also tarnished its reputation. While the JMC and UNTAG proved effective at overseeing Namibia's independence, they were nevertheless powerless to control the civil war in Angola which continued to rage for most of 1989 and 1990. With the FAPLA determined to crush UNITA now that it had lost its South African allies, the fighting in southern Angola escalated once more, hindering the Cuban withdrawal and, on more than one occasion, bringing it to a halt following UNITA attacks on Cuban personnel (see p. 269).

Gorbachev's visit to Cuba, 2–5 April 1989

The timing of SWAPO's bungled incursion into Namibia could not have been worse for Castro, as the next day he was due to host Gorbachev on his first visit to Cuba for crucial discussions on the future of the Cuban–Soviet alliance. Since their first meeting at the CPSU Party Congress in February 1986 (see Chapter 8), Castro's dispute with Gorbachev over his radical reform programme had deteriorated steadily. Though a keen advocate of economic restructuring loosely based on *perestroika*, Castro had blocked all attempts to introduce *glasnost* into Cuba, fearing the political consequences. By the time Gorbachev arrived in Cuba on 2 April 1989, the two men had become bitter opponents, and this put Castro in a weak position to negotiate future Soviet aid upon which Cuba depended.[4] Determined to scale down Soviet military adventurism which, over the previous decade, had cost billions of dollars, Gorbachev had started withdrawing Soviet forces from Afghanistan in February 1989, and he was keen to rein in Cuba which was Moscow's most expensive oversees satellite. During his visit, Gorbachev reaffirmed his opposition to the export of revolution – i.e. internationalism in the Guevarist mould – and, in private talks with Castro, he refused a request for upgraded MiG-29s,[5] hinting that trade talks scheduled for a fortnight later would involve a significant cut in Soviet aid.

The brewing clash in the Soviet Union between reformists and conservatives

The reforms Gorbachev was planning for the Soviet empire went beyond cuts in aid, however, and envisioned the removal of the conservative leadership of the socialist bloc and their replacement with like-minded reformers. Since the tempestuous Party Congress in February 1986, Gorbachev had emerged as the figurehead of the reformist wing of the CPSU, drawing much of his support from the KGB which was in favour of an overhaul of the Communist system.[6] Opposing them were the party's conservative wing and the Soviet military, both of which stood to lose influence if Gorbachev's reforms continued unabated. Castro naturally looked to them for support, having built up a close relationship with the Soviet military during the thirteen-year operation in Angola. The struggle between the reformists and the conservatives fed through into the Cuban political system, and it is no coincidence that, a little over a week before Gorbachev arrived in Havana, the Chief of MININT José Abrantes gave a speech supporting *glasnost* and Gorbachev's reforms.[7] Abrantes' speech – like Del Pino's defection two years previously – pointed to ideological divisions within the government, and the timing could not have been more critical as, earlier that month, Gorbachev had secretly given his backing to Hungarian plans to hold free elections, an event which was to precipitate the collapse of the Iron Curtain.

Radical changes would soon be sweeping through the socialist bloc, and it was clear from Gorbachev's visit to Cuba that the survival of Castro's regime did not feature in Soviet plans. Fears that the Soviets would pull the economic carpet were confirmed a fortnight later when Leonid Abalkin, Chairman of the Commission on Economic Reform, arrived in Cuba for a week of discussions. Although the trade agreement he agreed was better than might have been expected, it was nevertheless the start of a collapse in Soviet aid which would plunge Cuba into an economic crisis from which it has still not fully recovered. For Castro, the prospect of an end to the annual $4–5 billion Soviet aid package was disastrous, and he turned to his allies in the Soviet military for help, forming an alliance of interests which would prove crucial to his future survival. In the meantime Gorbachev's visit to Cuba fuelled Castro's suspicions of MININT, whose close association with the KGB and reformists (like Abrantes) threatened to create a competing power structure which might prove more attractive to Gorbachev than the current Cuban leadership.[8] In this atmosphere of intense mistrust of MININT, on 25 April (only five days after Abalkin's departure), Abrantes received a dossier revealing that drug-trafficking was taking place in Cuban waters, providing Castro with the pretext for the largest purge of Cuba's internal security apparatus in the Revolution's history.

The Ochoa scandal

It is unlikely that the truth behind the trial and execution of General Arnaldo Ochoa Sánchez and Tony de la Guardia will ever be known. On the one hand, the details of the case are tangled up in government cover-up and propaganda, and on the other in unrestrained rumour and hearsay.[9] In the lead-up to the trial, the Cuban government launched a fierce propaganda campaign to discredit the accused, but in its haste to condemn them before any evidence had even been heard, it prompted accusations that the exercise was a smokescreen for an internal coup. The subsequent purge of MININT – which was taken over by the FAR within days of the trial – seemed to confirm this view, as did rumours of hidden weapons caches which were to be used in a coup against Castro himself. The timing of the Ochoa trial – only weeks before a wave of revolutions swept across Eastern Europe – gave further credence to this theory and, given the KGB's orchestration of several revolutions (most notoriously in Czechoslovakia), this raises the suspicion that Cuba might have been one of their intended targets. The most controversial question raised by the Ochoa scandal – whether Castro knew about drug-trafficking operations prior to 1989 – has still not been satisfactorily answered, however, and will be discussed later in this chapter.

Background to MININT's smuggling operations

By the time the Ochoa scandal blew up in June 1989, MININT had become a separate elite in Cuba, running dozens of clandestine operations across the world, and providing Cuba with an economic lifeline through its smuggling operations in Panama. Founded in June 1961 (after the Bay of Pigs invasion), MININT was initially responsible for domestic law enforcement and crushing internal dissent. But, under the guise of Guevara's internationalism, it expanded its operations overseas, developing the covert Special Forces which spearheaded Operation Carlota. Following Reagan's election in November 1980, and the tightening of the embargo against Cuba, MININT's importance increased with the expansion of MC (Moneda Convertible, or Hard Currency), a secret department in MININT authorised to carry out smuggling to break the blockade.[10] A front company – CIMEX (Compañía de Importación y Exportación) – was set up in Panama to handle the export of Cuban cigars, sugar and rum in return for desperately needed hard currency, consumer goods and cutting-edge technology. Thanks to Castro's warm relations with Manuel Noriega, CIMEX soon became Cuba's main trading entrepôt in the Americas. The clandestine nature of MININT's operations – and the international business contacts its officers formed – created an elite of officers whose standard of living was the envy of every Cuban, and the cause of resentment in the FAR's highest ranks.

With authorisation to carry out smuggling in Cuban waters, it was inevitable that MININT would become involved in drug-trafficking – given Cuba's location between the main source of cocaine (Colombia) and its principal market (the USA).[11] Cuban fishermen had been smuggling marijuana and cocaine to the USA for well over a century, but it was not until the early 1980s that the Cuban government entered into dealings with the Medellín drug cartel, allegedly authorising Cuban air space for cocaine smuggling in return for flying weapons to M-19 guerrillas in Colombia.[12] In 1982 – during the Guillot Lara case – a Miami court heard how four Cuban officers smuggled 80 pounds of cocaine, 2.5 million pounds of marijuana and 25 million methaqualone tablets into the USA, but MININT nevertheless continued to expand its links with the Colombian cartels, relying on Noriega as its middle man. Indeed, so close did the Cuban–Panamanian connection become that Castro is alleged to have mediated in a dispute between Noriega and Pablo Escobar in 1984, following the destruction of a cocaine laboratory by the DEA (Drug Enforcement Administration).[13] Thus, by the time Tony de la Guardia was appointed head of CIMEX in 1986, there was already a culture of drug-trafficking within MC, even if most of its operations were concentrated on obtaining hard currency, consumer goods and technology.

Tony de la Guardia was a veteran of the Revolution and had been one of the first advisors to be sent to Nicaragua in 1978, assisting in the capture of Managua the following year. His involvement in money-laundering operations for the Argentine Montoneros in 1975 made him the ideal candidate to run CIMEX. Following his appointment in June 1986, he made a deal with a Cuban exile living in Panama – Reinaldo Ruiz – to ship five stolen IBM computers and two television de-scrambling boxes to Cuba. Ruiz was keen to do further deals and, through his cousin Miguel Ruiz (who worked as a visa official at the Cuban Embassy), he contacted Tony de la Guardia and proposed a drug-trafficking operation through Cuba. Tony de la Guardia readily agreed, as the operation would net MC vast amounts of hard currency, but it is unclear if he got authorisation from José Abrantes who was later accused of failing to keep tabs on his subordinate. The first smuggling operation, on 10 April 1987 – flying 300 kg of cocaine from Panama to Varadero (a resort 75 miles east of Havana) for transfer to launches for the crossing to Florida – was a failure, however. The US Coast Guard easily intercepted the launches whose crew threw a third of the cocaine overboard before they were apprehended. Ruiz was determined to try again but, in February 1988, he was arrested and extradited to the USA on drug-smuggling charges. With his Panama connection cut off, Tony de la Guardia made contact with Escobar's Medellín cartel, and this brought him into partnership with a Cuban general who had been carrying out black market deals for several years, General Ochoa.

Background to Ochoa's illicit deals

Ochoa first became involved in the international black market shortly after being appointed Vice-Minister of Overseas Missions in March 1986. Ochoa dispatched his aide, Captain Jorge Martínez, to Panama to make business contacts and, by the end of the year, he had established a friendship with Favel Pareja, a Colombian who worked for Escobar and who proposed drug-trafficking and money laundering operations in Cuba. Ochoa vetoed the idea, however, and instead closed an arms deal with the Sandinistas which allegedly netted over $150,000 and, following his posting to Angola in November 1987, his contacts with Pareja tailed off. With Cuban involvement in the Angolan *candonga* now firmly established, Ochoa was soon trading ivory, diamonds and rare woods, using the proceeds to buy building materials for the airbases at Cahama and Xangongo. During his time in Angola, Ochoa allegedly made a further $50,000 from the purchase of radios for the FAPLA and, in April 1988, he sent Martínez to Cuba with orders to contact Tony de la Guardia whose drug-smuggling operation had come to his attention via Tony's twin brother, Patricio (also a senior figure in MININT).

The Escobar connection

The meeting Martínez and Padrón held in Havana with four representatives of Escobar's drug cartel in April 1988 proved the most scandalous aspect of the Ochoa–De la Guardia case, and directly linked Cuba to a notorious international criminal.[14] The Colombians proposed setting up a processing plant and a dollar counterfeiting operation in Cuba, but Padrón rejected the idea, agreeing to ask Ochoa about setting one up in Angola (although he never did as he knew Ochoa would refuse). At a second meeting, the Colombians instead suggested using Cuba as a drug conduit, to which Ochoa agreed on the condition that the drugs never touched Cuban soil. In May, Martínez was dispatched to Escobar's Colombian hideout to close the deal. Escobar's interest in the Cubans went beyond drug-trafficking, however, and he asked Martínez if Cuba would provide him with ten SAMs to protect his ranch from air-attack, and to arrange for an aircraft to be permanently on standby for him in Cuba which could be sent to extract him at short notice. Ochoa even claimed that Escobar offered to invest millions in Cuban tourism in exchange for using Cuba as a drug conduit. But none of these deals materialised as both Ochoa and Tony de la Guardia were arrested before the drop-off points in Cuba were agreed. By the time Ochoa returned to Cuba in January 1989, he had amassed nearly $200,000 from illicit deals in Angola and Panama, all of which he later claimed was to be used to purchase new equipment for the Western Army. Thus when, on 25 April, Abrantes received a report on drug-smuggling, both Ochoa and the De la Guardias were caught off-guard, and Tony scrambled to cover up all trace of his operations.

The investigation into drug-smuggling

Following the report to Abrantes, a joint MININT–MINFAR investigation was set up, and two days later Furry and Abrantes chaired its first meeting, Tony de la Guardia listening to the report in silence. Within a fortnight the investigation had uncovered traces of drug-trafficking and, with suspicion gathering around Tony de la Guardia, Raúl Castro ordered a wire-tap of a dinner he was attending at the house of his father-in-law, Diocles Torralba (Cuban Transport Minister), along with his brother and Ochoa. Hidden microphones did not reveal anything about drug-trafficking, however, but instead a feeling of scepticism about the Cuban Revolution. Tony de la Guardia muttered that Del Pino had made the wisest move defecting, while Ochoa complained bitterly about the treatment of Cuban veterans returning from Angola. Furious at the content of the transcripts, Raúl Castro called Ochoa in for questioning three times over the next two weeks, each stormy meeting ending in bitter recriminations.[15]

Eventually, on the night of 9 July, Fidel Castro agreed that Ochoa and Tony de la Guardia should both be arrested, but in a peculiar move Ochoa was released for the weekend, and he immediately went to see Tony at his house on the coast.

The weekend before Ochoa's arrest

While Ochoa and the De la Guardia brothers conferred on the coast, back in Havana Castro was hosting the Panamanian president – Manuel Solís Palma – on his first visit to Cuba since Noriega had voided disputed elections in May 1989. Following Noriega's indictment in February 1988, the DEA had started to close in on his drug-trafficking operations and, in an effort to divert their attention, Noriega had handed over Reinaldo Ruiz (whose drug ring was separate from Noriega's). Ruiz's information on MININT – much of which came out later in his trial – enabled the DEA to get close to MC's operations and, by June 1989, they were planning to kidnap Abrantes and whisk him off for trial in the USA on drug-trafficking charges. Solís Palma's visit to Havana thus masked a hidden purpose, and it is likely he brought a message from Noriega warning Castro that the DEA was about to go public with Ruiz's information – and that he should act fast to minimise the damage. More controversially, it is rumoured that, on the same weekend, a group of MININT officers were arrested at a secret meeting at Padrón's house in Víbora Parque (northern Havana), Cuban Special Forces seizing large amounts of weaponry (including crates of RPGs) during the raid.[16] Coupled with the discovery of containers full of weaponry in the Ejército Rebelde dam several months later, this raises the possibility that MININT was plotting a coup against Castro, conceivably with the support of the KGB. Clearly the time had come for Castro to act and, on their return to Havana, Ochoa and the De la Guardias were arrested.

The trial of Ochoa, the De la Guardias and their accomplices

Following the arrest of Ochoa and the De la Guardia brothers, the Cuban government launched a heavily-biased 'trial by press' which made a mockery of the pseudo-legal proceedings which followed. Fourteen Cubans were charged with corruption and drug-trafficking, including Martínez, Padrón and even Tony de la Guardia's father-in-law, Diocles Torralba (who was tried separately). Raúl Castro opened the campaign to discredit them with a rambling speech on 14 June, which aside from revealing his anger at Ochoa's support for *glasnost*, also identified his most serious crime: calling Fidel's integrity into question. A chorus of disapproval followed from the FAR, most notably from the missions in Angola and Ethiopia (with which Ochoa was so closely associated) whose troops sent messages condemning Ochoa and demanding the full weight of the law be applied. Several articles in *Granma* outlined the government's case against the accused and, on 26 June, a Court of Honour – presided over by forty-four officers, at least half of them veterans of Angola – dishonourably discharged Ochoa and stripped of his 'Hero of the Republic' title. Three days later Abrantes was replaced as Chief of MININT by Castro's trusty subordinate Furry, a move which pre-empted the more complete purge he was planning.

On 30 June, a Special Military Court began the five-day trial of Ochoa and thirteen others, the majority of them from MININT.[17] Although nine lawyers were assigned to defend the accused, the proceedings had more in common with the scripted 'show trials' of Stalinist Russia than the Iran–Contra hearings on which they were modelled. There were widespread rumours that Ochoa and Tony de la Guardia were subjected to coercion behind the scenes,[18] both men delivering lengthy self-accusations which absolved their superiors of any knowledge of their dealings and called for the full weight of justice to be applied. But perhaps the most scandalous aspect of the trial was the so-called defence, which was in effect a second prosecution. The nine defence lawyers had accepted their roles under duress (they pointed this out to the court at every opportunity) and their unwillingness to upset the regime meant that at no stage during four days of questioning did they raise a single objection or even cross-examine their clients. Indeed, the entire defence consisted of half-an-hour of presentations on the last day, during which they admitted their clients' guilt but requested leniency in view of their previous good conduct.[19]

The verdict of the trial was never in any doubt, and during his closing remarks the Chief Prosecutor returned to a theme previously raised by Raúl Castro, accusing Ochoa of stabbing the fatherland in the back by assaulting Fidel's credibility. Although the prosecution had failed to prove that any of the accused had actually carried out drug-smuggling operations, the assault on Castro's integrity was sufficient for the Military Court to hand down death sentences on Ochoa, Tony de la Guardia and their two aides, and prison sentences from fifteen to thirty years for the other accused.[20] The verdicts still had to be confirmed by the Council of State, however, and determined to have the last word, Castro embarked on a four-hour diatribe aimed at destroying Ochoa's military reputation. Laboriously wading through dozens of military cables which revealed Ochoa's alleged incompetence, Castro heaped the blame for the setbacks of early 1988 on Ochoa, even reintroducing the attack on 14 February which his government had seen fit to cover up only a few months before.

Castro's knowledge of drug-smuggling and black-market operations

What Castro failed to address, however, were perhaps the most important questions raised by the Ochoa–De la Guardia scandal – namely how much Castro himself knew about drug-trafficking operations in Cuba and black-market dealings in Angola. The most controversial evidence emerged three years after the Ochoa trial. According to Patricio de la Guardia's wife, Abrantes confessed to her husband that Castro was aware that drug-smuggling operations were occurring in Cuban waters and, in 1988, had authorised the sale of ten tonnes of cocaine seized by the Cuban Coast Guard. Allegedly, Castro authorised Tony de la Guardia's first operation in 1987 as 'an exceptional, top-secret operation' and had warned Abrantes against carrying out further operations, hence his fury when he discovered the extent of MC's drug-trafficking in early 1989.[21] While such accusations lack substantiation, it is hard to imagine how Castro could have been unaware of drug-trafficking in Cuban waters when, throughout his tenure as Supreme Cuban leader, he has maintained an obsessive control of every aspect of Cuban life. Having established contact with M-19 in the late 1960s (ironically through Ochoa), the likelihood that Havana developed some form of cooperation with the Colombian drug cartels (whose links to the guerrillas are well documented) seems high, and this could not have occurred without authorisation from the highest levels of the Cuban political leadership.

By the same token, Castro's claims to have been unaware of Ochoa's black-market deals on the *candonga* strain credibility, particularly after the claims made by so many officers (and Castro himself) of his prodigious knowledge of every aspect of the Cuban operation in Angola.[22] With just about every Cuban officer (and many soldiers) regularly visiting the *candonga*, it is inconceivable that Castro was unaware of black-market activity in Angola, unless his knowledge of what was happening there was far weaker than he has consistently boasted. The decision to single out Ochoa for punishment when other contemporaries escaped even minor reprimand – most notably Polo who, as Chief of the ATS, had personally overseen the construction of the Cahama and Xangongo airbases – raises the suspicion that Ochoa was used as a scapegoat for the officer class, enabling them to side-step accusations of corruption when they returned to Cuba. In the final analysis, Ochoa's real crime was to call Castro's integrity into question – a treasonous offence in a regime which drew its legitimacy and ideological direction from that one man – although Ochoa's independent style and support for Gorbachev's reforms may have played a part in the decision to make an example of him. Insisting that public opinion forced him apply the maximum sentence, on 9 July Castro confirmed the death sentences, and four days later Ochoa, Tony de la Guardia, Martínez and Padrón were executed by firing squad.

The purge of MININT, July–August 1989

The executions on 13 July signalled the start of a purge of MININT and, the same day, seven senior MININT officers resigned their posts and were replaced by officers from the FAR, the majority of them veterans of Angola. These resignations were followed one week later by the trial of Diocles Torralba, who received a twenty-year sentence for corruption. Ten days later, Abrantes was arrested along with four other MININT officers and charged with negligence and tolerance of corrupt behaviour. The sentencing of Abrantes to twenty years in prison marked the completion of the purge,[23] and by the time Castro presided over the first meeting to reorganise MININT on 24 September, it had effectively been taken over by MINFAR. Whether MININT had been plotting to overthrow Castro and install a reformist regime in Cuba is open to question, but there is no doubt that the purge did not come a moment too soon. For, within weeks, the Soviet Empire started to crumble with the dismantling of the Iron Curtain and the removal of Eric Honecker as president of the GDR. As Cuban troops completed their withdrawal north of the 13th parallel and Namibia voted in its first free elections, the world's attention focused on Berlin where, on 9 November, the wall was torn down, triggering the collapse of the Soviet bloc.[24]

The end of the internationalist dream

With Cuba's alliances crumbling around it, plans were advanced for the return of the remains of Cuban internationalists. On 27 November (ironically the same day that the Communist government fell in Czechoslovakia), the first bodies arrived in Havana in preparation for a national ceremony on 7 December.[25] Since March, teams of forensic experts had been carrying out the difficult task of locating and recovering all the bodies of Cuban internationalists killed in Angola, a task made trickier by the fact that, until 1983, all Cubans killed in combat were buried near where they died. Great efforts were made to locate the remains of Cubans missing in action – some of whom were buried in mass graves with the FAPLA – and witnesses to the original burials were occasionally called back to help identify the sites.[26] In late November, the bodies were flown back in three Il-76 aircraft to Havana's San Antonio air base where they were laid out in four silos and divided into provinces and municipalities. Since April, pantheons had been ready in each of Cuba's provinces and, throughout December, the bodies were interred in dozens of ceremonies across the country.[27] On 6 December, the Cuban government declared two days of national mourning, and the following day sixteen internationalists (each one representing a province of Cuba) were buried in the Cacahual military monument in a ceremony attended by Castro and Dos Santos.

According to official figures published in *Granma* on 6 December 1989, 2,016 Cubans died on internationalist missions in Angola – 39 per cent in combat, 26 per cent of disease and 35 per cent in accidents. In addition, a further sixty-one Cubans died during the eighteen months of the withdrawal. This remarkably low figure for a sixteen-year operation contrasts starkly with claims from Castro's opponents that Cuba suffered up to 10,000 casualties during the Angolan intervention, including those wounded and MIA.[28] Attempts to estimate an accurate figure are hindered by Cuba's hesitancy in revealing casualties – arguing such information is advantageous to the enemy – and by its tendency to present the statistics in the most favourable light. Thus *Granma*'s figure of 2,016 fails to include those wounded, incapacitated by disease (in particular malaria and tropical fever) or any of the hundreds of MIAs, a figure which in a comparable military operation would be at least double the number of those killed.[29] A low Cuban casualty figure can in part be explained by Havana's policy of keeping its troops out of the front-line, hence the low percentage of combat deaths (versus accident and disease) and the accounts of Cuban veterans which consistently note the low number of fatalities suffered by their units. Nevertheless, the most recent figures – obtained from an ex-functionary of the FAR's Departamento de Abastecimiento – suggest that a total of 3,800 Cubans died in Angola, with around 10,000 wounded, incapacitated or MIA.[30]

The ceremonies across Cuba in early December were an overt gesture of recognition to the hundreds of thousands of Cubans who had taken part in the great internationalist experiment of the 1970s and 1980s, and redressed the grievances felt by relatives and widows of those who died overseas. Once the ceremonies were over, however, there was little disguising the fact that Havana was closing the book on its Angolan adventure and burying the ideology of internationalism along with the bodies of those who had died in its cause. From 1990 onwards, Cubans serving overseas would be '*colaboradores*' (aid workers) – earning hard currency for the Cuban regime – and, following the loss of Soviet aid, the widespread humanitarian missions of the 1980s would be scaled back dramatically. The precariousness of the Cuban regime was demonstrated less than a fortnight after the Cacahual ceremony when 24,000 American troops invaded Panama, capturing Noriega and flying him to the USA to stand trial on drug-trafficking charges. The overthrow of Noriega was a disaster for Havana, not only removing one of its last allies in the hemisphere, but more importantly cutting off Cuba's primary source of hard currency and foreign goods. With Cuba's isolation growing more acute by the day, in January 1990 Castro announced the start of the 'Special Period in a Time of Peace', inaugurating the most difficult period in the Revolution's history.

The final phase of the Cuban withdrawal,
January 1990–June 1991

Against this background of intensifying crisis in Havana and continuing fighting in Angola, the last phase of the Cuban withdrawal was completed, although it suffered a hiccough on 25 January 1990 when – in response to the deaths of four Cuban soldiers in a UNITA attack – Cuba suspended it. Since the signing of the New York Accords, the war between the FAPLA and UNITA had limped on in south-eastern Angola, and various peace initiatives launched by the MPLA and the Front-Line States (most notably the Gbadolite Agreement signed in Zaire on 22 June 1989) had failed to bring peace to Angola. In great part this was due to the intransigence of Savimbi, whose unwillingness to commit himself to a peace accord was frustrating his American backers and, in December 1989, the FAPLA launched an offensive with 5,000 troops against Mavinga nicknamed 'O Último Assalto' (The Final Assault).[31] Convinced that Cuban personnel were assisting the FAPLA – in direct contravention of the New York Accords – UNITA launched a retaliatory attack against Cuban troops, prompting an outraged response from Havana, which insisted its forces were not involved in any way. International pressure was brought to bear on UNITA and, after Havana received assurances that Cuban forces would not be attacked again, the withdrawal resumed on 20 February. Like its predecessors, the FAPLA offensive's success was short-lived and, after occupying Mavinga on 4 February 1990, the FAPLA was forced to withdraw due to strained supply lines and UNITA's encirclement of the town, its last forces reaching Cuito Cuanavale by 14 May.

While the fighting continued in south-east Angola, Cuba's crisis deepened with the surprise defeat of the Sandinistas in Nicaraguan elections on 25 February 1990. The loss of Havana's last remaining ally in the hemisphere was a demoralising blow and, within a month, Cuba's 160 advisers and their families had returned to Cuba, ending nearly three decades of Cuban involvement in Nicaragua.[32] Further cuts in Soviet aid in June increased the pressure on Cuba, although Castro's relationship with the Soviet military remained close as, only two months later, the first MiG-29s appeared in Cuba, a request previously vetoed by Gorbachev.[33] With Desert Storm raging in the Persian Gulf, the Cuban withdrawal entered its final phase (as on every previous occasion, ahead of schedule), and on 1 May Havana had a good turn of fortune with the signing of the Bicesse Peace Accord between the MPLA and UNITA, exactly one month before the withdrawal was due to be completed. Finally, on 25 May, the last Cuban, General Samuel Rodiles Planas, boarded an aircraft in Luanda waving the Cuban flag, and with the arrival of the last Cuban ship in Havana on 14 June 1991, Cuba's fifteen-and-a-half-year intervention in Angola came to an end.

269

Cuban presence in Angola after the withdrawal

Despite officially completing its withdrawal in 1991, Cuba secretly maintains military forces in Angola, although in such small numbers they have attracted little attention. Continuing a policy (introduced in the mid-1960s) of protecting Cuba's African allies from internal overthrow, Dos Santos' Presidential Guard is still made up of Cuban officers, the majority of whom are registered on the staff of the Futungo de Belas palace as gardeners and maintenance men.[34] It is also possible that Cuban military advisors assist the FAA garrisons protecting Cabinda's oil-fields, given previous Cuban experience and the enclave's crucial importance to the economic survival of the Luanda regime.[35] The MPLA has suppressed any suggestion that Cuban military personnel are still present in Angola, however, and in January 1999 it expelled two Portuguese journalists after they published an article claiming that hundreds of Cuban troops had recently arrived in Angola to fight alongside the FAA.[36] In addition to an unofficial military presence and a few dozen medical '*colaboradores*', there are around 150 Cuban–Angolan families in Angola, nearly all of them Cuban men married to Angolan women.[37] The circumstances under which these Cubans remained in Angola are exceptional (suggesting it was unusual),[38] just as conversely it was rare for Cubans to bring Angolan wives or children back to Cuba (see Chapter 7).

Cuba after the withdrawal from Angola

Within months of the return of the last internationalists from Angola, the Cuban regime suffered a blow which many predicted would finally topple it, when in August 1991 conservatives in the CPSU launched a coup against Gorbachev. Castro initially welcomed the hard-line government of the 'Gang of Eight' only for the coup to collapse two days later, a weakened Gorbachev returning to power under the shadow of Boris Yeltsin whose political stock had rocketed during popular demonstrations against the coup. With the conservative threat defeated, the pace of Soviet reform accelerated and, within a month, Gorbachev announced that the 2,800-man Soviet combat brigade in Cuba would be withdrawn, infuriating Castro who was not informed of the decision beforehand. At a sombre fourth Party Congress in October, Castro announced harsh austerity measures, and in December he declared that Cuba was undergoing the most difficult period in its history, prompting widespread predictions of his regime's imminent collapse.

Not for the first time in a political career spanning more than half a century, however, Castro would defy all predictions and, with a degree of expertise which outshone his handling of previous crises, he weathered the 'Special Period', emerging in the late 1990s with a stronger grip on power than at any previous stage in the Revolution. Refining his ability of converting defeat into victory into a political art, Castro's regime spent the 1990s careening from one crisis to the next, Washington's inept attempts to tighten the economic stranglehold merely strengthening Havana's hand and enabling it to mobilise international condemnation of the American embargo. Through the skilful use of mass demonstrations, currency manipulation and some of the fiercest propaganda campaigns in the Revolution's history, Castro saw off dozens of crises, any one of which would have brought down a similar dictatorship in another part of the world.[39] But few dictators are of the calibre of Castro, and he remains a thorn in the side of the Americans who have had three more presidents since 1989 but are no closer to removing him from power.

Although the Cuban regime has experimented with modest economic and political reforms – opening up Cuba's fledgling tourist industry to foreign investment and allowing the emergence of a small entrepreneurial class – its tenacious grip on every aspect of Cuban life has smothered internal opposition and promoted the emergence of a privileged elite in the FAR and PCC. Since the mediagenic Elián González case in 2000, Cubans have been subjected to a relentless campaign of propaganda and popular mobilisation, Castro giving lengthy speeches to the nation every weekend since early 2000. This culminated in the bizarre national petition signed by more than eight million Cubans in June 2002 which declared that the Cuban political system will never change, with or without Castro at the helm.[40] Apologists for the Cuban regime nevertheless continue to focus on the American embargo whilst glossing over the glaring absence of political and human rights in Cuba, but until Castro dies, it is unlikely that genuine political liberalisation will occur.

Aftermath in southern Africa

For the countries caught up in southern Africa's three decades of conflict, the New York Accords promised to leave behind Africa's 'Wasted Decade'. Political change occurred quickly in South Africa where, in September 1989 – following the surprise resignation of P.W. Botha after a stroke – the reformer F.W. De Klerk became president and set about dismantling the apartheid system. By the time Nelson Mandela was released from thirty years of detention on 11 February 1990, the trend of political reform had become irreversible and, in April 1994, he was elected president in South Africa's first free elections. Although the ANC has been accused of failing to meet the aspirations of South Africa's poorest, the Truth and Reconciliation Commission and projects to improve conditions in the illegal settlements ringing Johannesburg have done much to address the ghosts of the apartheid era.[41] The future holds far greater challenges for the government, however, in particular tackling the increase in crime and the appallingly high rate of HIV infection. But pockets of resistance to change remain and, until Savimbi's death in February 2002, some ex-SADF officers and arms dealers continued to provide UNITA with support.

Compared to South Africa, Zaire was not so lucky, and Mobutu's dictatorship limped on for another eight years, only to be replaced by an equally corrupt one under Laurent Kabila. Ironically, the catalyst for change did not come from within Zaire but from neighbouring Rwanda which sank into civil war in late 1990, the sporadic incursion of Tutsi rebels into Zaire destabilising the region. Following the shooting down of an aircraft bearing the presidents of Rwanda and Burundi on 6 April 1994, Hutu extremists launched a savage genocide against the minority Tutsi population, murdering 800,000 Tutsis and moderate Hutus over the next three months. In fear of reprisals, the Hutu militia (Interahamwe) fled into eastern Zaire, and in its pursuit of them the Rwandan government threw in its lot with Laurent Kabila's rebels, giving a boost to their ailing insurgency. In May 1997, Kabila overthrew Mobutu,[42] raising hopes that the Congo could shake off its past and enter an era of peace and democracy. But Kabila proved a huge disappointment, and fresh rebellions quickly broke out in eastern Congo which ended up drawing in troops from Rwanda, Uganda, Angola and Zimbabwe in 'Africa's first World War'.[43]

Of all the signatories of the 'peace without losers', Angola – which should have been the New York Accords' greatest benefactor – proved the most tragic loser, its warring leaderships repeatedly wasting the opportunity for reconciliation. While the Bicesse Accords gave a brief respite in Angola's thirty-year conflict, the elections held in September 1992 failed to bring about a peaceful transition to democracy, the MPLA's surprise victory prompting UNITA's return to war amidst claims of electoral fraud. To Washington's horror, UNITA unleashed a civil war in Angola more horrendous than anything that had preceded it, besieging several provincial capitals – most harrowingly Kuito-Bié, which was reduced to rubble in savage fighting – and bringing the government to the brink of collapse. By July 1993, nearly 1,000 Angolans were dying every day from war, famine and disease, but the peace talks started that October in Lusaka proceeded only at a snail's pace. It was not until 20 November 1994 that the second Lusaka Accord was signed, providing for a power-sharing Government of National Unity and Reconstruction (GURN) and free elections to be held in late 1995 (at the time of writing these have yet to take place).

Like its predecessor a decade before, however, the Lusaka Accord failed to bring peace to Angola as a result of two overwhelming factors. The first was Jonas Savimbi, who refused to abide by any of his commitments and who continued to rule what was left of UNITA as a ruthless (and possibly insane) warlord. The second was Dos Santos' regime in

Luanda, which allowed the war to limp on while plundering Angola's oil and diamond wealth, showing callous disregard for the dire situation of the millions of displaced civilians and '*mutilados*' (disabled war veterans). With the war benefiting only the MPLA and UNITA leaderships, one strongly suspects that Dos Santos' inability to crush UNITA was a deliberate ploy to safeguard the Luanda elite's dominance of Angola, allowing him to side-step repeated calls for political reform, free elections and an end to the egregious corruption which has come to characterise his government.

With Savimbi's death in a hail of bullets near Lucusse in February 2002, and the subsequent peace treaty signed with UNITA on 4 April, the prospects for long-term peace seem brighter than at any stage in Angola's forty-one-year conflict. Coupled with the recent rash of peace treaties across southern Africa – in the Congo, Rwanda and the Sudan – it promises to bring an end to another wasted decade and create the kind of regional peace Crocker had envisioned would develop as a consequence of the 'linkage' agreements. But the deepening crisis in Zimbabwe continues to threaten the stability of the region, and it remains to be seen if Luanda will relinquish control of Angola's oil and diamond wealth and allow genuine democracy to take root. Tackling corruption remains Angola's greatest challenge, after an estimated $4.2 billion went missing from government coffers between 1997 and 2002 (the equivalent to Angola's entire social budget).[44] Recent efforts by the Angolan government to introduce more transparency in its management of oil revenues and to commit to political reform look encouraging, but with oil revenues set to mushroom over the coming years, foreign governments are likely to find their influence over Luanda dwindling.[45] As in April 1974, Angola is at a crossroads, and it will require tremendous political will to overcome its many problems, not least of which are clearing the twelve million mines littering the countryside, finding employment for thousands of demobilised troops, and stamping out the deeply ingrained banditry outside the main cities.

CONCLUSION

The intervention in Angola was the result of one of the Cuban Revolution's most powerful ideologies – internationalism – and reflected not only the political changes taking place in Cuba, but also the many ups and downs in Havana's relationship with Moscow, its most important ally and patron. Castro's struggle to maintain hegemony over the Cuban Revolution and his international profile put enormous strain on the Cuban–Soviet alliance, and this was reflected in the operation in Angola which had as many moments of ascendancy for the Cuban leader as it did of weakness. The result of a desperate gamble in November 1975, the fifteen-year Cuban occupation became a potent example of Castro's opportunistic genius of converting defeat into victory, a skill he has further refined in the turbulent years following the withdrawal. The model of internationalism created by his former protégé, Che Guevara, proved a powerful ideology for politicising a generation of Cubans, and enabled Havana to project its influence on a scale unprecedented in its history, at times with a strong degree of independence from its Soviet patrons. But, ultimately, the promotion of internationalism as a national ideology depended on the political climate and, following the Cuban withdrawal, the regime would mothball it once more, concentrating instead on the more lucrative image of Che Guevara and the romantic ideal he championed.

The Cuban–MPLA alliance

Born almost by accident in the mid-1960s, the Cuban–MPLA alliance lasted for nearly thirty years. Though beset by periodic ruptures and strained relations between the FAR and FAPLA, it was held together by the thread of Castro's unwavering support for Neto and the liberation movement he led – support which proved critical to Neto's survival. While contacts between Havana and the MPLA remained at a low level throughout the early 1960s, the Cuban mission to Brazzaville (which was intended as a back-up for Guevara's Congo campaign) gave birth to a military alliance which was to endure – albeit shakily – the difficult years following

274

the death of Guevara and his internationalist ideal. By mid-1975 the groundwork had been laid for an identical follow-up mission in Angola itself, a country which was sinking into chaos even as the first Cuban instructors arrived. When events on the ground in Angola threatened to overwhelm the Cuban mission, the conditions were just right – on an international level (with a weak American presidency and a robust Soviet military) and on a technical level (the FAR having completed five years of re-training and re-armament) – for Cuba to launch the largest military intervention in its history, catapulting itself onto the world stage as a military power.

Victory in the 'Second Liberation War' proved illusory, however, and Cuba was quickly sucked into the war against UNITA as the FAPLA's unwilling partner, unable to withdraw for fear of triggering the collapse of the Luanda regime, and by the end of the intervention becoming 'hostages' to the Angolan War.[1] While there is no doubt that Castro capitalised on the prestige and influence the Cuban operations in Angola and Ethiopia afforded him, the evidence is overwhelming that, even before the fighting of the 'Second Liberation War' was over, he was looking to withdraw his troops. In the long-run, Castro envisioned reducing the intervention force to a small garrison – if only to maintain a foothold in the region – supplemented by a permanent training force for the FAPLA and the various guerrilla movements based in Angola. But, as Angola's security deteriorated, Cuban troops were drawn into the fighting, necessitating constant reinforcements and eventually forcing them to re-engage in the war in late 1987. The Cuban operation in Angola was thus one of changing goalposts. And, after starting out with the limited objectives of securing the MPLA in power and expelling foreign aggressors, it expanded to include the extinction of UNITA, the independence of Namibia and even the end of apartheid itself, locking the Cuban army in an uncomfortable alliance with the FAPLA under the increasing control of their Soviet overlords.[2]

Cuba as a proxy force for the Soviet Union

One of the most consistent accusations made against the Cubans is that they were a proxy force for the Soviet military – 'Moscow's Gurkhas' as Savimbi described them – who were sent into Angola to extend Soviet influence in the region under the false guise of 'internationalism'.[3] This common view does not, however, describe the complexity of the Cuban–Soviet relationship which developed in Angola over three decades. Nor does it take into account Cuba's contrasting moments of freedom from and total submission to Soviet control which swung back and forth like a pendulum. There is no denying that the Cubans were, in some respects, a proxy force for the Soviets in Africa. Moscow was, after all,

Cuba's most important ally, and the Cuban mission advanced Soviet interests in the region, helping to train liberation movements armed and supplied by Moscow and gaining the Socialist bloc new African allies. Although Cuba was not officially a member of the Warsaw Pact, its forces (which were armed and trained by the Soviet military) extended Soviet power into sub-Saharan Africa, and provided the Soviets with an opportunity to test the vast amount of military hardware accumulated over the previous decade, leading to the Soviet takeover of the FAPLA's operations in the mid-1980s. Indeed, so total did Soviet control become that, despite MMCA comprising more than 30,000 Cuban troops throughout the 1980s, the opinion of a dozen Soviet advisers was sufficient to overrule the FAPLA–Cuban commanders on at least three occasions, precipitating the series of offensives which culminated in the catastrophe of 1987.

On the other hand, the evidence is compelling that Havana sent Argüelles into Angola in August 1975 of its own accord, and that it launched Operation Carlota without informing its Soviet patrons who, at first, withheld technical assistance. Undoubtedly the Soviets were aware that Cuba was carrying out a training mission in Angola – Soviet specialists were, after all, delivering weapons to the MPLA recruits who were being trained by the Cubans. But the decision to escalate to a full-scale intervention appears to have been purely Cuban, as is suggested by recent interviews with former Soviet politicians who were working on Angola at the time. That the Soviets were not involved in the launch of Operation Carlota is hardly surprising as it was an eleventh-hour gamble to avert catastrophe. They chose to withhold their support until the tide of battle had turned in the Cubans' favour, and then adopted the role of principal benefactor of the operation in Angola while leaving its running in Cuban and Angolan hands. It was only the rekindling of the Cold War in the early 1980s that spurred the Soviet military into taking control of the FAPLA, with Cuban forces as a vital prop for their efforts again UNITA. It took the disaster at the Lomba river to provide Castro with the opportunity to seize back control of the operation, and enabled him to terminate it under favourable terms.

The Cuban–Soviet relationship in Angola was thus characterised by a constantly changing balance of power, and reflected the volatile political mood in Havana. In the early 1960s the internationalist ideal and the search for new allies gave birth to Cuba's fledgling alliance with the MPLA, quite independently of the Soviets. But this tailed off in the late 1960s as Cuba was sucked into the Soviet embrace, and then was reborn as the result of a military miscalculation even more disastrous than Guevara's campaign in the Congo a decade before. Castro's relationship with the Soviet Union gained him international prestige and influence, but there was a limit to his independence from Moscow, and when the Kremlin called in its favours, Castro complied. The most glaring example of this occurred in the wake of the Vietnamese invasion of Cambodia in January 1979 when – as president of the NAM – Castro manipulated the Havana summit to ensure that a resolution was passed leaving the Cambodian seat vacant, a solution which favoured Soviet policy but which tarnished Cuba's reputation as an independent force in the world.[4] When domestic crisis shook Havana – for example during the Mariel crisis in 1980 – the Cuban mission in Angola was reined in (hence the lack of retaliation against Operation Protea). But when the Cuban–Soviet military alliance peaked in the late 1980s, Cuba once more re-engaged in the fighting in Angola, its politically-skilled leader conjuring up an improbable victory against all the odds. The Cuban operation in Angola is thus perhaps best viewed as the African adventure of Moscow's most outspoken 'super-client', containing all the strains and tensions of their turbulent alliance which evolved over three decades.

Ultimately the Cuban operation in Angola fostered a close relationship between the FAR and the Soviet military, both on the ground in Angola and at the highest echelons of power. This alliance of interests proved crucial to Castro's future survival, and fed into his dispute with Gorbachev in the late 1980s. Indeed, by the late 1980s the war in Angola had become an extension of Castro's struggle against the reformist forces in the Kremlin, and possible moves by them to remove him from power might have been the motivation behind the highly-controversial trial of Ochoa and the De la Guardia brothers, and the purge of MININT which followed. In the final analysis, however, Castro's overriding concern in Angola was to terminate the military operation on terms which were acceptable to Havana. And, by the late 1980s, these included not only a military victory on the ground to justify more than a decade of fighting and casualties, but more significantly a seat for Cuba at the negotiating table, something which had been denied during the humiliating Cuban Missile Crisis. Castro was testing the extent of his independence to the limit – the Soviets could cut him off if they wished, but only at a great political cost – and, with Moscow and Washington pressuring all sides towards a settlement, he was astute enough to push for the maximum gains. What began as a mad scramble into Africa would finish as an orderly military withdrawal, and Cuban troops would return victorious to Cuba, even if, in reality, their 'victory' was at best ambiguous.

South Africa's involvement in Angola, 1963–88

South Africa's involvement in Angola was as traumatic and uneven as Cuba's. Yet, despite the many victories it achieved against its SWAPO, FAPLA and Cuban adversaries, its one outstanding characteristic was how little Pretoria learned from the experience. Unwilling to face up to the painful truth that its overhasty intervention in Angola had precipitated Operation Carlota – and brought 36,000 Cuban troops into Angola – Pretoria blamed its failure on the Americans and, following the withdrawal in March 1976, it backed off from further involvement in Angola. With the explosion of SWAPO's insurgency in early 1977, however, the SADF was drawn back in, re-igniting its military alliance with UNITA and leading to a carbon copy of Operation Savannah. Exactly like its predecessor, Operation Moduler was intended as a short-term intervention to shore up UNITA, but with the same lack of clearly defined objectives – and a day-to-day strategy which lagged weeks behind events – the small-scale operation rapidly escalated beyond Pretoria's control, unleashing a confrontation on a scale which dwarfed all previous encounters. Once more pursuing a strategy which played into Cuban hands, Pretoria could not resist extending its objectives whenever events on the ground turned in its favour, and this enabled Castro to set the political and military agenda when South African forces came up against the heavily-reinforced garrison at Cuito Cuanavale in early 1988.

In fairness to Pretoria, it was – like Havana and Luanda – reacting to events on the ground. But its unwillingness to engage in the propaganda war undermined SADF efforts to dominate the fighting, and handed Havana political opportunities which it exploited to the full.[5] From a military perspective, the SADF dominated the war from the moment its troops crossed into Angola. The few setbacks suffered over thirteen years of fighting fade in importance when set against its suppression of SWAPO's insurgency in Namibia (which at no stage threatened to take control of any part of the colony), or the many crushing victories it achieved over the FAPLA–Cubans with numerically smaller forces.[6] In the political arena, however, Pretoria was outclassed by Fidel Castro who remains a master in the equally-important battle of perceptions. Through his skilful manipulation of the interlinking alliances and strategies in Angola he conjured up an ersatz military victory for his forces, enabling Cuba to become the only foreign power ever to withdraw from Angola with an ostensibly victorious army. Failing to develop a complementary political strategy which could match the dominance and creativity of its forces on the ground, Pretoria threw away its victories on the battlefield, and throughout the 1980s its bungled strategy proved a major factor in the military stalemate which developed.

For all their mastery of the propaganda war, however, the Cubans little understood the South Africans (nor did they understand the Cubans for that matter). And at each stage in Angola's prolonged conflict, both sides were boxing with shadows, reacting to imagined (and often erroneous) reports that their opponents were escalating the fighting, which in turn led to both sides stepping up their involvement. This battle of perceptions periodically escalated the fighting in Angola and, by the early 1980s, had created two different wars being fought over the same territory. For the vast majority of Cuban troops, the Angolan War was part of a broader struggle against the forces of global imperialism and (especially in South Africa's case) racism. Their South African adversaries, on the other hand, saw the war against SWAPO and its allies as nothing less than a fight for the survival of apartheid against the forces of Communist imperialism. The extremity of each side's view was vividly illustrated by the ideologies they professed, the Cubans expounding an amalgam of Guevarist ideals, dubious historical precedents and emotions which converged to form 'Cuban internationalism', while the South Africans clung to the almost messianic and equally apocalyptic 'Total Onslaught' counter-theory, creating a refracted view of the war when viewed from both sides simultaneously.

Ultimately Cuba and South Africa claimed to have intervened in Angola to prevent the other side from taking over, but their justification for intervening was, in reality, dubious. After all, Pretoria's main objective in invading Angola in late 1975 was to install a pro-apartheid government in Luanda – thus ensuring South Africa's continued hold on Namibia – and the SADF's repeated incursions into the Front-Line States were motivated more by a desire to forestall political change than to prevent the spread of Communism. By the same token, Havana's decision to send 36,000 troops to prop up its Angolan ally was not a pure gesture of inter-nationalist solidarity, but actually the result of a catastrophic series of mis-calculations which ended up placing the Cuban military mission in the path of two foreign armies. Throughout the Angolan War, both Cuba and South Africa nevertheless insisted they were acting in their people's and their allies' interests, but it is hard to escape the conclusion that both were in reality proxy forces for the wider struggle being fought between the Soviet and Western blocs in the 1970s and 1980s. It is thus no coincidence that both Cuba and South Africa started withdrawing from Angola only months before the socialist bloc began to collapse, spawning the chaotic 'New World Order' which modern historians have yet to decipher.

The success and failure of 'linkage'

Of the many peace initiatives attempted in the 1980s, the most outstanding for its boldness, durability and sheer originality was Crocker's 'linkage' negotiations, which survived more than seven years of criticism, ruptures and broken promises. Launched in the shadow of the CIA's bungled Angolan operation – which handed Luanda and Havana a resounding pro-paganda victory whilst alienating Washington's most important ally in the region – Crocker's strategy defied all expectations, and established itself as the only credible peace process which addressed the interests of the three principal parties: South Africa, Angola and Cuba. Despite generating a vast amount of criticism and bile, 'linkage' had an underlying logic which was undeniable and, over the years, South Africa and Cuba came to recognise that, whatever their original motivations for intervening in Angola, they would have to address the legitimate security concerns of their adversaries before the withdrawal of military forces could be achieved. That Crocker's team managed to maintain consensus between the warring parties over more than seven years is a remarkable achievement, and the agreement signed in New York was a major success by any standards, providing for the independence of Namibia and the withdrawal of South African and Cuban forces from Angola – leaving southern Africa free of foreign troops for the first time since the Napoleonic Wars.[7]

In the long-term, however, the New York Accords failed to bring peace to Angola because they side-stepped the issue which had triggered foreign intervention in the first place – namely Angola's chronic civil war – and, within eighteen months of Cuba completing its withdrawal, fighting had broken out once more. In fairness to Crocker, the 'linkage' negotiations were about linking Namibian independence to the withdrawal of Cuban and South African forces from Angola, and this was achieved within the framework of the New York Accords. Nevertheless, the Accords were intended to create a wider context for peace across the whole of southern Africa, and in the months following New York it seemed as if this goal had been achieved with the Bicesse Peace Accords (May 1991) and Angola's first free elections (September 1992). What no one anticipated – least of all Washington which supported UNITA until polling day – was that Savimbi was using the lull in the fighting to rebuild his forces, and he re-launched hostilities only weeks after UNITA's defeat in the polls. While doubts remain over the validity of the MPLA's election victory in 1992, these do little to justify UNITA's return to war which, over the next two years, unleashed a man-made catastrophe on the Angolan population, killing hundreds of thousands of civilians and reducing to rubble what little remained of Angola's infrastructure.

The failure of 'linkage' thus lay in the handling of its aftermath, not only by its American authors but also by the international community which was, once again, nonplussed by the turn of events in Angola. Had the Bush administration appointed a replacement for Crocker (who resigned in April 1989) with the same vision and patience, it is arguable that the Americans could have steered the peace process to a more successful conclusion. By the same token, the UN's handling of Angola – one of several catastrophic peace-keeping missions it carried out in the 1990s (in Bosnia, Somalia and Rwanda) – contributed to the failure of the elections and UNITA's return to war. As the fighting escalated across Angola, the UNAVEM force could do little but stand by impotently, much as its successor MONUA did six years later before it was expelled by the MPLA in March 1999. In the final analysis, therefore, though Crocker's strategy was highly original, like so many peace initiatives launched during the last decade (for example in Northern Ireland and the Middle East), it failed to bring peace to the region, and could be said to have produced no more than could have been expected of it, but rather less than had been hoped for. And, while the New York Accords did succeed in removing South African and Cuban forces from Angola (bar a handful of Cuban military experts still present in Luanda), they failed to bring an end to Angola's internal conflict which raged on until Savimbi's death in February 2002.

The cost to Angola of the Cuban and South African interventions

Since the first uprisings against the Portuguese in 1961, Angola has suffered four decades of conflict, enjoying only brief respites (in 1974, 1991–2 and 1994–8) before sinking into fresh rounds of hostilities, each more destructive than the last. Between 1975 and 1989 (the period of the Cuban intervention), more than half-a-million Angolans were killed – in combat, or indirectly by bombing, landmines and starvation – with at least a further half-million injured or crippled.[8] In addition, a staggering two million Angolans were displaced by the fighting (nearly one-fifth of the population), the majority fleeing to Zaire and Zambia, or swelling the *musseques* in Luanda, Lobito and Benguela. By 1991 (when the last Cuban troops left Angola) over $30 billion of damage had been inflicted on Angola, and the few sources of income other than Cabinda oil (such as coffee exports or revenue from the Benguela railway line) had dried up completely.[9] In addition to the destruction of Angola's infrastructure, there are between five and twelve million landmines littering the countryside, the vast majority of them unmarked. Efforts by the international community to clear these mines have, for the most part, proved ineffective, in part due to renewed outbreaks of fighting (which led to fresh mines being laid) but also to the fact that many minefields overlap, or were laid with booby-traps and decoys to slow down the enemy advance (most notably east of the Cuito river).

No party bares the sole blame for the horrendous destruction wreaked on Angola throughout the interventionist war (1975–91). But all intervening parties share equal responsibility for escalating what had been a small-scale insurgency into a full-scale civil war, providing the Angolans with some of the most destructive military technology ever to see combat in Africa. The massive injection of Soviet military aid to the MPLA (totalling nearly $15 billion by 1988) radically altered the nature of the conflict, triggering a military escalation which continued unabated until the late 1980s. But the South African invasion in October 1975 provided Cuba with the pretext to launch the largest intervention in its history, converting Angola overnight into one of the central points of Cold War confrontation.

Despite more than thirteen years of intervention, however, Cuba and South Africa's only achievement was to restrict the civil war to Angola's remote periphery, for within eighteen months of Cuba completing its withdrawal, the fighting had spread to major population centres such as Kuito-Bié. Ultimately, the only enduring effect of Cuba and South Africa's intervention was to open up Angola to exploitation by foreign mining companies, black-marketeers and the MPLA regime itself, installing an elite in Luanda more corrupt than any administration in Angola's tragic history.

The disappearance of internationalism from the Cuban political agenda

Of all the issues raised by the Cuban intervention, perhaps the most striking is how quickly the Cuban regime has erased Angola from the public memory, despite the involvement of nearly 5 per cent of the Cuban population in Angola. Like dozens of other political experiments which litter the Revolution's forty-year history, internationalist service in Angola was promoted while it served the political agenda. But when Havana's objectives changed with the collapse of the Soviet bloc and the start of the 'Special Period', the internationalist ideal was rapidly replaced by the siege mentality of the early 1960s. In retrospect, it is clear that Cuba's withdrawal from Angola did not begin a moment too soon, for within months the Soviet bloc had collapsed, only to be followed by the Soviet Union itself a little over six months after the last Cuban troops returned to Havana. Although Castro maintains some support from sections of the Soviet military (which might explain how his regime survived the acute crises of the mid-1990s), the Cuban withdrawal marked the end of an era. Today – scarcely a decade after the last troops returned to Cuba – it would be inconceivable for Cuba to launch a similar military intervention.

Since the early 1990s, Havana has chosen to forget the internationalist operations in Angola, Ethiopia and Nicaragua, and has instead sought inspiration from its earliest years – concentrating on heroes and events from the 1960s (such as Guevara and the Bay of Pigs) – whilst making no reference to the thirty years of political and economic experimentation which followed. Government energies have been consumed by a series of crises which have swept through Cuba since 1989, creating a model of government geared almost exclusively towards crisis management and manipulation. Indeed, it is clear that major crises such as the '*balseros*' (1993–4), the shooting down of two Miami–Cuban aircraft (1996) and the Elián González case (1999–2000) have become the principal tools by which the Cuban regime maintains its grip on power. American moves to tighten the embargo (coupled with Washington's ambiguity over the controversial Helms–Burton law) have only served to strengthen Castro's grip on power, which must surely be stronger now than at any stage in the Revolution's chequered history. Barring a change of heart by the Bush administration – or the sudden onset of senility – there is little reason to doubt that Castro will remain president of Cuba for the foreseeable future, overseeing the wild experimentation and siege mentality of Cuba's unending 'Special Period'.

Cuban internationalist veterans today

Against this backdrop of deepening domestic crisis, Cuba's 450,000 internationalist veterans have struggled to come to terms with their experience of serving in Angola, having been given no public voice for their feelings, memories or frustrations.[10] Like the veterans of most wars, internationalists are divided over whether it was worth the human and material cost. While some doggedly cling on to the fading values of internationalism, others express bitterness and a sense of betrayal at the way they were used as proxy forces for the Soviet Union, and at their treatment since their return to Cuba. Unsurprisingly, those who still believe whole-heartedly in the cause predominantly come from the two groups which enjoyed the best conditions in Angola: the professional military and the civilian internationalists. For the FAR's officer ranks, service in Angola represented a golden opportunity for promotion, combat experience and adventure, and there is little doubt that Angola nurtured an entire generation of officers (as is reflected by their dominance of the Cuban government since the early 1990s). It is even easier to understand why civilian veterans view Angola in an overwhelmingly positive light, as the work they carried out there was humanitarian – working in hospitals, teaching children, building bridges and restoring water supplies – much like the foreign aid agencies which run Angola's starved social services today. However botched the decisions which brought them to Angola, there is no denying the humanitarian contribution they made there, and the affection with which they are remembered in Angola today is a testament to this fact.

Those who look back on Angola with bitterness are, for the most part, former ground troops – both reservists and national servicemen – who, with a few notable exceptions (such as the raid on Sumbe in 1984), bore the brunt of the fighting, and who returned to Cuba most drained by the experience. Many were affected by the loss of close friends – the vast majority in accidents – and a small proportion who saw combat were traumatised by the experience, in particular those who took part in the LCB and SAD operations (see Chapter 7). With the economy in crisis, many veterans look enviously on neighbours who escaped internationalist service and are now prospering in Cuba's black-market economy. Most feel (with some justification) that they have been abandoned by the government which did so much to promote the internationalist ideal throughout the late 1970s and the 1980s. Of course, the same could be said about any war, but what makes the Angolan War similar to recent conflicts – for example in the Persian Gulf (1990–1) or Kosovo (1999) – is that it ended with an equivocal victory, which in the case of Angola involved a peace treaty reeking of compromise. While publicly the Cuban regime has celebrated the 'victories' at Cuito Cuanavale and Calueque – and laid on grand ceremonies for the returning troops – to this day veterans are haunted by doubts that the operation in Angola achieved very little in the long-term, and might have been entirely in vain.

For, although the final settlement signed in December 1988 could be read as a Cuban victory – with the removal of the South Africans from Angola and the independence of Namibia (with a SWAPO-dominated government) – over the last decade Cuban veterans have watched impotently as the country they struggled to rebuild collapsed into chaotic warfare, savage fighting reducing to rubble the infrastructure and social services they had painstakingly constructed. Furthermore, veterans have witnessed the Dos Santos government – once proudly Marxist–Leninist and an outspoken champion of internationalism – degenerate into an elite cryptocracy whose venality far exceeds Batista's government of the late 1950s. Meanwhile Cuba has been consumed by the kind of power cuts, food shortages and political repression which characterised Angola at the peak of the war. With much of Angola in ruins, it is almost as if the Cubans had never been there at all, and little remains today of their sixteen-year presence bar Angolan children greeting foreigners with cries of '*Amigo!*', and fading slogans on the walls of derelict camps. That the great 'victories' at Cuito Cuanavale and Calueque have faded so rapidly from the public consciousness reveals how hollow a 'victory' the Angolan operation was, if it was a victory at all.

Since their return to Cuba, veterans have been sidelined by the regime which has excluded them from its annual roster of commemorations, failing to create an 'Internationalists Day' despite there being as many as half a million veterans of the internationalist missions which took place between 1959 and 1991. In contrast to the American government – which, after initially shunning its Vietnam veterans, has commemorated, acknowledged and even eulogised them – the Cuban government has allowed the veterans of Angola to fade from view, while the regime concentrates on its latest revolutionary offensives to boost domestic tourism and foreign investment. Many veterans nevertheless would gladly carry out another internationalist mission, as much motivated by a desire to recapture the youth, enthusiasm and sense of purpose of the internationalist ideal, as by a desire to escape the economic hardship and monotony of contemporary Cuba. But the veterans of Angola are not part of the Revolution's latest internationalist mission to Venezuela in support of Castro's closest regional ally, Hugo Chávez. For them the internationalist dream has given way to the politics of survival and the economics of the black market. Despite the sacrifice of hundreds of thousands of Cubans, the Havana regime is not interested in giving veterans a public voice, and has erased them from the national memory. The 'People's War' in Angola and its Cuban warriors have been swept under the carpet.

APPENDIX 1

CHRONOLOGY OF PRINCIPAL EVENTS IN THE ANGOLAN WAR, 1956–91

10 December 1956	MPLA formed in Luanda from amalgamation of radical nationalist movements (including the Angolan Communist Party) with Ilídio Machado Alves as president. Agostinho Neto becomes effective leader after Machado's arrest in May 1959.
1 January 1959	Castro's guerrillas seize power in Cuba, spawning Che Guevara's global internationalist mission. Cuba sets up contacts with African liberation movements, among them the MPLA (although contacts remain weak at this stage).
October 1959	The Castro brothers and Cuban Communists take over Cuban government, radicalising the Revolution.
3 February 1960	British Prime Minister Harold Macmillan's 'Winds of Change' speech at the South African parliament heralds the wave of nationalism which sweeps into southern Africa during the 1960s.
30 March 1960	Sharpeville massacre. Sixty-nine African demonstrators killed and 176 wounded in South Africa's first anti-colonial clash. Start of internal unrest in South Africa.
2 September 1960	First Declaration of Havana, proclaiming Cuba's determination to fight colonialism, capitalism and 'American neo-imperialism' in the world.
January 1961	First Angolan uprising: 'Maria's War' in Kassanje cotton-growing district (Malanje). Portuguese reprisals leave up to 7,000 Africans dead.
4 February 1961	Second Angolan uprising: 250 MPLA militants attack police station and São Paulo fortress in Luanda to free political prisoners. Seven Portuguese police officers and forty Angolans killed.
5 February 1961	After funeral of police officers, white vigilantes massacre Africans in *musseques* around Luanda. All MPLA activists expelled from Luanda over following weeks, the survivors fleeing north to the Dembos region to set up the '1st Military Region'.
15 March 1961	Third Angolan uprising: UPA launches rebellion in northern Angolan coffee plantation zone. Over 750 white settlers killed in a wave of violence. White troops and vigilantes kill up to 50,000 Africans in retaliation. 150,000

Africans flee across border into Zaire, swelling the UPA's ranks.

17 April 1961   Bay of Pigs invasion. 1,400 CIA-trained Cuban exiles invade Cuba at Playa Girón and Playa Larga. After three days they are surrounded and surrender. 114 invaders are killed, eleven aircraft shot down and 1,197 are taken prisoner (and later ransomed). At least 161 defending Cubans are killed.

October 1961   MPLA moves HQ to Léopoldville (Kinshasa), which becomes centre of operations for all the Angolan liberation movements. UPA has been operating there since the late 1950s.

9 October 1961   Ferreira Incident: Squadron of twenty-one MPLA guerrillas led by Tomás Ferreira captured and executed by UPA as they attempt to infiltrate northern Angola – start of open warfare between the MPLA and UPA (later FNLA).

27 March 1962   FNLA formed from merger of Kongo nationalist group PDA (Partido Democrático de Angola) and UPA. They form the Governo Revolucionário de Angola no Exílio (GRAE).

October 1962   Cuban Missile Crisis. Castro and Guevara are both furious at being excluded from the American–Soviet deal which removes the missiles in return for an American pledge not to invade Cuba.

20 January 1963   MPLA launches Cabinda front, supplied from its base in Dolisie (Congo-Brazzaville), but the guerrillas have little success in the exceptionally difficult terrain of the Mayombe jungle.

April 1963   Castro makes thirty-seven-day visit to the Soviet Union, returning with plans to boost sugar production to the detriment of Guevara's rapid industrialisation plans. Start of rift between Castro and Guevara.

29 June 1963   GRAE recognised by Zaire, which expels MPLA from Kinshasa. MPLA sets up in Brazzaville under the patronage of the Marxist president Massemba-Débat.

October 1963   Cuba sends contingent of 686 officers and soldiers, twenty-two T-34 tanks and artillery/mortars to defend Algeria from Moroccan invasion. They remain to train Algerian troops, solidifying Cuban–FLN alliance and setting up Algeria as the principal training ground for Cuba's internationalist guerrillas, among them Masetti's doomed Argentine column.

April 1964   Masetti's guerrillas are wiped out in Argentina, ending Guevara's plans to join them.

December 1964   Che Guevara embarks on African tour, meeting in January 1965 with Massemba-Débat and Neto in Brazzaville where he agrees to set up a Cuban training operation.

February 1965   Guevara's plans for a '*guerrilla madre*' in the Congo get a cold reception from Africa's liberation movements in Dar-es-Salaam, but he determines to go ahead with his operation regardless.

April 1965	Guevara arrives incognito in the Congo. Backed by *c.*120 Cubans, he tries to expand the CNL's war against the Léopoldville regime, but he fails to get anywhere with Kabila's guerrilla forces, leading to serious recriminations and the eventual collapse of the guerrilla front.
23 August 1965	Last 250 Cubans arrive in Brazzaville for triple mission: to train the Congolese militia, to prepare an MPLA relief column, and to train and fight alongside the MPLA's guerrillas in Cabinda.
24 November 1965	Mobutu seizes power in Zaire (with American and Belgian backing). FNLA's ties to Mobutu grow through his kinsman, Holden Roberto. Cubans are asked to leave eastern Zaire by Congolese allies, ending Guevara's operation.
January 1966	First Tricontinental Conference held in Havana. Guevara is conspicuously absent. Castro decides to concentrate Cuban internationalist efforts on his new protégé, Amílcar Cabral of the PAIGC. Neto meets with Castro in Cuba, but both the MPLA and Cuba are thinking of curtailing their Brazzaville operations. Castro offers training in Cuba, and by October the first MPLA cadres start training to become instructors themselves on the MPLA's 'Eastern Front'.
12 March 1966	UNITA founded in eastern Angola (Savimbi joins his guerrillas in October).
May 1966	MPLA launches 'Eastern Front' in Moxico from bases in Zambia.
27 June 1966	Attempted coup against Massemba-Débat's government by disaffected officers in Congolese army is put down by Cuban–MPLA personnel in Brazzaville.
July 1966	Guevara returns to Cuba to start planning Bolivian guerrilla operation.
August 1966	SWAPO launches guerrilla insurgency in Namibia.
September 1966	'Camilo Cienfuegos' Column brings the first reinforcements in four years to the stranded 1st Military Region in the Dembos.
October 1966	Guevara leaves for Bolivia incognito to set up guerrilla operation.
25 December 1966	UNITA carries out first major attack in Angola, interrupting the Benguela Railway and stopping Zambian and Zairian copper shipments for a week. UNITA expelled from Zambia a year later for jeopardising its main export income.
January–April 1967	Kamy Column attempts to bring reinforcements to 1st Military Region, but it is decimated en route, only twenty-one of its 150 guerrillas making it to Nambuangongo alive.
July 1967	Remaining Cuban instructors withdrawn from Brazzaville – MPLA–Cuban alliance weakens.
8 October 1967	Che Guevara is captured by the Bolivian army and taken to the village of La Higuera, where he is summarily executed the following morning. Death of the internationalist ideal.

APPENDIX 1

May 1968	MPLA completes its move from Brazzaville to Lusaka (Zambia) to concentrate its efforts on the 'Eastern Front' in Moxico.
August 1968	Castro gives public support to Soviet crushing of 'Prague Spring', signalling his compliance to Moscow after their bitter clash earlier in the year. Cuba embarks on 10 Million Ton Harvest.
19 May 1970	Castro reveals to crowds that the 10 Million Ton Harvest will not reach its target, and hints that radical economic and political changes will have to occur in Cuba. This leads to the 'Institutionalisation' process (1971–6), converting Cuba into a model Communist state.
February 1972	Portuguese–SADF forces launch third consecutive offensive against the MPLA in Moxico, triggering the collapse of the 'Eastern Front'. Recriminations in the MPLA leadership lead to a serious outbreak of factionalism.
17 March 1972	1,000 FNLA guerrillas mutiny in base at Kinkuzu, Zaire. Mobutu sends Zairian army to crush rebels and prop up Roberto.
May to June 1972	Castro makes first African tour, visiting Conakry and Algiers. He meets with Cabral to discuss progress of the Cuban mission in support of the PAIGC in Guiné, but talks with the MPLA are at a low level, reflecting the downgrading of the MPLA–Cuban alliance.
December 1973	Roberto heads FNLA delegation to China, leading to modest military training programme which starts in early 1974.
early 1974	Soviet military aid to MPLA halted due to factionalist disputes: Chipenda's 'Eastern Revolt' faction (founded 1973) and Mário de Andrade's 'Revolta Activa' (formed 11 May 1974).
25 April 1974	Carnation Revolution in Portugal – dictatorship overthrown by progressive officers of the MFA who favour rapid decolonisation from the Portuguese African Empire. The world is nonplussed by the news. General Spínola becomes president, but his desire to curtail full dismemberment of the Portuguese Empire quickly leads to his overthrow.
26 July 1974	MPLA delegation attending 26 July celebrations in Havana asks Cuba for military aid, and though the Cubans agree no action is taken.
30 September 1974	Leftist *Movimento das Forças Armadas* (MFA) seizes power in Lisbon, removing Spínola, and promises rapid independence for African colonies. Francisco da Costa Gomes assumes presidency.
November 1974	Soviet aid to MPLA resumes after Neto purges breakaway factions and is re-elected President of the MPLA at a Special Conference in September. Violence breaks out between FNLA and MPLA in Luanda and other provincial capitals, continuing up to and beyond independence.

15 December 1974	Chipenda expelled from MPLA. He takes his guerrillas and joins the FNLA (16 February).
31 December 1974	Cubans re-engage in Angola when a two-man delegation meets Neto for talks. They carry out a detailed reconnaissance of the MPLA's operations in Zambia and northern Angola, and write an optimistic report to the Cuban leadership. However Cuba, which is exclusively focused on the final stages of 'Institutionalisation', ignores their requests for military aid.
15 January 1975	Alvor Agreement signed. Angolan Independence Day is set for 11 November 1975.
22 January 1975	The CIA's 40 Committee approves $300,000 of covert support for the FNLA.
31 January 1975	Transitional Government set up in Luanda, but fighting breaks out within twenty-four hours.
13 February 1975	MPLA attack Chipenda's 'Eastern Revolt' offices for second time. Fifteen-to-twenty killed and thirty wounded. MPLA–FNLA–UNITA occupy Chipenda's office afterwards.
11 March 1975	Failed right-wing counter-coup to return Spínola to power further destabilises Portuguese authority in Angola, starting '*Verão Quente*' (Hot Summer) of Portuguese Revolution. Heavy factional fighting continues in Angola until July when Angola divides into different spheres of influence.
May 1975	Neto meets Major Flavio Bravo, Cuban Chief of Logistics, in Brazzaville and renews his requests for arms, supplies and financial assistance. Again they meet with no Cuban action.
12 July 1975	FNLA finally driven out of Luanda by MPLA after heavy fighting.
18 July 1975	President Ford approves Operation 'IA Feature' (covert military and financial support for FNLA and UNITA to overthrow MPLA) with eventual budget of $32 million (real value *c.*$65 million).
20 July 1975	FNLA launches offensive to capture Luanda before 11 November with *c.*17,000 troops, led by Roberto and supported by right-wing Portuguese military, PIDE officers and Zairian troops.
August 1975	Cuba finally decides to offer the MPLA military support, and sends investigative mission under Comandante Raúl Díaz Argüelles to Luanda to decide what form this support should take. He concludes Neto's request for aid is too modest and increases it to a 480-man mission with heavy equipment and weaponry to train sixteen battalions of the new FAPLA.
8 August 1975	Thirty-man SADF unit occupies Ruacaná hydro-electric complex and other installations on the Cunene River. Portugal protests, but weakly as its troops have withdrawn from the area.
14 August 1975	Luanda's Transitional Government collapses. The Portuguese High Commissioner officially takes over, but

in reality the MPLA fills up all the available posts in the Government. FNLA and UNITA form alliance and withdraw from Luanda.

18 September 1975   Portuguese High Commissioner announces that Portuguese troops are starting to withdraw from Angola, despite the collapse of the Alvor Peace Process.

mid-September 1975   First Cuban instructors start to arrive in Angola and set up training camps in Cabinda, Salazar (N'Dalatando), Benguela and Henrique de Carvalho (Saurimo).

14 October 1975   Zulu Force – two battalions (one Bushman, one FNLA) and fourteen SADF officers (c.500 men) – crosses into Angola. By 3 November it is at the outskirts of Benguela, having swept all before it.

3 November 1975   Zulu Force attacks FAPLA–Cuban defensive line at Caluita and Catengue, inflicting heavy casualties and taking Benguela. First officially recognised Cuban losses of the war: four killed, seven wounded and thirteen missing in action. In reaction, Luanda sends an urgent request to Havana to send massive reinforcements to prevent the fall of Luanda to Zulu Force.

4 November 1975   The Cuban leadership agrees to send reinforcements, launching Operation Carlota.

7 November 1975   Cuban troop airlift starts: first eighty-two-man contingent leaves Havana for Luanda on special Cubana de Aviación flight. 650 arrive by the end of the week, 2,000 by 15 November.

8 November 1975   Three ships with artillery regiment, motorised battalion and other military personnel leave Cuba for Angola. First aircraft with Cuban reinforcements (MININT Special Forces) arrives in Luanda.

10 November 1975   FLEC–Zairian force invades Cabinda, but is beaten back with heavy casualties by the FAPLA–Cubans. Roberto, against the advice South African advisors, orders disastrous attack against MPLA–Cuban positions in Quifangondo (just north of Luanda), and his army is beaten back with 120 dead. At noon Portugal grants independence to 'the people of Angola'.

11 November 1975   Independence Day. MPLA sets up People's Republic of Angola (PRA) in Luanda. UNITA and FNLA set up Popular Democratic Republic of Angola (PDRA) in Ambriz.

12 November 1975   Zulu Force starts to advance from Lobito towards Luanda, breaching Cuban–MPLA defensive position outside Novo Redondo (Sumbe).

13 November 1975   Cuban engineers blow up bridges over Queve river, bringing Zulu Force's advance to a halt. For the next two months both sides fight it out for dominance in Cuanza Sul.

23 November 1975   FAPLA–Cubans ambush Foxbat at Ebo as it advances on Gabela, killing c.50 and destroying seven armoured cars. Foxbat pulls back, its commander planning a revenge attack over the partially-destroyed 'Bridge 14' on the Nhia river.

27 November 1975	Nigeria recognises MPLA government in Luanda, citing SADF intervention as the reason for its change in policy. Three Cuban military supply ships arrive in Angola.
9 December 1975	Soviet airlift halted after meeting between President Ford and Soviet Ambassador Dobrynin.
10 December 1975	MPLA starts evacuation of Luso (Luena) as SADF–UNITA force approaches from west.
11 December 1975	Comandante Raúl Díaz Argüelles killed by land mine on Hengo track road in withdrawal from Nhia river. FAPLA–Cubans are driven off south bank of Nhia river, allowing South Africans to repair 'Bridge 14' in the night and launch a surprise attack the following morning.
12 December 1975	Zulu Force inflicts bloody defeat on FAPLA–Cubans north of 'Bridge 14', killing up to 400 FAPLA and Cuban troops and advancing as far as the Catofe river. They are prevented from going further, however, and eventually withdraw to Santa Comba (Uaco Cungo).
19 December 1975	US Senate votes 54–22 to attach Clark Amendment to Defence Appropriations Bill, cutting off CIA funds for covert operations in Angola.
24 December 1975	Fighting breaks out between UNITA and FNLA in Benguela with mortars and automatic weapons. Soviet airlift resumes after Clark Amendment passed in US Senate.
25 December 1975	Fighting between UNITA and FNLA breaks out in Huambo, at least twenty-five are killed. It soon spreads to Namibe and Lubango. General Viljoen informs Chipenda and Savimbi that the SADF is starting to withdraw from Angola.
12 January 1976	FNLA expelled from Ambriz by MPLA–Cuban forces. FNLA forces now in full retreat.
21 January 1976	South Africa finally starts withdrawing its troops from Angola.
23 January 1976	Last South African troops reach Cunene – the withdrawal has taken less than forty-eight hours. A residual rearguard numbering up to 5,000 men remains, protecting Calueque.
3 February 1976	Mobutu, Roberto and Savimbi confer in Kinshasa and Mobutu announces he is now 'neutral' in Angolan conflict. Cuban troop level in Angola now over 30,000.
8 February 1976	FNLA HQ at São António do Zaire (Soyo) falls to FAPLA–Cuban forces. UNITA HQ at Huambo falls to FAPLA–Cuban forces.
16 February 1976	FNLA expelled from its last foothold in Angola, São Salvador, after a last-ditch defence by foreign mercenaries. Ten mercenaries are captured, later tried and three are executed for war crimes.
29 February 1976	Neto and Mobutu meet in Brazzaville and establish short-lived diplomatic détente.
10 March 1976	Nito Alves and José van Dúnem return from Soviet Union and start plotting coup against Neto.
13 March 1976	Last UNITA stronghold at Gago Coutinho (Lumbala

N'Guimbo) falls to FAPLA–Cuban forces. Savimbi retreats into bush with a few hundred guerrillas.

14 March 1976 Castro and Neto meet in Conakry to draw up programme for gradual withdrawal of Cuban troops from Angola at a rate of 200 per week.

27 March 1976 Last elements of Zulu Force withdraw into Namibia after Angolan assurances on Calueque.

1 April 1976 UN Security Council condemns RSA's role in Angola in a 9–0 vote (five abstentions) but makes no mention of Cuba's intervention.

late July 1976 Neto visits Havana for 26 July celebrations and publicly thanks Castro for Cuban support. Series of economic and technical agreements signed.

October 1976 During a plenum of the MPLA Central Committee, the party formally adopts Marxism–Leninism. Neto moves against Nito Alves, setting up a Commission of inquiry chaired by José Eduardo dos Santos to investigate factionalism in the MPLA.

8 March 1977 'Shaba I': Katangese exiles (FNLC) invade Shaba province of Zaire from Angola and are quickly defeated by 1,500 Moroccan troops airlifted in by France and Belgium.

23 March 1977 Castro arrives in Luanda for first visit. He attends ceremonies at Quifangondo and speaks to huge crowds. Secretly he negotiates a deal with Neto to start withdrawing Cuban forces faster, but these plans get nowhere as the situation continues to deteriorate in Angola.

21 May 1977 Report into factionalism published, demanding expulsion of Alves and Van Dúnem from MPLA.

27 May 1977 Attempted coup by Nito Alves and José van Dúnem. Three Central Committee members and a large but unreported number of lesser officials, rebels and bystanders killed. Cuban tanks under Rafael Moracén re-capture radio station and put down mutinous 8th Brigade.

12 June 1977 Raúl Castro visits Luanda to personally show support for Neto regime. He agrees to Cuban reinforcements to counter new threats, ending Cuban plans for a rapid withdrawal.

late 1977 President Vorster authorises SADF raids over border into Angola against SWAPO bases, starting South Africa's eleven-year cross-border campaign.

4 May 1978 SADF launches Operation Reindeer. 300 paratroopers attack SWAPO bases at Cassinga and Chetequera. Over 600 Namibians killed, sparking international outrage. SWAPO claims those killed were civilians, women and children; the SADF insists they were all combatants. Global revulsion at the massacre leads to passing of Resolution 435.

11 May 1978 'Shaba II': Katangese exiles invade Shaba province of Zaire from Angola, capturing Kolwezi, but are again defeated in a few weeks by French and Belgian paratroopers.

July 1978	Neto and Mobutu sign deal to repatriate Katangese exiles to Zaire, Angolan refugees to Angola, and to re-open the Benguela railway line.
29 September 1978	UN Security Council Resolution 435 passed, demanding South African withdrawal from Namibia and free elections, and recognising SWAPO as the only genuine representative of the Namibian people. This Resolution becomes the backbone of (and principal obstacle to) the peace process.
September 1979	SAAF bomb Lubango and MK training camp at Novo Catengue (Benguela), killing many Angolan workers in factories.
10 September 1979	Neto dies of cancer in Moscow clinic. José Eduardo dos Santos becomes Angolan President.
November 1979	Holden Roberto exiled to Paris from Zaire. FNLA plays little further role in Angolan War.
February 1980	'Total Onslaught' adopted by Pretoria after Mugabe's Marxist government takes power in independent Zimbabwe. SADF steps up 'destabilisation' war against the Front Line States.
January 1981	Ronald Reagan sworn in as American President. Major change in American policy towards the Soviet Union and Africa, sparking the 'Second Cold War'.
April 1981	Chester Crocker proposes linking Cuban withdrawal from Angola to the Namibian peace process, triggering an angry rejection from Cuba and the Front Line States. Start of 'linkage' negotiating process which struggles on for more than seven years.
23 August 1981	SADF launches Operation Protea. 5,000 troops in tanks and armoured cars penetrate seventy-five miles into SW Angola to attack SWAPO bases and putting paid to Cuban withdrawal plans. SADF captures Xangongo and N'Giva, installing small garrisons. 16,000 Angolan refugees flee the fighting.
4 February 1982	Cuba and Angola make Joint Statement of Principles, laying down three conditions for Cuban withdrawal from Angola: Namibian independence under Resolution 435, free elections and SADF withdrawal. They insist that any Cuban withdrawal agreement will be bilateral. Paulo Jorge and Isidoro Malmierca (Foreign Ministers) sign for their governments.
2/10 August 1983	Bloody nine-day siege at Cangamba (Moxico) between UNITA and the surrounded FAPLA–Cuban garrison. 2,000 killed and 4,000 wounded in bitter fighting. The garrison is eventually relieved by reinforcement columns sent from Huambo and Menongue, then UNITA calls in SAAF bombers to flatten the town.
3 December 1983	SADF launch Operation Askari (twelfth incursion since independence). 2,000 troops invade Cunene to attack SWAPO bases, clashing violently with FAPLA–Cubans at Cuvelai, both sides sustaining heavy casualties. Both sides eventually agree to American-brokered ceasefire.

January 1984	Cuba, the MPLA and the Soviets agree in Moscow to increase Soviet military aid by $2 billion and to boost Cuban garrison by 7,000 troops in response to SADF invasion.
February 1984	Lusaka Accord: MPLA signs deal with RSA to ban SWAPO activity in southern Angola in return for pull-out of SADF troops from Angola. However, JMC fails to enforce ceasefire and, with SWAPO's insurgency continuing, the fighting soon restarts.
19 March 1984	Cuba and the MPLA issue second Joint Statement of Principles setting basic conditions for withdrawal of Cuban troops from Angola, including a hint that they might be prepared to negotiate within the 'linkage' framework.
25 March 1984	UNITA launch raid on Sumbe (Cuanzu Sul) to capture hostages. 200 Cuban civilian internationalists help defend Sumbe, driving off UNITA guerrillas in heavy street fighting. 100 UNITA guerrillas killed; eleven FAPLA–Cubans killed and twenty-three wounded.
March 1985	Crocker presents 'basis for negotiation' to Angolan and South African governments. They baulk at negotiating further, however, and the negotiations soon collapse.
21 May 1985	Two South African commandos from nine-man unit captured while sabotaging Cabinda oil installations. They reveal they have carried out three previous operations in Angola.
5 July 1985	Clark Amendment repealed – Reagan sanctions covert aid to UNITA. The MPLA withdraws from the 'linkage' negotiations in protest.
July to October 1985	First major Soviet-run offensive: Operation Congresso II. FAPLA–Cuban forces (supported by SWAPO/MK) attack Cazombo and Mavinga, capturing the former but are repulsed at the Lomba river by last-minute SADF intervention with MRLs and air power.
May to August 1986	Second major Soviet-run offensive is abandoned after SADF–UNITA sabotage supply lines, with a raid on shipping and oil storage tankers in Namiba and an SADF–UNITA attack on Cuito Cuanavale, destroying the bridge over the Cuito river.
28 May 1987	Brigadier-General Rafael del Pino defects to USA, criticising Havana for its Angolan operation which he claims is riven with corruption and incompetence. He warns of the rise of MININT.
27 July 1987	Castro makes bid to join American negotiations, but is made to wait by Crocker.
late July 1987	Third major Soviet-run offensive: Operation Saludando Octubre. 18,000 FAPLA troops, hundreds of tanks and Cuban-piloted MiG-23s advance east of Cuito Cuanavale, but are quickly bogged down in fighting with UNITA and forced to regroup.
4 August 1987	SADF launches Operation Moduler, sending a force which grows to 2,000 men, with tanks, MRLs, G-5s and

	SAAF fighter-bombers to assist UNITA in the defence of Mavinga.
September to October 1987	The Battle of the Lomba River. The SADF smashes the FAPLA advance on Mavinga as four brigades attempt to cross the Lomba river. 47 Brigade is annihilated and the remaining FAPLA forces are driven in headlong retreat towards Cuito Cuanavale.
6 November 1987	At a conference in Moscow, Castro urges Dos Santos and Gorbachev to adopt a more aggressive policy against the SADF in southern Angola.
15 November 1987	FAR General Staff decides to send reinforcements to shore up Cuito Cuanavale in the face of renewed SADF attacks on the area. 'Maniobra XXXI Aniversario' initially involves 3,000 troops, more than 700 combat/transport vehicles and supplies. Polo appointed Chief of ATS, Ochoa is in overall command of MMCA. Castro plans a separate move into south-west Angola to put pressure on the Namibian border.
13 January 1988	The Battle of Cuito Cuanavale starts. 6,000 UNITA troops, backed by c.2,500 South Africans launch a series of attacks to capture Cuito Cuanavale. First attack against 21 Brigade drives it back to the river, the FAPLA losing 250 troops, four tanks and various armoured cars/artillery. South African losses are one wounded and one Ratel-90 damaged.
29 January 1988	Cuba officially joins the 'linkage' negotiations in Luanda, agreeing to negotiate the withdrawal of all Cuban forces from Angola.
30 January 1988	Ochoa is summoned to Havana by Castro and ordered to implement his defence strategy for Cuito Cuanavale, which involves withdrawing all but one brigade from the east of the river. Ochoa does not comply with his orders, however.
14 February 1988	SADF–UNITA launch second attack on Cuito Cuanavale, penetrating between 21 and 59 brigades and driving them back. Cubans launch a desperate tank counter-attack to prevent the total collapse of the FAPLA's defence. The FAPLA lose 500 men, seventeen tanks and nine armoured cars, the Cubans at least fourteen men and five tanks, the South Africans four killed and seven wounded. Castro is furious at Ochoa for not having altered the defences, and he sends Polo to Cuito Cuanavale to take personal command.
25 February 1988	SADF–UNITA launch third attack on Cuito Cuanavale, assaulting 59 Brigade's positions during a tactical withdrawal. South African armour gets bogged down in minefields east of the FAPLA's positions and accurate artillery and MiG-23 air-strikes, and withdraws with several killed and wounded, not having taken the positions.
1 March 1988	SADF–UNITA launch fourth attack on Cuito Cuanavale, hoping to complete mission before demobilisation of 20

APPENDIX 1

Brigade. South African armour again gets bogged down in minefields and artillery bombardment east of 25 Brigade's positions, and is forced to call off the attack having suffered some casualties. 20 Brigade demobilised and replaced by 82 Brigade.

6 March 1988 — Cuban troops start to move into south-west Angola as part of Castro's carefully-orchestrated escalation of the fighting in Angola.

mid-March 1988 — Several rounds of talks between Crocker, the MPLA and Cuba on setting up tripartite talks.

22 March 1988 — Castro orders Ochoa to build up airbases at Cahama and Xangongo (Cunene) in preparation for advance up to the Namibian border.

23 March 1988 — SADF–UNITA launch final attack on Cuito Cuanavale, but their armour once more gets bogged down in the FAPLA's defensive positions, and they are forced to withdraw with heavy UNITA casualties, abandoning three immobilised tanks which the Cubans capture.

3/4 May 1988 — First of twelve rounds of tripartite talks under Chester Crocker starts in London, getting no further than the opening statements. General Jannie Geldenhuys and General Úlises Rosales del Toro hold a stormy meeting, both sides warning the other of the dangers of escalating the war into south-west Angola.

4 May 1988 — FAPLA–Cubans ambush South African force south of Donguena (Cunene), killing seven men from 101 Bn and destroying three Casspirs (capturing one other). Fifty-four Cubans are killed in close-quarter fighting.

22 May 1988 — South Africans launch bungled ambush south of Tchipa (Cunene), drawing in full Cuban company stationed nearby. Six Cubans killed, three South African Unimog trucks destroyed before South Africans withdraw to Calueque.

24/25 June 1988 — Round two of the 'linkage' negotiations in Cairo between Cuba, Angola and RSA. Initially there is a shouting match, but they agree at the end to persist with the 'spirit of London'.

27 June 1988 — Final Cuban–SADF clashes of the Angolan War. 61 Mech clashes with one of three 600-man FAPLA–Cuban columns coming from Tchipa, supported by thirty-five tanks. Two Ratel-90s destroyed, killing one and wounding three. The Ratels fight back, shooting out two T-55s, several vehicles and inflicting heavy casualties before withdrawing. South Africans lose two Ratels, one killed and four wounded. FAPLA lose two T-55s, two BTR-60s, eight trucks and c.300 killed. Cuban MiG-23s launch air-strike on Calueque, killing eleven SADF conscripts and destroying hydroelectric installations and bridge over Cunene river.

10/13 July 1988 — Round three of the 'linkage' negotiations on Governors Island, New York. A conciliatory gesture from the new Cuban delegation chief, Carlos Aldana, breaks the

297

	logjam, and on the last day Cuba, the MPLA and South Africa sign the 'New York Principles', establishing the framework for the final stages of the negotiating process.
2/5 August 1988	Round five of the 'linkage' negotiations in Geneva produces the 'Geneva Protocol', laying down the conditions for the South African withdrawal from Angola and the implementation of Resolution 435, leaving the Cuban withdrawal timetable as the only remaining sticking-point.
30 August 1988	Last South African troops withdraw over border into Namibia, ending nearly twenty-five years of military involvement in Angola.
11/15 November 1988	Round ten of the 'linkage' negotiations in Geneva produces a twenty-seven-month Cuban troop withdrawal timetable, with 3,000 troops to leave before implementation of Resolution 435.
22 December 1988	The MPLA, South Africa and Cuba sign the New York Peace Accords, providing for the implementation of Resolution 435, and the withdrawal of all Cuban and South African forces from Angola and Namibia. Cuba and the MPLA sign a separate Bilateral Agreement covering the twenty-seven-month Cuban troop withdrawal, to be completed by 1 July 1989.
10 January 1989	First 3,000 pre-implementation Cuban troops start to leave Angola.
1 April 1989	SWAPO attempts to infiltrate 1,200–1,800 guerrillas into Namibia before implementation of Resolution 435, sparking international crisis. The UN eventually authorises the SADF to remove the guerrillas from Namibia, and 250 guerrillas are killed in their sweep. Twenty-six South Africans killed and 145 wounded. Namibia's peace process re-starts on 19 May.
2/5 April 1989	Gorbachev visits Cuba, seeking to cut back Soviet aid. Start of major dispute between Castro and the reformist elements in the CPSU.
27 April 1989	Joint MINFAR–MININT investigation into drug-smuggling activities is launched, quickly honing in on Tony de la Guardia's operations as head of MC.
2 June 1989	Ochoa admits black-market dealings in Angola in private meeting with Raúl Castro, who subsequently decides to have him arrested.
9/10 June 1989	Ochoa is released for the weekend, and visits Tony de la Guardia's home, rejecting offers to escape by boat to Florida. Castro meets with Panamanian president Manuel Solís Palma who warns him DEA is closing in on MC's operations. MINFAR's Special Forces sweep on secret meeting of MININT officers at Padrón's house in Víbora Parque (northern Havana), seizing large amounts of weaponry (including crates of RPGs).
13 June 1989	Ochoa and Diocles Torralbas (vice-president of Council of Ministers and Transport Minister) are arrested on charges of corruption and illicit handling of resources.

22 June 1989	The Gbadolite peace agreement between the MPLA and UNITA signed in Zaire, backed by seventeen African nations, the USA, the Soviet Union and Cuba. Fighting soon breaks out again.
26 June 1989	Court of Honour dishonourably discharges Ochoa and strips him of his rank and 'Hero of the Republic' title.
30 June to 4 July 1989	Trial of Ochoa, the De la Guardia brothers and eleven other MININT/FAR officers. The judges recommend seven death sentences, two thirty-year, four twenty-five-year and one fifteen-year sentence.
9 July 1989	Council of State meets to decide final verdicts, Castro speaking for nearly four hours to destroy Ochoa's military reputation. Final verdict: Ochoa, Tony de la Guardia, Martínez and Padrón to receive the death sentence.
13 July 1989	Ochoa, Tony de la Guardia, Martínez and Padrón executed by firing squad. Seven senior MININT officers resign their posts, signalling start of MININT purge.
23 July 1989	Hungary has first free elections, leading to the dismantling of the Iron Curtain with Austria, and starting the refugee crisis which precipitates the collapse of the socialist bloc.
7/11 November 1989	Voting for Namibia's first free elections. SWAPO wins, but not by a large enough majority to form a government.
9 November 1989	Berlin Wall comes down, triggering the collapse of the socialist bloc.
17 December 1989	Ceausescu orders Romanian security forces to fire on anti-government demonstrators in Timisoara, starting the Romanian Revolution which ends with Ceausescu and his wife's execution on Christmas Day.
20 December 1989	24,000 US troops invade Panama, capturing Noriega and cutting off Cuba's main source of imports.
4 February 1990	FAPLA briefly occupies Mavinga during 'O Último Assalto', but is forced to withdraw due to strained supply lines.
21 March 1990	Namibia becomes independent.
April 1991	MPLA abandons Marxist–Leninism in favour of 'democratic socialism', rapidly evolving into a corrupt political elite.
1 May 1991	MPLA and UNITA sign ceasefire, leading to peace accord at the end of the month.
25 May 1991	Last Cuban troops leave Angola on flight to Havana.
31 May 1991	Bicesse Accords signed – MPLA and UNITA agree to end war and hold free elections.
14 June 1991	Last Cuban troop ship docks in Havana, officially ending the Cuban intervention.

APPENDIX 2

PRINCIPAL SADF OPERATIONS IN ANGOLA, 1975–88

Date	Code-name	Description
October 1975– April 1976	Savannah	Full-scale invasion of Angola, heavy clashes at Catengue, Ebo and 'Bridge 14' (Cuanza Sul) thirty-three SADF killed and many wounded
May 1978	Reindeer	Air-borne assault on SWAPO camps at Cassinga and Chetequera (Cunene), more than 600 SWAPO killed and 340 wounded, sixty Cubans and six SADF killed
March 1979	Rekstok/Saffron	Air-strikes against SWAPO camp at Novo Catengue (Benguela) and attack on base near Zambian border
September 1979	N/A	SADF Canberras bomb Lubango, killing many Angolan factory workers
June 1980	Sceptic	Three-week raid 110 miles into Angola against SWAPO base at Chifufua, 360 SWAPO and seventeen SADF killed, first SADF–FAPLA clashes
July 1980	Klipkop	Attack on SWAPO base at Chitado (Cunene) twenty-seven FAPLA–SWAPO killed
August 1981	Protea	Full-scale invasion of Cunene, FAPLA and SWAPO units engaged, radar systems at Cahama destroyed, SADF sets up two garrisons at N'Giva and Xangongo, 1,000 SWAPO–FAPLA casualties, ten SADF killed and many wounded
August 1981	Carnation	Offshoot of Operation Protea, 225 SWAPO killed
November 1981	Daisy	Attack on SWAPO bases at Bambi and Chetequera (Cunene), seventy SWAPO and three SADF killed
March 1982	Super	Attack on SWAPO assembly area near Iona (Namibe), 200 SWAPO killed, two SADF wounded

Date	Code-name	Description
July/August 1982	Meebos	Air and ground attacks against SWAPO command and control structures near Mupa (Cunene), 350 SWAPO and twenty-nine SADF killed (fifteen of them in Puma helicopter crash)
February 1983	Phoenix	Two-month operation to disrupt infiltration of 1,700-man SWAPO column into Namibia, 209 SWAPO, twenty-seven SADF and thirty-three civilians killed
December 1983	Askari	Full-scale invasion of Cunene, ferocious SADF–Cuban clash at Cuvelai and Cahama, SADF withdraw having destroyed SAM-8 air-defence system, 324 FAPLA, Cuban and SWAPO killed, twenty-four SADF killed and many wounded
May 1985	N/A	SADF commando raid on Calombo installations (Cabinda), two SADF killed and two captured
June 1985	Bush Willow	Twenty-five mile sweep inside Angola over two weeks against SWAPO, fifty-seven guerrillas killed
September 1985	Magneto	SADF provide artillery advisors, medics and air transport to UNITA to repel FAPLA's Operation Congresso II, one SADF killed
September 1985	Wallpaper	SADF provide MRLs and SAAF air support for UNITA, turning back the FAPLA at the Lomba river
June 1986	N/A	South African Navy Special Forces raid on Namibe harbour, destroying two fuel storage tanks, sinking the *Habano* and damaging two other Eastern bloc ships
August 1986	N/A	SADF–UNITA raid on Cuito Cuanavale, ammo dumps and bridge destroyed
June 1987	N/A	SADF provides MRLs and anti-tank teams to assist UNITA in *Operação Chuva*
4 August 1987	Modular	Invasion by 700-man force to support UNITA in defence of Mavinga, grows to 3,000 men, clashing with FAPLA during the 'Battle of the Lomba river', pushes FAPLA back towards Cuito Cuanavale
13 December 1987	Hooper	Extension of Operation Moduler, attempt to remove FAPLA from eastern banks of Cuito
12 March 1988	Packer	Final attempt dislodge FAPLA from the 'Tumpo triangle'
30 April 1988	Displace	Mining and holding operation east of Cuito river, ending with final SADF withdrawal into Namibia (August 1988)

APPENDIX 3

ANGOLAN PLACE NAME
VARIANTS

Name before independence	Current name	Province of Angola
Ambrizete	N'Zeto	Zaire
Artur de Paiva	Cubango/Kuvango	Huíla
Carmona	Uíge	Uíge
Cassai Gare	Caicumbo	Moxico
Catofe	Gumba	Cuanza Sul
Chipita	N'Gange	Cabinda
Duque de Bragança	Malanje	Malanje
Gago Coutinho	Lumbala N'guimbo	Moxico
General Machado	Camacupa	Bié
Henrique de Carvalho	Saurimo	Lunda Sul
João de Almeida	Chibia	Huíla
Lândana	Cacongo	Cabinda
Luso	Luena	Moxico
Moçâmedes	Namibe	Namibe
Ngunza	Sumbe	Cuanza Sul
Norton de Matos	Caluita	Benguela
Nova Lisboa	Huambo	Huambo
Novo Redondo	Sumbe	Cuanza Sul
N'to	Buca	Cabinda
Pereira d'Eça	Ongiva/N'Giva	Cunene
Porto Alexandre	Tômbua	Namibe
Portugália	Luachimo	Lunda Norte
Robert Williams	Caála	Huambo
Roçadas	Xangongo	Cunene
Sá da Bandeira	Lubango	Huíla
Salazar	N'Dalatando	Cuanza Norte
Santa Comba	Uaco Cungo	Cuanza Sul
São António do Zaire	Soyo	Zaire
São Salvador (do Congo)	Mbanza Congo	Zaire
Serpa Pinto	Menongue	Cuando Cubango
Silva Porto	Kuito-Bié	Bié
Subantando	Baca	Cabinda
Tando Zinze	Lucula	Cabinda
Teixeira da Silva	Bailundo	Huambo
Teixeira de Sousa	Luau	Moxico
Vila Nova de Seles	Uku	Cuanza Sul

APPENDIX 4

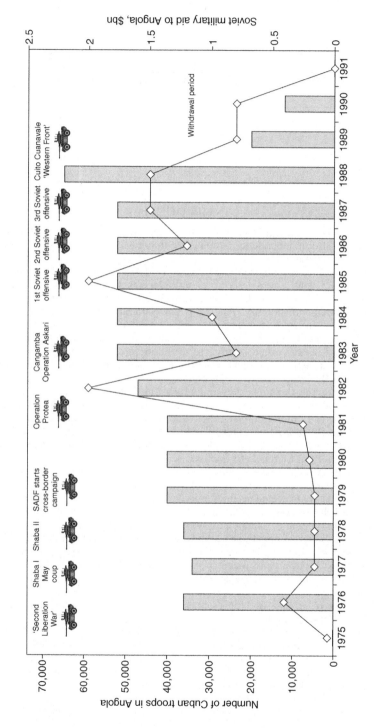

Cuban troop numbers and Soviet military aid to Angola, 1975–91.

NOTES

INTRODUCTION

1 The issue of place names in Angola is complex as many towns changed their names after independence (some more than once). See Appendix 3 for a list of the main variants.

2 See Thomas Pakenham, *The Scramble for Africa: 1876–1912* (London: Abacus, 1992), pp. 250–2, for a description of how the enclave of Cabinda emerged from negotiations between the French, Belgian and Portuguese governments in the late nineteenth century. Angola is sub-Saharan Africa's second largest oil-exporter, and by 2008 will be producing 2.2 million barrels per day.

3 The Belgian Congo has gone by four names since independence. I have used Congo-Kinshasa when relating to events before 1971, and Zaire in all other cases. The neighbouring Democratic Republic of the Congo is referred to as Congo-Brazzaville to avoid any confusion.

4 The 700-mile Benguela railway line was, until independence, one of Angola's principal sources of revenue, shipping copper from mines in Katanga (Belgian Congo) to Lobito. Following the withdrawal of the Portuguese, guerrilla activity brought traffic to a standstill, and by the mid-1990s, 385 of its *c.*390 bridges had been destroyed. Today the only operational section is the twenty-mile segment from Benguela to Lobito.

5 Due to the extended war and the displacement of the population into the cities (principally Luanda and Benguela) and neighbouring countries (Zaire and Zambia), there are no accurate population figures. In 1956, the Portuguese estimated the Angolan population at 4.4 million, and by 1979 this had grown to 6 million, topping 12.8 million in 2000 (EIU Country Report).

6 Angola's eight main ethnic groups are (in order of size): Ovimbundu, Mbundu, Bakongo, Lunda-Chokwe, Nganguela, Ovambo, Nyaneka-Humbe and Herero. The *mestiço* (mixed race) is considered a separate ethnic group, and there are many sub-groups and even undocumented tribes in the Angolan interior.

7 Figures from 1988 are representative of the Angolan population during the Cuban intervention.

8 *Assimilação* was a Portuguese policy to 'assimilate' Africans into the colonial regime. Candidates were expected to renounce all ties with Africa and fully embrace the Portuguese culture, customs and language. *Assimilados* were therefore natural targets for Angolan nationalists who viewed them with a hatred out of all proportion to their numbers.

9 David Birmingham, *Frontline Nationalism in Angola and Mozambique* (London: James Currey, 1992), p. 24. The effect these missionaries had in edu-

cating an indigenous elite cannot be understated. The fathers of the Neto, Roberto and Savimbi were ministers in each of the missionary churches.

10 Massive immigration during the 1950s boosted the white population from 80,000 to nearly 200,000 by 1961, and 320,000 by 1974. In the chaotic lead-up to Angolan independence, however, 90 per cent of the Portuguese settlers fled to Portugal and South Africa.

11 By 1973, Angola was the world's fourth largest exporter of coffee and sixth exporter of diamonds, providing Lisbon with US$70 million in revenues every year (John Marcum, *The Angolan Revolution: The Anatomy of an Explosion (1950–1962)* (Cambridge MA: MIT Press, 1969), p. 5, n11). Between 1960 and 1974 the Angolan economy grew at a robust 7 per cent per year.

12 The MPLA's nucleus was the *Partido Comunista de Angola* (PCA) which was founded by Viriato da Cruz and Mário de Andrade in October 1955. In January 1956 the PCA merged with other radical Angolan groups to form the PLUAA (*Partido da Luta Unida dos Africanos de Angola*, Party of the United Struggle of the Africans of Angola), finally taking the name MPLA on 10 December 1956. Neto became leader in May 1959 when the founding president, Ilídio Machado Alves, was arrested by the Portuguese. Following Neto's arrest in June 1960 he was elected Honorary President, and he formally took up the leadership of the MPLA in December 1962 after his escape from Portugal.

13 Eloy Concepción, *Por qué somos internacionalistas* (Havana: Ediciones Políticas, 1987), pp. 4–9 and Marcum, *The Angolan Revolution (1950–62)*, pp. 126–9.

14 Speaking of the massacre of Portuguese settlers, Roberto (in interview) said: 'When you have a frying pan on a fire and you close the lid, it is going to explode. We were surprised because we didn't expect such a massacre ... [but] there was an explosion after so many years of exploitation ... A popular revolution can't be controlled.'

15 Marcum (*The Angolan Revolution (1950–62)*, pp. 141–9) notes many reports by American missionaries of the wholesale massacre of the indigenous population. An estimated 20,000 Africans were killed in the first six months, rising to as many as 50,000 by the end of the Portuguese campaign.

16 It has been widely repeated that Roberto was a kinsman of Mobutu through his marriage to Mobutu's sister-in-law, but this is vehemently denied by Roberto (author's interview).

17 The FLEC (*Front de Libération de l'Enclave de Cabinda*) was founded in August 1963 and since that date has carried out a sporadic and mostly ineffective guerrilla insurgency in Cabinda.

18 In 1920, the League of Nations designated the South West Africa Protectorate a 'C' Mandate territory to be governed by South Africa as part of the British Commonwealth. After the Second World War, South Africa refused to hand over the territory to UN trusteeship, and, in 1968, the UN General Assembly passed a resolution demanding Namibia's independence. The following year the UN Security Council endorsed this resolution, and in June 1971 the International Court of Justice ruled that South Africa's occupation was illegal and ordered its immediate withdrawal.

19 W.S. Van der Waals, *Portugal's War in Angola, 1961–1974* (Rivonia: Ashanti Publishing, 1993), p. 134. Vice-Consul Ben de Wet Roos was appointed in November 1963, and was succeeded in December 1965 by Jannie Geldenhuys. Both men would play pivotal roles in Operation Savannah (1975–6) and the 1987/8 campaign.

20 Most notable among them were Ben Bella in Algeria (19 June 1965), Nkrumah in Ghana (24 February 1966) and Keita in Mali (19 November 1968).

21 John Stockwell, *In Search of Enemies: A CIA Story* (New York: W.W. Norton & Co., 1978), p. 51.
22 Author's interview with Roberto.

1 INTERNATIONALISM IN THE CUBAN REVOLUTION AND THE BIRTH OF THE ALLIANCE WITH THE MPLA, 1959–65

1 Castro's longest recorded speech is fourteen hours, and he still holds the record for the longest speech to the UN General Assembly (four-and-a-half hours).
2 See Jon Lee Anderson, *Che Guevara: A Revolutionary Life* (London: Bantam Press, 1997), pp. 71–127, for an account of Guevara's political radicalisation during his journey through Latin America.
3 In June 1958, Castro wrote to Celia Sánchez that it was his 'true destiny' to fight the Americans and make them 'pay dearly for what they are doing' (quoted in Tad Szulc, *Fidel, A Critical Portrait* (Bungay: Coronet Books, 1989), p. 482).
4 Rodríguez talked for two days with Castro in the Sierra Maestra, and after conferring in Havana with two other Cuban Communists (Blas Roca and Juan Marinello), he returned to the Sierra Maestra in early September where he remained at Castro's side for the remainder of the war.
5 O. Drugov, *Proletarian Internationalism: Yesterday and Today* (Moscow: Novosti Press Agency Publishing House, 1984), p. 5.
6 The first – involving the landing of eighty Cubans in Panama on 24 April 1959 – was embarrassing for Castro who was on a tour of the USA and Canada, and he publicly offered help to capture the insurgents. On 7 May, a twenty-two-man force bound for Nicaragua was apprehended before it left Cuba. Again the operation had been planned without the sanction of the Cuban regime (Jorge I Domínguez, *To Make a World Safe for Revolution: Cuba's foreign policy* (Cambridge, MA: Harvard University Press, 1989), pp. 117–18).
7 '*Foquismo*' was originally sketched out in an article in 1959 and, after its publication in 'La guerra de guerrillas', it was adapted by Guevara into what was effectively a manual for guerrilla warfare: *Guerrilla Warfare: A Method*, published in September 1963.
8 Cuban-trained guerrilla '*focos*' in Argentina (1958–63), Paraguay (1958–9) and Ecuador (1962) were easily crushed, in most cases as a result of poor preparation by the guerrillas.
9 Luis Báez, *Secretos de Generales* (Havana: Editorial Si-Mar, 1996), p. 24 and William Gálvez, *El Sueño Africano de Che: ¿Qué sucedió en la guerrilla congolesa?* (Havana: Casa de las Américas, 1997), p. 35.
10 These included a group from the Zanzibar National Party under 'Field Marshal' John Okello who went on to overthrow the Sultan of Zanzibar in January 1964.
11 Piero Gleijeses, 'The First Ambassadors: Cuba's Contribution to Guinea-Bissau's War of Independence', *Journal of Latin American Studies*, 29 (February 1997), p. 47.
12 The Cuban ship – *Bahía de Nipe* – returned to Cuba with seventy-six wounded guerrillas and twenty Algerian orphans who were educated in Cuba (Piero Gleijeses, 'Havana's Policy in Africa: New Evidence from Cuban Archives', Cold War International History Project (CWIHP), 6, 1996).
13 The medical team's arrival was timed to coincide with Castro's visit to Algeria, but it was sent at such short notice that no one was there to meet it, forcing the Cubans to fend for themselves for the first weeks of their mission (Piero Gleije-

NOTES

ses, *Conflicting Missions: Havana, Washington, and Africa, 1959–1976* (Chapel Hill and London: University of North Carolina Press, 2002), p. 37).

14 For a full account of the Cuban intervention in Algeria, see Gisela García Blanco, *La Misión Internacionalista de Cuba en Argelia (1963–1964)* (Havana: Imprenta de la Dirección Política Principal de las FAR, 1990).

15 My account of Guevara's meetings in Congo-Brazzaville is taken from interviews with Jorge Risquet by David Deutchmann, *Changing the History of Africa* (Melbourne: Ocean Press, 1989), pp. 1–40 and by Drumond Jaime and Helder Barber, *Angola: Depoimentos para a História Recente, 1950–76* (Lisbon: Istoé Comunicações, 1999), pp. 330–46.

16 Paulo Jorge, who from 1957–62 was a leading MPLA activist at the Casa dos Estudantes, recalled Dr Arménio Ferreira who politicised African students while giving them free medical consultations (author's interview with Paulo Jorge, Luanda, October 1998).

17 Paulo Jorge (in interview) recalled reading and discussing Castro's '*La historia me absolverá*' speech at the Casa dos Estudantes in 1957/8.

18 Risquet (in Deutchmann, *Changing the history of Africa*, p. 1) dates the first official contacts with the MPLA in 1962. However, letters published by Lúcio Lara reveal contacts between Cuba and the MPLA as early as March 1960, although there are few details (Lúcio Lara, *Um Amplo Movimento ... Itinerário do MPLA através de documentos e anotações, Vol. 1 (até fev. 61)* (Luanda, 1998), pp. 309 and 319).

19 Author's interview with Paulo Jorge.

20 Gleijeses, *Conflicting Missions*, p. 82.

21 See, for example, Thomas H. Henriksen (ed.), *Communist Powers and Sub-Saharan Africa* (Stanford: Hoover Institution Press, 1981), p. 61 and Marcum, *The Angolan Revolution: Exile Politics and Guerrilla Warfare (1962–76)* (Pittsburgh: University of Pittsburgh, 1978), p. 161.

22 Interview with author in Luanda, May 1998: '[Guevara] sent me a letter, but I didn't meet him. Because he was in Brazzaville, and he went to see an MPLA camp in Cabinda and was very unimpressed. And he wrote me a letter in Kinshasa saying he wanted to meet me and that I should come over to see him and that he wanted to help the FNLA ... And I refused, saying this was a national liberation war and we didn't want any foreigners involved. And he said that I would regret that decision' (author's translation).

23 Quoted in Fred Bridgland, *Jonas Savimbi, A Key to Africa* (Edinburgh: Mainstream Publishing, 1986), p. 192.

24 Marcum, *The Angolan Revolution (1950–62)*, p. 161.

25 Castro later revealed: 'I myself suggested the idea to Che. He had time on his hands; he had to wait. And he wanted to train cadres, to get experience' (quoted in Gleijeses, *Conflicting Missions*, p. 101).

26 Dreke was a veteran of the Revolutionary War and in 1965 was Vice-Chief of the LCB in the Central Army. Following the Congo mission, from 1967–8 he commanded the Cuban internationalist operation in Guiné (Gálvez, *El Sueño Africano de Che*, p. 44 and Gleijeses, 'Havana's Ambassadors', pp. 52–4). 'Papi' Tamayo served with Raúl Castro during the Revolutionary War, and during the 1960s was an important part of Barba Roja's intelligence apparatus, fighting alongside Turcios Lima in Guatemala and Héctor Béjar in Peru (Anderson, *Che Guevara*, p. 575). He later accompanied Guevara on his ill-fated mission to Bolivia where he was killed on 30 July 1967.

27 Kindelán fought alongside Camilo Cienfuegos during the Revolutionary War (Luis Báez, *Secretos de Generales*, p. 61). Risquet worked in M–26–7's underground and spent five months in jail where he was tortured. In mid-1958 he

joined Castro's guerrillas in the Sierra Maestra, and in 1965 he was secretary of the fledgling Communist Party in Oriente (Gleijeses, *Conflicting Missions*, p. 160).

28 Anderson, *Che Guevara*, p. 639. Although Castro told Alexiev not to communicate this information to the Kremlin, he could have been in little doubt that Alexiev would do so (that was precisely his job).

29 Gleijeses, 'The First Ambassadors', p. 48.

30 Jaime and Barber, *Angola: Depoimentos para a História Recente*, pp. 333–4 and Báez, *Secretos de Generales*, pp. 61–2 and 261–4.

2 THE CUBAN MISSION TO BRAZZAVILLE AND THE COLLAPSE OF THE ALLIANCE, 1965–74

1 Báez, *Secretos de Generales*, pp. 261–3.

2 Quoted in Gleijeses, 'Havana's Policy in Africa'.

3 Ibid.

4 Author's translation of Moracén (in Báez, *Secretos de Generales*, p. 263). Intertribal conflict was still prevalent on the Cabinda front six years later when Pepetela wrote his acclaimed novel *Mayombe*. The novel, which centres on a group of MPLA guerrillas fighting in the Mayombe forest in the early 1970s, explores the divisive effects of tribalism which must be overcome to create the new Angolan nation. So controversial were the book's themes that only the personal intervention of Neto led to its belated publication in 1980.

5 As one Cuban who later served in Guiné put it: 'All I knew about Africa [before I went there] was the Tarzan movies' (quoted in Gleijeses, 'The First Ambassadors', p. 65).

6 Báez, *Secretos de Generales*, p. 263.

7 See Gálvez, *El Sueño Africano de Che*, pp. 84–5, for Guevara's bemused description of '*dawa*', a magic potion applied by the Congolese before battle which they believed made them impervious to bullets.

8 Anderson, *Che Guevara*, pp. 655–6.

9 See Gálvez, *El Sueño Africano de Che*, pp. 272–3 and Gleijeses, *Conflicting Missions*, p. 141 for full text of cables.

10 It was not until June 1966 that two of the missing Cubans were found seriously ill in a hut. The other – Aurino – was never found and was presumed dead (Gálvez, *El Sueño Africano de Che*, pp. 349–50).

11 Following Guevara's withdrawal, the remnants of the CNL were swiftly crushed. Ironically, Kabila did eventually overthrow Mobutu – thirty-two years later – and ruled for four chaotic years until his assassination in January 2001.

12 Castro had read out Guevara's letter the previous October at the founding congress of the PCC (Cuban Communist Party) – probably as a means of quashing persistent rumours that Guevara had been removed in a coup. But the timing could not have been worse for Guevara as scarcely a month later the Congo front started to collapse.

13 Carmelo Mesa-Lago and June S. Belkin (eds), *Cuba in Africa* (Pittsburgh: University of Pittsburgh Press, 1982), p. 19 and Gleijeses, *Conflicting Missions*, pp. 163 and 166.

14 Guinean president Sékou Touré's Cuban Presidential Guard saved his life during a Portuguese commando raid on Conakry on 22 November 1970. Moracén later set up and ran Neto's Presidential Guard in Angola, and this unit still protects president Dos Santos today.

15 Cole Blasier and Carmelo Mesa-Lago (eds), *Cuba in the World* (Pittsburgh: University of Pittsburgh Press, 1979), p. 91.

16 Báez, *Secretos de Generales*, p. 264.

17 My account of the 'Camilo Cienfuegos Column' is taken from interviews with Jorge Risquet in Jaime and Barber, *Angola: Depoimentos para a História Recente* and Deutchmann, *Changing the History of Africa*, pp. 2–5 and Gleijeses, *Conflicting Missions*, pp. 178–81.

18 Monstro Imortal (from Piri in the Dembos) underwent guerrilla training in Brno (Czechoslovakia) before commanding the 1st Military Region from 1966–70. He went for further training in Yugoslavia, and served in Cabinda before his election to the MPLA Politburo and appointment as Chief of Staff in 1974 (Marcum, *The Angolan Revolution (1962–76)*, p. 387, n345).

19 The First Conference of Solidarity for the Peoples of Africa, Asia and Latin America (the 'First Tricontinental') met from 2–15 January 1966.

20 OSPAAAL (Organisation of Solidarity between the Peoples of Asia, Africa and Latin America) has been described as 'Cuba's first stable "front organisation" to support revolution' (Domínguez, *To Make a World Safe for Revolution*, p. 270).

21 The MPLA's key role in OSPAAAL was confirmed two years later when Paulo Jorge was elected chairman, holding the position from March 1968 to November 1969 (author's interview).

22 The Cubans intended to run the operation from Accra, but when President Nkrumah was overthrown on 24 February 1966 they had to find another location. Brazzaville was too far away to be practical, so the Cubans chose Conakry (having established a good relationship with President Sékou Touré). In May, the first five Cuban instructors of the fledgling MMCG (Misión Militar Cubana en Guiné) arrived in Conakry, and by June it had grown to a contingent of around sixty instructors (plus fifteen-to-twenty doctors and nurses) which remained constant for the next eight years. See Gleijeses, *Conflicting Missions*, pp. 185–211, for a full account of the Cuban mission in Guiné.

23 President Kaunda's government was still fairly new and weak, and given Zambia's geographical location – flanked by Mobutu's Congo-Kinshasa to the north and Ian Smith's Southern Rhodesia (later Zimbabwe) to the south – he was anxious to avoid antagonising his neighbours by placing Cuban troops near their borders (Risquet in Jaime and Barber, *Angola: Depoimentos para a História Recente*, p. 338).

24 Mesa-Lago and Belkin, *Cuba in Africa*, p. 20.

25 My account of the attempted coup is taken from the interview with Jorge Risquet in Jaime and Barber, *Depoimentos para a História Recente*, Gleijeses, *Conflicting Missions*, pp. 166–73 and interview with Moracén in Báez, *Secretos de Generales*, p. 263.

26 The Cuban journalist Limbania Jiménez Rodríguez (Nancy) interviewed members of the Kamy Column during their training. Ten years later she wrote up her notes in the book *Heroínas de Angola* (Havana: Ediciones Políticas, 1985).

27 Kamy trained in Ghana and Morocco, specialising in mine-laying and ambush tactics. In 1965 – aged 23 – he was killed when his own mine exploded accidentally (Nancy, *Heroínas de Angola*, p. 57).

28 Author's translation from Nancy, *Heroínas de Angola*, p. 62.

29 Over the following months the MPLA made strenuous efforts to get the guerrillas released, but when an OAU commission visited Kinkuzu it could find no trace of them. Years later the FNLA revealed the location of the bodies which had been buried in shallow graves near the Angolan border, and they were disinterred and reburied in Angola (Nancy, *Heroínas de Angola*, pp. 53–5).

30 Gleijeses, *Conflicting Missions*, p. 183.
31 Under pressure from the OAU – which insisted the weaponry belonged to the Angolan people – Mobutu handed it over to the FNLA, insisting the FNLA 'represented the Angolan people too'.
32 Risquet in Jaime and Barber, *Depoimentos para a História Recente*, pp. 337–8 and Gleijeses, *Conflicting Missions*, p. 182.
33 A small group of Cuban military advisors remained in Brazzaville until 22 September 1968, nearly three weeks after Massemba-Débat had been overthrown (Gleijeses, *Conflicting Missions*, p. 183).
34 Gleijeses, 'Havana's Policy in Africa'. In addition, 254 Congolese students had completed their studies in Cuba (Gleijeses, *Conflicting Missions*, p. 168).
35 See, for example, Gleijeses, 'Havana's Policy in Africa' and William M. LeoGrande, *Cuba's Policy in Africa, 1959–1980* (Berkeley: University of California Press, 1980), p. 10.
36 Quoted in Marcum, *The Angolan Revolution (1962–76)*, p. 174.
37 In particular Guevara failed to appreciate the popularity of Bolivian President Barrientos who came to power in democratic elections in July. A native Quechua, Barrientos was popular among the Indian population and had already carried out substantial land reform in the Santa Cruz area by the time Guevara's guerrillas arrived there. Thus there was little local support for Guevara, and during his campaign not a single Bolivian joined his guerrillas. Guevara was also hindered by poor intelligence (most of his Cubans had learnt Quechua only to discover that the language of southern Bolivia is Guaraní), betrayal by dozens of deserters, and Guevara's ill health (caused by acute asthma) which by the final days forced him to ride a donkey. In retrospect Guevara's Bolivian campaign more resembles a seven-month retreat through hundreds of miles of wilderness than a military offensive, although this is not the picture painted by the Cuban government.
38 Escalante led the Popular Socialist Party (PSP) before the Cuban Revolution and was a figurehead for orthodox Cuban Communists who looked towards Moscow rather than Castro for their ideological orientation. Forty-three PCC members were arrested during the purge, and thirty-five of these were imprisoned.
39 In the end 8.5 million tons were produced, although this included husks and off-cuts. There are even rumours that the 8.5 million ton figure included the previous year's harvest.
40 The reorganisation of the PCC culminated in the first Party Congress of December 1975, and the adoption of a new constitution in 1976 (W. Raymond Duncan, *The Soviet Union and Cuba: Interests and Influence* (New York: Praeger Publishers, 1985), p. 108).
41 Duncan, *The Soviet Union and Cuba*, p. 101. The new hardware included MiG-23 fighter-bombers, T-62 tanks and BM-21 missile launchers.
42 See Jorge I. Domínguez, 'Cuban Foreign Policy', *Foreign Affairs*, 57, 1 (Fall 1978), p. 90 for details of the agreement.
43 In September 1969, Cuba set up a medical training centre in Mostaragem (Algeria), signalling the revival of the Cuban–FLN alliance (Sergio Díaz-Briquets (ed.), *Cuban Internationalism in Sub-Saharan Africa* (Pittsburgh: Duquesne University Press, 1989), p. 19).
44 Unknown to Spínola, secret negotiations did take place between Lisbon and the PAIGC in late 1972, but they were abandoned when the PAIGC demanded Cape Verde form part of an independent Guiné, a concession Caetano would not grant (author's conversations with Professor Fernando Rosas, Bristol, November 1999).

NOTES

45 See Gleijeses ('The First Ambassadors', pp. 78–80) for an account of the war's closing stages.
46 Risquet said of the Cuban–MPLA relationship after the Brazzaville mission: 'Our support was continuous, although with occasional ups and downs' (in Deutchmann, *Changing the History of Africa*, p. 6). Paulo Jorge claims that there was 'never any weakening in our relations [with Cuba]' (author's interview). However, he is contradicted by Neto who, in March 1972, told the Cuban chargé d'affaires in Brazzaville that 'while one cannot say that the relations between Cuba and the MPLA are bad or cold, it's obvious that they are not like what they were a few years ago' (quoted in Gleijeses, *Conflicting Missions*, p. 244).
47 Domingo Amuchástegui Álvarez, *XX Años del inicio de la lucha armada en Angola* (Havana: Facultad de Historia y Ciencias Sociales, 1981), p. 198 and Deutchmann, *Changing the History of Africa*, p. 45.
48 Henda was killed in an attack on the Karipande barracks (Moxico) on 14 April 1968.
49 Marcum, *The Angolan Revolution (1962–1976)*, p. 199 and Van der Waals, *Portugal's War in Angola*, p. 145.
50 Author's interview with Paulo Jorge.
51 In September 1972, a 500-man Cuban mission under the command of Arnaldo Ochoa Sánchez began training the militia in Sierra Leone. In early 1973, 100 Cuban instructors started training guerrillas in South Yemen, and this was expanded to 600–700 during the Dhofari rebellion which lasted until 1975. By November 1974, there were 400 Cubans in Equatorial Guinea, 80 of them military advisors (Duncan, *The Soviet Union and Cuba*, p. 125, William Ratliff, 'Política Militar Cubana en el África Subsahariana', *Revista Occidental*, 2 (1989), p. 147 and LeoGrande, *Cuba's Policy in Africa*, p. 12).
52 Between November 1973 and May 1974, three Cuban T-54 tank units engaged the Israelis in artillery duels in the Golan Heights. Following a ceasefire between Syria and Israel, Cuban forces were withdrawn in February 1975 (Gleijeses, *Conflicting Missions*, p. 226).

3 THE CARNATION REVOLUTION AND THE FAILURE OF ANGOLA'S DECOLONISATION, APRIL 1974–OCTOBER 1975

1 The MPLA received aid from the Soviet Union, Cuba, Yugoslavia, Algeria, Vietnam, North Korea, the PALOPs, Congo-Brazzaville, Guinea-Conakry, East Germany; the FNLA received aid from the CIA, Zaire, China, Romania, Tunisia, Tanzania, France, Britain (mercenaries), Belgium, Zambia, India; and UNITA received aid from South Africa, Côte d'Ivoire, the Arabian states, Morocco, Senegal, Cameroon, Central African Republic, Togo. Most of the FNLA's backers also gave aid to UNITA, and some (such as Romania, Guinea, Tanzania and Zambia) switched sides on at least one occasion.
2 My account of the Carnation Revolution is taken from Van der Waals, *Portugal's War in Angola*, p. 244 and a paper by Professor Fernando Rosas entitled 'Failed Transition: Portugal from Caetano's Spring to the Revolution of 25 April 1974' given at the University of Bristol on 2 November 1999.
3 *Resenha Histórico-Militar das Campanhas de África (1961–1974)* (Lisbon: Commissão para o Estudo das Campanhas de África, 1988), pp. 240 and 246.
4 The FNLA received a contingent of 112 Chinese military instructors following Roberto's visit to China in January 1973 (Stockwell, *In Search of Enemies*, p. 67 and author's interview with Roberto).

311

5 These included the 'Poder Popular' pilot scheme in Matanzas (April to July 1974) and the drafting of a new constitution (October 1974 to April 1975).

6 In late July 1974, an MPLA delegation attending the Moncada celebrations in Havana requested Cuban economic aid, military training and weaponry, but despite agreeing to their requests, the Cubans took no action (Gleijeses, Conflicting Missions, p. 245).

7 On 28 July 1974, Neto, Roberto and Savimbi signed an OAU-brokered agreement at Bukavu (Zaire), pledging to form a common front for independence negotiations with Portugal. However, the agreement fell apart as a result of (mostly white-instigated) rioting in Luanda, which killed thirty-seven Africans and sparked the exodus of up to 70,000 others from Luanda (Africa Contemporary Record (1974–75), p. B542).

8 Odd Arne Westad, 'Moscow and the Angolan Crisis, 1974–1976: A New Pattern of Intervention', CWIHP.

9 China was never comfortable with its involvement in Angola and, on 24 October 1975, it formally withdrew from the conflict (the only foreign power to do so).

10 Africa Contemporary Record, 1975–6, Colin Legum (ed.) (London: Rex Collings), p. B424.

11 See Jan Breytenbach, Forged in Battle (Capetown: Saayman & Weber, 1986), p. 4, for a description of his first meeting with Chipenda's guerrillas in August 1974.

12 Arthur J. Klinghoffer, The Angolan War: A Study in Soviet Policy in the Third World (Boulder: Westview Press, 1980), p. 21.

13 Stockwell (In Search of Enemies, p. 67) also notes that the Soviets started flying large quantities of military supplies to Dar-es-Salaam for unspecified liberation movements in August 1974, the same month that the CPSU announced its support for the MPLA as the true representative of the Angolan people.

14 Author's interview with Paulo Jorge.

15 Africa Contemporary Record (1974–75), p. B534.

16 FLEC, the 'Eastern Revolt' and 'Active Revolt' factions were excluded from the talks, forcing Chipenda to merge his forces with the FNLA six weeks later.

17 See Colin Legum and Tony Hodges, After Angola: The War Over Southern Africa (London: Rex Collings, 1976), p. 47 for details of the Alvor Accords.

18 See www.cubangola.com for a full discussion of when Cuban personnel first arrived in Angolan territory.

19 Gleijeses, 'Havana's Policy in Africa'.

20 Ibid.

21 See www.cubangola.com for full text of letter dated 26 January 1975.

22 Gleijeses, 'Havana's Policy in Africa'.

23 In the words of Jorge Risquet: '[1975] was a year of never-ending work. This may have played a role. And the situation in Angola was quite confused. In the first months of 1975 there was very little discussion in the sessions of the Political Bureau about Angola. Our focus was on domestic matters' (quoted in Gleijeses, 'Havana's Policy in Africa').

24 According to Lúcio Lara, Cuban inaction was the result of the MPLA's 'pride, self-confidence and miscalculation', its leadership viewing Havana as a minor source of aid compared to Belgrade and Moscow (Gleijeses, Conflicting Missions, p. 250).

25 The 40 Committee has been described as a 'crisis-management committee of the senior policymakers charged with overseeing covert operations' (LeoGrande, Cuba's Policy in Africa, p. 16).

26 Westad, 'Moscow and the Angolan Crisis'.

27 The MPLA accused the FNLA of massacring fifty-one MPLA recruits who were on their way to a training camp in Caxito on 26 March 1975. UNITA later claimed that FAPLA soldiers massacred 150 UNITA recruits on 9 August 1975.

28 Legum and Hodges, *After Angola*, p. 54.

29 There is some dispute over the value of Soviet aid to the MPLA prior to independence. Stockwell (*In Search of Enemies*, pp. 207 and 216) claims the MPLA received $225m of Soviet military equipment, while the CIA did not even manage to spend all of its $31.7m budget. Whereas Gleijeses (*Conflicting Missions*, pp. 350–1) states that total Soviet aid to the MPLA did not exceed $81m, and that as a result of the CIA's tendency to undervalue the surplus weaponry it provided to the FNLA, Soviet and American aid were on a par.

30 Mobutu was partly responsible as most of the weaponry sent by the CIA passed through his hands first, and he was not averse to keeping the most modern for his own army while handing on their ageing surplus to the FNLA.

31 *Africa Contemporary Record (1975–76)*, p. A13.

32 Legum and Hodges, *After Angola*, p. 20, *Africa Contemporary Record (1975–76)*, p. B426 and K. Chipipa, 'Angola moves towards peace or war', UNITA pamphlet, November 1975.

33 Gleijeses, *Conflicting Missions*, pp. 262–5, Westad, 'Moscow and the Angolan Crisis' and Klinghoffer, *The Angolan War*, p. 54.

34 Stockwell, *In Search of Enemies*, pp. 45–6 and 55.

35 During a visit to Caracas in February 1976, Henry Kissinger admitted to the Venezuelan president: 'Our intelligence services have grown so bad that we only found out that Cubans were being sent to Angola after they were already there' (quoted in García Márquez, 'Operation Carlota', 1976, South Africa Military History Website, home.wanadoo.nl/rhodesia/samilhis.htm).

36 Stockwell, *In Search of Enemies*, p. 68.

37 Calueque performed two functions: it regulated the flow of water to the underground generating plant at Ruacaná (Namibia), and it pumped water from the Cunene river along 200 miles of canals into arid areas of Ovamboland.

38 From April 1974, the SADF carried out numerous incursions into southern Angola in pursuit of SWAPO, some allegedly against the MPLA. See Nerys John, *Operation Savannah* (unpublished Masters ms, University of Cape Town, 2002), pp. 23–4, Michael Wolfers and Jane Bergerol, *Angola in the Frontline* (London: Zed Press, 1983), pp. 13–14 and A. Muatxiânvua, 'Metamorfoses da agressão a Angola', *Jornal de Angola*, Luanda, 20 December 1987, for reports of South African attacks on Pereira d'Eça (N'Giva) and Chiede in early 1975.

39 Breytenbach, *Forged in Battle*, pp. 4–6, Gleijeses, *Conflicting Missions*, pp. 276 and 294, Klinghoffer, *The Angolan War*, p. 44 and Steenkamp, *South Africa's Border War, 1966–1989* (Gibraltar: Ashanti Publishing, 1989), p. 44.

40 Legum and Hodges, *After Angola: The War Over Southern Africa*, p. 50.

41 Gleijeses, 'Havana's Policy in Africa'.

42 Klinghoffer, *The Angolan War*, pp. 25 and 119. The Soviets again suggested that the MPLA ask Cuba for instructors during 'Iko' Carreira's visit to Moscow in August 1975 (Marcum, *The Angolan Revolution (1962–1976)*, p. 443, n257).

43 Gleijeses, 'Havana's Policy in Africa'.

44 Blasier and Mesa-Lago, *Cuba in the World*, p. 98, Chester A. Crocker, *High Noon in Southern Africa: Making Peace in a Rough Neighborhood* (New York: W.W. Norton & Co., 1992), p. 47 and Marcum, *The Angolan Revolution (1962–76)*, p. 443, n257.

45 The arrival of these Cubans was cited by the American government as its first

'indication' that Cuban personnel were involved in the Angolan War (Marcum, *The Angolan Revolution (1962–1976)*, p. 443, n256).

46 Argüelles was a veteran of the Havana underground, smuggling arms for Castro's guerrillas and taking part in an assassination attempt on Batista. He was part of the landing force at Santa Lucía (Camagüey) which joined the guerrillas in the Escambray mountains. He fought in Guevara's assault on Santa Clara, and after the fall of Batista held several positions in the National Police and FAR. From 1971, he served on internationalist missions in Africa, the Middle East and Guiné.

47 According to Gleijeses (*Conflicting Missions*, p. 250), Yugoslavia had already given the MPLA $100,000 to transport its arms to Luanda in April, so Neto probably pocketed the funds himself.

48 Jaime and Barber, *Depoimentos para a História Recente*, p. 340.

49 Blasier and Mesa-Lago, *Cuba in the World*, p. 100.

50 Westad, 'Moscow and the Angolan Crisis'.

51 Under an agreement made with Moscow in 1965 (which prevented Cuba passing Soviet weaponry to a third party), no Soviet weaponry was issued to the Angolans. The only Soviet weapons used were the Cubans' own AKMs (a modified version of the AK-47).

52 Furry was a founding member of M–26–7 and joined Castro's guerrillas in the Sierra Maestra in March 1957. He took part in the attack on Uvero (Oriente) before joining Raúl Castro's front in the Sierra Cristal. After the fall of Batista, Furry was sent to Bolivia and Argentina to prepare Masetti's guerrilla operation, and following its collapse he returned to Cuba where he held several posts in the government and army. In December 1975, he was named Chief of MMCA, and in 1986 he was promoted to the Politburo, the Council of State and (in 1989) to Chief of MININT. Furry is the only Cuban officer to have attained the rank of General de Cuerpo Ejército (Field Marshal), and is one of only five to be made 'Hero of the Republic', Cuba's highest honour.

53 It is also likely that – as on previous Cuban missions in Africa – there was a preference for black Cubans who would not stand out in Angola.

54 Báez, *Secretos de Generales*, pp. 453–4.

55 Ramón Espinosa Martín joined M–26–7 in late 1956, and carried out arms-smuggling and sabotage operations before joining the guerrillas in the Sierra Escambray in October 1957, taking part in the capture of Santa Clara. After helping round up officers loyal to Huber Matos in October 1959, Espinosa was sent to the Isle of Pines for specialist training alongside his superior, William Gálvez. Espinosa was on a military course in Cuba when he was appointed to MMCA.

56 Among those Espinosa met were Pedalé (MPLA Minister of Defence and Cabinda Chief) and Eurico (FAPLA political commissar for Cabinda) (Marina Rey Cabrera (ed.), *La Guerra de Angola* (Havana: Editora Política, 1989), p. 28).

57 Although Cuban personnel steered clear of the American-owned oil installations, Espinosa kept the airstrip under observation in case it was used for enemy landings. In October 1975 the Americans withdrew their personnel, leaving the Cubans to protect the installations from FLEC attack.

58 They were followed a few days later by a second group of seventy Cuban instructors (Jaime and Barber, *Depoimentos para a História Recente*, p. 342 and Rey, *La Guerra de Angola*, p. 29).

59 The other two ships were *La Plata* and *Coral Island* (*aka* the *Oceano Pacífico*).

60 Gleijeses, 'Havana's Policy in Africa'.

61 *Africa Contemporary Record (1975–76)*, p. A8.

62 MMCA was made up of 480 Cubans, including 390 instructors and seventeen doctors. This was supplemented by a small contingent of civilian pilots to fly the MPLA's aircraft, and several air traffic control and cargo handling specialists (Gleijeses, 'Havana's Policy in Africa').

63 Quoted in Gleijeses, 'Havana's Policy in Africa'.

4 OPERATIONS SAVANNAH AND CARLOTA, OCTOBER–NOVEMBER 1975

1 Steenkamp, *South Africa's Border War*, p. 44, Van der Waals, *Portugal's War in Angola*, p. xii and Gleijeses, *Conflicting Missions*, p. 294.

2 Stockwell, *In Search of Enemies*, p. 45.

3 Interview in 'Cold War'. P.W. Botha – at the time Minister of Defence and from September 1978 President of South Africa – insists that the CIA and Henry Kissinger knew about Pretoria's plan to invade Angola and fully supported it. He put the invasion's failure solely down to American refusal to honour its commitments (author's interview with P.W. Botha, Wilderness (RSA), 10 November 1998).

4 The African leaders were Mobutu (Zaire), Kaunda (Zambia), Senghor (Senegal) and Houphouët-Boigny (Ivory Coast). See Nerys John, *Operation Savannah*, pp. 84–91 for a discussion of the decision-making process which led to the South African invasion.

5 Data on Task Force Zulu is taken from Ian Uys, *Bushman Soldiers: Their Alpha and Omega* (RSA: Fortress, 1993), pp. 26–8 and Steenkamp, *South Africa's Border War*, p. 46.

6 There is much dispute over Zulu Force's size. However, recent evidence suggests that Zulu Force started with around 500 men and grew to 2,900 with the formation of Battle Groups Foxbat, Orange and Elk. This figure was only exceeded in early 1976 when a rear-guard of 4,000–5,000 troops occupied positions within thirty miles of the Namibian border (Steenkamp, *South Africa's Border War*, pp. 56 and 59).

7 Breytenbach notes several occasions when his arrival was greeted with jubilation by FAPLA troops who thought he was Cuban (see *Forged in Battle*, pp. 88–9).

8 Quoted in Breytenbach, *Forged in Battle*, p. 29.

9 Cuban accounts make no reference to these fatalities. According to the official version, the first Cuban casualties occurred in a skirmish the following day at Quifangondo, and there were no fatalities until 2 November (Risquet, in Jaime and Barber, *Depoimentos para a História Recente*, p. 343).

10 Breytenbach, *Forged in Battle*, p. 50.

11 Risquet, in Jaime and Barber, *Depoimentos para a História Recente*, p. 342.

12 Rey, *La Guerra de Angola*, pp. 44–5 and 50–1.

13 Wolfers and Bergerol, *Angola in the Frontline*, p. 23.

14 Quoted in Gleijeses, 'Havana's Policy in Africa'.

15 Uys, *Bushman Soldiers*, p. 33.

16 My account of the battle of Catengue is taken from Breytenbach, *Forged in Battle*, pp. 69–79 and Gleijeses, *Conflicting Missions*, p. 303.

17 Between 1966 and 1974, nine Cubans died on the Cuban mission to Guiné (Gleijeses, 'The First Ambassadors', p. 74). The Cubans admit only four fatalities prior to 3 November, but South African accounts suggest that perhaps a dozen Cubans were killed in separate incidents south of Rotunda (22 October), south of Quilengues (31 October) and at Catengue itself.

18 According to Wolfers and Bergerol (*Angola in the Frontline*, p. 30) and Jorge

Risquet (in Jaime and Barber, *Depoimentos para a História Recente*, p. 343), Neto sent a trusted cadre (Onambwe, who studied in Cuba during the 1960s) to Havana to make the request in person. However, recent research by Gleijeses (*Conflicting Missions*, pp. 305–6) has shown this story to be false.

19 Complaining about the state in which many of the trucks arrived in Angola, Argüelles moaned: 'this is the largest operation we have ever undertaken and we are doing it in the worst conditions and circumstances. With little time for planning and with almost no knowledge of and experience in the country . . . we have had to improvise as we go along' (Gleijeses, 'Havana's Policy in Africa').

20 In 1989, Jorge Risquet claimed that '[it] was a sovereign decision made in response to a request for aid by Agostinho Neto. Not only was it our decision, we didn't even consult the Soviet Union. There was a communication – that is something different – to the Soviet Union, after our troops were on the way' (interview in Deutchmann, *Changing the History of Africa*, pp. 16–17).

21 Author's translation of interview with Castro in 'Cold War'. On 17 April 1976, Castro declared that 'Cuba alone bears the responsibility for taking the decision. The USSR . . . never requested that a single Cuban be sent to that country' (Deutchmann, *Changing the History of Africa*, pp. 71–2).

22 Westad, 'Moscow and the Angolan Crisis'. Many in the Soviet Central Committee were unenthusiastic about getting involved in Angola; for example Karen Brutents, First Deputy Head of its International Department: 'In Moscow [news of Operation Carlota] was greeted without enthusiasm. It was only when the Cubans had landed that we got involved. . . . Once we started sending things to Angola, we were soon in over our heads – even though it wasn't in our plans to go there' (from 'Cold War'). Former Soviet Ambassador to Washington Anatoly Dobrynin backs up this view, insisting that Cuba sent troops into Angola 'on their own initiative and without consulting us' (quoted in Gleijeses, 'Havana's Policy in Africa, 1959–76').

23 Klinghoffer (*The Angolan War*, p. 18) and Mesa-Lago and Belkin (*Cuba in Africa*, p. 25) date their arrival on or around 12 November, whereas Gleijeses ('Havana's Policy in Africa') claims to have seen Cuban documents proving Soviet personnel took no part in planning the FAPLA campaigns in Angola.

24 Westad ('Moscow and the Angolan Crisis') recounts that, on 5 November, the Soviet Ambassador to Brazzaville suggested to his Cuban counterpart that Cuba should get more involved in helping the MPLA, to which he replied that Cuba already had an artillery regiment fighting in Luanda!

25 Gabriel García Márquez, 'Operation Carlota'.

5 THE 'SECOND LIBERATION WAR', NOVEMBER 1975–MARCH 1976

1 My account of the fighting in Cabinda is taken from an interview with Espinosa in Báez, *Secretos de Generales*, pp. 452–9, José M. Ortiz, *Angola: un abril como Girón* (Havana: Editora Política, 1979), pp. 31–9 and Rey, *La Guerra de Angola*, pp. 25–41.

2 Author's translation from Rey, *La Guerra de Angola*, p. 32.

3 Author's translation of Espinosa in Báez, *Secretos de Generales*, p. 458.

4 Author's translation from Rey, *La Guerra de Angola*, p. 38.

5 Ortiz (*Un abril como Girón*, p. 39) estimates 600 FLEC–Zairian casualties for the entire invasion, 250 of those during the last day's fighting. FAPLA–Cuban casualties are not mentioned in any accounts, so the figure is a best estimate.

6 My account of the battles of Quifangondo is taken from Rey, *La Guerra de Angola*, pp. 43–56, Wolfers and Bergerol, *Angola in the Frontline*, pp. 17–19,

Jaime and Barber, *Depoimentos para a História Recente*, pp. 343–4, Steenkamp, *South Africa's Border War*, pp. 48–53, Stockwell, *In Search of Enemies*, pp. 213–15 and author's interview with Holden Roberto (May 1998, Luanda).

7 See, for example, Steenkamp, *South Africa's Border War*, p. 48 and Robin Hallet, 'The South African Intervention in Angola, 1975–1976', *African Affairs*, 309, October 1978, p. 376.

8 Author's interview with Roberto. Steenkamp (*South Africa's Border War*, p. 48) concurs with Roberto, noting that in early November Zulu Force's commander drew up plans for a simultaneous river crossing and parachute assault on Luanda by elite SADF forces, but was overruled by the High Command.

9 Roberto described the battle of Quifangondo as 'the worst day in my life'. Watching missiles raining down on his troops from a distance, he told me that he wished the ground had opened up and swallowed him (author's interview).

10 Figures from Gleijeses, *Conflicting Missions*, p. 310.

11 Total FNLA–Zairian casualties at Quifangondo were 100–150 killed and c.200 wounded. Roberto (in interview) admitted that up to 120 men were killed, with twice as many wounded.

12 The defeat also shattered the alliance with the CIA and South Africa. Within a fortnight both teams of instructors had withdrawn from Angola, fuelling rumours they had sabotaged the attack.

13 Jorge Risquet (in Jaime and Barber, *Depoimentos para a História Recente*, p. 344) describes a counter-attack by ten Cuban commandos, whereas Wolfers and Bergerol (*Angola in the Frontline*, p. 25) describe a three-pronged FAPLA attack on the airport.

14 Breytenbach, *Forged in Battle*, p. 99.

15 Wolfers and Bergerol (*Angola in the Frontline*, p. 51) claim that, in the three months UNITA was occupying Benguela, over 500 MPLA supporters were murdered under the orders of UNITA chief Jorge Valentim (currently Angolan Minister for Tourism).

16 Steenkamp, *South Africa's Border War*, p. 54.

17 Breytenbach, *Forged in Battle*, p. 108.

18 Jaime and Barber, *Depoimentos para a História Recente*, p. 344.

19 The Cubans claim that their BM-21s destroyed five South African armoured cars during the engagement (Wolfers and Bergerol, *Angola in the Frontline*, p. 39).

20 Linford planned an amphibious landing at Porto Amboim using the SAS *President Steyn* which was patrolling off the coast, but the navy refused. Several attempts to send commandos over the Queve in boats were abandoned when they drew heavy fire from the other shore (Uys, *Bushman Soldiers*, pp. 37–8 and 42).

21 Due to the scepticism of his editors, Bridgland's claims that South African troops were fighting in Angola were toned down, and it was not until 23 November that they appeared in full in *The Washington Post*. See Nerys John (*Operation Savannah*, pp. 63–6) for a full account of the breaking of this story.

22 My account of the ambush at Ebo is taken from Breytenbach, *Forged in Battle*, pp. 130–2, Gleijeses, *Conflicting Missions*, pp. 316–7, Ortiz, *Un abril como Girón*, p. 65 and Wolfers and Bergerol, *Angola in the Frontline*, p. 42.

23 Breytenbach, *Forged in Battle*, p. 132.

24 Foxbat's casualties included four South African dead and eleven wounded.

25 Author's translation of Furry, in Báez, *Secretos de Generales*, p. 26.

26 García Márquez, 'Operation Carlota'.

27 Risquet, in Jaime and Barber, *Depoimentos para a História Recente*, p. 344 and Gleijeses, *Conflicting Missions*, p. 317.

28 According to García Márquez ('Operation Carlota'), during the battle at Catengue some FAPLA soldiers had had so little training that their Cuban instructors shouted out instructions to them during brief lulls in the fighting.

29 Quoted in García Márquez, 'Operation Carlota'.

30 Pilots who were normally restricted to seventy flying hours per month ended up doing 200, one pilot flying the entire fifty-hour round trip without a rest.

31 Christopher Stevens, 'The Soviet Union and Angola', *African Affairs*, 229 (April 1976), p. 142.

32 Stockwell, *In Search of Enemies*, p. 22.

33 Gleijeses also notes that between 9 and 24 December the Soviets suspended all weapons deliveries to Angola (*Conflicting Missions*, pp. 333 and 371).

34 The Il-62 can carry over 200 men up to 6,400 miles without refuelling, a significant improvement on the Britannia which could carry at most 100 men for around half of that distance (Blasier and Mesa Lago, *Cuba in the World*, p. 104).

35 Gleijeses, *Conflicting Missions*, pp. 368–9.

36 In the meantime, Cuba had to make do with its ageing Britannias in the face of American efforts to deny them landing rights. When, in late January 1976, Canada withdrew its landing rights, Cuba had no choice but to fly the 3,500 miles from Holguín to Bissau non-stop – an extremely risky option. Once there were sufficient Cubans in Angola, capacity was sacrificed for safety and the Britannias were fitted with four extra petrol tanks, reducing the number of passengers by thirty but enabling the aircraft to fly directly to Sal with sufficient reserves (García Márquez, 'Operation Carlota').

37 Rey, *La Guerra de Angola*, p. 60.

38 My account of the attack is taken from Richard Allport, 'The Battle of Bridge 14', home.wanadoo.nl/rhodesia/bridge14.htm and John, *Operation Savannah*, pp. 31–2. Cuban and Angolan accounts make only muted references to the disaster they suffered.

39 Breytenbach, *Forged in Battle*, p. 142.

40 García Márquez ('Operation Carlota') gives the following account:

> On December 11 at Hengo ... a Cuban armoured car with four commanders on board ventured on to a track where sappers had previously detected a number of mines. Although four vehicles had already passed through safely, the sappers advised the armoured car not to take that particular route, whose only advantage was to save a few minutes when there seemed to be no need for great haste. Hardly had the car started on the track when it was blown up by a mine. Two commanders of the Special Forces battalion were seriously wounded. Raúl Diaz Argüelles ... was killed on the spot.

Concepción (*Por qué somos internacionalistas*, p. 162) claims Argüelles was killed as his armoured car crossed the Calengue river, while Allport ('The Battle of Bridge 14') and Steenkamp (*South Africa's Border War*, p. 54) claim he was killed at Bridge 14.

41 The South Africans claimed that over 400 FAPLA–Cuban soldiers were killed in the fighting, among them Argüelles himself (John, *Operation Savannah*, p. 32). Steenkamp (*South Africa's Border War*, p. 54) further notes: 'the exact number will never be known because the bush was so thick that enemy dead and wounded were being found for days afterwards.' Although South African estimates may be inflated, Risquet's assertion (in Jaime and Barber, *Depoimentos para a História Recente*, p. 345) that Foxbat 'didn't cause us heavy casualties' is not credible.

42 Jannie Geldenhuys, *A General's Story: From an Era of War and Peace* (Johannesburg: Jonathan Ball Publishers, 1995), p. 54.

43 Cuban sources make oblique references to a military setback on 12 December, but are coy with details. García Márquez ('Operation Carlota') describes the battle as 'perhaps the biggest setback of the war' and concludes that an '[a]nalysis of the incident shows it to have been the result of a Cuban error'. Brigadier-General Orlando Almaguel Vidal admits that 'some errors were committed, principally through lack of experience, and Colomé [Furry] criticised us for them' (author's translation from Báez, *Secretos de Generales*, p. 208), but gives no other details. According to the official history of the war (Rey, *La Guerra de Angola*, p. 84), the South Africans penetrated the Cuban line of defence at Catofe, leading to a new line being set up which held them three miles south of the river. Like Risquet (in Jaime and Barber, *Depoimentos para a História Recente*, p. 345), Wolfers and Bergerol (*Angola in the Frontline*, p. 42) and Ortiz (*Un abril como Girón*, p. 58), he gives the impression that the main fighting took place just south of Catofe, when it actually took place on the Nhia river. No mention of Cuban casualties is made in any of these accounts.

44 See Steenkamp (*South Africa's Border War*, pp. 54–5) for details of Orange and X-Ray's frustrating campaign in the Angolan interior.

45 See CWIHP for full text of his letter dated 30 December 1975.

46 Rey, *La Guerra de Angola*, p. 243 and Gleijeses, *Conflicting Missions*, p. 340.

47 Steenkamp, *South Africa's Border War*, p. 59.

48 Battle-Group Bravo became 32 Battalion (the 'Buffalo Battalion') which saw plenty of action during the Angolan War. The Bushman soldiers of Battle-Group Alpha eventually became 201 Battalion which gained an equally fierce reputation in Angola and Namibia.

49 My account of the Northern Front is taken from Rey, *La Guerra de Angola*, pp. 57–63, Ortiz, *Un abril como Girón*, pp. 69–76, Raúl Valdés Vivó, *Angola: Fin del mito de los mercenarios* (Havana: Empresa de Medios de Propaganda, May 1976), author's interview with Roberto, Stockwell, *In Search of Enemies*, pp. 243–6, Peter Tickler, *The Modern Mercenary: Dog of War, or Soldier of Honour?* (London: Guild Publishing, 1987), pp. 62–99 and Gleijeses, *Conflicting Missions*, p. 338.

50 Stockwell, *In Search of Enemies*, p. 215.

51 Rey, *La Guerra de Angola*, p. 61.

52 Operation IAFeature included a mercenary programme, but it met with little success. Despite strenuous efforts and a $2 million budget, only twenty French mercenaries ever reached Angola (two were killed in combat before they were withdrawn) (Stockwell, *In Search of Enemies*, pp. 243–6).

53 Author's interview with Roberto; John Stockwell and unnamed mercenary in 'Cold War'.

54 There is much confusion over the exact sequence of events surrounding Callan's execution of the mercenaries. I have used the most accurate version in Tickler, *The Modern Mercenary*, pp. 76–87, while drawing some details from the more garbled accounts in Ortiz, *Un abril como Girón*, p. 236, Valdés Vivó, *Angola*, p. 84 and by Roberto himself (in interview).

55 The execution of these Cuban prisoners was noted in Fred Bridgland's book *Savimbi: A Key to Africa*, pp. 191–2, but was considered controversial enough to be censored from Cuban accounts. Gleijeses (*Conflicting Missions*, p. 326) suggests that the entire story was disinformation designed to undermine Cuban morale.

56 '*Kwacha*' is Umbundu for 'cockerel' (a reference to the motif on UNITA's flag), and was used by FAPLA and Cuban troops to refer to UNITA guerrillas.

57 They were watched by P.W. Botha, General Viljoen, Magnus Malan (SADF Chief) and Brigadier Roos (who had been Roberto's SADF advisor at Quifangondo).

58 Washington did not formally recognise the PRA until 19 May 1993.

59 On 22 January 1976, the OAU roundly condemned the South African invasion of Angola, but made no mention of Cuba's intervention. On 31 March, the UN Security Council issued its own condemnation of the South African invasion, again without censuring Cuba.

60 Legum and Hodges, *After Angola*, p. 36.

61 On 1 February 1976, President Vorster appeared on television blaming the Americans for reneging on their promises of support (Wolfers and Bergerol, *Angola in the Frontline*, p. 55). He was followed in May by Defence Minister P.W. Botha who claimed that Zulu Force could have captured Luanda in early November but pulled back because the Americans pleaded against such a move (Marcum, *The Angolan Revolution (1962–1976)*, p. 443, n261). P.W. Botha later claimed that the decision to withdraw from Angola was taken once the Americans reneged on their promise to mine Luanda harbour (which would have prevented Cuban reinforcements unloading). When Botha hosted Kissinger at a banquet in South Africa several months later, Kissinger said to him: 'I owe you an apology' (author's interview).

62 Quoted in Steenkamp, *South Africa's Border War*, p. 60.

6 THE FAILED WITHDRAWAL FROM ANGOLA, 1976–81

1 In an interview with Gianni Miná in June 1987, Castro claimed that 'around 130' Cubans had been killed during the 'Second Liberation War' (*Un Encuentro con Fidel* (Havana: Oficina de Publicaciones del Consejo del Estado), 1987, p. 208). American officials estimated that 200 Cubans died in the fighting and nineteen were taken prisoner, sixteen of whom were handed over to UNITA and executed. The remaining three were exchanged for eight SADF prisoners in September 1978 (Gleijeses, *Conflicting Missions*, p. 380). Pamela Falk ('Cuba in Africa', *Foreign Affairs*, 65, 5 (Summer 1987), p. 1083) puts total Cuban casualties at 400, Klinghoffer (*The Angolan War*, p. 134) at over 500, and the SADF as high as 2,000 (cited in Marcum, *The Angolan Revolution (1962–76)*, p. 444, n281). Given that Cuban troops were involved in defensive battles and only suffered one major setback (the 'Battle of Bridge 14'), a figure of 300 killed for the whole 1975/6 campaign may be closer to the mark.

2 Báez, *Secretos de Generales*, p. 209.

3 My account of the fighting in Cabinda is taken from Galo Antonio Carvajal García, *Recuerdos de una campaña: Premio Testimonio 1981* (Havana: Editorial 13 de marzo, 1982) and interviews in Báez, *Secretos de Generales*, pp. 199–201, 210–11 and 459–63.

4 Risquet, in Jaime and Barber, *Depoimentos para a História Recente*, p. 345.

5 For a full account of this incident, see interview with Espinosa in Báez, *Secretos de Generales*, pp. 459–63.

6 Espinosa never served on an internationalist mission again and is currently Commander of the Eastern Army, one of the FAR's most senior positions.

7 The term was Cuban, and referred to the FAR's successful campaign against anti-Castro guerrillas (many of them his former comrades) in the Sierra Escambray between 1959 and 1966.

8 The Cuban LCB training unit based in Funda (Luanda) was reputed to be the toughest in the Cuban army, and by the early 1980s internationalists were

making concerted efforts to avoid a posting there (author's interviews with Cuban veterans, Havana, 1997–2000).

9 Lubango, Jamba, Cuchi and Menongue had the largest Cuban regiments in the ATS, with smaller Cuban outposts at Humpata and Quipungo. By January 1985, Castro admitted the ATS had grown to 30,000 men (Deutchmann, *Changing the History of Africa*, pp. 94–5), and it may have exceeded 45,000 in the final months of the war.

10 When Castro met with Eric Honecker on 3 April 1977, he told him there were 36,000 Cuban troops in Angola (CWIHP).

11 I obtained this figure from a former officer in the FAR who served in southern Angola between 1983 and 1985. Allowing for the overlap of Cubans arriving with those who were about to leave, it is possible that, at some points in the 1980s, there were as many as 100,000 Cubans in Angola (interview with author, Havana, September 1999).

12 Castro emphasised this point in 1987: 'There has been an internal war, but the internal war is fundamentally an activity of the Angolans. Our task is to defend the south of the country to prevent another large-scale foreign invasion' (author's translation from Miná, *Un Encuentro con Fidel*, p. 208).

13 Figure from Klinghoffer, *The Angolan War*, p. 27. Soviet aid to the MPLA from 1960 to March 1975 totalled only $54 million.

14 Domínguez, 'Cuban Foreign Policy', p. 95. Ultimately divisions in the FAPLA were beyond Cuban control, and one of the units they trained – the 8th Infantry Brigade – mutinied in support of Nito Alves in May 1977 (see pp. 129–30).

15 Information on Novo Catengue is taken from Ronnie Kasrils, *Armed and Dangerous: From Undercover Struggle to Freedom* (Johannesburg: Jonathan Ball, 1998), pp. 171–88.

16 Cuba opted to back Joshua Nkomo's ZAPU as it was already receiving Soviet aid, whereas Robert Mugabe's ZANU relied on Chinese support. In February 1976, however, Cuba sent a small contingent of military advisors to Mozambique to start a modest training programme for ZANU (Klinghoffer, *The Angolan War*, p. 136).

17 Following the success of Operation Carlota, in August 1976 Cuba was elected to chair the next NAM Conference, a move which enabled Castro to challenge Yugoslavia's Marshal Tito as the Third World's unofficial spokesman.

18 According to Neto's statement on 24 February 1977, Operation Cobra 77 was to involve an invasion by 1,800 FNLA troops (under American and Zairian officers) and the Zairian army's Ditrala battalion, with air support from F-104 bombers which had been on standby at the American Kitona base since May 1975. The main target was the Cabinda oil fields, but the SADF would also attack along the Cunene border to cut the Benguela railway line and destabilise Angola (Wolfers and Bergerol, *Angola in the Frontline*, p. 218). Neto's revelations about Cobra 77 were never proven.

19 Author's translation from Barbara Walters' interview with Castro printed in *Bohemia*, 1 July 1977.

20 My account of the Nito Alves coup is taken from David Birmingham, 'The Twenty-Seventh of May, An Historical Note on the Abortive 1977 Coup in Angola', *African Affairs*, 77, 308 (July 1978), pp. 554–63, Wolfers and Bergerol, *Angola in the Frontline*, pp. 73–98, Anatolii Mikhailovich Khazanov, *Agostinho Neto* (Moscow: Progress Publishers, 1986), pp. 262–7, Báez, *Secretos de Generales*, pp. 265–7 and author's interview with Paulo Jorge.

21 For a brief biography of Alves, see the preface to his collection of poetry *Memória da longa resistência popular* (Lisbon: Africa Editora, 1976), pp. 9–16.

22 Van Dúnem was head of the 'São Nicolau Group', an elite of MPLA cadres who served time together in the PIDE's harsh São Nicolau prison camp (in southern Angola) and who had their own grievances against the leadership.

23 Writing before the coup, Marcum (*The Angolan Revolution (1962–76)*, p. 442, n246) noted that Alves 'emerged in 1975 as an ambitious spokesman for black as against *mestiço* power and was regarded by some as second only to Neto in influence within the MPLA.'

24 Castro mentioned the Nitistas' approach in his meetings with Honecker one month later. See CWIHP for transcripts.

25 Birmingham, '27th May', p. 555.

26 Alves would be President, Van Dúnem Prime Minister, Monstro Imortal Minister of Defence, and Bakalof FAPLA Chief of Staff.

27 The seven were Saydi Mingas (Minister of Finance), António Garcia Neto (Director of International Cooperation), Comandante N'zaji (DISA Chief), Comandante Dangereux (FAPLA Chief of Staff), Comandante Bula (FAPLA Deputy Chief of Staff), Comandante Eurico (FAPLA General Staff) and Comandante Gato (Director of the Port of Luanda).

28 According to the FNLA (in its fortnightly bulletin 'Folha 8', 26 May 1998), up to 40,000 Angolans were arrested in Sambizanga and over 30,000 killed in the purge which followed the coup, many being buried in mass graves. The MPLA denies these accusations, but on 10 April 1992 it admitted that 'regrettable excesses' had occurred, and promised to set up a commission of enquiry. Following the outbreak of war in November 1992, however, the idea was shelved indefinitely.

29 Van Dúnem and Cita Vales were the first to be captured when they were found hiding in a barn in the Dembos. On 7 July, Alves was arrested by villagers in his home town, allegedly hiding up a tree. Bakalof was the last to be captured on 9 November in the Palanca suburb of Luanda.

30 Jay Mallin, *Cuba in Angola* (Miami: Research Institute for Cuban Studies, University of Miami, 1987), p. 9.

31 Paulo Jorge (in interview) recalled that, in tense negotiations with the Soviets, Neto shouted: 'We didn't fight for independence to submit ourselves to you!' As MPLA President, Neto fought for relations with the Soviets based on reciprocal interests, and despite substantial Soviet aid he refused their repeated requests for bases in Angola.

32 Neto switched from labelling the Nitistas 'ultra-leftists' to 'right-wing imperialists' so as not to implicate the Soviets in the coup. But it is clear from several sources (Paulo Jorge in interview and Klinghoffer, *The Angolan War*, p. 130) that Neto was privately convinced the Soviets had been involved. *Pravda* referred to the Nitistas as 'rightist' when – aside from the racial tone of their politics – they were more pro-Soviet and 'ultra-leftist' than Neto. By the time Khazanov produced his hagiography of Neto in 1986, the Nitista coup was described as 'part of a broad imperialist plot against the young republic', with no mention of Soviet involvement (*Agostinho Neto*, p. 267).

33 For a full account of the intervention in Ethiopia, see Nelson P. Valdés, 'Cuba y la guerra entre Somalia y Etiopía', *Estudios de Asia y Africa*, XIV, 2, Mexico (April–June 1979), pp. 244–66.

34 Domínguez, *To Make the World Safe for Revolution*, pp. 138 and 156.

35 The Cuban contingent in Ethiopia dropped to 11,000 troops by 1982, 8,000 by 1983, and 4,000 by 1984. The last 3,609 were withdrawn from October to November 1989 during 'Operación Solidaridad'.

36 My account of the raid on Cassinga and Chetequera is taken from Steenkamp *South Africa's Border War*, pp. 71–80, Geldenhuys, *A General's Story*,

pp. 90–4), Rey *La Guerra de Angola*, p. 232, Jim Hooper, Anthony Rogers and Ken Guest, *Flashpoint! At the Front Line of Today's Wars* (London: Arms and Armour Press, 1994), pp. 117–18, author's interview with Cuban stationed in Otchinjau during the Cassinga raid (Havana, September 1999) and author's interview with Helmoed-Römer Heitman, Cape Town, November 1998.

37 Reindeer also had a third target – Charlie – which was a series of SWAPO bases ten-to-fifteen miles east of Chetequera. These were attacked by part of the mechanised force which broke off from the main group as it approached Chetequera.

38 The death of so many Cubans at Cassinga has been omitted from Cuban accounts. For example, Rey (*La Guerra de Angola*, p. 232) refers only to Cuban forces rushing to Cassinga to prevent the SADF finishing off the wounded, but makes no mention of casualties. However, one Cuban officer who commanded a gun emplacement at Otchinjau during the attack claimed that at least sixty Cubans were killed in the reckless attack from Tchamutete. Following the Cassinga raid, the FAR set up a commission of enquiry, but its findings were kept secret (author's interview with FAR officer, Havana, September 1999). Hooper (*Flashpoint!*, p. 118) puts 'Known Cuban losses' at sixteen killed and sixty-three wounded, implying that many more were killed.

39 Cuban officer (in interview) who visited the camp after the attack.

40 Heitman (in interview) claims to have seen SADF photos taken during the attack which show all the bodies wearing uniform (none had boots, but this is common in African armies) and no children among them. He suggests that the carnage was caused by the surprise air-strike which caught the camp's inhabitants in the open at the same moment.

41 My account of Shaba II is taken from LeoGrande, *Cuba's Policy in Africa*, p. 27, Mesa Lago and Belkin, *Cuba in Africa*, p. 144, Helen Kitchen (ed.), *Angola, Mozambique and the West* (New York: CSIS, 1987), p. 23 and Crocker, *High Noon in Southern Africa*, p. 54.

42 Nelson P. Valdés, 'Cuba y Angola: Una Política de Solidaridad Internacional', *Estudios de Ásia y África*, XIV, 4 (Mexico, 1979), p. 667.

43 For example, author's interview with FAR historian, Havana, September 1997.

44 The MPLA also agreed to take back tens of thousands of Angolan refugees living in Zaire in exchange for an estimated 250,000 Zairian refugees (most of them Lundas) living in north-eastern Angola.

45 The fate of the Katangese is unclear, but the majority appear to have returned to Zaire where, according to a FAR historian (in interview with author, Havana, September 1997), they were murdered on Mobutu's orders. According to W. Martin James, *A Political History of the Civil War in Angola: 1974–1990* (New Brunswick: Transaction Publishers, 1992), p. 218, in 1987 there were still 1,400 Katangese fighting with the FAPLA in Angola.

46 See www.cubangola.com for full text of UNSCR 435.

47 UNITA had its HQ in Jamba (Cuando Cubango), less than twenty miles north of the border with the Caprivi Strip, and over 350 miles south of the FAPLA's nearest base (Cuito Cuanavale). Its proximity to SADF bases in Caprivi made supplying UNITA easy, and throughout the war dozens of journalists were flown in from Johannesburg for lengthy briefings by Savimbi.

48 Crocker, *High Noon in Southern Africa*, p. 56.

49 Nine years later, in an interview for *Paris Match* (Jean Letarguy, 'Jonas Savimbi: Comment j'ai vaincu les russes d'Angola', 18 March 1988), Savimbi claimed that Neto had attempted a reconciliation with UNITA through the Senegalese president Léopold Senghor, and that to block it the Kremlin ordered Neto's Soviet doctors to ensure he did not recover from his cancer.

50 Little is known about Dos Santos' background. He was the son of a Luanda bricklayer and joined the MPLA in his teens. He saw some action against the Portuguese, and later took a degree in petroleum engineering in Baku (Azerbaijan). After undergoing a telecommunications course, he joined Cabinda's communications unit (his radio van can still be seen in Luanda's castle) and, in September 1974, he was elected to the Politburo. Following independence, Dos Santos held a number of government posts – including Foreign Minister – before rising to prominence in the lead-up to the Alves coup when he chaired the commission into factionalism. He was confirmed as President of the MPLA–PT at the First Extraordinary Party Congress in December 1980.

51 Crocker, *High Noon in Southern Africa*, p. 145.

52 Under the 'Reagan doctrine' the American administration offered covert military assistance to dozens of anti-Communist forces. These included the Mujahideen in Afghanistan (many of them later members of the Taleban and Al-Qaeda), the Contras in Nicaragua, the '*Mano Blanco*' death squads in El Salvador and UNITA in Angola.

53 These included the Belgian Congo (1960), Northern Rhodesia (1964), and Portuguese Angola and Mozambique (1975).

54 My account of Operation Sceptic is taken from Steenkamp, *South Africa's Border War*, pp. 92–3, Geldenhuys, *A General's Story*, pp. 120–4 and Horace Campbell, *The Siege of Cuito Cuanavale* (Uppsala: Scandinavian Institute of African Studies, 1990), p. 14.

55 My account of Operation Protea is taken from Geldenhuys, *A General's Story*, pp. 144–5, Steenkamp, *South Africa's Border War*, pp. 98–9, Campbell, *The Siege of Cuito Cuanavale*, pp. 14–15 and Muatxiânvua, 'Metamorfoses da agressão a Angola'.

56 The area under SADF control stretched from Uia and Mucope (north-west of Xangongo) to Evale and Mupa (north-east of N'Giva).

7 'THE PEOPLE'S WAR'

1 In a speech to returning internationalists on 27 May 1991, Raúl Castro declared that 377,033 Cuban troops had served in Angola, in addition to 'almost 50,000' civilians.

2 García Márquez, 'Operation Carlota'.

3 This figure includes the thousands of Cubans involved in logistics, transport and administration in Cuba itself. Indeed, one would be hard pressed to find a single Cuban whose relative or friend had not served in Angola.

4 The majority of this chapter is based on interviews carried out by the author with Cuban internationalist veterans during research trips to Cuba in 1997, 1999, 2000 and 2002.

5 Previous operations included Algeria (1963–4), Congo (1965), Congo-Brazzaville (1965–7), Guiné (1966–74), Venezuela (1967) and Syria (1973–4).

6 When they reach eighteen, all Cuban males must do three years of military service (*Servicio Militar General*) during which they receive basic training and some specialised skills. They then become part of the 'reserve' until the age of forty-five or fifty, undergoing a two-week refresher course every other year (the length and frequency of this course varies greatly).

7 Initially reservists represented 70 per cent of Cuban troops in Angola (Domínguez, *To Make a World Safe for Revolution*, p. 275), but by 1980 this had dropped to around 10 per cent (author's interview with Lieutenant-Colonel Montpier, President of the Municipal Association of Ex-Combatants, Víbora Parque, Havana, October 1997).

8 Risquet, in Deutchmann, *Changing the History of Africa*, p. 26.

9 One veteran of Cuba's first internationalist mission to Algeria in 1963 commented: 'Nowadays when you say that you have been on an internationalist mission people understand what you mean; there is a history, a tradition. Back then there wasn't any. We were taking a first step; we were launching out in to the unknown' (Gleijeses, *Conflicting Missions*, p. 36).

10 Information on the slave trade in Cuba is taken from a lecture given by Lopes Váldez, an ethnologist from the Cuban Academy of Sciences (summarised on www.batadrums.com).

11 Concepción, *Por qué somos internacionalistas*, p. 115.

12 During a speech in July 1978 Castro claimed that '[w]ithout internationalism the Cuban Revolution wouldn't even exist. To be an internationalist is to pay our debt to humanity'.

13 This section is based on the replies given by two dozen internationalist veterans on why they chose to go to Angola.

14 One Cuban was unable to sleep his first night in Cabinda after the tales he heard on the way over about snakes attacking at night (Carvajal García, *Recuerdos de una campaña*, p. 16). Several veterans said they were disappointed to find that Angola's greatest natural danger was not lions or elephants but the mosquito.

15 Officers – including pilots and weapons specialists – were selected from the FAR's own ranks. Very few declined an internationalist mission as it was not only an honour but also offered the prospect of rapid promotion.

16 During the latter stages of the war, it was not uncommon for internationalists to spend up to thirty-two months in Angola, a situation which caused some resentment.

17 Lieutenant-Colonel Montpier (in interview) said that refusing to serve on an internationalist mission was looked on as being 'very low' ('*muy ínfima*'). García Márquez ('Operation Carlota') notes that several Cubans who refused the call-up for Operation Carlota 'were exposed to all kinds of public scorn and private contempt'.

18 Cuban veterans have consistently noted the lack of *habaneros* in their units. For example, Salvador (in interview with author, Havana, September 1997) noted that when he sailed to Angola in June 1988 on the Soviet ship *Fedor Shaliapin*, only eight of the 1,100 men on board were from Havana (less than 1 per cent). Similarly Héctor (in interview with author, Havana, September 1999) recalled that only four of his 450-man contingent were from Havana (again just under 1 per cent).

19 Havana has five police forces operating on the streets in addition to the *Departamento de Seguridad del Estado* (G-2) – Cuba's secret police – which has many officers patrolling the city centre. With so many police forces in Havana it is not uncommon to see policemen on every street corner. Social tensions in Havana are often at boiling-point, and it is no coincidence that the first riot in the Revolution's history (in August 1994) took place on Havana's sea-front boulevard, the Malecón. In the centre of a sizeable city like Santa Clara (population 175,000), however, a police presence is almost nowhere to be seen.

20 The official ethnic breakdown of Cuba's population is 51 per cent mulatto, 37 per cent white, 11 per cent black and 1 per cent Chinese. Since 1959 the Cuban population (particularly in Havana) has grown markedly darker with the flight of the 'white' community to Miami.

21 From *General del Pino Speaks* (Washington: The Cuban–American National Foundation, 1987), p. 14.

22 Andrés Oppenheimer, *Castro's Final Hour: The Secret Story Behind the*

NOTES

Coming Downfall of Communist Cuba (New York: Touchstone, 1992), pp. 89–90.

23 Secrecy surrounding the missions was rather lax, however. One veteran recalled that even though he kept his destination secret, his family and friends knew where he was going because two of the ships in his convoy – the *Habano* and *Trece de marzo* – were known to be involved in the Angolan operation.

24 Cubans wishing to defect en route had no chance to do so. The most common refuelling stop was Sal, a remote island in Cape Verde over 400 miles from the nearest (African) coast.

25 In an interview in 1985 (reprinted in Deutchmann, *Changing the History of Africa*, p. 96) Castro declared that '[o]ur military cooperation has never been paid for in any country in the world where we have given it'. This contrasts with Díaz-Briquets, *Cuban Internationalism*, p. 137 and Anthony G. Pazzanita, 'The Conflict Resolution Process in Angola', *Journal of Modern African Affairs*, 29, 1 (1991), p. 96 who claim that Cuban soldiers, lieutenants and colonels cost $1,000, $2,000 and $5,000 per day respectively.

26 Castro's interview with Eric Honecker (CWIHP).

27 By 1987, Cuba was providing internationalist aid to nearly thirty countries, but only Libya, Algeria and Iraq were asked to pay for it (Iraq received the aid free after the war with Iran began). All were oil-exporting countries which had benefited from the 1973 OPEC price rise.

28 *Case 1/1989: End of the Cuban Connection* (Havana: José Martí Publishing House, 1989), p. 396.

29 Estimates from Crocker, *High Noon in Southern Africa*, p. 341 and William Ratliff, 'Política Militar Cubana en el África Subsahariana', *Revista Occidental*, 2 (1989), p. 141. Díaz-Briquets (*Cuban Internationalism*, p. 54) notes that a Cuban doctor with eight years' experience cost the Angolan government around $1,000 per month. Cuban doctors received a salary of 350 pesos per month in Cuba (about $450 at official rates), suggesting that the Cuban government pocketed the difference.

30 *Case 1/1989*, p. 396.

31 Typical Cuban units enduring these conditions were at Cangamba (Moxico), Jamba and Tchibemba (Huíla) and Cuchi (Cuando Cubango).

32 One veteran recalled that, during a cholera outbreak in Luanda in 1986, Cuba donated four million antibiotic tablets. At least half of these 'disappeared' from Luanda's docks, only to turn up on the *candonga*.

33 Luanda has two enormous *candongas*: the largest, 'Roque Santeiro' was named after a popular Brazilian soap opera and is located to the north of Luanda along the road to Cacuaco; the other is the humorously-named 'Tira Bikini' ('Take off your bikini').

34 The Cuban spirit of survival and adaptability is encapsulated by the three most commonly used verbs in Havana: '*resolver*', '*inventar*' and '*escapar*'. '*Resolver*' ('to resolve') roughly translates as 'to sort out' or simply 'to find', as in '*resolví unos zapatos para mi hija*' ('I managed to get some shoes for my daughter'). '*Inventar*' is the art of creating a meal for a family while lacking most (or even all) of the ingredients. And '*escapar*' is to 'get by', as in '*me escapo*' ('I get by'), the only way to survive in Cuba.

35 Oppenheimer, *Castro's Final Hour*, p. 79.

36 The main Cuban garrisons along the Namibe–Menongue railway line were at Namibe, Humpata, Lubango, Matala, Dongo, Jamba, Kuvango, Cuchi and Menongue, with smaller units scattered to the north and south.

37 By following in the bulldozer's tracks, other vehicles were unlikely to set off

undiscovered mines. Tanks were wider than bulldozers, however, and occasionally set off mines laid on the edge of the road.

38 The order of the *caravanas* varied enormously, and each may also have contained 0.80 mm and 120 mm guns, BM-21s, bridge-laying vehicles and jeeps.

39 Travelling between Cuatir and Cuito Cuanavale in early 1988, Cuban journalist César Gómez Chacón counted 165 wrecks (*Cuito Cuanavale: viaje al centro de los héroes* (Havana: Editorial Letras Cubanas, 1989), p. 128). The wrecks of thirty-six petrol tankers still litter the road between Longa and Cuito Cuanavale (just east of Masseca). According to FAPLA veterans they were a supply column which was betrayed to UNITA by a local commander (see www.cubangola.com for photographs).

40 Gómez Chacón, *Cuito Cuanavale*, pp. 126–7.

41 Roger Ricardo Luis, *Prepárense a vivir: crónicas de Cuito Cuanavale* (Havana: Editora Política, 1989), p. 107 and García Márquez, 'Operation Carlota'.

42 On 16 March 1968, American troops from the 11th Brigade under Lieutenant William Calley entered the village of My Lai (Quang Ngai province, Vietnam) and massacred over 500 unarmed Vietnamese villagers. When the story broke a year later it caused a scandal in the USA, but in the end only twelve low-ranking officers were brought to trial, and their ring-leader, Lieutenant Calley, served no more than three years under house arrest before he was paroled in 1974.

43 One Angolan veteran who was involved in joint SAD operations claims that the Cubans were strongly opposed to atrocities, and often restrained FAPLA troops who were about to go on the rampage (author's interview with FAPLA veteran, Luanda, May 1998).

44 Author's interview with a former judge who served on a Cuban military tribunal in Angola in 1978.

45 A former FAR judge told me that during a year-long stint in southern Angola in 1985, around fifty offences were brought to trial, an 'insignificant' number considering there were over 20,000 Cuban troops in the region.

46 Many Angolans who were trained by the Cubans still remember them with affection. The most common phrases which cropped up in interview were 'they got on well with everyone', 'they behaved very well towards us' and 'we miss them' ('*sentimos saudades deles*').

47 According to Cuban propaganda Angolans referred to Cubans as *primo* (cousin), acknowledging their shared historical struggle. One FAR officer I interviewed, however, refused to let the Angolans call him *primo*, insisting that they used the term sarcastically and almost as an insult, a view echoed by several other veterans.

48 One veteran recalled finding FAPLA tanks and armoured cars abandoned by their Angolan crews only to discover that they had simply run out of diesel. By the time his unit found them, however, they had been cannibalised by the locals for spare parts and then booby-trapped by UNITA. One group of forty rusting hulks can still be seen ten miles west of Menongue (at Missombo) where they were abandoned by the FAPLA in November 1992. According to locals, the convoy stopped on hearing the war had broken out again, and the troops simply left their vehicles and returned home.

49 Several Cubans (both civilian and military) witnessed these press gangs rounding up Angolan males, a practice one described as 'brutal and savage'. The memory of these round-ups left a deep scar, and until recently there were no public cinemas in Angola (Luanda's *Cine Loanda* was converted into a smart restaurant).

50 Many veterans told stories of FAPLA soldiers defecting to UNITA, betraying

military information and even murdering Cubans (although no specific case has come to my attention). A phrase which frequently cropped up was '*nunca me confía en ellos*' ('I never trusted them').

51 See www.cubangola.com for a study of MK mutinies in Angola in the early 1980s.

52 While in Santa Clara I heard of a Cuban doctor who had brought a young Angolan boy back to Cuba and adopted him as his son. The man was a local hero because he had twice written to Castro asking for permission, suggesting it was a rare occurrence.

53 Information on the *Departamento de Abastecimiento* was given to me by a Cuban who worked there between 1977 and 1984.

54 The *Leonid Sovinov* was a luxury cruise ship which was built in England, bought by the Soviet navy and then handed on to Cuba. It had a swimming pool and a tropical hothouse, and was a popular posting. The ship never docked in an Angolan port, however, and many Cubans' only view of Angola was of its coastline.

55 Soldiers received a salary of seven Cuban pesos (US$7 at the official rate) and 150 kwanzas (*c.*US$1) per month, while senior officers received twenty-four pesos and 3,000 kwanzas per month (plus a better ration of luxuries). Stipends varied during the mission but never exceeded 1,500 kwanzas per month (*c.*$11) for soldiers and 4,000 (nearly $30) for officers.

56 Following the Ochoa scandal in 1989, which revealed the extent of Cuban dealings on the *candonga*, the stipend system was reformed and Cubans were paid their stipends in goods.

57 Domínguez, *To Make a World Safe for Revolution*, p. 275.

58 Figures from Muatxiânvua, 'Metamorfoses da agressão a Angola' and Concepción, *Por qué somos internacionalistas*, p. 17. In Luanda the 'skeleton building' – the shell of a high-rise office block opposite the National Assembly – stands as a symbol of the Portuguese exodus. Its Portuguese owners allegedly poured concrete down the lift shafts so that building work could never be completed.

59 Like the reservists, civilian internationalists were guaranteed their job back once they returned, and their salary was paid to their families while they were abroad. Food and lodging were provided, plus a small stipend – about 1,500 kwanza (around US$30) – to buy small luxuries and extra food.

60 Domínguez, *To Make a World Safe for Revolution*, p. 168. During the Angolan War many Cuban civilians took part in the fighting, among them journalists (e.g. César Gómez Chacón who directed artillery at Cuito Cuanavale), doctors, cameramen, construction workers and even cooks.

61 In his interview with Barbara Walters (*Bohemia*, 1 July 1977) Castro claimed that 'Cuba's role in Africa is principally of a civilian character, and not a military character' (author's translation). By that stage, however, there were at least 36,000 Cuban troops in Angola versus 5,000 civilians (just over 12 per cent). By late 1988 the military contingent had grown to over 65,000 troops while the civilian contingent remained the same, a more accurate measure of Cuban priorities.

62 According to one engineer who was working in Luanda, groups of Cubans were kept in the same building for easier protection. One six-floor building he lived in housed 800 Cuban nurses and teachers (author's interview, Havana, August 1997).

63 Alfredo Fumero Castro and Mariano Mijares Tabares, *Tergiversaciones del imperialismo norteamericano sobre la práctica del internacionalismo proletario de la revolución cubana con Angola* (Havana: Escuela Superior del PCC Ñico López, 1982), p. 55.

64 The first medical teams arrived in Benguela and Cabinda in March 1976.
65 For example, between January and September 1977 (the first year of the programme) Cuban doctors carried out one million consultations and 16,000 operations (Concepción, *Por qué somos internacionalistas*, p. 22).
66 This may be the main reason why, in the 1980s, Cuba had more medical staff working overseas than the WHO.
67 Díaz-Briquets, *Cuban Internationalism*, pp. 56 and 58.
68 In the early 1960s vast citrus fruit plantations were set up on the Isle of Pines, swelling its population from 10,000 to 70,000. From September to December, foreign students studying there were obliged to help with the harvest. Following the collapse of the Soviet bloc in 1989 many of the schools were shut down, and today only a handful of foreign students are still studying there.
69 Jane Franklin, *Cuba–Angola: A Chronology, 1961–1988* (New York: Center for Cuban Studies, 1989).
70 Of the 580 Cuban teachers polled by Félix Manuel Valdés Márquez for his thesis (*Problemática Lingüística y Colaboración Educacional Cubana en Angola* (Havana: Instituto Superior Pedagógico Enrique José Varona, 1983), pp. 43–5), three-quarters knew no Portuguese before arriving in Angola, and one-third of those who did were self-taught. Of the 462 Angolan school children polled, 48 per cent said they understood their Cuban teachers after one month, rising to 88 per cent after two months. By the end of the first year only 1.29 per cent of students could still not understand their teachers.
71 Díaz-Briquets, *Cuban Internationalism*, pp. 75–6.
72 Cuban assistance enabled the sugar industry to produce 40,000 tonnes of sugar for the 1976/77 harvest, an impressive feat only three months after end of the 'Second Liberation War' (Concepción, *Por qué somos internacionalistas*, p. 21). By the late 1980s, however, the sugar and coffee industries had all but collapsed.
73 Concepción, *Por qué somos internacionalistas*, pp. 108–9.
74 Jeremy Harding, *The Fate of Africa, Trial by Fire* (New York: Simon & Schuster, 1993), p. 72, Larteguy, 'Jonas Savimbi' and Duncan, *The Soviet Union and Cuba*, p. 145.
75 According to the Cuban government (*Granma*, 6 December 1989), 39 per cent were killed in combat, 26 per cent died of disease and 35 per cent were killed in accidents.
76 Some veterans put the high incidence of driving accidents down to the youth of the Cuban drivers who had never handled military vehicles of the size the Soviets were providing.
77 One Cuban sapper recalled that, during two years in Angola (including a dozen *caravanas*), nobody in his platoon was killed or wounded, a not untypical story. Figures given to me by Lieutenant-Colonel Montpier from Havana's Víbora Parque municipality show that, out of the 2,752 men who carried out internationalist missions in Angola, only thirty-six died there (or less than 1.5 per cent).
78 The most common ailments were malaria (perhaps 90 per cent of cases), tropical fever, unknown strains of hepatitis, obscure eye and skin diseases, and cirrhosis.
79 In December 1986, the FAR also issued a decree forbidding Cuban soldiers in Angola from having blood transfusions from Africans to avoid the risk of infection.
80 The state-of-the-art HIV treatment centre in Los Cocos (on Boyeros, near the old airport) was opened with great fanfare in the mid-1980s. Following the collapse of Soviet aid to Cuba, it fell into disrepair, and the current conditions are

rumoured to be terrible. Del Pino (*General del Pino Speaks*, p. 34) bluntly described the facility as 'a jail'. The Cuban government is extremely secretive in its handling of AIDS, and though it claims the virus's spread is under control, there is a huge amount of denial for the magnitude of the problem facing ordinary Cubans (whose most common form of contraception is abortion).

8 ABORTIVE PEACE NEGOTIATIONS AND THE PATH TO FULL-SCALE WAR, 1981–5

1 James, *A Political History of the Civil War in Angola*, p. 213. See Appendix 4.
2 James Hamill, *The Challenge to the MPLA: Angola's war: 1980–1986*, Politics Working Papers 41, University of Warwick, 1986, p. 6.
3 The SADF liaison officer – Johann Smith – spent most of the 1980s by Savimbi's side and was adopted by his entourage, spending Christmas 1985 in Jamba with the UNITA leader (author's interview with Johann Smith, Johannesburg, October 1998).
4 See Geldenhuys, *A General's Story*, p. 146 and Hooper, *Flashpoint!*, pp. 124–5 for details of Operations Daisy (November 1981), Super (March 1982) and Meebos (July–August 1982) which destroyed four large SWAPO camps in Cunene.
5 Bridgland, *Jonas Savimbi*, pp. 344–5.
6 Owen Ellison Kahn, *Disengagement from Southwest Africa: the Prospects for Peace in Angola and Namibia* (New Jersey: Transaction Publishers, 1991), p. 100. Under the deal Cuba agreed to send 7,000 reinforcements to Angola.
7 Data on UNITA's 1983 campaign is taken from Hamill, *The Challenge to the MPLA*, pp. 7–10 and Muatxiânvua, 'Metamorfoses da agressão a Angola'.
8 In November a UNITA missile brought down a Boeing 737 as it took off from Lubango, killing all 126 passengers on board (many of whom it claimed were FAPLA soldiers). Three months later, UNITA shot down another Boeing 737 as it took off from Huambo, but its claims that over 100 FAPLA and Cuban soldiers were killed were rejected by the FAPLA which insisted there were no fatalities.
9 My account of the siege of Cangamba is taken from highly contradictory sources: Rey (*La Guerra de Angola*, pp. 116–25), Luis (*Crónicas de Cuito Cuanavale*, pp. 99–101), Steenkamp (*South Africa's Border War*, pp. 109–10) and interviews with UNITA, FAPLA and Cuban soldiers who either fought in the battle or were involved in the relief (see other footnotes for details).
10 One Cuban veteran claimed that the garrison was made up of 156 FAPLA soldiers and their forty-to-sixty Cuban instructors (interview with author, Havana, September 2000). Steenkamp (*South Africa's Border War*, p. 109) claims there were at least 3,000 FAPLA troops in Cangamba, but the combined defending force probably did not exceed 1,000 troops.
11 According to Eduardo António 'Matamata', a UNITA commander at Cangamba, UNITA used six battalions (c.3,000 men) for the attack (interview with author, 30 March 1998, Jamba [Cuando Cubango]). Other sources put the figure much higher, at between 5,000 (Muatxiânvua, 'Metamorfoses da agressão a Angola') and 6,000 (Campbell, *The Siege of Cuito Cuanavale*, p. 16).
12 One Cuban veteran who examined the battlefield after the air attack found hundreds of dismembered body parts, calculating by the number of severed heads that as many as fifty guerrillas had been blown apart by each missile. From the body count, his team calculated that UNITA had used over 3,000 men in its attacks.

13 Most sources put the number of UNITA dead at 1,100, with around the same number wounded. UNITA's figure of sixty-three killed and 250 wounded seems fictitiously low (Crocker, *High Noon in Southern Africa*, p. 175). A more accurate figure was offered by a Cuban veteran who counted UNITA corpses after the battle and concluded that 500–700 UNITA soldiers had been killed.

14 Cuba maintains that only fifty-three FAPLA and Cuban soldiers were killed at Cangamba (Concepción, *Por qué somos internacionalistas*, p. 151), while UNITA claims to have killed 719 FAPLA soldiers and 120 Cubans, and to have captured 328 (Steenkamp, *South Africa's Border War*, p. 110). A Cuban who formed part of the reinforcement column estimates that around twenty Cubans and 100 FAPLA soldiers died, with up to three times that number wounded.

15 Kahn, *Disengagement from Southwest Africa*, p. 73.

16 Steenkamp, *South Africa's Border War*, p. 110.

17 The UN Contact Group – made up of the USA, Britain, West Germany, Canada and France – was formed in the mid-1970s to mediate between SWAPO and South Africa in negotiations over Namibia. Discussions chaired by the Contact Group in early 1978 led to the passing of Resolution 435.

18 Crocker, *High Noon in Southern Africa*, p. 398.

19 Crocker, *High Noon in Southern Africa*, p. 302.

20 See Round Eleven of the final negotiating phase (Chapter 11).

21 Crocker, *High Noon in Southern Africa*, p. 184.

22 The Front-Line States comprised Angola, Botswana, Mozambique, Tanzania, Zambia and Zimbabwe, and were so named because they were in the front-line of the war against apartheid.

23 These included discreet peace overtures to Savimbi (via the Senegalese president Abdou Diouf) and meetings between the Angolan Defence Minister Pedalé and the SADF in Brazzaville in January 1982.

24 See www.cubangola.com for full text of the first 'Joint Statement of Principles'.

25 Vernon 'Dick' Walters was Washington's ambassador-at-large, and often acted as Reagan's presidential emissary (for example, during the Falklands crisis in 1982). Formerly deputy CIA director, he had worked in some capacity for every president since Franklin D. Roosevelt. Frank Wisner was part of Operation IAFeature's team and then Ambassador to Zambia, and was reputed to know southern African politics better than anyone in the State Department.

26 The root of discontent in the MPLA came from two new factions, the black nationalist 'Catete group' and the Marxist 'internationalists' who were unhappy that Dos Santos was negotiating with UNITA and the Americans (Crocker, *High Noon in Southern Africa*, p. 157).

27 Kito was Angolan Minister of Interior, and often acted as unofficial presidential stand-in when Dos Santos was abroad.

28 Steenkamp, *South Africa's Border War*, pp. 112–13.

29 Ironically, the departure of France (and, shortly afterwards, Canada) was not viewed by Crocker as a negative turn of events. In his view this 'left a compatible rump of three like-minded allies who held *ad hoc* encounters whenever there was a need', and whose behind-the-scenes diplomacy during crucial moments in the negotiations proved invaluable (Crocker, *South Africa's Border War*, p. 178).

30 Operation Phoenix (13 February–13 April 1983) was intended to disrupt the infiltration of 1,700 SWAPO guerrillas into Namibia. After two months of fighting, 309 guerrillas had been killed for the loss of twenty-seven South Africans (Geldenhuys, *A General's Story*, p. 147).

31 My account of Operation Askari is taken from conflicting sources: Steenkamp, *South Africa's Border War*, pp. 112–18, Geldenhuys, *A General's Story*,

pp. 154–7, Colonel C.J. Nöthling, 'Military Chronicle of South West Africa (1915–1988)', http://home.wanadoo.nl/rhodesia/swatf.htm, Campbell, *The Siege of Cuito Cuanavale*, pp. 16–19, Robert Jaster, *The 1988 Peace Accords and the Future of South-Western Africa* (London: Brassey's, 1990), p. 14 and interviews with Cuban veterans (Havana, September 1999).

32 According to South African sources, G-5s were not used in Angola until August 1987.
33 Crocker, *High Noon in Southern Africa*, p. 171 and Jaster, *The 1988 Peace Accords*, p. 14.
34 Geldenhuys, *A General's Story*, p. 155.
35 Geldenhuys (*A General's Story*, p. 158) recalls that, because the Angolans refused to believe that the SADF had withdrawn, 'we actually had to send troops back into Angola so that we could withdraw them in terms of the agreement!'.
36 Crocker, *High Noon in Southern Africa*, p. 191.
37 See www.cubangola.com for an outline of the nine points of the 'Mulungushi Minute' (named after the conference centre in which the talks were held) and the six points of the Lusaka Accord.
38 Crocker, *High Noon in Southern Africa*, p. 195.
39 Jaster, *The 1988 Peace Accords*, p. 14 and Campbell, *The Siege of Cuito Cuanavale*, p. 23.
40 The Lusaka Accord was followed one month later by the Nkomati Accord between Mozambique and South Africa which raised the prospect of détente between Pretoria and its African neighbours.
41 See www.cubangola.com for the full text of the 'Second Joint Statement of Principles'.
42 Steenkamp, *South Africa's Border War*, p. 119.
43 In November 1983 and in February 1984, UNITA shot down two Boeing 737s – allegedly killing over 200 FAPLA and Cuban troops.
44 Hamill, *The Challenge to the MPLA*, pp. 10 and 15.
45 My account of the Sumbe raid is based on official Cuban accounts in Rey, *La Guerra de Angola*, pp. 126–32 and Concepción, *Por qué somos internacionalistas*, pp. 166–86.
46 There were 230 Cuban internationalists in Sumbe at the time (including forty-three women), 206 of whom fought on 25 March. Most belonged either to UNECA (the Cuban construction company) or to the Health and Education missions.
47 On 19 April 1984, a white Ford Cortina packed with over 300 kg of TNT exploded outside the entrance of the eleven-story building housing 198 Cuban internationalists. The bomb was timed to explode as the Cubans were returning from work, and fourteen Cubans and ten Angolans were killed with hundreds injured. South African claims that nearly 200 people died in the explosion, including forty Cubans and three Soviet officers, are unsubstantiated.
48 In June, UNITA attacked a troop train on the Benguela railway line, killing over 130 FAPLA troops. In July, UNITA attacked the Gulf Oil complex in Cabinda, blowing up a pipeline and killing twenty-four Angolans (Hamill, *The Challenge to the MPLA*, p. 16).
49 Crocker, *High Noon in Southern Africa*, p. 203.
50 At a meeting of the Contact Group in June 1983 Crocker had rashly predicted he would have Angola's first bid within a fortnight (Crocker, *High Noon in Southern Africa*, p. 166). The bid finally came fifteen months later.
51 These were the implementation of Resolution 435, an SADF–SWAPO cease-fire, the SADF's complete withdrawal from Angola and an end to South African support for UNITA.

52 Crocker, *High Noon in Southern Africa*, p. 212.
53 Details of the 'basis for negotiation' are taken from Crocker, *High Noon in Southern Africa*, p. 228.
54 Possibly in reply to the American proposal, three days later UNITA set off a bomb outside the Almirante Hotel in Huambo, killing seventy-five soldiers, among them eleven Cubans, several high-ranking FAPLA officers and several Bulgarians (Rafael Fermoselle, *The Evolution of the Cuban Military: 1492–1986* (Miami: Ediciones Universal, 1987), p. 421). Cuban sources make no reference to this bomb.
55 My account of the commando raid on Cabinda is taken from Soule, Dixon and Richards, *The Wynand du Toit story* (Johannesburg: Hans Strydom Publishers, 1987), Kitchen, *Angola, Mozambique and the West*, p. 48 and Campbell, *The Siege of Cuito Cuanavale*, p. 19.
56 Captain du Toit admitted to having taken part in three previous raids, destroying the Giraul bridge (Namibe, 1980), damaging Luanda's oil refinery (1982) and sinking two ships in Luanda harbour (1984). His unit was also responsible for an attack on the ANC's offices in Maputo in 1983. Captain du Toit was eventually released as part of a prisoner exchange on 7 September 1987.
57 South African Special Forces operated deep within Angola for most of the war and very few were detected. In Johannesburg, I met an SADF veteran who spent two years in the mid-1980s as part of a clandestine observation team on the outskirts of Luanda, reporting on troop movements and the arrival of military equipment. Throughout the war his unit was never detected.
58 In a further irony, some of the $20 million Luanda annually paid Cuba for its civilian internationalists came from royalties paid by Gulf Oil which inadvertently became one of the Cuban mission's principal sponsors.
59 The day after the Clark Amendment was repealed, the Senate voted 80–12 to impose economic sanctions on South Africa, shattering Washington's alliance with Pretoria.

9 THE BIG OFFENSIVES, 1985–7

1 My account of Congresso II is taken from Steenkamp, *South Africa's Border War*, pp. 133–6, Helmoed-Römer Heitman, *War in Angola: The Final South African Phase* (Gibraltar: Ashanti Publishing, 1990), pp. 13–15, Rey, *La Guerra de Angola*, pp. 133–4, Hooper, *Flashpoint!*, pp. 45–6, Kahn, *Disengagement from Southwest Africa*, pp. 90 and 97, Campbell, *The Siege of Cuito Cuanavale*, pp. 19–20 and author's interviews with Angolan veterans (Menongue and Cuito Cuanavale, March 1998).
2 One FAPLA commander who took part in the offensive (Major Mateus Timóteo in interview with author, Cuito Cuanavale, March 1998) admitted that FAPLA losses were so heavy that the bulk of the force never returned.
3 Figure from Heitman, *War in Angola*, p. 15.
4 The SADF suffered one fatality during the operation, medical orderly Lance-Corporal Hans Fidler who was killed on the Cazombo front.
5 Geldenhuys, *A General's Story*, p. 190 and Steenkamp, *South Africa's Border War*, pp. 142–3.
6 Three years later, Castro insisted that his commanders had opposed the Soviet plans, and that as a result there were 'no such offensives in 1986' (in Deutchmann, *Changing the History of Africa*, p. 107). Castro's claim is contradicted by a wealth of evidence, however (see pp. 197–99).
7 My account of the 1986 offensive is taken from Heitman, *War in Angola*,

pp. 15–18, Steenkamp, *South Africa's Border War*, pp. 142–4 and author's interview with FAPLA Major Timóteo.

8 Between 1986 and 1991, UNITA received between $15m and $30m of American military aid per year, scarcely 1 per cent of what the FAPLA received from the Soviets (Kahn, *Disengagement from Southwest Africa*, p. 155 and Steenkamp, *South Africa's Border War*, p. 139).

9 Author's interview with Timóteo.

10 See www.cubangola.com for an account of the many attempts to destroy and repair the Cuito river bridge during the war. When I visited Cuito Cuanavale in March 1998 little more than one-third of the bridge's eastern section was still standing.

11 Castro's first gaffe came at the 3rd Party Congress in February when he declared that only now would the party begin constructing socialism in Cuba, leaving many baffled as to what they had been doing for the previous twenty-five years.

12 Del Pino, *General del Pino Speaks*, p. 65.

13 Kasrils had been liaising with the FAPLA for two years, and obtained his information from ANC sympathisers in the SADF after it started planning joint operations with UNITA in April (*Armed and Dangerous*, pp. 268 and 278).

14 According to Cuban accounts (e.g. Rey, *La Guerra de Angola*, pp. 219–20 and Risquet in Deutchmann, *Changing the History of Africa*, p. 30), the Cubans opposed the Soviet plan and stopped their troops from playing any part in the offensive. Castro later claimed that Cuban warnings of a South African intervention 'were not heeded sufficiently in 1987 and [that] events unfolded just as we expected' (in Deutchmann, ibid., p. 107). However, a wealth of evidence suggests that Cubans played a prominent role in the offensive (see pp. 206–10).

15 Heitman, *War in Angola*, p. 31.

16 Rafael del Pino joined the Revolutionary Air Force prior to 1961 and shot down two enemy aircraft during the Bay of Pigs invasion. Following training as a MiG pilot in the Soviet Union, he served two years on an internationalist mission in Angola before returning to Cuba in mid-1976 to take up his post in the DAAFAR.

17 The full text of the interview Del Pino gave to Radio Martí is published by the Cuban–American National Foundation (CANF) in a pamphlet entitled *General del Pino Speaks: an Insight into Elite Corruption and Military Dissension in Castro's Cuba* (Washington, 1987).

18 See Del Pino (pp. 6, 13, 15 and 18) for allegations against MMCA's Commander Colonel Tomás Benítez Martínez, and for claims that high-ranking Cuban officers forged the service records of a faulty An-26 which Del Pino's son force-landed in Zaire.

19 Del Pino alleged that Luís Orlando Domínguez used 'Micro-Brigade' (MICON) gangs to build his luxury mansion in Guanabo (Habana del Este). Domínguez was subsequently imprisoned.

20 Crocker, *High Noon in Southern Africa*, pp. 348–51 and Geldenhuys, *A General's Story*, p. 205.

21 It is not coincidental that Castro made the request the day after his annual 'Moncada Speech' (on 26 July), as major policy decisions are often made prior to this speech every year.

22 The FAPLA's 8th Brigade was in charge of protecting the *caravanas* from Menongue, 13 Brigade defended Cuito Cuanavale itself, 25 Brigade protected the Tumpo logistic base (three miles to the east) and ferried supplies to the front-lines, and 66 Brigade guarded the bridges over the Chambinga river once the offensive had moved off (Heitman, *War in Angola*, p. 34).

23 Due to unexpected extensions, Operation Moduler became Operation Hooper on 13 December, Operation Packer on 12 March 1988 and Operation Displace (to cover the withdrawal) on 30 April 1988.

24 Following Operation Savannah, the SADF developed weaponry to respond to the BM-21, producing the 127 mm MRL and 122 mm G-5 gun. The MRL fires twenty-four rockets up to fourteen miles at a rate of one per second, while the G-5 fires up to three rounds per minute to a maximum range of twenty-five miles. Both weapons saw plenty of action during Operations Moduler and Hooper, as did the modified G-6 (a self-propelled version of the G-5) which joined 32 Battalion in Mavinga on 30 October 1987.

25 Operation Moduler had the initial operational limit of the Chambinga river (fifteen miles east of Cuito Cuanavale), but this was extended continually during the year-long operation.

26 Uys, *Bushman Soldiers*, p. 173.

27 My account of the battle of the Lomba river is based on Heitman, *War in Angola*, pp. 40–79, Allport, *The Battle of Cuito Cuanavale: Cuba's Mythical Victory*, http://home.wanadoo.nl/rhodesia/cuito.htm, Geldenhuys, *A General's Story*, pp. 213–16, Hooper, *Flashpoint!*, pp. 47–8, Nöthling, *Military Chronicle of South West Africa* and author's interview with Major Timóteo.

28 Bravo sustained only two wounded in the fighting. According to Geldenhuys (*A General's Story*, p. 214), during the fighting Cuban MiGs deployed chemical weapons, and subsequently many UNITA troops needed treatment for respiratory illnesses. These allegations have been denied by the Cubans.

29 My account of the destruction of 47 Brigade is taken from Heitman, *War in Angola*, pp. 74–8, Nöthling, *Military Chronicle of South West Africa* and author's interviews with Johan Lehman (Pretoria, October 1998) and author's interview with surviving veterans of 47 Brigade (Cuito Cuanavale, March 1998).

30 Johan Lehman (who visited the battlefield the next morning) reckoned that two thirds of the troops in 47 Brigade – i.e. roughly 600 men – were killed in the fighting, and recounted having to step over piles of bodies by the river (interview with author).

31 FAPLA losses included eighteen T-54/55s, twenty-six armoured vehicles, four SAM-8 launchers, four BM-21s and eighty-five trucks. Of that number, twelve tanks, twelve armoured cars, one SAM-8, two BM-21s and forty-five trucks were captured intact and handed over to UNITA. Crocker (*High Noon in Southern Africa*, p. 360) later noted that, as a result of the Lomba river battle 'the Soviet Union had become the largest external source of arms to UNITA and South Africa'.

32 Two SADF officers – Johan Lehman and Piet van Ziel – were entrusted with recovering the SAM-8 and returned to the Lomba at first light on 4 October. Two SAM-8 vehicles were found stuck in the mud and both were towed away using an abandoned T-55. By the afternoon the area was under artillery and aerial bombardment, but they nevertheless went back four times to salvage supplies. The SAM-8 was hidden inside a camouflaged trailer for two days, and then driven to the SADF's HQ half-an-hour south of Mavinga where it remained for two weeks while UNITA and the SADF wrangled over its fate. The Americans were keen to get hold of the SAM-8 as the others captured from 47 Brigade had been severely damaged and were of little use. But the South Africans refused and the SAM-8 was flown to South Africa, its subsequent fate remaining unknown (author's interview with Johan Lehman).

33 Kahn, *Disengagement from Southwest Africa*, p. 78 and Crocker, *High Noon in Southern Africa*, p. 346.

34 Helmoed-Römer Heitman, 'Operations Moduler and Hooper (1987–1988)', *South African Defence Force Review*, 1989.
35 Juan Bautista Benítez Suárez, *Equinoccio de los héroes* (Las Tunas: Editorial Sanlope, 1993), p. 11.
36 Ironically the day Castro launched the new intervention, American and Soviet delegations met for talks in Geneva, Crocker noting that the Soviets were 'humiliated, trapped, and at odds with themselves' after the disaster at the Lomba (Crocker, *High Noon in Southern Africa*, p. 361).
37 The code-name '31st Anniversary Manoeuvre' referred to the foundation of the FAR in 1956.
38 Benítez Suárez, *Equinoccio de los héroes*, pp. 11–12.
39 Throughout the 1970s, Cuito Cuanavale was a backwater, with only 16 Brigade defending the town and 36 Brigade in support at Longa. With the rise in UNITA activity in 1982/3, the town's defences were bolstered, and a contingent of three Cuban and four Soviet advisors were posted there to oversee operations. Cuba's 70th Brigade guarded the airbase at Menongue, but did not get involved in the fighting until the 1987 offensive (Timóteo in interview).

10 THE BATTLE OF CUITO CUANAVALE, NOVEMBER 1987–MARCH 1988

1 During the attack Combat Group Bravo managed to advance only 800 yards in nearly four hours of fighting (Heitman, *War in Angola*, p. 166).
2 Heitman, *War in Angola*, pp. 177 and 183 and Gómez Chacón, *Cuito Cuanavale*, p. 112.
3 By this stage Operation Moduler had become Operation Hooper after the bulk of 20 Brigade's troops completed their military service and were replaced with troops from 4 SAI and 61 Mech.
4 *Case 1/1989*, p. 393.
5 Ochoa joined Castro's guerrillas at the age of eighteen and rose through the ranks, fighting in the Revolutionary War, the Bay of Pigs and the LCB. He served on internationalist missions in Venezuela (1965), Congo-Brazzaville (1967), Sierra Leone (1972), Syria (1973), Angola (1975–6), Ethiopia (1977–8) and Nicaragua (1983–6), and in 1984 was made a Hero of the Cuban Republic, Cuba's highest decoration. Ochoa was a member of the Central Committee and served as Deputy Defence Minister and Vice-Minister of Overseas Missions.
6 Polo served as Chief of the Southern Front (later ATS) during Operation Carlota, representing Cuba at the ceasefire signed with the South Africans on 27 March 1976. He was a tank commander in Ethiopia in 1978, and was appointed Chief of the ATS in late 1987.
7 My account of the reinforcement of Cuito Cuanavale is taken from Gómez Chacón, *Cuito Cuanavale*, pp. 75, 94, 108–16, Rey, *La Guerra de Angola*, pp. 148–9 and Luis, *Prepárense a vivir*, p. 6.
8 Lieutenant-Colonel López had served in Angola during Operation Carlota and in 1978 was Chief of the BM-21 regiment in Ethiopia.
9 Figures from Heitman, *War in Angola*, p. 159.
10 After the attack Cuban engineers rigged up a walkway with rope and wooden planks for soldiers to cross (Luis, *Prepárense a vivir*, p. 48).
11 Heitman, *War in Angola*, p. 296.
12 *Case 1/1989*, p. 383.
13 My account of the attack of 13 January 1988 is taken from Heitman, *War in Angola*, pp. 206–10, Rey, *La Guerra de Angola*, p. 150 and author's interviews with veterans of 21 Brigade (Menongue, March 1998).

14 Heitman (*War in Angola*, p. 210) recounts that one South African saw thirty naked FAPLA troops emerge from the bush (they had read a UNITA leaflet telling them to take off their uniforms to surrender), before scuttling back when the fighting got closer.
15 Gómez Chacón, *Cuito Cuanavale*, p. 126 and Rey, *La Guerra de Angola*, p. 151.
16 *Case 1/1989*, p. 385.
17 Heitman, *War in Angola*, p. 217.
18 The talks did little more than establish that total Cuban withdrawal was on the agenda, however, and Crocker cut them short to prevent being drawn into a discussion on American aid to UNITA (Crocker, *High Noon in Southern Africa*, pp. 374–5).
19 *Case 1/1989*, pp. 385–6.
20 My account of the attack of 14 February is taken from Heitman, *War in Angola*, pp. 227–35, Rey, *La Guerra de Angola*, pp. 150–1, Gómez Chacón, *Cuito Cuanavale*, pp. 83 and 100–2, Luis, *Prepárense a vivr*, pp. 33–7 and *Case 1/1989*, p. 386.
21 Cuban troops fought in the defence of the brigade's Forward Command Post, fighting off UNITA from their trenches for over an hour before being overwhelmed by mortars. See interview with Lieutenant Benito Tena Macías in Gómez Chacón, *Cuito Cuanavale*, pp. 95–9, for a description of his nail-biting escape.
22 Luis, *Prepárense a vivir*, p. 33 and *Case 1/1989*, p. 386.
23 'Ciro' recounted being asked by one of the wounded for a knife 'to cut off something which was in the way: his left arm which was still hanging by a piece of skin from his shoulder'. When they had been loaded onto his tank it set off in the wrong direction, doubling back under artillery fire and braving a FAPLA minefield before it reached 16 Brigade's positions (author's translation from Luis, *Prepárense a vivir*, pp. 35–7 and Gómez Chacón, *Cuito Cuanavale*, p. 102).
24 Heitman, *War in Angola*, p. 235 versus Gómez Chacón, *Cuito Cuanavale*, p. 101.
25 *Case 1/1989*, p. 386.
26 Marina Rey Cabrera (ed.), *La Guerra de Angola* (Havana: Editora Politica, 1989).
27 Ibid., pp. 149–50.
28 For example, Chapter 14 describes the 'violent and agonising attacks' of 14/15 February (author's translation from Rey, *La Guerra de Angola*, p. 168).
29 *Case 1/1989*, pp. 386 and 388.
30 My account of the attack of 19 February is taken from Heitman, *War in Angola*, pp. 242–3 and Rey, *La Guerra de Angola*, pp. 151–2.
31 My account of the attack of 25 February is taken from Rey, *La Guerra de Angola*, pp. 152–3, Gómez Chacón, *Cuito Cuanavale*, pp. 84–9 and Heitman, *War in Angola*, pp. 245–53.
32 The text of the cable is reproduced in Gómez Chacón, *Cuito Cuanavale*, p. 91.
33 In recognition of this error, for the attack on 29 February the approaches were not marked until only a few hours before it was launched.
34 My account of the fourth South African attack is taken from Heitman, *War in Angola*, pp. 253–62, Gómez Chacón, *Cuito Cuanavale*, pp. 92–4 and Rey, *La Guerra de Angola*, p. 153.
35 The Cuban MiGs had a disastrous morning, first accidentally bombing several FAPLA 23 mm gun positions, and then losing a MiG either to UNITA Stingers or possibly their own SAMs.
36 Commandant Muller in Heitman, *War in Angola*, p. 261.
37 Gómez Chacón, *Cuito Cuanavale*, pp. 129 and 172.

38 My account of the American-brokered talks in March 1988 is taken from Crocker, *High Noon in Southern Africa*, pp. 377–85 and Geldenhuys, *A General's Story*, pp. 226–7.

39 The interventions in Algeria, Congo and Venezuela were not publicly revealed until the late 1970s, while the intervention in Ethiopia was not announced until 14 March 1978, ten days after Cuban forces fought their final clashes with the Somalis. Similarly, Castro chose to announce that Cuban troops were in Angola on 22 December 1975, seven weeks after the first reinforcements were sent (and over four months after the first instructors arrived in Angola).

40 Heitman, *War in Angola*, pp. 264–6 and 274.

41 Cuban engineers partly repaired the crossing, installing a suspension footbridge over which troops could cross. Heavy supplies, tanks and trucks were brought across by PTS ferry, two of which were destroyed on 18 March by G-5s.

42 My account of the final South African assault is taken from Heitman, *War in Angola*, pp. 267–80 and interview, Luis, *Prepárense a vivir*, pp. 136–41, Gómez Chacón, *Cuito Cuanavale*, pp. 67–70, Benítez Suárez, *Equinoccio de los héroes*, pp. 47–8 and Rey, *La Guerra de Angola*, p. 154.

43 Heitman, *War in Angola*, p. 279.

44 See Rey, *La Guerra de Angola*, p. 196, Gómez Chacón, *Cuito Cuanavale*, p. 68 and Benitez Suarez, *Equinoccio de los héroes*, p. 48 for details of these allegations.

45 Although Cuban accounts claim that the South Africans suffered heavy casualties, 82 Brigade's only losses were the three Olifants and several armoured cars and tanks damaged (Geldenhuys, *A General's Story*, p. 222).

46 Combat Group 20 comprised one anti-tank squadron, C Company of SWATF (motorised infantry), Quebec Battery (G-5s), two engineer troops and (after 26 May) one MRL battery. See Heitman, *War in Angola*, pp. 281–94 for details of Operation Displace.

47 See www.cubangola.com for a map of the minefields in this area.

48 Following the journalists' visit, the Olifant was brought across the Cuito river and placed in the Cuban Command Post as a war trophy (Gómez Chacón, *Cuito Cuanavale*, pp. 57–9). Photos of the Olifant – the only South African tank captured during the Angolan War – appear in all Cuban accounts.

49 For examples, see Crocker, *High Noon in Southern Africa*, pp. 367–71, Geldenhuys, *A General's Story*, pp. 208 and 224–31 and Heitman, *War in Angola*, p. 285.

11 THE FIGHTING IN SOUTH-WEST ANGOLA AND THE NEGOTIATING END-GAME, MARCH–DECEMBER 1988

1 Luis, *Prepárense a vivir*, p. 13.

2 *Case 1/1989*, p. 389.

3 *Case 1/1989*, pp. 92, 97 and 103.

4 Rey, *La Guerra de Angola*, pp. 199–200.

5 Kahn, *Disengagement from Southwest Africa*, p. 84.

6 My account of the ambush is taken from Uys, *Bushman Soldiers*, pp. 187–9, Geldenhuys, *A General's Story*, p. 238 and Heitman, *War in Angola*, p. 298.

7 My account of the Cuban ambush on 4 May is taken from Rey, *La Guerra de Angola*, pp. 178–89 and 234, Uys, *Bushman Soldiers*, pp. 190–3 and Geldenhuys, *A General's Story*, p. 242.

8 The delegations were: Cuba – Jorge Risquet (chief), Carlos Aldana Escalante

(political representative) and General Úlises Rosales del Toro (military representative); South Africa – Neil van Heerden (Foreign Affairs), Dr Neil Barnard (National Intelligence Agency), General Jannie Geldenhuys (military representative) and Derek Auret (Foreign Affairs); Angola – Afonso van Dúnem (Minister of Foreign Affairs) and N'dalu (Deputy Minister of Defence). Crocker chaired the tripartite meetings, while Adamishin, the unofficial Soviet representative, advised from the wings.

9 Crocker, *High Noon in Southern Africa*, p. 393.
10 See Geldenhuys, *A General's Story*, pp. 3–4 for his account of their stormy encounter.
11 Heitman, *War in Angola*, p. 297 and Báez, *Secretos de Generales*, p. 43.
12 Geldenhuys, *A General's Story*, p. 244.
13 My account of the bungled ambush is taken from Rey, *La Guerra de Angola*, pp. 180–1, Heitman, *War in Angola*, pp. 300–1, Geldenhuys, *A General's Story*, pp. 244–5 and Uys, *Bushman Soldiers*, p. 194.
14 *Case 1/1989*, pp. 390–1 and Rey, *La Guerra de Angola*, p. 181.
15 See Uys, *Bushman Soldiers*, pp. 196–7 and Rey, *La Guerra de Angola*, pp. 181–2 for conflicting accounts of this clash twelve miles south-east of Tchipa.
16 Uys, *Bushman Soldiers*, p. 197, Heitman, *War in Angola*, p. 303 and Rey, *La Guerra de Angola*, p. 182.
17 Crocker, *High Noon in Southern Africa*, p. 394.
18 Crocker, *High Noon in Southern Africa*, pp. 413 and 428.
19 My account of the final clash on 27 June is taken from Heitman, *War in Angola*, pp. 303–5 and interview, Rey, *War in Angola*, pp. 182–3, Geldenhuys, *A General's Story*, pp. 247–8, Benítez Suárez, *Equinoccio de los héroes*, pp. 15–16, Uys, *Bushman Soldiers*, p. 198 and *Case 1/1989*, p. 391.
20 See *Case 1/1989*, p. 391 for text of Castro's dispatch to Ochoa and Polo.
21 My account of the air-strike on Calueque is taken from Benítez Suárez, *Equinoccio de los héroes*, pp. 16–18, Heitman, *War in Angola*, pp. 306–7, Rey, *La Guerra de Angola*, pp. 184–6, Geldenhuys, *A General's Story*, pp. 248–9 and Crowther, Heitman and Timóteo (all in interview).
22 Cuban accounts make no mention of casualties, but Crocker (*High Noon in Southern Africa*, p. 372) records that the Cubans admitted to him that ten Cubans had been killed. Heitman (*War in Angola*, p. 305) and Geldenhuys (*A General's Story*, p. 248) estimate 302 FAPLA–Cuban fatalities based on intercepts of FAPLA signals.
23 Cuban troops who occupied Calueque one week later vividly described the carnage of the MiG-23 strike. One reported that 'pieces of flesh and bomb fragments were still hanging from the tangled wreckage caused by the explosions; the enormous engines of the sluice-gates had been thrown about like toys and there were blood, shreds of clothing, wrecked equipment and supplies all over the place' (author's translation from Benítez Suárez, *Equinoccio de los héroes*, pp. 17–18).
24 10 Division comprised three mechanised battalion groups, one tank regiment, three armoured car squadrons and an artillery brigade (Heitman, *War in Angola*, p. 308).
25 See, for example, Rey, *La Guerra de Angola*, p. 184 and Benítez Suárez, *Equinoccio de los héroes*, p. 18.
26 *Case 1/1989*, pp. 391–2.
27 My account of the final phase in the negotiations is taken from Crocker, *High Noon in Southern Africa*, pp. 392–446, Jaster, *The 1988 Peace Accords*, pp. 23–8 and Benítez Suárez, *Equinoccio de los héroes*, p. 18.
28 So important did Crocker consider Cuban involvement in this final round that

he later commented that '[w]e might still be at the table today were it not for the Cuban factor'.

29 See www.cubangola.com for full text and summary of the New York Principles.
30 Crocker, *High Noon in Southern Africa*, p. 394.
31 Crocker later quantified the Soviets' contribution to the negotiations as not opposing them, associating themselves with them, and clearing up misunderstandings between the Americans and Angolans (*High Noon in Southern Africa*, p. 423).
32 The seven-point South African proposal is summarised in Crocker, *High Noon in Southern Africa*, p. 432.
33 See www.cubangola.com for full text and summary of the Geneva Protocol.
34 As examples, Crocker lists the starting point, the duration of the withdrawal, the degree of front- or back-loading, the pace of the withdrawals, which benchmarks would be used to link it to the Namibia process, who and what exactly would be withdrawn, and what verification regime would be adopted (*High Noon in Southern Africa*, p. 434).
35 See *Case 1/1989*, p. 392 for text of Castro's cable to Ochoa and Polo.
36 Jaster (*The 1988 Peace Accords*, p. 27) notes that, in October, the National Party won municipal elections it had been expecting to lose, increasing Pretoria's room for compromise. Conversely, recent FAPLA victories against UNITA (which the SADF had not stepped in to take away) boosted Angolan confidence, and made it more likely to compromise on the withdrawal timetable.
37 Crocker (*High Noon in Southern Africa*, p. 441) recalled that Jim Woods achieved the breakthrough by making complex charts and graphs for both delegations which showed that the differences between them were arithmetical rather than over principles.
38 The number of Cuban troops was taken to be 50,000, although all sides were aware that there might have been substantially more in Angola. Ultimately, the redeployment of these forces northwards and the specific benchmarks for their withdrawal enabled Crocker to side-step this issue.
39 Crocker, *High Noon in Southern Africa*, p. 394.
40 See www.cubangola.com for full text and summary of the Brazzaville Protocol.
41 My account of the signing is taken from Félix Pita Astudillo, 'Olive Green Thursday at the UN', *Granma*, 26 December 1988 and Crocker, *High Noon in Southern Africa*, p. 446.
42 The Cuban delegation included Carlos Aldana (Chief of DOR), Jorge Risquet, Isidoro Malmierca (Foreign Minister), Ricardo Alarcón (Vice Foreign Minister), Divisional-General Rosales del Toro and Furry, Divisional-General Pascual Martínez Gil (Vice Foreign Minister of MININT), Divisional-General Ramón Espinosa Martín (Chief of the Eastern Army), Divisional-General Víctor Schueg Colás, Brigadier-General Rafael Moracén Limonta, Brigadier-General Bermúdez Cutiño and Brigadier-General Rubén Martínez Fuentes (Chief of DAAFAR). Ochoa and Polo were notable absentees, remaining at their posts in Angola.
43 See www.cubangola.com for full text and summary of the New York Peace Accords. The USA did not sign the New York Accords – hence their qualification as 'tripartite' – and acted instead as their broker. This stance allowed the Reagan administration to bypass the Senate (which might have buried the treaty in ratification debates) and protected the negotiations from overt Soviet pressure (Crocker, *High Noon in Southern Africa*, p. 395).

12 THE STING IN THE TAIL

1 On 30 December 1988, Castro also promoted twelve officers to the rank of general in recognition of their internationalist services.

2 My account of SWAPO's incursion in April 1989 is taken from Jaster, *The 1988 Peace Accords*, pp. 36–9, Crocker, *High Noon in Southern Africa*, pp. 421–2, Geldenhuys, *A General's Story*, pp. 266–9 and Heitman (in interview).

3 Twenty-six South Africans were also killed in the fighting and 145 wounded.

4 By 1989, Cuba was receiving 90 per cent of its oil, 100 per cent of its wheat and 40 per cent of its basic foodstuffs from the Soviet Union. It is even alleged that Cuba was making up to $500m per year by selling excess Soviet oil on the world market (Oppenheimer, *Castro's Final Hour*, p. 227).

5 Author's interview with Víctor Veras (Havana, September 1997).

6 Author's conversations with Octavio Guerra Royo, Havana, December 2000.

7 Although he never fought in the Sierra Maestra, in 1959 Abrantes was appointed Chief of Castro's personal escort and was incorporated into his inner circle. In December 1985, Abrantes replaced Ramiro Valdés as Interior Minister following the latter's violent dispute with Raúl Castro.

8 Del Águila (in Díaz-Briquets, *Cuban Internationalism*, p. 141) noted in 1988 – prior to the Ochoa scandal – that a Cuban defector, Major Florentino Azpillaga, had warned that elements in the security and intelligence agencies were conspiring against Castro. According to him, the Castro brothers were 'surrounded by influential enemies who may at some point force a showdown with the political leadership'.

9 My account of the Ochoa scandal is taken from ideologically opposed sources including Oppenheimer, *Castro's Final Hour*, pp. 18–128, the Cuban government's transcript of the trial (*Case 1/1989*), José F Alfonso, 'The Ochoa Affair: A Majority Faction in the Revolutionary Armed Forces?', Cuban Armed Forces Review Website and author's conversations with Víctor Veras, Havana, December 2000.

10 MC was set up around 1970 to smuggle tobacco and rum to the USA in exchange for hard currency, technology (in particular computer chips) and drugs which were prohibited by the American embargo.

11 By the late 1980s, MC's association with the Medellín drug cartels had earned it the nickname '*Marijuana y Cocaína*'.

12 Oppenheimer, *Castro's Final Hour*, p. 41.

13 According to José Blandón – one of Noriega's advisers who defected to the USA in January 1988 – Castro persuaded Noriega to return $4.6m he had been paid by Escobar to protect the laboratory, and to release several Colombians who were detained in the raid.

14 My account of the meeting is taken from Oppenheimer, *Castro's Final Hour*, pp. 81–2.

15 Ochoa admitted to carrying out deals on the *candonga*, but insisted all profits were used exclusively for the construction of the Cahama air base. According to Oppenheimer (*Castro's Final Hour*, pp. 91–3), Ochoa accused the entire officer class of corruption, including Raúl Castro himself.

16 My account of the raid on Víbora Parque is taken from conversations with a Cuban resident from the area who witnessed it (but does not wish to be identified).

17 With the exception of Ochoa and his two aides (Martínez and Estupiñán), all the accused were from MININT. The Court was presided by Divisional-General Ramón Espinosa Martín (Chief of the Eastern Army), and Cuba's Minister of Justice – Brigadier-General Juan Escalona Reguera – was Chief Prosecutor.

18 See, for example, Oppenheimer, *Castro's Final Hour*, pp. 106–11.
19 The paucity of the defence can be seen in the Cuban government's publication of transcripts from the trial – *Case 1/1989* – where the prosecution takes up over 200 pages (pp. 82–299), while the defence takes up only four (pp. 299–303).
20 Ochoa's aide José Llicas – who had sold Cuban sugar on the *candonga* – was never charged, probably because his action was such a common occurrence in Angola.
21 Oppenheimer, *Castro's Final Hour*, pp. 127–8.
22 For examples, see Furry in Báez, *Secretos de Generales*, p. 27 and Castro in *Case 1/1989*, p. 395.
23 Abrantes remained in prison until his death on 21 January 1991 from a heart attack. Given his age (58) and his previous good health, some view his death as suspicious. Abrantes' death came only three weeks after Reinaldo Ruiz died of a heart attack in a Miami jail on 31 December 1990.
24 The tearing down of the Berlin Wall on the night of 9/10 November was followed on 17 November by student demonstrations in Prague, the overthrow of the Czechoslovak government on 27 November, and the bloody overthrow of Ceausescu in Romania in late December.
25 Details on the return of Cuba's internationalist dead are taken from Benítez Suárez, *Equinoccio de los héroes*, pp. 23–9.
26 Some bodies were inevitably missed, and when I travelled through Longa (Cuando Cubango) in March 1998, I found the grave of a Cuban MiG-23 pilot. According to the local FAA commander, he was shot down in 1988 and was not disinterred because so little of his body had survived the crash. His grave remains untended and marked only by a blank plinth (see www.cubangola.com for photo).
27 All remains were buried alphabetically, irrespective of rank. The idea was that, in the future, any Cuban killed in the defence of Cuba would be buried there – including officers, soldiers, MININT personnel and militia (even if they died on exercise).
28 Del Pino (*General del Pino speaks*, p. 15) put total Cuban casualties at 'about 10,000' and Ratliff ('Política Militar Cubana', p. 145) at 12,000. Both figures predate the bloody confrontations of 1987/8 in which several hundred Cubans were killed.
29 The government's policy of recording internationalist casualty figures separately in each municipality is also an effective way of preventing an accurate national estimate.
30 Figures from author's interview. One FAR historian (in interview with author, Havana, September 1997) claimed to have seen documents recording the return of 4,000 bodies to Cuba. This figure compares favourably with a former FAR officer who served in Angola in the mid-1980s and who estimated that around thirty Cubans were killed every month (interview with author, Havana, June 2002). According to Víbora Parque's municipal register of internationalists, thirty-six men were killed out of 2,752 who served in Angola (or 1.3 per cent). If this percentage is applied to official figures for Cubans who served in Angola (377,000), it suggests that around 5,000 Cubans died in Angola, with twice as many wounded or MIA.
31 My account of this offensive is taken from author's interview with a veteran of the offensive, Major Mateus Timóteo (Cuito Cuanavale, March 1998).
32 Cuba's first ties with Nicaragua started in the early 1960s when Rodolfo Romero, one of the founding members of the Sandinistas, was trained in Cuba.
33 Author's conversations with Víctor Veras (Havana, September 1997).

34 I obtained this information 'off the record' from a reliable military source in Luanda. One Cuban internationalist veteran – an electrical engineer – recounted that while in Luanda in the late 1970s he was called in to repair the electricity supply at the Futungo de Belas palace, under the watchful eye of a dozen heavily-built black soldiers. Growing tired of their looming presence he started to make disparaging comments about them in Spanish, only for one of the guards to step forward and tell him in perfect Cuban Spanish to watch his mouth (interview with author, Havana, September 1997).

35 By the late 1990s, the Cabinda oil fields were providing the Luanda regime with an annual revenue of around $5 billion, or 95 per cent of Angola's hard currency earnings (EIU Country Report, 2000).

36 These allegations – made by drunken ex-mercenaries in Luanda's infamous French Club – remain unsubstantiated, and most informed sources in Luanda dismiss them as recycled rumours.

37 In Luanda the small Cuban community is based around a group of shops on the Rua da Missão (by Kinaxixi square). Each month the Cuban Embassy in Luanda holds a party for Cuban expatriates.

38 According to a Cuban doctor who is married to an Angolan and lives in Lubango (Huíla), Cubans needed special permission to remain in Angola, and those who stayed on illegally (perhaps 100 in total) were granted an amnesty in the late 1990s.

39 The most dramatic crisis came in August 1994 when rioting in Havana led to the exodus of at least 30,000 Cubans on makeshift rafts, 5,000 others perishing in the attempt. The crisis end in September 1994 with an agreement from Washington to repatriate all future 'balseros' (raft people).

40 Castro's petition was in response to another petition containing 11,000 signatures which demanded genuine democracy in Cuba. Inevitably all Cubans eligible to sign Castro's petition were put under considerable pressure to do so, and the few who refused are still feeling the repercussions (author's conversations with Víctor Veras, Havana, June 2002).

41 In late 1998 I visited two de-densifying projects in the Saandspruit and Phola Park illegal settlements (near the airport) where basic houses with running water, electricity and gas were being built. Although Johannesburg's illegal settlements continue to grow uncontrollably, the tangible improvement in living conditions in these settlements was apparent. Conditions in Soweto's Nelson Mandela Transit Camp remain desperate, however.

42 Mobutu fled to southern France and then to Rabat (Morocco) where he died from cancer on 7 September 1997.

43 Between 1998 and 2003 an estimated 3.3 million Congolese died as a result of this war.

44 'Some Transparency, No Accountability: the Use of Oil Revenue in Angola and its Impact on Human Rights', *Human Rights Watch*, January 2004.

45 In the late 1990s the Angolan government earned around US$2.5bn per year from oil. By 2008 it is estimated that Angola will be producing 2.2m barrels per day, generating annual revenues in excess of US$8bn (Tony Hodges, *Angola: Anatomy of an oil state* (Oxford: James Currey, 2004).

CONCLUSION

1 This description was used by the Soviet Deputy Foreign Minister Adamishin to Crocker during their talks in July 1987 (Crocker, *High Noon in Southern Africa*, p. 349).

2 When Cuban forces intervened in Angola in 1975 there was no mention of

NOTES

the Namibia question or of Cuba's support for SWAPO (which was still allied to UNITA at the time). However, following the passing of Resolution 435 the independence of Namibia became a sine qua non for a Cuban withdrawal.

3 For example, Crocker, *High Noon in Southern Africa*, p. 36 and Steenkamp, *South Africa's Border War*, pp. 52–3.

4 LeoGrande, *Cuba's Policy in Africa*, p. 64.

5 As former SADF Chief General Geldenhuys puts it: 'We regarded propaganda as a distasteful word' (*A General's Story*, pp. 135).

6 These included Catengue (November 1975), Cassinga (May 1978), Cuvelai (January 1984), the Lomba river (September–October 1988) and Tchipa (June 1988).

7 Crocker, 'Peacemaking in Southern Africa'.

8 Data for this section are taken from Jeremy Harding, *The Fate of Africa: Trial by Fire* (New York: Simon and Schuster, 1993), p. 25, Falk, 'Cuba in Africa', p. 1094, Wolfers and Bergerol, *Angola in the Frontline*, p. 157, Benítez Suárez, *Equinoccio de los héroes*, p. 20, Concepción, *Por qué somos internacionalistas*, pp. 59 and 98–100 and Hamill, *The Challenge to the MPLA*, p. 64.

9 According to a UN report published in the late 1980s, between 1974 and 1989 South Africa caused nearly $60 billion worth of damage to the economies and infrastructures of the Front-Line States.

10 The remainder of the conclusion is based on interviews carried out by the author with internationalist veterans during visits to Cuba in 1997, 1999, 2000 and 2002.

11 Following an accord signed by Castro and Chávez in 2000, Venezuela provides up to 53,000 barrels of crude oil per day to Cuba in return for humanitarian assistance. By late 2004 there were over 13,000 Cuban doctors running clinics in the slums of Caracas, as well as a contingent of at least 200 Cuban advisors working in military intelligence, the ministry of interior and immigration. Some estimates put the number of Cuban doctors in Venezuela as high 35,000 (author's conversations with Cuban doctor, Havana, September 2004).

SELECT BIBLIOGRAPHY

Publications in English

Anderson, Jon Lee, *Che Guevara: A Revolutionary Life* (London: Bantam, 1997).

Birmingham, David, 'The Twenty-Seventh of May, an Historical Note on the Abortive 1977 Coup in Angola', *African Affairs*, 77, 308 (July 1978): 554–63.

Birmingham, David, *Frontline Nationalism in Angola and Mozambique* (London: James Currey, 1992).

Blasier, Cole and Mesa-Lago, Carmelo (eds), *Cuba in the World* (Pittsburgh: University of Pittsburgh Press, 1979).

Breytenbach, Jan, *Forged in Battle* (Capetown: Saayman & Weber, 1986).

Bridgland, Fred, *Jonas Savimbi, A Key to Africa* (Edinburgh: Mainstream, 1986).

Campbell, Horace, *The Siege of Cuito Cuanavale* (Uppsala: The Scandinavian Institute of African Studies, October 1990).

Crocker, Chester A, *High Noon in Southern Africa: Making Peace in a Rough Neighborhood* (New York: W.W. Norton & Co., 1992).

Deutchmann, David (ed.), *Changing the History of Africa* (Melbourne: Ocean Press, 1989).

Díaz-Briquets, Sergio (ed.), *Cuban Internationalism in Sub-Saharan Africa* (Pittsburgh: Duquesne University Press, 1989).

Domínguez, Jorge I., 'Cuban Foreign Policy', *Foreign Affairs*, 57, 1 (1978): 83–106.

Domínguez, Jorge I., *To Make a World Safe for Revolution: Cuba's Foreign Policy* (Cambridge, MA: Harvard University Press, 1989).

Falk, Pamela S., 'Cuba in Africa', *Foreign Affairs*, 65, 5 (1987).

Franklin, Jane, *Cuba–Angola: A Chronology, 1961–1988* (New York: Center for Cuban Studies, 1989).

Geldenhuys, Jannie, *A General's Story: From an Era of War and Peace* (Johannesburg: Jonathan Ball, 1995).

George, Edward, 'Moscow's Gurkhas or the Tail Wagging the Dog? Cuban Internationalism in Angola, 1965–1991', Occasional Papers Series, 29, Department of Hispanic Studies, University of Bristol (August 1999), 39pp.

Gleijeses, Piero, 'The First Ambassadors: Cuba's Contribution to Guinea-Bissau's War of Independence', *Journal of Latin American Studies*, 29 (February 1997): 45–86.

Gleijeses, Piero, *Conflicting Missions: Havana, Washington, and Africa, 1959–1976* (Chapel Hill and London: University of North Carolina Press, 2002).

Hamill, James, *The Challenge to the MPLA: Angola's War: 1980–1986*, Politics Working Papers, 41, University of Warwick (1986).

Heitman, Helmoed-Römer, *War in Angola: the Final South African Phase* (Gibraltar: Ashanti Publishing, 1990).

Jaster, Robert S., *The 1988 Peace Accords and the Future of South-Western Africa* (London: Brassey's, 1990).

José Martí Publishing House Committee, *Case 1/1989: End of the Cuban Connection* (Havana, 1989).

John, Nerys, *Operation Savannah*, unpublished Masters ms, University of Cape Town, 2002.

Kahn, Owen Ellison (ed.), *Disengagement from Southwest Africa: The Prospects for Peace in Angola and Namibia* (New Jersey: Transaction Publishers, 1991).

Khazanov, Anatolii Mikhailovich (Cynthia Carlile [trans.]), *Agostinho Neto* (Moscow: Progress Publishers, 1986).

Kitchen, Helen (ed.), *Angola, Mozambique and the West* (New York: CSIS, 1987).

Klinghoffer, Arthur J., *The Angolan War: a Study in Soviet Policy in the Third World* (Boulder: Westview Press, 1980).

Legum, Colin and Hodges, Tony, *After Angola: the War Over Southern Africa* (London: Rex Collings, 1976).

LeoGrande, William M. (ed.), *Cuba's Policy in Africa, 1959–1980* (Berkeley: Institute of International Studies, University of California, 1980).

Mallin, Jay, *Cuba in Angola* (Miami: University of Miami Press, 1987).

Marcum, John A., *The Angolan Revolution: the Anatomy of an Explosion (1950–1962)* (Cambridge, MA: MIT Press, 1969).

Marcum, John A., *The Angolan Revolution: Exile Politics and Guerrilla Warfare (1962–1976)* (Pittsburgh: University of Pittsburgh, 1978).

Mesa-Lago, Carmelo and Belkin, June S. (eds), *Cuba in Africa* (Pittsburgh: Center for Latin American Studies, University of Pittsburgh, 1982).

Oppenheimer, Andrés, *Castro's Final Hour: the Secret Story Behind the Coming Downfall of Communist Cuba* (New York: Touchstone, 1992).

Pino Díaz, Rafael del, *General del Pino Speaks: an Insight into Elite Corruption and Military Dissension in Castro's Cuba* (Washington, DC: The Cuban–American National Foundation, 1987).

Steenkamp, Willem, *South Africa's Border War, 1966–1989* (Gibraltar: Ashanti, 1989).

Stockwell, John, *In Search of Enemies: a CIA Story* (New York: W.W. Norton & Co., 1978).

Szulc, Tad, *Fidel, A Critical Portrait* (Bungay, Suffolk: Coronet Books, 1989).

Uys, Ian, *Bushman Soldiers: their Alpha and Omega* (South Africa: Fortress, 1993).

Van der Waals, W.S., *Portugal's War in Angola, 1961–1974* (Rivonia: Ashanti Publishing, 1993).

Viney, Graham Elliott, *Angola: a Study in Foreign Intervention, 1974–1976*, Faculty of Social Studies, University of Oxford (thesis), August 1978.

Wolfers, Michael and Bergerol, Jane, *Angola in the Frontline* (London: Zed Press, 1983).

Publications in Spanish and Portuguese

Báez, Luis, *Secretos de Generales* (Havana: Editorial Si-Mar, 1996).

Benítez Suárez, Juan Bautista, *Equinoccio de los héroes* (Las Tunas: Editorial Sanlope, 1993).

Carvajal García, Galo Antonio, *Recuerdos de una campaña: Premio Testimonio 1981* (Havana: Editorial 13 de marzo, 1982).

Castro, Fidel, *Angola Girón africano* (Havana: Ediciones Políticas, 1976).

Concepción, Eloy, *Por qué somos internacionalistas* (Havana: Ediciones Políticas, 1987).

Gálvez, William, *El Sueño Africano de Che: ¿Qué sucedió en la guerrilla congolesa?* (Havana: Casa de las Américas, 1997).

Gómez Chacón, César, *Cuito Cuanavale: viaje al centro de los héroes* (Havana: Editorial Letras Cubanas, 1989).

Guevara, Ernesto 'Che', *Diario de la campaña en el Congo* (Cuba, 1968).

Jaime, Drumond and Barber, Helder, *Angola: Depoimentos para a História Recente, 1950–76* (Lisbon: Istoé Comunicações, 1999).

Luis, Roger Ricardo, *Prepárense a vivir: crónicas de Cuito Cuanavale* (Havana: Editora Política, 1989).

Miná, Gianni, *Un Encuentro con Fidel* (Havana: Ediciones Políticas, 1987).

Muatxiânvua, A, 'Metamorfoses da agressão a Angola', *Jornal de Angola*, 1987.

'Nancy' (Limbania Jiménez Rodríguez), *Heroínas de Angola* (Havana: Ediciones Políticas, 1985).

Nazario, Olga, 'La operación de Cuba en Angola', *Revista Occidental* (1989): 65–91.

Ortiz, José M., *Angola: un abril como Girón* (Havana: Editora Política, 1979).

Pérez Guerra, Elsa and Hernández Fhan, Minerva (eds), *Cronología de la Revolución (1984–1989)* (Havana: Editora Política, 1991).

Pino-Santos Navarro, Carina (ed.), *Cronología: 25 años de Revolución (1959–1983)* (Havana: Editora Política, 1987).

Ramos, Dalie (ed.), *La Paz de Cuito Cuanavale: documentos de un proceso* (Havana: Editora Política, 1989).

Ratliff, William, 'Política Militar Cubana en el África Subsahariana', *Revista Occidental*, 2 (1989): 139–59.

Rey Cabrera, Marina (ed.), *La Guerra de Angola* (Havana: Editora Política, 1989).

Rius, Hugo, *Angola: Crónicas de la esperanza y la victoria* (Havana: Ediciones Políticas, 1982).

Valdés, Nelson P., 'Cuba y la guerra entre Somalia y Etiopía', *Estudios de Ásia y África*, XIV, 2, Mexico (April–June 1979): 603–67.

Valdés, Nelson P., 'Cuba y Angola: Una Política de Solidaridad Internacional', *Estudios de Ásia y África*, XIV, 4, Mexico (October–December 1979).

Valdés Vivó, Raúl, *Angola: Fin del mito de los mercenarios* (Havana: Empresa de Medios de Propaganda, May 1976).

Walters, Barbara, 'La entrevista de Fidel con la periodista norteamericana Barbara Walters', *Bohemia*, Havana (1 July 1977): 47–65.

Publications on the Internet

Cold War International History Project (CWIHP), cwihp.si.edu

1   Brenner, Philip and Blight, James G., 'The Crisis and Cuban–Soviet Relations: Fidel Castro's Secret 1968 Speech.'
2   Domínguez, Jorge I., 'Cuba as Superpower: Havana and Moscow, 1979.'
3   'Fidel Castro's 1977 Southern Africa Tour: a Report to Honecker.'
4   Gleijeses, Piero, 'Havana's Policy in Africa, 1959–76: New Evidence from Cuban Archives.'
5   Soviet documents on Angola and Southern Africa, 1975–79.
6   Westad, Odd Arne, 'Moscow and the Angolan Crisis, 1974–1976: a New Pattern of Intervention.'

CNN 'Cold War' website, edition.cnn.com/SPECIALS/cold.war.
Crocker, Chester, 'Peacemaking in Southern Africa: the Namibia–Angola Settlement of 1988', 1998, Georgetown University website (www.georgetown.edu).
Cubangola, www.cubangola.com, website containing original documents, maps, graphic images, interviews and links to other websites related to Cuba and Angola.
South Africa Military History Website, home.wanadoo.nl/rhodesia/samil-his.htm.

1   Allport, Richard, 'The Battle of Bridge 14.'
2   Allport, Richard, 'The Battle of Cuito Cuanavale: Cuba's Mythical Victory.'
3   García Márquez, Gabriel, 'Operation Carlota', 1976.
4   Heitman, Helmoed-Römer, 'Operations Moduler and Hooper (1987–1988).'
5   Moss, Robert, 'Castro's Secret War Exposed: How Washington Lost its Nerve and How the Cubans Subdued Angola' (first printed in the *Sunday Telegraph*, 20 February 1977).
6   Nöthling, Colonel C.J., 'Military Chronicle of South West Africa (1915–1988).'

Newspapers and journals

African Affairs
Africa Contemporary Record
The Economist
Foreign Affairs
Granma
Journal of Modern African Studies

INDEX

INDEX

Lucusse 197, 273
Ludy (Rodrigues João Lopes) 37
Luena 166, 167, 193, 197
Lumbala N'Guimbo 165, 166, 170, 192
Lusaka 34, 40, 45, 46, 182
Lusaka Accord (1994) 272

M–26–7 (Movimento 26 de julio) 14, 22
Malange 73, 94
Mariel (Cuba) 27, 141, 163, 173, 176
Martínez Sánchez, Augusto 37
Marxist-Leninism 8, 10, 11, 128, 139
Masetti, Ricardo 20
Massemba-Débat, Alphonse 21, 26, 32; coup
  against 35–6, 40
Matthews, Herbert 16
Mavinga 140, 164, 165, 191, 192–5, 200,
  203–5, 269
May 1977 coup 126–30
Mayombe jungle 3, 23, 29–30, 66, 161
M'bridge river 37–8
Mbundu ethnic group 5, 6, 8, 29
Mengistu, Haile Mariam 124, 132–3
Menongue 5, 120, 167–8, 203, 211, 216, 218,
  220, 232
mercenaries 83–6, 89–91, 108–10
mestiço 6, 127
MFA (Movimento das Forças Armadas) 50,
  51, 54
Mingas, Saydi 44
MININT (Ministerio del Interior) 143, 211,
  256, 260–7, 277; involvement in smuggling
  and black market deals 261–7; Special
  Forces 81, 82, 88, 94–6
MK (Umkhonto weSizewe) 123–4, 135,
  137–8, 139, 142, 155, 171, 176, 184, 191,
  197, 200, 257
MMCA (Misión Military Cubana en
  Angola) 65, 67, 77–8, 88, 98, 101, 103, 107,
  141, 144, 210, 239, 276
Mobutu, Joseph 10, 12, 31, 61, 112, 117–18,
  126, 136, 272
Moçâmedes 5, 71–2, 75, 111
Moncada barracks (Santiago) 14
Monje, Mario 42
Monstro Imortal (Jacob Alves Caetano) 33,
  129–30
Moracén Limonta, Rafael 27, 28–9, 36, 99,
  129–31, 148, 257
Morro do Cal, 73–5, 77, 86–8,
Moxico province (Angola) 5, 52, 166, 191,
  197–9
Mozambique 44, 49, 52, 63
MPLA (Movimento para a Libertação de
  Angola) 8; alliance with Cuba (*see*
  Cuban–MPLA alliance); alliance with
  Soviet Union 12, 46–7, 54, 91, 101, 125,
  165, 170, 180 (*see also* Soviet military aid);

factionalism 46–7, 52–3, 55, 113, 126–31;
  First Party Congress 132; guerrilla activity
  3, 5, 8, 9, 10; Luanda uprising (1961) 9; 1st
  Military Region (Dembos) 9, 10, 23, 33,
  36–9, 40, 127, 128; 2nd Military Region
  (Cabinda) 11, 22–3, 28–9, 40; 3rd Military
  Region or 'Eastern Front' (Moxico) 23,
  34, 39, 40, 41, 44, 45–7, 66; rivalry with
  FNLA 11, 22, 33, 37, 71–2
Mugabe, Robert 139, 171
Mukwidi 39
Mussende (Cuanza Norte) 111, 166, 170,
  musseques 9, 281

Nambuangongo 33
Namibe 5, 197–8, 239, 242
Namibia 11, 62, 106, 123, 133–4, 137, 171,
  189, 200, 205, 210, 237, 241–6, 250, 257–8,
  267, 275, 284
Nascimento, Lopo do 8, 57, 59, 138
Nasser, Gamal Abdel 19, 25
Neto, Agostinho 8, 9, 13, 22–3, 37, 57, 66, 86,
  99, 113, 119, 124–32, 136; death 138;
  relationship with Castro 34, 46–7, 77–8,
  117, 131, 136; relationship with Soviets
  46–7, 127, 138
N'Giva 140–1, 164, 181–2
Ngouabi, Marien 35–6, 40, 61
Nhia river 97, 102–3, 110
Nicaragua 17, 139, 262, 269, 282
Nitistas see Nito Alves
Nixon, Richard 50–51
Nkrumah, Kwame 8, 29
Noriega, Manuel 261, 264, 268
North Korea 89–90
Nova Lisboa (Huambo) 5, 69, 73, 74, 111
Novo Redondo (Sumbe) 93–4, 96

OAU (Organisation of African Unity) 12,
  23, 30, 39, 46, 47, 53, 93, 104, 106, 113
Ochoa Sánchez, Arnaldo 98, 133, 148, 152,
  210, 215–25, 236–7, 248, 252, 255, 256, 257,
  260, 262–7, 277
OMA (Organização da Mulher Angolana)
  37, 39
Onanbwe 22
Operación Triángulo 27, 34
Operation Carlota 3, 82, 116, 143, 188, 211,
  231, 278; decision to launch 77–80, 276;
  defence of Cabinda 82–6; defence of
  Luanda 80–1; the Northern Front 101,
  106–10; logistics 81, 99–101; the Southern
  Front 72, 75, 94, 110–12; Soviet
  involvement 65, 79–80, 88, 101
Operation IAFeature *see* CIA
Operation Savannah 68–77, 91–8, 101–6, 110,
  111, 114–15, 123, 173, 203–4, 213, 206, 230,
  278; ambush at Ebo 97–8, 101–2; Battle-

352